Frank P. Harvey is Associate Professor in the Department of Political Science and Centre for Foreign Policy Studies at Dalhousie University, Halifax, Nova Scotia, Canada. His most recent work is *The Future's Back: US-Soviet Rivalry, Nuclear Proliferation and Crisis Stability after the Cold War*. He has published articles on nuclear and conventional deterrence theory, US-Soviet rivalry and crisis decision-making, and protracted ethnic conflict in the former Yugoslavia in *The Canadian Journal of Political Science*, *Security Studies*, the *Journal of Politics*, and *The Journal of Conflict Management and Peace Science*. His current research interests include ethnic conflict and peacekeeping.

Ben D. Mor is a Lecturer in International Relations in the Department of Political Science at the University of Haifa in Israel, where he also teaches in the MA Program on National Security for the Israel Defense Forces. He previously taught at the University of Nebraska, Lincoln and New York University. Dr Mor is the author of *Decision and Interaction in Crisis* and has published articles on applied game theory, the evolution of enduring rivalries, and the Middle East peace process.

CONFLICT IN WORLD POLITICS

Advances in Political Science: An International Series

As an expression of its commitment to global political science, the International Political Science Association initiated this series to promote the publication of rigorous scholarly research by its members and affiliated groups. Conceptual and theoretical developments in the discipline, and their explication in various settings, represent the special focus of the series.

Members of the editorial board are Asher Arian (general editor), Luigi Graziano, William Lafferty, Theodore Lowi and Carole Pateman.

Titles include:

Christa Altenstetter and James Warner Björkman (*editors*)
HEALTH POLICY REFORM, NATIONAL VARIATIONS AND GLOBALIZATION

Frank P. Harvey and Ben D. Mor (*editors*)
CONFLICT IN WORLD POLITICS: Advances in the Study of Crisis, War and Peace

Klause von Beyme
TRANSITION TO DEMOCRACY IN EASTERN EUROPE

Conflict in World Politics

Advances in the Study of Crisis, War and Peace

Edited by

Frank P. Harvey
Associate Professor
Department of Political Science
University of Dalhousie
Halifax
Nova Scotia, Canada

and

Ben D. Mor
Lecturer in International Relations
Department of Political Science
University of Haifa
Israel

First published in Great Britain 1998 by
MACMILLAN PRESS LTD
Houndmills, Basingstoke, Hampshire RG21 6XS and London
Companies and representatives throughout the world

A catalogue record for this book is available from the British Library.

ISBN 0–333–68198–3

 First published in the United States of America 1998 by
ST. MARTIN'S PRESS, INC.,
Scholarly and Reference Division,
175 Fifth Avenue, New York, N.Y. 10010

ISBN 0–312–17668–6

Library of Congress Cataloging-in-Publication Data
Conflict in world politics : advances in the study of crisis, war and
peace / edited by Frank P. Harvey and Ben D. Mor.
p. cm. — (Advances in political science)
Includes bibliographical references and index.
ISBN 0–312–17668–6 (cloth)
1. International relations.   2. World politics—1989–   3. War.
4. Peace.   I. Harvey, Frank P.   II. Mor, Ben D.   III. Series:
Advances in political science (New York, N. Y.)
JZ5595.C66 1997
327.1'01—dc21   97–18969
                                                                CIP

© International Political Science Association 1998

All rights reserved. No reproduction, copy or transmission of this publication may be made without written permission.

No paragraph of this publication may be reproduced, copied or transmitted save with written permission or in accordance with the provisions of the Copyright, Designs and Patents Act 1988, or under the terms of any licence permitting limited copying issued by the Copyright Licensing Agency, 90 Tottenham Court Road, London W1P 9HE.

Any person who does any unauthorised act in relation to this publication may be liable to criminal prosecution and civil claims for damages.

The authors have asserted their rights to be identified as the authors of this work in accordance with the Copyright, Designs and Patents Act 1988.

This book is printed on paper suitable for recycling and made from fully managed and sustained forest sources.

10   9   8   7   6   5   4   3   2   1
07   06   05   04   03   02   01   00   99   98

Printed in Great Britain by
The Ipswich Book Company Ltd
Ipswich, Suffolk

To our children

Adi
Dana
Jayden
Kalli G
Yaniv

Contents

List of Figures ix

List of Tables x

Notes on the Contributors xii

Acknowledgments xvi

Abbreviations xvii

INTRODUCTION

1 Conflict, Crisis and War: Cumulation, Criticism, Rejoinder 3
  Michael Brecher and Frank P. Harvey

PART ONE: CONFLICT

2 Satisfaction, Capabilities, and the Evolution of Enduring Rivalries, 1816–1990: A Statistical Analysis of a Game Theoretic Model 33
  Zeev Maoz and Ben D. Mor

3 Foreign Policy Choices and Domestic Politics: A Re-examination of the Link Between Domestic and International Conflict 62
  Paul K. Huth and Ellen Lust-Okar

4 Loss Aversion, Framing, and Bargaining: The Implications of Prospect Theory for International Conflict 96
  Jack S. Levy

PART TWO: CRISIS

5 Crisis Escalation: A New Model and Findings 119
  Michael Brecher

6 Nuclear Crisis as a Multi-Stage Threat Game: Toward an Agenda for Comparative Research 142
  Frank P. Harvey and Patrick James

| 7 | Interstate Rivalry and the Study of Militarized Conflict
Paul R. Hensel | 162 |

PART THREE: WAR AND PEACE

8	The Steps to War in Europe, 1933–41 *John A. Vasquez*	207
9	Threat Perception and Surprise: In Search of the Intervening Variable *Abraham Ben-Zvi*	241
10	Democratic Change and Defense Allocation in East Asia *Steve Chan*	272
11	A Prospect-Based Analysis of War Termination *Alex Mintz and Nehemia Geva*	288
12	Camp David: Was the Agreement Fair? *Steven J. Brams and Jeffrey M. Togman*	306

Appendix
Survey of War Literature by Category — 324

Bibliography — 326

Index — 356

List of Figures

1.1	Conflict, crisis, war	10
2.1	EIRs: a game-based theoretical framework	37
2.2	A schematic structure of a rivalry game	38
2.3	Flow chart of rivalry calculus	39
2.4	The supergame of enduring rivalries	42
3.1	The interaction between domestic conflict and foreign policy	68
3.2	Domestic factors influencing response to domestic opposition	73
4.1	A value function	99
5.1	Crisis escalation model	121
6.1	The multi-stage threat game	147

List of Tables

2.1	Enduring rivalries, 1816-1986	47
2.2	Relationship between game type and dyadic conflict by rivalry and non-rivalry years	53
2.3	Effects of strategic game and control variables on dispute behaviour: an event-history analysis	54
2.4	Relationships between game transitions and conflict	56
2.5	Effects of strategic game transitions and control variables on dispute behaviour: an event-history analysis	57
3.1	Simplified payoffs for challenger state	71
3.2	Influence of domestic and foreign policy variables on the likelihood of international conflict	89
5.1	International crises: findings on Hypothesis 1	134
5.2	Violence in escalation of international crises: findings on Hypothesis 2	135
5.3	Severe violence in international crises: findings on Hypothesis 3	136
5.4	Proneness to foreign policy crisis: findings on Hypothesis 4	138
5.5	Proneness to violent crisis escalation: findings on Hypothesis 5	139
6.1	Outcomes and payoffs in the multi-stage threat game	149
6.2	Threshold conditions for preference orderings	149
6.3	Possible preference orderings for row player	150
6.4	Possible preference orderings for column player	150
6.5	Profile of outcomes	151
6.6	Intensity of superpower bargaining techniques	154
7.1	Frequency of militarized interstate disputes and wars	189
7.2	Frequency of international crises	190
7.3	Frequency of homeland territorial changes	191
7.4	Frequency of militarized interstate disputes and wars in enduring rivalries	193
7.5	Frequency of international crises in enduring rivalries	193
7.6	Frequency of homeland territorial changes in enduring rivalries	193
7.7	Militarized dispute recurrence	194
7.8	Dispute outcomes and militarized dispute recurrence	195
7.9	Contentious issues and militarized dispute recurrence	196

List of Tables

7.10	Logistic regression analysis of militarized dispute recurrence	197
8.1	Typical path associated with world war	211
8.2	Factors related to onset and expansion of war: the Second World War in Europe	237
10.1	Democratic change and defense allocation	281
11.1	Proportion of students choosing the 'Stop the War' alternative	298
11.2	Proportion of adult subjects choosing the 'Stop the War' alternative	299
12.1	Hypothetical Israeli and Egyptian point allocation	316

Notes on the Contributors

Abraham Ben-Zvi received his PhD in political science at the University of Chicago in 1973. He is a Professor in the Department of Political Science and a Senior Research Fellow in the Jaffee Center for Strategic Studies at Tel-Aviv University. In the 1995–6 academic year, he was the Goldman Visiting Professor in the Department of Government at Georgetown University. He has published extensively on a variety of strategic and security issues. His most recent book is *The United States and Israel: The Limits of the Special Relationship* (1993).

Steven J. Brams is Professor of Politics at New York University. He is the author or co-author of 12 books that involve applications of game theory and social choice theory to voting and elections, international relations, and the Bible and theology. His two most recent books are *Theory of Moves* (1994) and, with Alan D. Taylor, *Fair Division: From Cake-Cutting to Dispute Resolution* (1996). He is a fellow of the American Association for the Advancement of Science, a Guggenheim fellow, and a past president of the Peace Science Society (International).

Michael Brecher is the R.B. Angus Professor of Political Science at McGill University. He is the author or co-author of 17 books that focus on South Asian politics, international relations, political biography, comparative foreign policy, the Arab/Israel conflict, and conflict, crisis and war. His most recent books are *Crises in World Politics* (1993) and *A Study of Crisis* (1997). He is a Fellow of the Royal Society of Canada, recipient of Killam Awards from the Canada Council, fellowships from the Nuffield, Guggenheim, and Rockefeller Foundation, the Distinguished Teaching Prize from McGill University (1986), Distinguished Scholar Award from the International Studies Association (1995).

Steve Chan is Professor of Political Science at the University of Colorado (Boulder). His research interests cover political economy, conflict management, defense economics, and democratic peace. He has published nine books and numerous articles in the fields of international relations and comparative politics.

Notes on the Contributors

Nehemia Geva is an Assistant Professor of Politicial Science at Texas A&M University. He is the author of articles on cognitive processes in decision-making, experimental analyses of choice and democratic peace.

Frank P. Harvey is Associate Professor of Political Science at Dalhousie University. His most recent book is *The Future's Back: US–Soviet Rivalry, Nuclear Proliferation and Crisis Stability after the Cold War* (McGill-Queen's University Press, 1997). He has published articles on nuclear and conventional deterrence theory, US–Soviet rivalry and crisis decision-making, and protracted ethnic conflict in the former Yugoslavia in the *Canadian Journal of Political Science*, *Security Studies*, the *Journal of Politics*, and the *Journal of Conflict Management and Peace Science*. His current research interests include ethnic conflict and peacekeeping.

Paul R. Hensel is an Assistant Professor of Political Science at Florida State University. His research has appeared in the *Journal of Conflict Resolution*, *Journal of Peace Research*, *International Organization*, *Conflict Management and Peace Science*, and *Political Geography*. His current research interests include the evolution of interstate rivalry and the causes and implications of territorial conflict between states.

Paul K. Huth is Associate Professor of Politicial Science and Associate Research Scientist in the Institute of Social Research at the University of Michigan. He is the author of *Extended Deterrence and the Prevention of War* (1988) and most recently *Standing Your Ground: Territorial Disputes and International Conflict* (1996). He is also the author of articles appearing in the *American Political Science Review*, *World Politics*, *Journal of Conflict Relations*, and *International Studies Quarterly*. He has been the recipient of numerous grants from the National Science Foundation to support his research on the causes of international conflict.

Patrick James is Professor and Chair of the Department of Political Science at Iowa State University. His fellowships and awards include the Louise Dyer Peace Fellowship of the Hoover Institution and the Merrill Chair in the Department of Political Science, Utah State University. He is the author of many articles on the subjects of international relations and Canadian politics. His most recent book, co-edited with David Carment, is *Wars in the Midst of Peace: The International Politics of Ethnic Conflict* (1997).

Jack S. Levy is Professor of Politicial Science at Rutgers University. He is the author of *War in the Modern Great Power System, 1495–1975* (1983) and of numerous articles. His research interests include the causes of war and theories of decision-making.

Ellen Lust-Okar is a doctoral candidate in the Department of Politicial Science at the University of Michigan with a specialization in comparative politics and the Middle East. Her dissertation research focuses on the political response of regimes in Morocco and Jordan to economic crises and policies of attempted economic reform. She has been awarded research fellowships and grants from the United States Information Agency, the Social Science Research Council, the MacArthur Foundation, and the Council of American Overseas Research Centers. She is the author of an article published in *Middle Eastern Studies*.

Zeev Maoz is a Professor of Politicial Science and Head of the Jaffee Center for Strategic Studies at Tel-Aviv University. He is the author of several books including *National Choices and International Processes* (1990), *Paradoxes of War* (1990), and *Domestic Sources of Global Change* (1996). His articles have been published in the *American Politicial Science Review, World Politics, Journal of Conflict Resolution*, and *International Studies Quarterly*, among others. He is currently engaged in a project with Ben D. Mor on the strategic evolution of enduring rivalries.

Alex Mintz is the Cullen-McFadden Professor of politicial science and director of the Program in Foreign Policy Decision Making at Texas A&M University. He is the author of numerous books and articles on political decision making, simulation and experimentation, and defense politics and economics.

Ben D. Mor holds a PhD in international relations from New York University and is since 1991 a Lecturer in the Department of Politicial Science at the University of Haifa, Israel, where he also teaches in the MA Program on National Security for the Israel Defense Forces. He has previously taught at the University of Nebraska, Lincoln (1988–9) and New York University (1989–91). He is the author of *Decision and Interaction in Crisis* (1993) and has published articles on applied game theory, the evolution of enduring rivalries, and the Middle East peace process.

Jeffrey M. Togman received his PhD from New York University and is Assistant Professor of Politicial Science at Seton Hall University. He is co-author, with Steven J. Brams, of 'The Dynamics of the Northern Ireland Conflict,' *Oxford International Review* 7, no. 2 (Spring 1996). His research interests include comparative politics, philosophy of the social sciences, and international migration.

John A. Vasquez is Professor of Politicial Science at Vanderbilt University. He is a specialist in peace research and in international relations theory. His publications include *The War Puzzle* (1993), *In Search of Theory: A New Paradigm for Global Politics* (co-authored with Richard W. Mansbach (1981), and *The Power of Power Politics: A Critique* (1983). He is also editor of *Classics of International Relations*, 3rd edn (Prentice-Hall, 1996) and co-editor of *Beyond Confrontation: Learning Conflict Resolution in the Post-Cold War Era* (1995). He is currently working on an appraisal of neotraditional realist research and on a series of articles testing the steps to war model.

Acknowledgments

We would like to thank Michael Brecher and Zeev Maoz for their support and for encouraging us to take on this project. We are grateful to Asher Arian, general editor of the new 'Advances in Political Science' series, and Sunder Katwala, assistant editor, for their help and guidance in preparing the manuscript. GregoryWitol's excellent research and technical assistance was instrumental in producing the final draft. Frank Harvey was supported by a grant from the Social Science and Humanities Research Council of Canada.

Abbreviations

ABM	Anti-ballistic missiles
AMAN	Israeli military intelligence
AW	Adjusted Winner
C^3I	Command, control, communication, and intelligence
COPDAB	Conflict and Peace Data Bank
COW	Correlates of War
CREON	Comparative Research on the Events of Nations
EBA	Elimination by aspects
EIR	Enduring international rivalry
ICB	International Crisis Behaviour
ICBM	Intercontinental ballistic missile
ICCW	International conflict, crisis, and war
IR	International relations
IWC	Intra-war crisis
MAD	Mutual Assured Destruction
MID	Militarized interstate dispute
MTG	Multi-stage threat game
NME	Nonmyopic equilibrium
PA	Proportional allocation
PC	Protracted conflict
PLO	Palestine Liberation Organization
SAM	Surface-to-air missile
TOM	Theory of moves
WEIS	World Event Interaction Survey

Introduction

1 Conflict, Crisis and War: Cumulation, Criticism, Rejoinder

Michael Brecher and Frank P. Harvey

The expansion of violent international conflict and war in central and eastern Europe at the outset of the 1990s, previously repressed by bipolar ideological battles, is now emerging in the absence of these Cold War restraints as a significant threat to global peace and security. Evidence from the most recent cases of protracted violence in the former Yugoslavia appears to confirm suspicions that international organizations and multistate coalitions are not well suited to handle these newly developing threats. Unfortunately, the academic community remains ill-equipped to provide persuasive answers to pressing questions about the causes and consequences of *international conflict, crisis* and *war* (ICCW). Even more disturbing is that answers to these questions are becoming crucial at a time when international relations theory is being criticized for its lack of cumulativeness, or worse, relevance.

The challenge of this project is to uncover theoretical and empirical knowledge about ICCW by probing the strengths and weaknesses of existing theories, and by exploring and applying new avenues of research and testing. The objective is to develop a stronger foundation for answering pressing questions about the onset, escalation and de-escalation of different forms of international violence. Meeting this particular challenge in the context of ICCW, however, will not be easy. As a community of scholars we have yet to agree on either the nature of progress and cumulation in the field, or on appropriate methods for collecting and assimilating significant contributions and important theoretical insights. Notwithstanding the tremendous amount of time and energy spent on developing ICCW theory and evidence, there remains no clear indication of *integrative* cumulation.[1] While one can easily list important advances in communications technology, gene splicing, artificial intelligence, space flight, heart surgery, robotics, and so on, one would be hard pressed to cite many examples of this kind of cumulation in the social sciences or, more specifically, the field of international relations. On the other hand, scholars in the latter area of research seem to have a much harder time acknowledging progress even when it has occurred.

In the conviction that progress is not an achievement confined to the 'hard' sciences, and that we have indeed produced cumulative findings, this introductory chapter unfolds in three stages. The first evaluates the relative importance (relevance) of alternative explanations for the lack of integrative cumulation in the field of ICCW. Two impediments in particular – the sheer complexity of the field, and methodological constraints (namely the sustained disagreement over the proper nature of inquiry) – are identified as the most compelling explanations. As a first step towards addressing these impediments, and in order to set the stage for the chapters to follow, section two offers a comprehensive review of theory, methods and evidence in each of the three substantive areas of the literature. The chapter concludes by introducing the eleven contributions to the volume.

I. IMPEDIMENTS TO CUMULATION

Some observers have pointed to the expansion of the field as a key explanation for the lack of *integrative* cumulation on ICCW. Over thirty years ago, Platig (1966:182) observed that developments in international relations (IR) 'may have outrun the capability of any one person to evaluate [progress] ... in adequate depth.' If this was not an accurate assessment of the discipline's complexity then, it certainly is true today. In addition to the diversity of professional tasks, intellectual approaches and research objectives (e.g. historical, theoretical, methodological and policy-oriented), the field today encompasses a variety of substantive foci: international law; international organizations and regimes; international political economy; international communication; comparative foreign policy; comparative decision-making; international conflict, crisis and war; conflict and crisis prevention, management and resolution; arms control and disarmament; security studies, etc. Cumulation in the midst of this sectoral diversity, even if it is occurring, has become increasingly difficult to identify.

Aside from several very competent literature reviews and research surveys, the IR community continues to search for a method of compiling, evaluating and linking theoretical accomplishments. Occasionally there is some measure of progress through an assortment of compilations, but more often than not these projects fail to assess research adequately in terms of its overall contribution to knowledge. This volume applies a more systematic approach to evaluating cumulation by limiting the search to three substantive areas: *conflict, crisis* and *war*. This approach allows for assessment of a more manageable portion of the entire research program and facilitates the compilation, evaluation and synthesis of what we have discovered about the conduct of states by making cumulation an explicit objective.

For others, it is not so much the complexity of the field but endless debate about appropriate methodology that explains the lack of integrative cumulation. Scholars approaching the subject from one perspective frequently disregard the findings from another simply by virtue of the approach. One important implication of these more than lingering divisions is that the field inevitably becomes saturated with efforts to falsify theories by pointing out flaws inherent in the methods used. Indeed, among leading criticisms of research efforts over the last 40 years, the following top the list: too many cases were used and were not subject to in-depth examination; not enough cases were used to permit valid generalizations; the study lacked the rigor of deductive theorizing; mathematical models and game theory are too abstract and require an empirical referent; the time frame for the analysis was inappropriate – either too long or too short; the statistical procedures were flawed, given the type of variables used; operationalization of variables was either unreliable or invalid; the level of analysis (system, state or individual) was inappropriate; the level of analysis was appropriate, but the inferences drawn were not; and so on. The assumption underlying almost all of these criticisms is that cumulation is a product of the techniques and methods employed, and by overcoming these technical obstacles theoretical progress should follow. Unfortunately, many of these criticisms serve to perpetuate debates that contribute only a little to the growth of a discipline. Cumulation should be measured within the context of specific methodological approaches, not on the basis of the approach selected. With this in mind, the present volume includes contributions from scholars who employ a variety of methods (game theory, formal modeling, aggregate data analysis, in-depth case studies) and levels of analysis.

The more recent, although less convincing, postmodern explanation for the lack of integrative cumulation in international relations emphasizes problems inherent in the methods, applications and entire research product over the past five decades.[2] The non-cumulative nature of the discipline, in other words, is due to a fundamentally mistaken epistemology, namely the dominant, scientific vision of reality that continues to provide the basis of knowledge construction in the field. This position is hardly surprising given that postmodernism is an intellectual movement that is highly critical of any effort to develop 'theories' of social action.

As a whole, this critique encompasses three distinct strands, all rooted in critical social theory, and all emphasizing the inadequacy of the prevailing logical positivist/empiricist approach. While some base their critique on 'language' and linguistic determinants of reality (Phillips, 1977; Giddens, 1979; George and Campbell, 1990), others stress problems stemming from the cultural bias of social research, and a final set of criticisms focuses on 'change' and the 'time specific' (or historical) limitations of IR theory (George and Campbell, 1990:270). Each of these arguments has received detailed treatment elsewhere (Harvey, 1997), so only the third will be discussed here, given its relevance to the 'New Directions' theme of the current project.

With respect to the failure of the dominant approach to appreciate the impact of *change*, the main problem here concerns the 'conceit of scholars' – the belief that our social theories somehow transcend history and that 'what (we) know is as old as the world' (Cox, 1986:212–214). According to critics, like Cox, there is a 'time specific' nature to all social theory (particularly in the field of international relations), simply because everything we know as 'theory' can only be understood with reference to a particular environment, system or historical period.[3] The drive to rewrite IR textbooks in the aftermath of the Cold War exemplifies this position.

There is a fundamental contradiction in the argument that the process of 'change' is sufficient to render specific IR theories invalid and cumulation impossible. After all, the very same process of change that presumably has rendered theories obsolete can, at some future point in time, create conditions that reestablish a theory's relevance and, by implication, its significance as a basis for valid explanation. Even if social theories are not universally relevant across time, the universal applicability of a validated theory remains constant. Ironically, postmodernists are guilty of the same crime for which they condemn international relations scholarship; their interpretation of change is far too restrictive.

More importantly, although the international system may have undergone significant change recently, it is not clear how these transformations are 'theory damaging'. Postmodern critics, and those who share their views regarding the time-specific nature of social theories, must explain the impact 'change' has on particular theories, and must go beyond arguments that change, in and of itself, is sufficient to render these theories (or research programs) obsolete. The process of change, after all, is not boundless – some things change more than others, though the impact of relatively stable forces (structures) rarely is acknowledged by critics.

Finally, the extent to which change has rendered existing ICCW theory less relevant today is an empirical question. The answer can only be found by identifying the factors that promoted or inhibited violent conflict in the past, and by determining whether similar forces present comparable opportunities and constraints on states and peoples today. The most relevant question as we approach the twenty-first century is this: would we know more or less about international conflict, crisis and war, or how to handle newly developing threats, if we accept these criticisms and continue to repudiate the entire positivist enterprise? The answer, which underscores the epistemological foundation of the current volume, is 'much less'.

The purpose of the following review is to illustrate how 'much more' we have accomplished than critics acknowledge, and to encourage recognition of cumulation and consensus while identifying new avenues for research and testing.

II. INTERNATIONAL CONFLICT, CRISIS AND WAR: A SURVEY OF PROGRESS

Concepts, Definitions and Linkages

Conflict, crisis and war are intricately related, in theory and reality. All are characterized by mistrust between adversaries, turmoil, tension and hostility. Violence, an essential trait of war, is often, though not necessarily, present in crisis and conflict. Although societal *conflict* is as old as human history, serious inquiry began only in the mid-nineteenth century, notably by Marx and Engels, Spencer, Darwin, and theorists of *power and influence*, namely, Mosca, Michels, Pareto and Sorel. In the twentieth century, this continuing inquiry has generated a large body of knowledge.

In the broadest sense, '[c]onflict phenomena are the overt coercive interactions of contending collectivities' (Gurr, 1980:1–2). Further, they are characterized by two or more parties engaged in mutually hostile actions and using coercion to injure or control their opponents. Thus conflict encompasses political riots, insurrection, revolution, crisis and war.

What is an *international crisis*, and how does it begin? There are two defining conditions: a change in type and/or an increase in intensity of disruptive interactions between two or more states, with a heightened (higher-than-normal) probability of military hostilities (war); that, in turn, destabilizes their relationship and represents a challenge to the structure of an international system. The change or increase in intensity is usually triggered by an external act or event: a threatening statement; the severance of diplomatic relations; a trade embargo; the movement of troops; violence against an ally or client state; or a direct military attack. An international crisis can also be initiated by an internal challenge to a regime, or an act to strengthen the position of those in power. It may also arise from a technological or geopolitical change that weakens a state's capacity to protect its vital interests, including independence.

An international crisis begins with a *foreign policy crisis* for one or more states. The trigger to a foreign policy crisis is a hostile act, disruptive event or environmental change that creates three interrelated perceptions by a state's decision-maker(s): of threat to one or more basic values; finite time for response; and heightened probability of involvement in military hostilities before the challenge is overcome. The most crucial is the third condition: a higher-than-normal perception of war likelihood includes a perceived higher-than-normal threat to values; but threat can exist without the expectation of violence. In sum, a foreign policy crisis is catalyzed by a decision-maker's image of pressure to cope with externally focused stress. This, in turn, marks the beginning of an international crisis. Herein lies the link between the two levels of crisis. An international crisis erupts when there is behavioural change by one or more states leading to more hostile interaction. The change in A's behaviour triggers a foreign policy crisis for B, through its perception of threat, time pressure and heightened war likelihood. Thus perception and behavior, state level and system/interactor level, foreign policy crisis and international crisis, are intertwined.

International conflict and international crisis, too, are related but not synonymous. In essence, every crisis reflects a 'state of conflict' between two or more adversaries; but not every conflict is reflected in crisis. Moreover, the focus of crisis is, usually, a single issue, whether a border dispute, economic boycott, alleged mistreatment of a minority group, threat to a political regime, etc. Crises are episodes that occur within, as well as outside, protracted conflicts or enduring rivalries, for example, the 1960, 1964 and 1977–8 Ethiopia–Somalia crises over the disputed Ogaden territory, and the Iceland/UK 'cod wars' of 1973 and 1975–6 over fishing rights. Even when an international crisis is very long it can be distinguished from an international conflict, as with the Jordan Waters crisis of 1963–4, which was part of the Arab–Israeli protracted conflict over many issues since the end of the British Mandate over Palestine in May 1948.

Protracted conflict is the conceptual link between international conflict and international crisis. Such conflicts have been defined as 'hostile interactions which extend over long periods of time with sporadic outbreaks of open warfare fluctuating in frequency and intensity. [Protracted conflicts] are conflict situations in which the stakes are very high. . . . While they may exhibit some breakpoints during which there is a cessation of overt violence, they linger on in time and have no distinguishable point of termination. . . . Protracted conflicts, that is to say, are not specific events or even clusters of events at a point in time; they are processes' (Azar et al., 1978:50).[4]

There have been many protracted conflicts in the twentieth century – 31 from the end of 1918 to the end of 1994. These include conflicts between Ethiopia and Somalia, France and Germany, Greece and Turkey, India and Pakistan, Israel and the Arab states, etc. Most exhibit all of the traits specified above. In others, notably the East–West conflict from 1945 to 1989, direct violence between the principal adversaries was conspicuously absent, though proxy wars were widespread, e.g. in Angola, Afghanistan, the Middle East; that is, there were no 'sporadic outbreaks of open warfare' between the United States and the Soviet Union. So too with the Italy–Yugoslavia conflict over Trieste from 1945 to 1953. In others, violence was intense and persistent, notably the long-war conflicts: between China and Japan from 1937 to 1945; World War II from 1939 to 1945; the Yemen War from 1962 to 1967; the Vietnam War from 1964 to 1975, and the Iran–Iraq War from 1980 to 1988. Thus 'sporadic warfare' is not a necessary condition of protracted conflict.

Many crises, too, occur without violence, for example, Germany's remilitarization of the Rhineland in 1936, and Iraq's threat to Kuwait's territorial integrity in 1961 and 1994. Some are characterized by minor or serious clashes, such as a border dispute between Cambodia and Thailand in 1958–9, and the second Congo crisis in 1964. Others are accompanied by war.

Conflict and crisis are also closely linked to *war*. Among many definitions of war, the most widely-accepted is a 'conflict involving at least one member of [the] interstate system on each side of the war, resulting in a total of 1000 or more battle deaths' (Singer and Small,

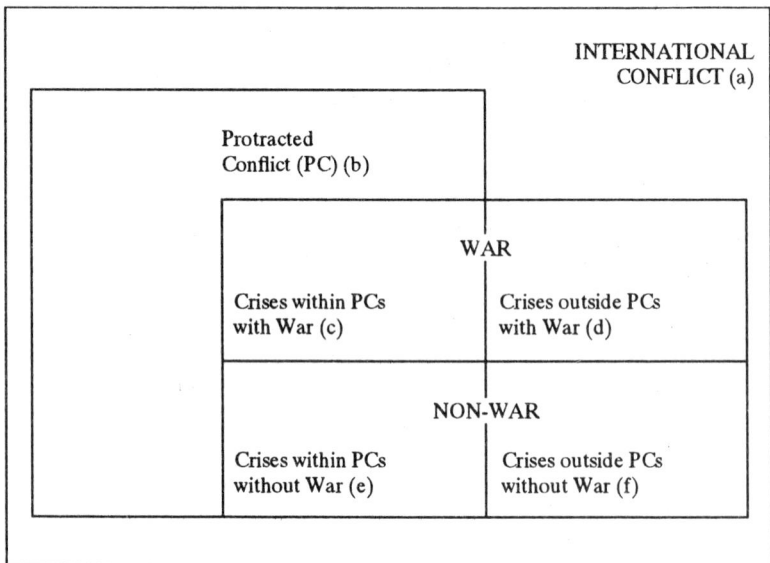

Figure 1.1 Conflict, Crisis, War

1972:381). Crises are generally identified with acts, events or environmental changes that occur prior to the outbreak of military hostilities (Snyder and Diesing, 1977; Lebow, 1981). However, crises can be triggered by the outbreak of war, for example, the German attack on 22 June 1941 ('Operation Barbarossa'), catalyzing a crisis for the Soviet Union. Crises can also escalate to war, as with the India/China border crisis of 1959–62. And developments during a war can trigger a crisis for a warring state, as for Germany following the decimation of its VI Army at the Battle of Stalingrad (1942–3). In short, a crisis can erupt, persist and terminate with or without violence. War does not eliminate or replace crisis. Rather, crisis is accentuated by war.

The links among these three concepts are evident in Figure 1.1.

Not all crises escalate to war. Some crises occur within, others outside, protracted conflicts (enduring rivalries). Some crises within and some outside protracted conflicts escalate to war. Both crisis and war are segments of international conflict; that is, in spatial terms, international conflict comprises, in descending order, protracted conflict, crisis, war, along with other kinds of transnational or interstate disputes over territory, resources, human rights, etc.

International Crisis: Theory, Methods and Evidence

There are many ways to classify works on crisis. One is in terms of substance, with half-a-dozen strands. The first is *crisis anticipation*, of which McClelland was the pioneer: his use of events data – the *World Events Interaction Survey* (WEIS) – to map the flow of system-level transitions (1961, 1964, 1968, 1972, 1977) generated early warning indicators for crisis forecasting. A second substantive focus is *crisis decision-making*, pioneered by Snyder, Bruck and Sapin (1962 [1954]). Paige (1968, 1972) applied their general framework to the US response to the outbreak of the Korean War in June 1950. And a plethora of books and articles examined US decision-making in crises: Allison (1971) and Herek (1989) on Cuban Missiles; Shlaim (1983) on the Berlin Blockade; Dowty (1984) on the Lebanon crisis of 1958, the Jordan–Syria confrontation of 1970, and the superpower nuclear alert crisis of 1973; and Burke and Greenstein (1989) and Steinberg (1996) on presidential decisions during the Vietnam War. Similarly, Soviet crisis decisions were examined by Adomeit (1982 [the Berlin crises of 1948–9, 1961]); Glassman (1975) and Golan (1977 [the 1973 October/Yom Kippur crisis-war]); and Dawisha (1984 [the Prague Spring crisis of 1968]).

A third cluster of works examined *crisis management*, by intermediaries (Young, 1967; Haas, E.B., 1983, 1986; Brecher and Wilkenfeld, 1989), and by states (George, Hall and Simons, 1971; George and Smoke, 1974; George, 1991). Others (Bracken, 1983; Lebow, 1987) focused on crisis management in the nuclear sphere. Research on the related theory and practice of deterrence was even more abundant, notably Kahn (1960), Schelling (1960), and G.H. Snyder (1961), the pioneers, followed by George and Smoke (1974) and Morgan (1977), and a third wave in the 1980s and 90s, noted in the earlier discussion of works on war.

The *crisis bargaining* sector of the literature has generated a large number of works, notably Young (1968), Snyder and Diesing (1977), Allan (1983), Powell (1987, 1988), Leng (1983, 1988, 1993), Brams (1994), Morgan (1994). *Crisis diplomacy* was examined through the lens of comparative history (Richardson, 1994). The study of *crisis initiation* has been less developed: notable are Bueno de Mesquita's expected utility theory of the initiation of war (1981, and Bueno de Mesquita and Lalman 1992); and Maoz's (1982) study of the initiation of 'serious international disputes'. Finally, little attention has been devoted to *crisis abatement*, that is, the winding down of crises (Brams and Kilgour, 1987a; Brecher, 1993).

Another general mode of grouping works on crisis is in terms of *crisis decision-making models*. The pioneer was the 'Stanford School,' whose Studies in Conflict and Integration in the 1960s and 1970s employed a 'mediated stimulus-response' (or hostile interaction) model, with perception as the key variable explaining state behaviour under high stress (Holsti, 1965, 1972; Nomikos and North, 1976). This posits that an expression of hostility by state A towards state B, and reciprocity by B at a higher level of hostility, leads to a spiral of increasingly intense hostility and escalation to violence. A variant is the 'conflict-begets-conflict' model, which asserts that state behaviour, like human behaviour, is likely to be a proportional response to an environmental stimulus, more precisely, that the total conflict sent by states approximates the total conflict received (Wilkenfeld, 1975).

The 'individual stress' model identifies stress as the derivative of perceptions – of threat, time pressure, and, in the Hermann (1969) version, surprise, or, in Brecher's (1977) definition of a foreign policy crisis, probability of war. There is a wide diversity of views regarding the effects of stress on the quality of decision-making (Holsti and George, 1975; Brecher 1993). Closely related is the 'cognitive' model, which argues that psychological biases make rational choice a chimera (Lazarus, 1966; Jervis, 1976; Janis and Mann, 1977; Lebow and Stein, 1989a), and 'psychoanalytic' models that emphasize the role of shame and humiliation in crisis decision-making (Steinberg, 1991a,b, 1996), and the role of leader personality (Post, 1991).

The 'organizational process' or 'cybernetic' model (Steinbruner, 1974) argues that the constraints imposed by threat, time and surprise lead decision-makers to rely on standard operating procedures of organizations rather than to engage in a careful search for, and evaluation of, alternatives based upon multiple sources of information. And these decisions tend to be 'satisfying,' not 'optimizing.' The decisive role of constraints in obstructing vigilant problem-solving – 'cognitive,' 'affiliative,' and 'egocentric' (self-serving and emotive) constraints – is evident in Janis's (1989) 'constraints model' of policy-making processes.

The 'cost-calculation' model under its various names – rational actor (Allison, 1971), analytic (Stein and Tanter, 1980), expected utility (Bueno de Mesquita, 1981) – postulates that crisis decisions emerge from a careful assessment of the risks and benefits of alternative options; that is, decision-makers choose the option that has the greatest expected utility. This they do by multiplying the subjective value of each possible outcome of an action by the probability that it will occur.

Moreover, they continuously revise their estimates in the light of new information.

A contrasting approach to probability assessment and risky choice is provided by 'prospect theory' (Kahneman and Tversky, 1979). Discussed at length in Chapters 4 (Levy) and 11 (Mintz and Geva), its main thesis – and major findings – are 'that people tend to overweight losses with respect to comparable gains, that they are generally risk-averse with respect to gains and risk-acceptant with respect to losses, that they respond to probabilities in a non-linear fashion, and that how they frame a problem around a reference point has a critical influence on their choices' (see also Quattrone and Tversky, 1988).

A third general approach to classifying works on crisis is *levels of analysis*, with many variations: two levels – global systemic and state (Singer, 1961); three levels – systemic, nation-state, decision-making (Spanier, 1974); four levels – state, bureaucratic organization, decision-making group, individual (Holsti, 1989); and five levels – global systemic, inter- and/or multistate composite group (state), group, individual (Andriole, 1978). Some extend their analysis to ten levels (Deutsch, 1974).

Crisis research can also be grouped in terms of the *methodology* employed. It may be historical description. It may be 'critical case' study (Eckstein, 1975), or 'comparative case' study, using a framework such as 'structured focused comparison' (George, 1979) or 'structured empiricism' (Brecher, 1972), or some other variant of comparative analysis (e.g., Lebow, 1981). It may be quantitative, aggregate study of a large number of cases (Singer and Small, 1972; Small and Singer, 1982; Gochman and Maoz, 1984; Leng and Singer, 1988; Brecher and Wilkenfeld, 1989, 1997). Or it may be a game theory approach to the dissection of crisis (Brams and Kilgour, 1988; Mor, 1993; Brams, 1994; the chapters by Harvey and James, and Maoz and Mor in this volume).

As with the state level of analysis, there are competing definitions of crisis at the interactor-system level. Those emphasizing the *process* dimension, view international crisis as a turning point: 'a "change of state" in the flow of international political actions..., "short burst" affairs... marked by an unusual volume and intensity of events' (McClelland, 1968:160–1); 'Interaction above the present upper critical threshold... (of the Normal Relations Range [NRR]) for more than a very short time implies that a crisis situation has set in' (Azar, 1972:184); a 'militarized interstate dispute' 'evolves into a militarized interstate crisis when a member of the interstate system on each side of the dispute indicates by its actions its willingness to go to war to defend its interests or to obtain its objectives' (Leng and Singer, 1988:159; also Gochman and Maoz, 1984). These definitions tend to emphasize various stages of conflictive behavior among states; to characterize different types of activity; to measure the direction and speed of behavioral change; and to locate shifts that indicate changes in interaction processes. They are all important aspects of crisis analysis at the interactor-system level.

Structural-interaction definitions go further: they identify an international crisis as a situation characterized by basic change in processes that might affect structural variables of a system. Typical is Young's view (1968:15): 'A crisis in international politics is a process of interaction occurring at higher levels of perceived intensity than the ordinary flow of events and characterized by ... significant implications for the stability of some system or subsystem.' Such definitions exhibit three weaknesses. They do not integrate all the key concepts related to international crisis – change in interaction, type of structure, disequilibrium, and instability. They focus excessively on process, with little explanation of its effects on the structure of a system. And they merge systemic concepts with unit-level concepts – perception, stress and value. This mixture of levels, conditions and indicators creates conceptual ambiguity.

Several works analyzed crisis at both state and system levels and integrated their findings, while treating foreign policy crisis and international crisis as conceptually distinct (George and Smoke, 1974; Tanter, 1974; and Snyder and Diesing, 1977). Yet in all of these the primary focus was other than crisis: for George and Smoke, deterrence theory; for Tanter, the East–West conflict; and for Snyder and Diesing, a synthesis of systems, bargaining and decision-making theory.

A qualitatively different conception of crisis is attributed to Chinese communist leaders by Bobrow et al. (1977:204, 205): first, '[w]hile international crises indicate periods of stress and danger, they may also signal opportunities to advance one's interests'; second, '[t]hey are recurrent phenomena generated by long-term economic processes and are not unpredictable, sudden flares of belligerency among actors'; third, '[t]hey are, at least at their initial stage of development, primarily domestic phenomena and not foreign relations phenomena'; and fourth, '[t]hey are protracted phenomena ... and their resolution requires persistent struggle, perseverance and patience....'

The term, crisis, has a fundamentally different meaning for the *world system* approach to world politics. According to Wallerstein (1983:21): 'By crisis in a historical system I shall mean ... a structural strain so great that the only possible outcome is the disappearance of the system as such, either by a process of gradual disintegration ... or by a process of relatively controlled transformation.... In this sense, a crisis is by definition a "transition" ... medium-long in length, taking often 100–150 years.'

In response to conceptual inadequacies and ambiguities, a new definition of international crisis was created: it incorporates change in process and structure, and links them to stability and equilibrium, the four crucial elements of an international system. In international crises, change varies in quantity and quality; that is, few distortions in process or few challenges to the structure of a system denote low instability, whereas many changes indicate high instability. By contrast, reversible changes in process or challenges to structure indicate equilibrium, while irreversible changes identify disequilibrium. That, in turn, may or may not lead to system transformation (Brecher and Ben Yehuda, 1985). This definition of international crisis has the additional merit of facilitating the study of change in world politics.

From this review it is clear that, despite abundant theorizing and research, perhaps because of the plethora of definitions, approaches and conceptual frameworks, a theory of crisis, encompassing both international and foreign policy dimensions, has not yet been universally accepted. In the quest for a consensus theory, three guidelines merit attention:

1. the concepts of international and foreign policy crisis denote dynamic processes over time, with separate phases (periods) – onset (pre-crisis), escalation (crisis), de-escalation (end-crisis), and impact (post-crisis);
2. the distinguishing trait of each phase – incipient distortion, peak distortion, accommodation, and non-crisis interaction – and of each period – low, high, declining, and non-crisis stress – can be explained by different sets of enabling variables: system, interactor, actor and situation attributes, acting through perceptions of threat, time pressure and war likelihood; and
3. the two levels of crisis are analytically distinct but interrelated processes, each helping to explain the other, and both are integral parts of a larger unified whole.

The task of achieving a theoretical consensus on crisis, as on war and conflict, is, in one sense, made easier by the impressive cumulation of data on conflict, crisis and war: a large number of datasets facilitate the testing of models and hypotheses.

Escalation from Crisis to War

It remains to address two closely-related aspects of conflict, crisis and war: the meaning of escalation, and competing explanations of escalation from crisis to war. As a point of departure, escalation in interstate relations denotes a pattern of rising tension, growing military preparedness, and increasingly hostile actions. These are often accompanied by an arms race, unproductive negotiations, verbal abuse, and extreme tactics, often leading to violence. Escalation occurs both prior to, and during, a war.

The idea of escalation before a war is central to the literature on arms races, as in Richardson's pioneering arms race model (1960a, 1960b). In essence, it argued that any change in an existing military balance enhances the security of one adversary and the threat perceived by the other. More important, both are prisoners of assumptions and misperceptions that tend to become self-fulfilling and thereby induce an *escalation spiral* in the search for superior power; that is, they engage in an arms race. State A may not contemplate a preemptive attack on B, or vice-versa; but each may – in an anarchical state system, is likely to – assume that the other will so contemplate and so act, if it has a sufficient margin of military capability. Thus A will assume that B will attempt to alter the arms balance in its favour. A's assumption will, in turn, predispose it to increase its arms potential. Such behaviour will lead B to perceive threat and to respond in kind. In short, the assumptions of A and B become self-fulfilling, driving both to an escalatory arms race. For Richardson, in sum, escalation is built into the dynamics of the arms race.[5]

For Rapoport (1960, 1987), escalation is built into the dynamics of system instability: the arms system, like any other, becomes unstable when the rates of change in the military balance, not its level, are not constant. In the nuclear era, with the exponential increase in destructive power, escalation is an integral part of the dynamics of non-war superpower confrontation. The idea of escalatory steps to war is also embedded in Lebow's (1987) concept of 'miscalculated escalation', one of three sequences from crisis to nuclear war (the others are 'preemption' and 'loss of control').

Leng (1983) found that escalation from crisis to war was driven much more by developments in the international environment and the behaviour of one's adversary than by domestic stimuli. James (1987, 1988) discovered that states were more likely to escalate a military dispute, that is, initiate war, when the dispute coincided with an increase in international turmoil and an opportunity to use force successfully. And Huth, Gelpi and Bennet (1993:619), found that 'rational deterrence theory provides a much more compelling explanation of great-power decisions to escalate militarized disputes [from 1816 to 1984] than does structural realism.'

The idea of escalation during a war is evident in von Clausewitz's *On War* (1976 [1832]; Paret, 1985). For him, the essence of war is to compel one's enemy to do one's will. Thus the aim of the adversaries is total victory; moderation in war is a contradiction. To that end both must act so as to maximize their military power by mobilizing and using all possible resources. And since victory is the shared yet conflicting goal, the logic of war makes (reciprocal) escalation inevitable: each will raise the stakes and intensity of the contest until one side triumphs. For Clausewitz, in short, escalation is built into the dynamics of war.[6]

Among strategic theorists of the contemporary era, escalation is clearly implied in Schelling's *The Strategy of Conflict* (1960). But this book focuses primarily on *limited war* and on bargaining, via tacit communication, between adversaries in a conflict/war situation. Victory is best achieved through deterrence, or 'the skillful non-use of military capacity to pursue a nation's objective' (1960:6). However, in the contest over resolve each party will raise the stakes, that is, escalate, to compel the other to yield. For Schelling, then, escalation is built into the dynamics of bargaining in limited war.

The link between escalation and war was cogently formulated by Smoke (1977:17): 'Escalation is the process by which the previous limits of a war are crossed and new ones established.... Conversely, the (expanding) limits of a war are the barriers or thresholds or stages of the escalation process. [That is], limited war and escalation are coextensive.... But limited war is the static term; escalation is the dynamic term.'

An all-encompassing view of escalation was presented by Herman Kahn, another leading strategist of the post-World War II era. *On Escalation* (1965), which followed his even more controversial *On Thermonuclear War* (1960), was — and remains — innovative in two respects. First, in contrast to the view of escalation as a purely intra-war phenomenon, that is, 'the development of small wars into larger ones' (Pruitt and Snyder, 1969:57), Kahn discerned the roots of escalation and its early stages in a pre-war environment of crisis. Second, he created an elaborate and complex *escalation ladder* of 44 rungs, from non-war to nuclear war. For Kahn, escalation is built into the dynamics of interstate conflict.

Finally, escalation is attributed by many to behaviour by a single state, which initiates war to attain one of several goals: economic gain; political aims, such as the acquisition or restoration of territory (irredentism), the liberation of oppressed groups, or the creation of friendly governments in other states; ideological ends, such as the spread of communism or democracy and market economies; the enhancement of national security or military power in anticipation of future wars; influence; prestige, etc.

International War

What factors induce states to attempt to achieve political, economic or military objectives through war? In addition to pioneering works by Sorokin (1937), Wright (1942), and Richardson (1960a, 1960b), there have been virtually thousands of books and articles on the subject, a vast literature exhibiting an array of approaches, methods, theories and substantive foci, as evident in the brief selection of relevant works listed by category in Appendix I. A brief review of the more prominent areas of research and findings will follow.

With respect to *regime type*, there is little evidence that internal conflict is linked to external conflict behaviour (e.g. Rummel, 1963; Tanter, 1966; Wilkenfeld, 1968). Following a review of the literature on the subject, Huth and Lust-Okar (Chapter 3 in this volume) recommend a new approach that may account for the inconsistent findings, one that considers domestic political variables in the decision calculus. There is strong evidence and a near-consensus that democratic regimes do not engage in war with each other (a list of works on regime type and war will be found in the Appendix). Nor do they initiate foreign policy crises with other democratic regimes (Brecher and Wilkenfeld, 1989, 1997). There also is growing evidence that war results from an exponential *growth in military and economic capability* by a regime unaccompanied by higher status in the system, that is, 'power transitions' (Organski and Kugler, 1980; Howard, 1984: Kugler and Organski, 1989).

Another explanation of escalation to war emphasizes *interactive behavior* that generates a spiral of mutually-reinforcing hostility culminating in war. This process is closely linked to the 'security dilemma': 'Wherever ... anarchic society has existed ... there has arisen what may be called the "security dilemma" of men, or groups, or their leaders ... [who] must be, and usually are concerned about their security from being attacked, subjected, dominated, or annihilated.... Since none can ever feel entirely secure in such a world of competing units, power competition ensues, and the vicious circle of security and power accumulation is on' (Herz, 1950:157; 1951; see also Jervis, 1976, 1978; Snyder, 1984).

For some (Lenin, 1939 [1917]; Choucri and North, 1975, 1989), interstate war may be caused by a conflict over scarce resources. It may be due to unanticipated effects of coercive diplomacy (George, Hall and Simons, 1971), or unstable military balances resulting from arms races (Brown, 1987). Among these structural factors there is an ongoing debate over the likely effect of power distribution in an international system on peace and war. Balance of power theorists (Morgenthau, 1960; Claude, 1962) argue that relative equality, that is, balanced power, is more likely to produce peace. Preponderant power theorists (Organski, 1958) argue the reverse, on the grounds that a strong power need not employ war to attain its objectives.

Another explanation of escalation to war emphasizes the role of *threat perception*. At one level, war may ensue when decision makers perceive their goals as incompatible with those of their adversary(ies). Threat perception may lead to preemptive war. And misperception – of one's intentions and/or capability, or of the adversary's intentions and/or capability – is viewed by some as the primary source of escalation to war (Jervis, 1976; Lebow, 1981; Vertzberger, 1990). This school emphasizes the cognitive dimension of behaviour: distrust generates counter-mistrust and a spiraling process of mutual misperception leading to war.

The assertion, common in most political psychology literature, that decision-makers are more likely to fall prey to these subconscious psychological and cognitive pressures, and less likely to decide rationally, often lacks a compelling defence. Consequently, proponents of political psychology are often criticized for failing to explain why their models provide a more plausible set of assumptions upon which to develop explanations for crisis escalation and war. The mere likelihood that decision pathologies may take over during a crisis is not sufficient to render alternative, rational choice models trivial. Since the publications of Bueno de Mesquita's *The War Trap* (1981), several scholars have compiled an impressive body of evidence (both formal and empirical) demonstrating that positive expected utility is a necessary condition for crisis, escalation and war. Although the model has since been refined (Bueno de Mesquita, 1985; Bueno de Mesquita and Lalman, 1986, 1992), the core 'rational choice' proposition continues to receive widespread empirical support (Ray, 1994).

What has been learned about the outbreak of war by quantitative research? Zinnes (1980:359–60) acknowledged that 'the mystery is a long way from being solved'. And Midlarsky (1989) was no more sanguine: 'Overall, these studies show that there are many ways to investigate the phenomenon of international warfare, ways that are both analytically rigorous and empirically valid.' In sum, the explanation and prediction of war, even more so than of crisis, remains elusive. Although we have compiled an impressive body of theory and evidence on international conflict, crisis and war, and answered several important questions about onset, escalation and de-escalation in each domain, we have also produced additional questions and puzzles. Each of the eleven chapters that follow in this volume builds on this body of research in an effort to enhance our explanatory power with respect to the conflict domain of world politics. Summaries of their contributions are presented below.

III. NEW APPROACHES

Part One of the volume, on international *conflict*, encompasses three chapters. In Chapter 2, Maoz and Mor develop a game theoretic model to explore questions about the evolution of rivalries, a subject that has received comparatively little attention in the literature on protracted conflict and enduring rivalry. Their research addresses several important and interrelated questions about the link between three phases of rivalry, from onset to development to termination: How does the evolution of enduring rivalry differ from incidental rivalries? Why do some conflicts repeat themselves while others terminate before they become enduring? What are the temporal relations between disputes over time? How is the outbreak of one dispute linked to the process and outcome of previous dispute(s)? And finally, how do enduring rivalries terminate?

With respect to the temporal domain between crises in rivalries, the exclusive focus of their chapter for this volume, the occurrence or non-occurrence of a dispute in any given year is a function of two key variables: *capabilities and satisfaction*. Among the many hypotheses the authors subject to empirical verification, one is that leaders are more likely to initiate crises when they are not satisfied with the status quo while holding a favorable balance of power. Outcomes in these disputes change the status quo, both in terms of satisfaction levels and capabilities, which in turn increases the probability of crisis escalation and sets in motion subsequent stages of rivalry. Their analysis demonstrates, in part, that actors change their preferences 'in accordance with outcomes they obtain in previous disputes and in response to changes in the balance of capabilities.' The findings also help to explain why some rivalries are protracted: neither side manages to obtain outcomes in previous disputes that are sufficient to satisfy key demands and core values.

In Chapter 3, Huth and Lust-Okar address the many inconsistent findings on the relationship between internal and external conflict behaviour (i.e. externalization, contagion, and scapegoat theories), a subject that has received detailed treatment in the literature. Their objective is to evaluate two opposing arguments: (1) 'domestic unrest leads to more aggressive and confrontational foreign policy behaviour as ruling elites seek to divert political attention at home away from internal problems by rallying nationalist political support behind a policy of conflict and crisis with an external adversary'; versus (2) 'domestic political instability and turmoil cause state leaders to withdraw from foreign affairs as they focus state resources and their attention on dealing with internal political and economic problems.' Since existing evidence appears to support both positions, Huth and Lust-Okar assume both sides are right, under some conditions, and set out to reconcile opposing arguments by analyzing a more restricted set of political conditions – related to a leader's preference for *suppressing* or *accommodating* domestic opposition.

The potential of prospect theory as a theory of choice under conditions of risk is the focus of Chapter 4: Jack Levy's 'Loss Aversion, Framing, and Bargaining: The Implications of Prospect Theory for International Conflict.' The first half of his paper presents the essence of prospect theory and its major findings based on laboratory evidence: 'that people tend to overweight losses with respect to comparable gains, that they are generally risk-averse with respect to gains and risk-acceptant with respect to losses, that they respond to probabilities in a non-linear fashion, and that how they frame a problem around a reference point has a critical influence on their choices.' In the course of this presentation he notes prospect theory's 'rich and intriguing set of hypotheses about international relations,' and highlights what he regards as 'anomalies' in expected-utility theory.

Some implications of prospect theory for bargaining, deterrence and system stability in international politics are explored in the second half of the paper. Levy also addresses some of the 'difficult methodological problems' arising from efforts to apply prospect theory to international conflict. And he concludes on a note of caution, calling for 'a great deal of theoretical and empirical research ... before we can be confident that prospect theory constitutes a generalizable and empirically valid theory of behaviour.'

Part Two, on *Crisis*, includes three chapters, each attempting to account for crisis escalation in three distinct domains: conventional (Brecher), nuclear (Harvey and James) and protracted conflict (Hensel) settings. In Chapter 5, 'Crisis Escalation: Model and Findings', Brecher focuses on the peak stress stage of an interstate crisis. As specified elsewhere (Brecher, 1993), a crisis unfolds in four phases (onset, escalation, de-escalation and impact), and, at the state level, four periods (pre-crisis, crisis, end-crisis and post-crisis). Escalation refers to three distinct but related processes: 'change from embryonic to full-scale crisis ..., from low to peak stress; change from non-violent to violent crisis; and change from no/low violence to severe violence.' Each of these taps a distinct dimension of escalation. Together they are parts of a holistic view of this phase of crisis.

The inquiry is guided by a set of questions about the most likely conditions for escalation: at the interactor/system level, escalation from the onset phase to a full-scale international crisis, violent escalation, and severe violence; at the actor level, escalation of a foreign policy crisis for state A by state B, the use of violence by the escalating state, and vulnerability to violent escalation; and, finally, how states cope with the high stress of escalation. To uncover these most likely conditions the chapter specifies a model of crisis escalation, setting out the independent, intervening and dependent variables, and their relationships; frames hypotheses derived from the model; and tests them with aggregate data, from 400 international crises and 800+ foreign policy crises from 1918 to 1988. The expectations from the model are tested. Strong support is reported for all seven hypotheses. Finally, the evidence from ten case studies reveals a widely shared pattern of coping during the escalation phase. This finding challenges conventional wisdom and compels rethinking about how states cope in foreign policy crises.

Harvey and James employ game theory in Chapter 6 to probe crisis interaction by the superpowers. They begin 'Superpowers at the Brink' with a critique of the literature and aggregate studies of nuclear deterrence. Several obstacles to cumulative knowledge are noted: lack of consensus on superpower crises; lack of clarity in designating attackers and defenders; failure to distinguish general from immediate deterrence; conceptual and empirical confusion between deterrence and compellance; disputes over the criteria for success and failure in crisis behaviour.

'Disagreements about the historical record' emerge with stark clarity from a review of 15 studies.

To overcome this core problem Harvey and James opt for an 'alternative strategy which focuses on strategic interaction in crises as discrete events.' This is operationalized in a multi-stage threat game, designed to achieve 'simplification' and 'a greater sense of reality.' Propositions and possibilities for testing are discussed briefly. A 15-point scale of intensity of superpower bargaining techniques ranges from a nuclear strike to cooperation. They conclude that their crisis-based approach is a more promising test of rational deterrence theory than others used hitherto. And they report that preliminary evidence points to learning by the superpowers of vital rules of prudence, promoting de-escalation and stability in crises, rather than the reverse.

In Chapter 7, Hensel provides additional evidence about the differences in conflict behaviour between enduring rivals and non-rival adversaries. Following a detailed review of the enduring rivalry literature, Hensel examines how the impact of confrontations on subsequent relations between states changes as the rivalry relationship evolves. With this as a starting point, Hensel adds original empirical analysis of crisis frequency and recurrence to illustrate the important contributions of *rivalry* and *evolution* concepts to our understanding of interstate conflict, militarized interstate disputes, international crises and interstate wars.

Hensel accomplishes this task by empirically comparing rivalry-based and evolutionary perspectives on international conflict to more traditional approaches. The analysis employs recently updated Correlates of War (COW) Project data on militarized interstate disputes from 1816 to 1992, covering 16 more years than previous data sets, with roughly twice as many militarized disputes. The new data are used to reexamine some of the most important findings from the current published research on rivalry. The chapter also employs a recently updated version of the International Crisis Behaviour (ICB) data base that runs to 1988, unlike earlier studies which ended in 1979. Hensel uses the updated data sets to explore the conflict behaviour of 103 enduring rival dyads in three evolutionary phases, thus allowing comparison of how conflict behavior changes as the disputes evolve through the different phases of rivalry. The analysis expands on the existing literature 'by controlling for the effects of the issues at stake between two rivals and the outcomes of their confrontations as well as the history of past conflict between them.' The conclusion summarizes a number of potential contributions and offers suggestions on how the concepts can help to shape conflict research in the future.

Part Three, on *War and Peace*, includes five chapters, encompassing three strands in the literature: escalation, de-escalation and resolution. The scope of Chapter 8, by John Vasquez, is both very narrow and very broad, as evident in its title, 'The Steps to war in Europe, 1933–41.' Its aim is two-fold: to explain the outbreak of a European war in 1939 and its enlargement to global war in 1941; and to test the fit between a general theory of the causes and expansion of major power war and the evidence of one of the two cataclysmic wars of the century. The analysis is theoretically, not empirically, driven; that is, it employs the method of explaining a specific war in light of what are 'theoretically known' general causes of war.

Vasquez begins with a brief presentation of his theory of 'steps to (world) war,' defined elsewhere (Vasquez, 1993:63) as 'a large-scale severe war among major states that involves the leading states at some point in the war and most other major states in a struggle to resolve the most fundamental issues on the global political agenda.' The 'typical path' to war between equally powerful states – no other type of war is embraced by his theory – comprises six steps. The underlying cause is a physical threat to the territory of a major power by one of its rivals. The 'proximate causes' are: a 'power politics' response, that is, formation of an alliance by the threatened state against its rival; and a military buildup by the threatened state; successive crises between the protagonists; escalatory bargaining by both parties during these crises; a hostile spiral; and the wielding of authority by hardliners on at least one side. Vasquez poses – and answers in the affirmative – the question, did the outbreak of World War II fit these steps to war?

He then addresses the related question of war expansion and cites six sufficient conditions: the presence of alliances that draw allied non-belligerents into the war, the most important factor in war expansion; territorial contiguity, facilitating spillover of the war to bordering states; bandwagon effects associated with the weakening of norms prohibiting violence; the breakdown of the political order; and the bringing of economically dependent states into the war. Finally he specifies three necessary systemic conditions for expansion to global war: a multipolar distribution of capability; the reduction of multipolarity, through alliances, to bipolarity; and the absence of power preponderance by either bloc.

The bulk of the chapter applies this theory to the cause of the European War in 1939 and its expansion to World War II in 1941. The reader is taken through the steps to war as they unfolded in the 1930s, and its transformation to World War II with Germany's invasion of the

Soviet Union and Japan's attack on Pearl Harbor in 1941. The conclusion is unqualified: 'The path states took to the dyadic war and the path that led that war to expand to a world war were not unique to 1939–1941, but typical of how world wars begin. This shows that a scientific analysis can clearly identify the underlying factors guiding states along the paths to war.'

Chapter 9, by Ben Zvi, addresses war through the prism of 'Surprise Attacks'. In-depth case studies of the Yom Kippur War and the attack on Pearl Harbor are used to probe for evidence about the dynamics of escalation from the perspective of decision making in the defending state (Israel and the US, respectively). The focus is on the nature of 'surprise' and the cognitive forces that explain the failure to predict, respond to, or prepare for the impending attack. The main purpose for comparing Pearl Harbor and the Yom Kippur War is 'to proceed beyond the parameters and bounds of the existing cognitive explanations by focusing on two neglected dimensions: the role of processes which took place after the recognition of war as imminent had permeated the thinking of the leadership of the defending state, and the role of capability assessment as a variable which contributed most decisively to the initial success of the challenger.'

The author divides intention assessment into two subcategories: (1) perceptions of the adversary's *basic intentions* (derived from the opponent's general behavioral style, approach to calculating political action, motivational calculus and ideology, all of which comprise 'a coherent set of beliefs and expectations concerning the opponent's operational code, frame of reference, and overall cultural and conceptual frameworks') and (2) *immediate intentions* (derived from information about the challenger's strategic interests – i.e. does the challenger actually intend to 'attack?'). The findings suggest that: 'while perceptions of the enemy's immediate intentions were revised and updated in view of the accumulating tactical indicators of the approaching war, no such change took place in the perceptions of the adversary's capabilities, which remained largely outdated.' The implications for crisis management are described in the conclusion.

The subject of the Democratic Peace is covered in Chapter 10, 'Democratic Change and Defense Allocation in East Asia', by Steve Chan. Using quasi-experimental research, the author undertakes 'a preliminary analysis to clarify the effects, if any, of the "democratic opening" in four East Asian countries on their military expenditures.' Chan tests several key expectations, derived from the democratic peace thesis, that 'democratization can simultaneously influence these expenditures by promoting a more relaxed international environment and by altering domestic priorities for resource allocation.'

Building on previous applications of the thesis to questions of war and peace, Chan extends the investigation by probing several additional propositions about the impact of democratic changes on military expenditure choices. Four East Asian countries are examined – Malaysia, the Philippines, South Korea, and Taiwan – three of which feature 'simultaneously rapid and sustained economic expansion, substantial armament in the midst of seemingly intractable enduring rivalries, and significant democratic opening in the recent past', with Malaysia serving as the 'control case'. Several important hypotheses about regime change and policy shifts are explored. The findings suggest that expectations about defense allocations are influenced by several factors beyond the democratic opening, including 'the interaction effect between the source of political change, the strength of the new regime's political control, and the depth and extent of its institutional ties with the armed forces.' Studying the democratic peace from the perspective of democratization and armaments helps to clarify the dynamics of democratic peace thesis and points in new and interesting directions for research on the subject.

Turning from escalation to termination, Mintz and Geva, in Chapter 11, apply prospect theory and the non-compensatory principle of decision-making to the study of war termination. Three substantive assumptions set the stage for their research: as with decisions to start a war, the domain in which a leader operates (gain vs. loss) also affects the decision to terminate a war; the loss–gain domain is defined by political leaders in political terms; and decisions made by political leaders often correspond to expectations derived from the non-compensatory principle of decision-making.

The authors explore risky decisions in one arena (foreign policy), proposing that the utilities assigned to war termination are derived from another arena (domestic politics). Political currency, rather than monetary currency (which traditionally has been used in experimental research on prospect theory in the realm of economics), serves as the empirical base. Risk aversion in the domain of gain and risk seeking in the domain of loss are explained using fluctuations in levels of public approval.

The contribution of the chapter is unique in that it introduces a prospect-based theory of war termination and tests it using quasi-experimental methods. Based on a simulated international crisis involving the United States and an 'aggressive' non-democratic regime, the experiment varies the domains in which the decision-maker operates by defining gains and losses in terms of an increase or decrease in public support. The authors hypothesize that there is a direct association 'between the domain in which the decision maker operates and his or her choice, and that this association is contingent on the salience of the political dimension.' The findings from two experiments appear to conform to prospect theory explanations – decisions to terminate a war 'are not always based on a comprehensive and comparative evaluation of all alternatives along all dimensions, but often rely on cognitive shortcuts and heuristics.' The experiments reported in this chapter provide support for the notion that 'where you stand in the polls determines where you stand on the issues.'

In Chapter 12, Brams and Togman mount a very compelling case in favor of a new procedure for arriving at an 'envy-free' division of goods (including territory) to resolve interstate conflicts and wars. The benefits of the Adjusted Winner (AW) strategy, both in terms of theory and policy, are described in detail and evaluated with reference to a real-world territorial dispute in the Middle East, namely the Camp David Accords of 1978. Their objective is 'to compare the resolution that AW hypothetically would have given with the agreement that was actually reached,' and to develop a straightforward procedure that guarantees certain properties of fairness. While AW is applicable to numerous types of disputes, the Camp David Accord was especially useful to draw out its relevance in the context of an international crisis with a significant territorial component. AW produced an outcome that mirrors quite closely the actual agreement reached by Egypt and Israel, demonstrating quite convincingly that deductive analysis can contribute to both normative as well as explanatory theory. Additional conclusions are drawn about the potential use of AW in aiding negotiators to resolve disputes more generally.

In sum, each of the chapters in this volume confronts important facets of conflict, crisis and war. Together their diverse theoretical approaches and methods contribute to our growing cumulative knowledge and our ability to explain parts of this domain of world politics. Clearly, much remains to be done before we can comprehend the whole and thereby make possible more effective crisis and conflict management, and the lessening, if not eradication, of the scourge of war. The contributions to this volume move us one step closer to that end.

NOTES

1. In this context, an important distinction must be drawn between *expansive* and *integrative* (or selective) cumulation. The former can be understood as 'an expanding, commonly perceived catalogue of models, concepts, variables, indices, relationships, data, and techniques' that are shown to be useful under certain circumstances (Ashley, 1976:152), that is, a storehouse of research options, puzzles and problems that guide inquiry in the field. In contrast, integrative cumulation encompasses a set of 'shared expectations (of) the explanatory, predictive . . . and problem solving promise of alternative models, data sets, and techniques' (Ashley, 1976:152). Expansive cumulation occurs as available research options increase, whereas integrative (selective) cumulation occurs when a community's expectations about the promise and value of these options approach consensus.

   Although terminology may differ observers agree that while the field has performed adequately in the expansive or additive sense, it has not fared well with respect to selective or integrative cumulation. There may be an abundance of facts and information out there, large impressive data bases on conflict, war, crises and militarized interstate disputes (e.g. *Dimensions of Nations, Correlates of War, International Crisis Behaviour*, etc.), and four 'events' data banks on interstate conflict and cooperation (*Conflict and Peace Data Bank* [COPDAB]; *Comparative Research on the Events of Nations* [CREON]; and *World Event Interaction Survey* [WEIS]), still we seem unable to tie findings into a framework that explains how all of these variables are related. Moreover, scholars continue to have trouble agreeing on the methods to use when developing theory, or the standards to apply when accepting or rejecting evidence.

2. The terms 'poststructural' and 'postpositive' have also been used to describe this intellectual movement, although postmodernism and poststructuralism refer to slightly different strands of critical theory. The purpose here is to extract the broad criticism implicit in both schools. Rosenau (1992:3) distinguishes between the two in terms of emphasis, arguing that '[P]ostmodernists are more oriented towards cultural critique while the poststructuralist emphasizes method and epistemological matters.' George and Campbell (1990:281) noted additional differences between hermeneutics and poststructuralism. While hermeneutics and other critical theories expose the so-called 'rotten foundations and the ideological function of traditional theory . . . to enable people to overcome the power structures that oppress them', poststructuralism focuses 'less on attempting to secure emancipation through the unmasking of power, oppression, and ideology, and more . . . on concrete examples of the way power is used in all of societies sites . . . and how to effectively resist the imposition of power articulated via the privileged "logocentric" discourses of modern scientific rationality.'

   Since we are concerned primarily with the application of these arguments to the field of international relations, emphasis will be placed on contributions to two special editions of *International Studies Quarterly* (1989, 1990). Contributions by George (1989), Der Derian (1990), George and Campbell (1990), Lapid (1989), K.J. Holsti (1989), Biersteker (1989), and

Ashley and Walker (1990) provide a good illustration of priorities among postmodern critics of IR.
3. Even 'facts' and 'empirical evidence' must be considered time-specific. Nicholson's (1992:34) discussion of the 'telephone' illustrates the argument. The existence of a telephone depends on the acceptance of a particular conceptual framework, in this case one that is apparent to most people in the twentieth century but not to someone in the sixteenth century – '[they] have no sets of concepts to recognize it or relate to it..., no conceptual framework into which it fits.... Facts are only understood in some sort of context, and are not free-floating, simply waiting to be observed.... It is only when one gets to the point of being able to say that one sees the object "as a telephone" that it makes sense and that a "fact" such as "X percent of households in Britain have telephones" becomes meaningful.'
4. On the concept of protracted conflict, see also Azar (1979, 1985), Azar and Farah (1981), Brecher (1984), Brecher and Wilkenfeld (1989: chaps 9–11; 1997: part IV). 'Protracted conflict' is related to, but not identical with, the concept of enduring rivalry, which is highly visible in the International Relations literature of the 1990s; see, for example, Goertz and Diehl, 1992a, 1992b; Huth and Russett, 1993.
5. The postulated link between an arms race and the outbreak of war was strongly supported by Wallace (1979, 1981, 1982); Weede (1980), Altfeld (1983), and Diehl (1983) dissented sharply on methodological grounds, as did Intriligator and Brito (1984). The controversy remains unresolved. For comprehensive surveys of the literature on arms races, see Moll and Luebbert (1980), Isard and Anderton (1985), Intriligator and Brito (1989), and Siverson and Diehl (1989).
6. For other allusions to intra-war escalation in strategic thought during the past two centuries see Earle (1943) and Paret (1986).

Part One
Conflict

2 Satisfaction, Capabilities, and the Evolution of Enduring Rivalries, 1816–1990: A Statistical Analysis of a Game Theoretic Model[1]

Zeev Maoz and Ben D. Mor

I. INTRODUCTION

There is renewed interest in the study of Enduring International Rivalries (EIRs) in recent years, due to the realization that many conflicts in the contemporary international system have taken place between the same pairs of states. Fourteen per cent out of a total of 171 nations that have been involved in militarized interstate disputes over the period 1816–1986 accounted for more than 58 per cent of all dispute initiations (Maoz, 1982, 1993). The very same nations were primary targets of over 50 per cent of all disputes. Over 450 disputes out of 960 (44 per cent) were repeated disputes between the same states. Moreover, 266 out of 731 primary dyads in militarized disputes (36.3 per cent) were between states that had five or more disputes between them (Geller and Jones, 1991).

In spite of the recent proliferation of studies on various aspects of EIRs, we still lack a general explanation of the strategic evolution of EIRs. In this article, we propose a bargaining framework for the study of EIRs and develop a game-theoretic model of their evolution. The model seeks to address three issues: (1) How does the evolution of EIRs differ from incidental rivalries? Why do some conflicts repeat themselves while others terminate before they become enduring? (2) Within EIRs, what are the temporal relations between disputes over time? How is the outbreak of one dispute linked to the process and outcome of previous dispute(s)? (3) How do EIRs terminate? What are the strategic conditions under which a pattern of repeated conflict changes into a stable, non-conflict relationship?

These research questions cover the entire evolution of EIRs, from initiation to development to termination. In this chapter, however, we deal primarily with the second issue, namely explaining the temporal sequence of disputes, that forms the core of an evolving rivalry.[2] We conceive the dynamics of this interaction to involve *preference formation and change*, and accordingly pose three questions: (1) What factors influence actors' conflict-related preferences over time? (2) How do these preferences affect actors' choices during the rivalry? (3) What governs changes in these preferences over time? We attempt to answer these questions by introducing a preference-formation component into a game-theoretic model of EIRs. This model is tested by means of event data analysis, conducted on a population of 105 rivalries from 1816 to 1990.

The paper is organized as follows: Section 2 looks at the game-theoretic literature on extended play that is relevant to the study of long-term interactions, and discusses the required characteristics of an evolutionary, strategic approach to the study of EIRs; Section 3 introduces a game-theoretic model of EIRs that is based on this approach; Section 4 lays out the research design; Section 5 discusses the empirical results; and Section 6 concludes this study by examining the implications of the findings and by suggesting some possibilities for future research.

II. THEORETICAL BACKGROUND

An *Enduring International Rivalry* (EIR) is defined as a set of repeated militarized interstate disputes between the same set of states over time. To be classified as an EIR, these disputes must meet *all* of the following conditions.

The Severity Condition: There must be at least five reciprocated Militarized Interstate Disputes (MIDs) between the same two states, lasting for at least thirty days each.
The Durability Condition: There must be at least 25 years between the outbreak of the first dispute and the termination of the last dispute.
The Continuity Condition: The gap between any two disputes (i.e. the termination date of the first dispute and the starting date of the second dispute) does not exceed ten years. Alternatively, if the gap between two disputes is greater than ten years, two disputes between the same states will be considered as part of the same EIR only if the territorial domain and the issues at stake remain unresolved

and there is at least one dispute within a period of 25 years (Huth, Jones, and Maoz, 1990; Geller and Jones, 1991; Goertz and Diehl, 1992).

These conditions identify as EIRs a set of conflicts that has good face validity (Goertz and Diehl, 1993).[3]

We turn next to a discussion of the game-theoretic literature that serves as the foundation of our theory of the strategic evolution of enduring rivalries. For a comprehensive review of the general literature on EIRs, see the chapter by Paul Hensel in this volume.

Existing research on EIRs suggests that a *bargaining perspective* could be a productive approach to theory building. EIRs could be understood in terms of the bargaining strategies of participants, the outcomes they obtain, and the lessons they draw from their interaction. At the same time, preferences and perceptions may also be affected by events, the origin of which is not necessarily rivalry-related, such as power transitions and political shocks (Geller and Jones, 1991; Goertz and Diehl, 1995a).

Supergame-theoretic models address at a general level situations in which players are thought to interact over time. In these models, players' strategies control not only their payoffs but also the probabilities of playing some other game at the next stage (Luce and Raiffa, 1957). Alternatively, a supergame may consist of repeated play of the same game, with future play discounted and the number of iterations either known or governed by an exogenous probability (Axelrod, 1984, 1986; Taylor, 1976).

Snyder and Diesing (1977:182) found that 'supergame considerations were prominent and consistent in the calculations of crisis bargainers.' Mor's (1991, 1993) multi-stage game analysis of the 1967 Middle East crisis showed that long-term strategic calculations accounted for behaviour that seemed inexplicable when interpreted from a myopic perspective. Taylor (1976) and Axelrod (1984), who studied iterated Prisoners' Dilemma supergames, showed that, under certain conditions, mutual cooperation could be established as an equilibrium point. Others applied this conception to study international cooperation and collective action problems (e.g. Oye, 1988).

Play over time can also be captured by two other dynamic approaches. First, games of incomplete information analyze play through time by modelling how players update their perception of the opponent's type in response to its previous strategic choices. Applications included studies of nuclear deterrence and crisis bargaining (e.g. Morrow, 1989; Powell,

1990; Wagner, 1989). Second, the theory of moves (TOM) extends the rules of classical game theory to define sequential play within fixed-matrix games (see Brams, 1994, 1993; Brams and Mattli, 1993; Brams and Mor, 1993; Mor, 1995).

Maoz (1990b:464–530) discussed two general explanations of long-term international processes. The *ad hoc* approach assumes that decision-makers apply single-shot problem-solving reasoning. Hence, choices at one point in time are influenced by the outcomes of the immediately preceding events, as well as by the interpretation of the current decision problem. The *strategic* approach assumes that decision makers use long-term reasoning of a supergame nature, and wish to maximize gains over an envisioned series of interactions that extends over a relatively long period of time.

Game-theoretic conceptions are both strategic and dynamic. Yet they advance a restricted notion of learning, referring only to changes in the perception of the opponent (which in turn affect game perception and strategy choice). These approaches do not allow for players to change their *preferences* in response to previous outcomes (Goertz and Diehl, 1993:153).

The assumption that preferences are invariant over time is not supported by empirical data.[4] By definition, EIRs are long-term processes during which major events transpire: wars may be fought, territory may be lost, leaders and governments may be overthrown – even the structure of the international system itself may transform. It is implausible to assume that the preferences of national decision-makers remain the same throughout such changes. Moreover, preference change may be required for EIRs to resolve peacefully. Hence, for an EIR model to be truly dynamic, preference change must be allowed for, at least as a theoretical possibility.

Given these considerations, a game-based framework of EIRs must meet three criteria: (1) it should provide for repeated play; (2) it should provide for dependence between play at one point in time and play at a subsequent point; and (3) it should provide for variability in the structure of games (i.e. shifts in alternatives and preferences over time). In sum, such a framework must allow for the representation and analysis of *game transformations*. Accordingly, the model we present below proceeds from the assumption that the play of a game at any given point in time may affect the *structure* of games played at a subsequent point in time. This conception is described in Figure 2.1.

As Figure 2.1 shows, the play of any component game in a temporally related game series produces an outcome that leads to a subsequent

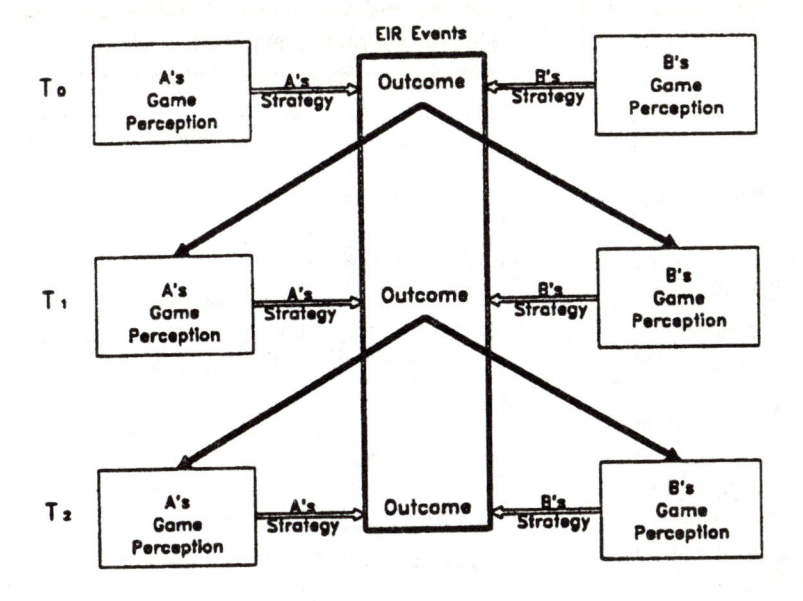

Satisfaction, Capabilities, and the Evolution of Rivalry

Figure 2.1 EIRs: a game-based theoretical framework

game.[5] This game, in turn, also produces an outcome, which leads to another, consecutive game, and so on. Any two adjacent games in this series may be structurally identical or different. If different, prior outcomes may be responsible for the change. The series either does or does not terminate in a final game. This is analogous to EIRs, some of which are resolved and some of which continue to simmer and perhaps explode.

III. ENDURING INTERNATIONAL RIVALRIES: A GAME-THEORETIC MODEL

The Formation of Preferences in a Rivalry

It is useful to start an analysis of EIRs from an abstract description of a generic situation wherein two states first come to consider one another as strategic partners/rivals (e.g. when one or both states acquire independence). We assume that the parties need to define their attitudes towards the territorial, political, social, or other aspects of this situation. This is the 'generic' status quo, which serves as a situational

		COLUMN State	
		Non-Initiation	Initiation
ROW State	Non-Initiation	CC Status quo is maintained	COLUMN gets its way CD ROW loses
	Initiation	COLUMN loses DC ROW gets its way	DD Escalation

Figure 2.2 A schematic structure of a rivalry game

anchor and as a starting point for behaviour. Thus, regardless of the specific options available to parties at any given point in time, they can always do nothing, that is, refrain from action designed to change this status quo. We label this the *non-initiation* strategy. At the same time, parties have a wide spectrum of options designed to bring about a change in the status quo. For the sake of simplicity, we assume that each party has the alternative of initiating a demand (whether or not this demand is backed by some action) designed to change this status quo. We label it the *initiation* strategy. The intersection of these two alternatives yields a 2 × 2 game, a schematic representation of which is given in Figure 2.2.

The four outcomes in this game can be defined as follows:

(a) *Status Quo* (CC): None of the parties acts to change the status quo, and thus the status quo is maintained.

(b) *One-Sided Victory/Defeat* (DC or CD): One party initiates a demand and the other party does not resist. Thus, the initiator gets to change the status quo in accordance with its demand. A demand by the *row* player that is met by a concession of the *column* player represents a victory for *Row* (DC), while a demand by the *column* player met

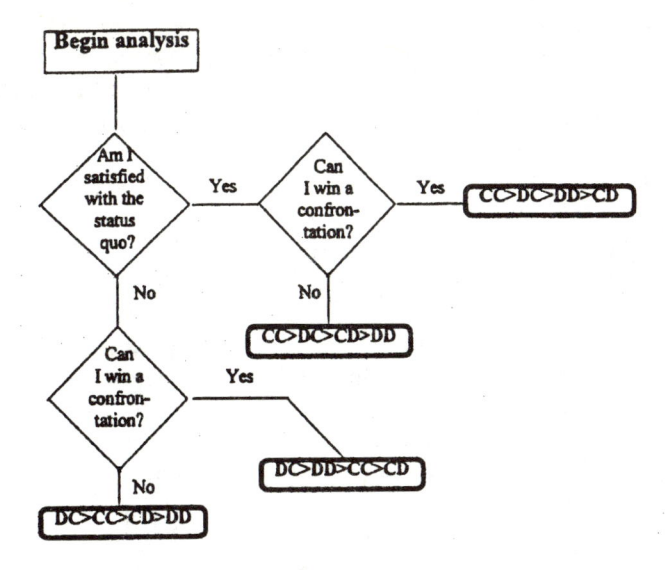

Satisfaction, Capabilities, and the Evolution of Rivalry

```
                    Begin analysis
                         │
                         ▼
                    ╱ Am I ╲
                   ╱satisfied╲   Yes      ╱  Can  ╲   Yes
                  ╲ with the ╱─────────▶ ╲ I win a ╱─────── [ CC>DC>DD>CD ]
                   ╲ status ╱              ╲confron-╱
                    ╲ quo? ╱                ╲tation?╱
                         │                      │
                         │ No                   │ No
                         ▼                      ▼
                    ╱  Can  ╲           [ CC>DC>CD>DD ]
                   ╱ I win a ╲   Yes
                  ╲ confron- ╱──────────
                   ╲ tation? ╱          │
                         │              ▼
                         │ No     [ DC>DD>CC>CD ]
                         ▼
                  [ DC>CC>CD>DD ]
```

Figure 2.3 Flow chart of rivalry calculus

by a concession of the *row* player results in a victory for *column* (CD).

(c) *Escalation* (DD): If both parties initiate demands and if neither is willing to concede the other's demand, then escalation ensues. This may mean a crisis or an all-out war.[6]

In order to develop preferences for these outcomes, we assume that the attitudes of the parties towards the generic status quo are based upon two principal factors: satisfaction with the status quo and a capability to change it. It is reasonable to expect that a party that is satisfied with a certain situation has little incentive to change it. An actor may be satisfied with the status quo even if it is not seen as ideal. Rather, the status quo may be seen as an acceptable constellation. The actor believes that, on balance, an uninterrupted continuation of the present state of affairs serves its goals.

The capability factor deals with a subjective perception by the actor of whether it can withstand or win a conflict with the opponent. Following Bueno de Mesquita (1981), we posit that capability is seen as an ability to bring a military confrontation to a favourable political conclusion.[7] From this scheme follows a fairly simple calculus, which produces four types of preference sets, as shown in the flow diagram of Figure 2.3.[8] The reasoning behind these preference structures is as follows:

1. *Satisfaction with the status quo*: When an actor is satisfied with the status quo, it is likely to prefer it to any situation that may involve change. This puts CC at the top of this actor's preference ordering. Thus, for this actor, CC > CD, DC, DD. It follows that for an actor not satisfied with the status quo, DC > CC. However, we cannot say anything more about these actors' preferences without knowing how they perceive their ability to win a militarized confrontation.

2. *Capability*: If an actor thinks that it possesses the capability to withstand and/or win a militarized conflict or war with its opponent, then it clearly prefers confrontation to surrender. Thus, it must have a preference structure in which DD > CD. This applies whether or not an actor is satisfied with the status quo. On the other hand, an actor that thinks it cannot withstand a conflict must have the opposite preference, that is, CD > DD. Moreover, whether or not an actor has the capability to withstand a militarized conflict, it prefers a political outcome where it gets its way without entering into conflict (DC) to a conflict (DD) or to surrender (CD). Hence, for an actor that believes it possesses the capability to win a militarized conflict, DC > DD > CD. For an actor that does not have the capability to win a militarized conflict, DC > CD > DD.[9]

3. *Satisfaction overrides capability*: Given that political aims are defined by factors other than capabilities, and capabilities are typically taken as means to political ends, we assume that political motivations – defined in terms of satisfaction with the status quo – override capabilities in terms of their impact on the overall preference structure of actors. This assumption is consistent with findings regarding crisis behaviour (see Leng, 1993:193; Maoz, 1983:195–229).[10] This assumption permits a lexicographic combination of satisfaction with capability, to produce four types of actors:

(a) *Satisfied without capability*: This actor would rather have the status quo maintained, but it feels that it cannot resist an attempt by the opponent to change it. The preference structure of this actor is straightforward: CC > DC > CD > DD.

(b) *Satisfied with capability*: This actor sees the status quo as satisfactory and thinks that if a challenge arises due to a demand by an opponent, it would rather fight than permit a change in the status quo. Obviously, it prefers winning over escalation. Such an actor's preference order is CC > DC > DD > CD.

(c) *Dissatisfied without capability*: This actor does not like the status quo but thinks it could not win a war. Thus, even if confronted

Satisfaction, Capabilities, and the Evolution of Rivalry 41

with a demand by the opponent that would further worsen its political situation, it is not inclined to fight. However, it would clearly prefer changing the status quo if it believed that doing so would not trigger escalation. The resulting preference structure is DC > CC > CD > DD.

(d) *Dissatisfied with capability*: This actor does not like the present situation and thinks it can change it successfully even if doing so may entail a war. This leads to a preference order of DC > DD > CC > CD.

The Strategic Configuration of EIRs

When we juxtapose the four types of actors in a larger, composite matrix, we obtain the supergame shown in Figure 2.4.[11]

Before analyzing the supergame, some remarks are in order. First, we display both Nash and nonmyopic equilibria (NME) in each of the games making up the supergame, but use only the nonmyopic equilibrium as the solution concept of these games.[12] The latter concept, which is based on a long-term strategic calculus, may be more appropriate for capturing the decision logic of states engaged in a long-term strategic relationship.[13] Second, we assume that the CC outcome of each game is the initial state at which actors make their strategic calculations. This assumption derives from the logic of our preference-formation scheme. By assuming a single initial state, we induce a unique nonmyopic equilibrium for each of the component games of the supergame. Third, we assume that the supergame represents an *objective set of possible strategic configurations*, namely that the parties know, at each given point in time, which of the games reflects their situation. Thus, in the remainder of the chapter we analyze and test the model under the assumption of complete information.[14]

Given the above assumptions, let us note some interesting characteristics of the supergame:

1. *Mutual satisfaction with the status quo is a sufficient condition for stability.* Regardless of actors' perceptions of their own capabilities or their opponents' capabilities, if both actors are satisfied with the status quo, they have no incentive to change it.[15]

2. *Satisfaction with the status quo by one actor and lack of capability by the other are sufficient conditions for stability.* The satisfied actor has no incentive to depart from the status quo; the other actor cannot do so without hurting itself. Examples are games III, VII, IX, and X.

Row Player			Column Player							
Satisfaction			Satisfied				Not Satisfied			
Capability			No Capability		Capability		No Capability		Capability	
		Strategy	Non Init.	Init.	Non Init.	Init.	Non Init.	Init.	Non Init.	Init.
Satisfied	No Cap.	Non Init.	i 4 *F 4	3 2	ii 4 *F 4	3 2	iii 3 F 4	4 * 2	iv 2 4	4 *F 2
		Init.	2 3	1 1	1 3	2 1	2 3	1 1	1 3	3 1
	Cap.	Non Init.	v 4 *F 4	3 1	vi 4 *F 4	3 1	vii 3 F 4	4 1	viii 2 4	4 1
		Init.	2 3	1 2	1 3	2 * 2	2 3	1 2	1 3	3 *F 2
Not Satisfied	No Cap.	Non Init.	ix 4 F 3	3 2	x 4 F 3	3 2	xi 3 F 3	4 * 2	xii 2 3	4 *F 2
		Init.	2 * 4	1 1	1 4	2 1	2 * 4	1 1	1 4	3 1
	Cap.	Non Init.	xiii 4 2	3 1	xiv 4 2	3 1	xv 3 2	4 1	xvi 2 2	4 1
		Init.	2 *F 4	1 3	1 4	2 *F 3	2 *F 4	1 3	1 4	3 *F 3

Figure 2.4 The supergame of enduring rivalries

Key:

1. Preferences represent ordinal ranking of outcomes. Row's preferences are given in the lower left corner of each cell. Column's preferences are given in the top right corner of each cell. The roman numerals in the upper left hand corner of each game give the order number of the game in the supergame.
2. Preference rankings are 4 = best, 3 = next best, 2 = next worst, 1 = worst.
3. Shaded games are distinct games. Unshaded games are mirror images of the shaded games.
4. * = Nash-equilibrium; F = Nonmyopic equilibrium.

3. *Dissatisfaction with the status quo and a perception of capability are a sufficient condition for change (i.e. initiation).* If an actor has both the motivation to change the status quo and the (perceived) capability to do so, then change follows. This is shown by games IV, VII, XII, and XVI.

4. *Mutual lack of satisfaction with the status quo is neither a necessary nor a sufficient condition for conflict.* Mutual dissatisfaction with the status quo tends to induce change, but not deterministically so. If both parties dislike the status quo but lack the capability to change it, in the long run they are better off maintaining the status quo in order to avoid mutual disaster. This is given by game XI, Chicken, which has a nonmyopic status quo equilibrium.

Transition Across Games: the Dynamics of Enduring Rivalries

As noted, we assume that the rivalry preferences of actors are determined by two parameters: their satisfaction with the status quo and their (relative) capability to change it (or defend it). The intersection of actors' preferences defines the game being played at any given point during an evolving rivalry. Given complete information, players always know which parameter values apply for the opponent and hence the opponent's preferences. In other words, players always know which game in the supergame they are playing. Once a given game applies, we expect the actors to choose their equilibrium strategies, and this choice defines their behaviour at this stage of the rivalry and produces the rivalry 'event' (or outcome).

This description provides a static, snapshot picture of the rivalry at a given point in time. We are interested, however, in explaining the *evolution* of rivalries, which requires that behaviour and outcomes be related over time. To provide the necessary dynamics, we assume that actors' preferences are not necessarily fixed but may evolve as the rivalry unfolds. Because we have a preference-formation component in the model, this assumption in turn implies that the parameter values which determine preferences may undergo change during the course of the rivalry. The question, then, is what triggers such change and how it affects the subsequent preferences of players.

We assume that there are two mechanisms that govern changes in parameter values:

Exogenous changes in capabilities. These are shifts in relative capabilities that cannot be derived from the model. Such shifts may be a *consequence* of events that do fall within the purview of the model and are predicted by it (i.e. dispute, crisis, or war outcomes) or the result of events that the model does not address (i.e. technological developments, arms transfers, alliances, and the like). In either case, data on changes in capabilities must be supplied exogenously; once they are given, they can be fed into the model in order to determine their effect on preferences and on the nature of the subsequent game to be played.

Endogenous changes in satisfaction. These are changes in actor satisfaction that are endogenous to the model. To obtain these predictions, we add an assumption about the relationship between outcomes and subsequent satisfaction with the status quo. Specifically, we assume that if, in a given game, a satisfied player obtains an outcome that is (at least) two ordinal ranks below the status quo, that player becomes dissatisfied; and, vice versa, a dissatisfied player that obtains an outcome at least two ordinal ranks above the status quo becomes satisfied.[16]

Applying these mechanisms (and exogenous data on relative capabilities), we are in a position to predict, for any given game n, what the $n + 1$ game will be. To take an example (using Figure 2.4), suppose that at a certain stage in an unfolding rivalry the game played is VIII, in which *Row* is satisfied with capability and *Column* is dissatisfied with capability. In this game, according to the nonmyopic solution, both players select their D strategy, and the outcome is therefore DD, a conflict event. This outcome is one ordinal rank above *Column*'s valuation of the status quo (i.e. outcome CC is ranked next worst) and so there is no change in this player's satisfaction. For *Row*, however, DD is two ordinal ranks below its valuation of the status quo. Therefore, this player, who was satisfied until now, becomes dissatisfied, and this change in the parameter value shifts the game to XVI and to another conflict event (DD) – say, war. Assume now that *Row* wins the war and that this victory tilts the balance of power unambiguously in its favour. Given this change in the capabilities parameter, the new game becomes XV, where the outcome is DC. This outcome is two ordinal ranks above *Row*'s valuation of the status quo ante, which makes this player satisfied and shifts the game to VII. In this game, the nonmyopic solution indicates that the status quo (CC) should persist; thus, if there are no further exogenous changes in capabilities, the rivalry ends at this point.

Note that by applying the two mechanisms, we arrive at a sequence of games (VIII, XVI, XV, VII) and rivalry events (DD, DD, DC, CC) that describe one possible evolutionary pattern of a rivalry. In the remainder of the paper, we analyze aggregate empirical data in order to determine whether real-life rivalries in fact evolve according to the patterns predicted by the model.

IV. RESEARCH DESIGN

Hypotheses

From our model, we can deduce some fairly simple, yet interesting propositions. We wish to remind the reader that all of these deductions are based on an assumption that objective games are also subjective games. This is a tenuous assumption, as we have shown elsewhere (Maoz and Mor, 1996a). Yet we justify this assumption on grounds that could be seen as plausible in terms of the measures we use to tap our key variables.

Specifically, we argue that, under certain circumstances, there is a high likelihood that subjective and objective games may converge. This takes place when the objective circumstances that affect the two key parameters of the model assume sufficiently clear values so that the likelihood of misperception decreases. For example, when the disparity in military capabilities is large, the likelihood that a given state would misperceive the balance of capabilities is low. Likewise, when a conflict ends in a clear one-sided victory, the likelihood that the perceptions of satisfaction would differ from rivals' actual valuations is also not very high.

By definition, when moving from a fairly simple abstract model which focuses only on two factors to the more complicated and multivariate empirical domain, we need to incorporate other issues that are known from the literature on international conflict to increase or decrease the probability of dyadic conflict. These are incorporated into the empirical analysis.

The three propositions to be tested are:

1. When the objective game has a conflict NME (e.g. when either one rival initiates and the other does not or when both initiate), the probability of conflict goes up significantly.
2. The effect of the objective game outcome on conflict is statistically significant even when we control for factors that are known to increase (e.g. contiguity) or decrease (e.g. joint democracy, alliance) the probability of conflict between rivals.

3. Transitions of game-configurations have a significant impact on the probability of conflict between rivals. Specifically, transitions of games from a conflict to a non-conflict structure reduces the probability of conflict. Transitions from non-conflict to conflict games raises the probability of conflict and war.

Spatial and Temporal Domain

There are various definitions of enduring rivalries, each generating a slightly different universe of cases for the period under investigation (1816–1986). Goertz and Diehl (1993) discussed these definitions and provided a tentative list of rivalries based on the definition discussed above (Huth, Jones, and Maoz, 1990).

For reasons explained below, we are working with a newly developed militarized interstate dispute dataset. We had therefore to produce a new list of rivalries and rivalry periods. This dataset contains 105 rivalry dyads (or 5.6 per cent) out of a population of 1846 dyadic disputes included in the general MID dataset. These dyads were involved in a total of 1501 disputes during rivalry periods (making for a total of 1890 dispute-years) and 44 disputes during periods that were not rivalry periods. (For example, disconnected disputes separated by long periods of no dispute activity.) Table 2.1 lists the rivalries and some of their characteristics.

Measurement of Variables

Dependent Variable: The dependent variable is the occurrence or nonoccurrence of a dispute (or war) at a given year during the rivalry period. A separate analysis is conducted for: (a) all disputes treated equally, with the dispute outbreak year treated as one and a non-outbreak year as zero; and (b) reciprocated disputes only.[17]

Independent Variables: The key variables that drive our model are satisfaction with the status quo and the capability to change it. We then develop a composite measure that describes the game which combines these two variables. In order to explain our game construction, we discuss each of these variables in some detail below.

Capability to change the status quo: As is customary in the quantitative international politics literature, we use the Correlates of War military capability index to measure capabilities (Singer, Bremer, and Stuckey, 1972; Singer, 1990). We develop our dichotomous index of

Satisfaction, Capabilities, and the Evolution of Rivalry 47

Table 2.1 Enduring rivalries, 1816–1986

Rivalry	Rivalry years	Non-rivalry years	No. of MID years	No. of war years	Match with Goertz-Diehl list?
USA–Cuba	61	19	18	0	Yes
USA–Haiti	49	61	10	0	Yes
USA–Dom	39	46	9	0	
USA–Mex	89	67	37	6	Yes
USA–Nicar	23	64	7	0	
USA–Ecuad	35	98	10	0	
USA–Peru	40	106	11	0	
USA–Eng	67	104	14	0	Yes
USA–Spain	83	88	21	1	Yes
USA–Germ	59	112	18	7	Yes
USA–Russ	70	101	37	0	Yes
USA–Libya	14	21	8	0	
USA–China	88	39	27	5	Yes
USA–N. Kor	39	0	23	4	
USA–Japan	35	86	13	6	Yes
Guat–Salv	68	34	7	3	
Hond–Nicar	87	0	14	1	Yes
Col–Peru	36	110	11	0	
Ecu–Peru	131	0	38	0	Yes
Peru–Chile	83	65	20	6	Yes
Braz–Parag	25	111	13	7	
Braz–Argen	24	122	6	2	Yes
Braz–GBR	26	135	16	0	
Boliv–Parag	58	76	21	5	Yes
Boliv–Chile	109	30	20	6	Yes
Parag–Argen	107	30	20	6	
Chile–Argen	111	37	35	0	
Argen–GBR	80	66	16	1	Yes
GBR–Fran	81	89	10	2	Yes
GBR–Germ	83	88	23	12	Yes
GBR–Italy	56	115	15	4	Yes
GBR–Greece	94	63	15	0	Yes
GBR–Russia	154	17	43	5	Yes
GBR–Iran	46	86	9	2	Yes
GBR–Turk	119	52	26	5	Yes
GBR–Egypt	56	27	9	3	Yes
GBR–China	110	17	19	2	Yes
GBR–Japan	45	76	15	6	Yes
Belg–Germ	30	82	17	7	Yes
Fran–Germ	116	55	33	14	Yes
Fran–Aust	65	95	10	6	Yes

(continued on page 48)

Table 2.1 continued

Rivalry	Rivalry years	Non-rivalry years	No. of MID years	No. of war years	Match with Goertz-Diehl list?
Fran–Italy	86	85	16	4	Yes
Fran–Russia	156	14	21	5	Yes
Fran–Turk	124	45	26	6	Yes
Fran–China	94	32	18	8	Yes
Fran–Japan	43	78	12	2	Yes
Fran–Thai	46	53	6	3	
Spn–Morro	67	30	17	4	
Germ–Italy	32	129	13	7	
Germ–Grce	59	102	9	5	
Germ–Russ	32	129	18	6	Yes
Germ–Swdn	32	129	11	0	
Germ–Nrwy	37	124	8	2	
Germ–Den	46	115	10	6	
Germ–China	66	95	9	2	
Aust–Italy	106	50	15	8	Yes
Hung–Romn	38	30	10	3	
Italy–Alban	40	29	10	0	
Italy–Yugos	32	75	9	0	
Italy–Russia	134	37	18	9	Yes
Italy–Ethiop	25	59	8	4	
Italy–Turkey	61	110	23	6	Yes
Alban–Yugo	69	0	11	0	
Yugos–Bulg	77	0	16	6	
Yugos–Rom	43	34	9	2	
Grce–Bulg	43	34	13	5	Yes
Grce–Turk	132	25	47	11	Yes
Bulg–Russia	37	42	11	8	
Bulg–Turk	59	20	10	2	
Russ–Finlnd	25	43	10	6	
Russ–Swdn	31	127	12	0	
Russ–Norwy	31	127	7	0	
Russ–Iran	79	53	23	0	
Russ–Turk	171	0	35	11	Yes
Russ–Isr	31	8	10	0	
Russ–China	127	0	44	2	Yes
Russ–Korea	38	0	6	0	
Russ–Japan	121	0	48	7	Yes
Ghn–Togo	27	0	8		
Chad–Libya	27	0	8		
Cong–Zaire	25	0	8	0	
Zaire–Zamb	23	0	6	0	
Ugnd–Tanz	24	0	8	2	
Somal–Ethio	27	0	19	2	Yes

Satisfaction, Capabilities, and the Evolution of Rivalry

Table 2.1 continued

Rivalry	Rivalry years	Non-rivalry years	No. of MID years	No. of war years	Match with Goertz-Diehl list?
Ethio–Sudan	31	0	6	0	
Zamb–Zimb	21	0	10	0	
Zamb–SAfr	31	0	9	0	
Zimb–Bots	21	0	7	0	
Mor–Alger	21	0	7	0	
Libya–Egypt	12	23	9	0	
Iran–Iraq	57	0	24	9	
Iraq–Isr	39	0	10	3	
Iraq–Kuwt	26	0	9	0	
Egy–Isr	32	7	30	11	Yes
Egy–Saudi	25	25	6	0	
Syria–Jord	39	0	9	0	
Syria–Isr	39	0	35	9	Yes
Lebn–Isr	29	0	12	2	
Jord–Isr	39	0	19	5	Yes
Isr–Saudi	39	0	8	3	
Saud–S.Yem	60	0	12	0	
Afgn–Pakis	41	0	16	0	
Chna–Taiwn	38	0	14	0	Yes
Chna–Korea	38	0	12	4	
Chna–Japn	101	20	39	13	Yes
Chna–India	40	0	20	2	Yes
Chna–Thai	18	82	9	4	
Chna–N.Viet	13	21	10	3	
Chna–S.Viet	22	0	8	0	
N.Kor–S.Kor	38	0	28	4	Yes
Korea–Jpn	35	0	13	0	
India–Pk	38	0	31	3	Yes
Burm–Thai	40	0	13	0	
Thai–Camb	35	0	24	0	
Thai–Laos	33	0	15	0	
Cam–N.Viet	22	0	16	5	Yes
Total	6527	4931	1890	84	

capability starting with the generation of a capability ratio of state A to state B. This index goes from zero up and is not bound at its upper range. We determine a non-symmetrical capability situation if the capability ratio is larger than 1.5 or lower than 0.67 (which is the reciprocal of the first number). This implies that if one of the states has a capability of 1.5 times that of its rival (and thus the rival has a capability which is less than two-thirds the capability of the first rival), then it is clear to both actors that one is much stronger than the other. In such situations it is evident that the stronger does have the capability to change the status quo and the other rival does not.

On the other hand, in situations when the capability ratio is lower than 1.2 but higher than 0.825, both actors may think that they do not have the capability of changing the status quo. This is a situation where both appear roughly equal and believe that they will pay a very high cost if they attempt to change the status quo forcefully.

Turning to symmetrical capabilities, we make here an assumption that allows us to model the Deadlock game (game xvi), but it is a tenuous assumption, because it contradicts what we have just stated regarding relatively symmetrical capabilities. We assume that if, and only if, both actors are dissatisfied with the prevailing status quo and their capabilities are roughly equal (capability ratio of 0.825 to 1.2), they will both perceive that they possess the capability for changing the status quo.[18]

Satisfaction with the status quo: In order to develop this measure, we must make some measurement assumptions. First, without more detailed knowledge about actors' valuations of the status quo, we assume that their initial attitude towards it is neutral – they neither dislike nor like the status quo. Once a dispute breaks out, the outcome of that dispute determines their attitude toward the subsequent status quo. In principle, winners of disputes develop a positive attitude toward the status quo, while losers develop a negative attitude. However, the extent of satisfaction or dissatisfaction with the post-dispute status quo varies with the extent to which the dispute was severe. A one-sided victory in a low-level dispute is typically not associated with a drastic shift in the *status quo ante*, thus it is unlikely that the basic attitudes of the victor and loser would change. On the other hand, victory or defeat in a major dispute is likely to generate a fundamental alteration in the nature of the status quo. Typically, this alteration is made in the direction of the winner's interests and in opposition to the loser's interests. Likewise, a symmetrical outcome in a dispute (e.g. a draw or a stalemate) is also not associated with a major shift in the status quo. Again, no fundamental alteration is expected in the attitude of the parties.

Hence to measure satisfaction, we first assigned a score of +1 to a victory in a dispute and a score of −1 to a defeat. A draw or stalemate received a score of zero. Thus, obviously, if one rival won, the other lost, and vice versa. Next, we multiplied the dispute outcome score by the highest level of hostility reached in the dispute, with these levels ranging from 1 (no military confrontation action taken by a rival) to 5 (war). This gave us a scale of satisfaction ranging from −5 to +5. We then determined that a weighted dispute outcome which is larger than 2 renders a rival satisfied with the prevailing status quo, while an outcome of less than −2 renders an actor dissatisfied.

This is the first step in the process of establishing an empirically observable rivalry supergame. We now have a combination of parameter values that allows generation of several games that are represented by asymmetrical parameter values of satisfaction and capability (e.g. games iv, xiii, vii, xiv). However, in order to get a more realistic representation of the supergame, we need to make assumptions that allow for symmetric parameter values. Let us consider first situations of symmetrical values for the satisfaction parameter, and then for the capability parameter.

First, we start tracing relationships between states not when the first rivalry-related dispute breaks out, but rather when the 'youngest' of the two states enters the system. Hence, without prior information about the states' attitudes towards the status quo, we assume that both states are satisfied. This causes us to 'miss' the first dispute between the two states,[19] but there is no reason to assign dissatisfaction to one of the states prior to a conflict outcome. Another post-conflict situation that is likely to induce mutual satisfaction with a given outcome is when a conflict between two states ends in a compromise. Although a compromise may benefit one of the states more than the other, we assume that states do not make compromises that they are not satisfied with.

On the other hand, quite a few disputes end in stalemates. This kind of outcome stipulates that no explicit resolution of the dispute was reached. Rather, hostilities ceased, but the issues at stake remain open. Such an outcome is likely to leave both parties dissatisfied.

These assumptions allow generation of games that are both symmetrical and asymmetrical in terms of satisfaction (e.g. games ii, v, x, xv and xvi, in addition to the above-mentioned games).

Finally, for the multivariate analyses, we code a game as a conflict game if it has a conflict equilibrium (i.e. games iv, viii, xii–xvi), and a non-conflict game otherwise. This enables us to test the impact of the general conflict-related predictions on the probability of conflict.

Control Variables

As noted above, we must control for empirically proven factors that affect the probability of disputes within rivalries. Since all the measures of these variables have been developed elsewhere (e.g. Maoz and Russett,

1993; Maoz, 1996a), we will just mention them briefly here.

Contiguity: Contiguity is perhaps the best predictor of the probability of dyadic conflict (Bremer, 1992, 1993; Vasquez, 1993). Contiguity allows a clear distinction between 'high-risk' dyads and 'low-risk' ones. While it does not vary within dyads, it is a useful control variable for the present population. Contiguity is categorized as zero for no contiguity and one for direct contiguity.

Alliance: Joint alliance membership is a good predictor of lack of conflict. This variable may vary within a given rivalry, and needs to be inserted as a measure of common interests of the parties. These common interests may overshadow any bilateral grievances or conflicts. Thus, it is important to investigate the extent to which our model is sensitive to externally-induced circumstances that produce joint alliance.

Joint Democracy: The democratic peace literature needs no introduction. Recent investigations of this issue in the context of enduring rivalries (Hensel, Goertz and Diehl, 1996; Maoz, 1996b) revealed that democracy is a powerful predictor of peace in enduring rivalries. Thus, it is essential to control for joint democracy in the context of enduring rivalries.[20]

Research Methods

We test our hypotheses first in a bivariate context, and subsequently in a multivariate context, controlling for the impact of the control variables. We use simple contingency tables for the bivariate tests. The association between our predictions and the data is computed using the m_b statistic (Maoz and Abdolali, 1989; Maoz, 1996a) which computes a bi-directional association between predicted and observed frequencies. It assesses the strength of association (or proportionate reduction in error) between predicted and observed frequencies in terms of how each contributes to the chi-square score.[21] For the multivariate test we use the Cox regression model that tests event-history data (Allison, 1984). This model allows us to trace when, in a context of a given rivalry, a dispute breaks out as a function of the strategic game being played, as well as of the control variables.

V. RESULTS

As noted, we first examine the relationship between the strategic game being played and the frequency of dispute and war between the states. We divide our analysis to rivalry and non-rivalry periods of the dyads

Table 2.2 Relationship between game type and dyadic conflict by rivalry and non-rivalry years

	Non-rivalry years				Rivalry years			
	MID		War		MID		War	
Game no.	No MID	MID	No war	War	No MID	MID	No war	War
2	83	4	87	0	95	31	125	1
	(95.4)	(4.6)	(100.0)	(0.0)	(75.4)	(24.6)	(99.2)	(0.8)
4	597	1	598	0	615	153	724	44
	(99.8)	(0.2)	(100.0)	(0.0)	(80.1)	(19.9)	(94.3)	(5.7)
5	244	4	248	0	104	72	173	3
	(98.8)	(1.2)	(100.0)	(0.0)	(59.1)	(40.9)	(98.3)	(1.7)
6	0	0	0	0	7	0	7	0
	(0.0)	(0.0)	(0.0)	(0.0)	(100.0)	(0.0)	(100.0)	(0.0)
7	1353	11	1360	4	1279	238	1428	89
	(99.2)	(0.7)	(99.8)	(0.2)	(84.3)	(15.7)	(94.1)	(5.9)
8	104	1	105	0	215	55	255	15
	(99.0)	(1.0)	(100.0)	(0.0)	(79.6)	(20.4)	(94.4)	(5.6)
10	608	9	617	0	777	137	875	39
	(98.5)	(1.5)	(100.0)	(0.0)	(85.0)	(15.0)	(95.7)	(4.3)
12	384	5	389	0	256	274	517	13
	(98.7)	(1.3)	(100.0)	(0.0)	(48.3)	(51.7)	(97.5)	(2.5)
13	1129	4	1133	0	1207	233	1364	76
	(99.6)	(0.4)	(100.0)	(0.0)	(83.8)	(16.2)	(94.7)	(5.3)
14	124	0	124	0	136	35	218	13
	(100.0)	(0.0)	(100.0)	(0.0)	(84.8)	(15.2)	(94.4)	(5.6)
15	486	10	496	0	516	601	1089	28
	(98.0)	(2.0)	(100.0)	(0.0)	(46.2)	(53.8)	(97.4)	(2.6)
16	31	2	33	0	32	70	98	4
	(93.9)	(6.1)	(100.0)	(0.0)	(31.4)	(68.6)	(96.1)	(3.9)
Total	5143	51	5190	4	5299	1899	6873	325
	(99.0)	(1.0)	(99.9)	(0.1)	(73.6)	(26.4)	(95.5)	(4.5)

$\chi^2 = 39.09$ $\chi^2 = 11.24$ $\chi^2 = 987.04$ $\chi^2 = 35.84$
$m_b = -0.19$ $m_b = -0.63$ $m_b = 0.55$ $m_b = -0.10$
$p = NS$ $p = NS$ $p < 0.001$ $p < 0.05$

noted in Table 2.1 above. The results of this analysis are given in Table 2.2.

This analysis reveals several things. First, during non-rivalry years, the same states, irrespective of the strategic game they were playing, had a low likelihood of dispute involvement. Hence the predictions of the strategic model of rivalry were not significant. Second, during rivalry years, the dispute-related predictions of the model performed

Table 2.3 Effects of strategic game and control variables on dispute behaviour: an event-history analysis

Variable	Stratum	MID Years Param	Std. Err.	Δ Prob. disp.	War Years Param	Std. err.	Δ Prob. war
N=14,822	General	−2 LL +	999.40		−2 LL	219.27	
Joint dem.		−1.75	0.16**	−70%	−3.55	1.00**	−94%
Alliance		−0.52	0.06**	−25%	−1.42	0.21**	−61%
Contiguity		0.44	0.05**	22%	0.58	0.13**	28%
Cum. conf.		0.04	0.01**	4%	0.05	0.01**	2%
Conf. game		0.68	0.04*	33%	0.06	0.12	3%
N=6,045	Non-riv	−2 LL	9.73		−2 LL	4.53	
Joint dem		−0.76	0.54	−36%	NA	NA	NA
Alliance		−0.42	0.37	−21%	NA	NA	NA
Contiguity		0.68	0.32*	33%	NA	NA	NA
Cum. conf.		0.01	0.02	0%	NA	NA	NA
Conf. game		0.26	0.32	13%	NA	NA	NA
N=8,777	Rivalry	−2 LL	440.00		−2 LL	111.62	
Joint dem.		−1.39	0.17**	−60%	−3.08	1.01**	91%
Alliance		−0.38	0.06**	−19%	−1.26	0.21**	56%
Contiguity		0.24	0.05**	12%	0.41	0.13**	20%
Cum. conf.		0.02	0.01**	2%	0.03	0.01**	4%
Conf. game		0.78	0.04**	28%	−0.03	0.12	−2%

quite well. The m_b score suggests a moderately high fit between the model's predictions and the data. However, in the case of war-related predictions, the model did very poorly. The m_b score suggests that the relationship between the predictions and the data is in the opposite direction. Two major 'miss' games in this respect are games 7 and 15. In game 7, the frequency of war years is considerably higher than the expected one (the expected/observed ratio is 0.77), and in game 15, the observed frequency of war years is considerably lower than the expected one (the expected/observed ratio is 1.8). These residual games disrupted the otherwise generally accurate model predictions.[22]

We now move to the multivariate analysis. This is done in Table 2.3 above. The results of this analysis suggest that, even when controlling for those variables that have been shown to affect the likelihood of dyadic conflict, the effect of the strategic configuration – as indicated in the strategic game being played by the rivals – is consistently and significantly related to the nature of the actual interaction. The likelihood of a conflict outcome goes up by 70–80 per cent when the game moves from a non-conflict game to a conflict game.

As was the case in the bivariate analysis, the strategic configuration did not significantly affect the probability of war outbreak. Here too, it seems that the principal reason for this is that games 7 and 15 had a strong residual effect on the whole analysis. Without the cases corresponding to these games, the effects of the strategic configuration on the escalation of disputes to war becomes statistically significant.[23]

The effects of all the control variables on the probability of conflict and war is statistically significant. Democracy has a consistently strong effect on non-conflict and non-war outcomes, reducing the probability of conflict by 75–83 per cent for disputes and by 95–97 per cent for wars. Contiguity and alliance also affected the probability of conflict in the expected direction.

The last item on our agenda concerns the relationship between game-related transition and conflict outbreak. The general focus of our study is on the dynamics of enduring rivalries. Thus, it is important to investigate whether, given a transition in the structure of the strategic configuration, the probability of conflict goes up or down, or remains the same. The transition of games was modelled by comparing the game that characterized the strategic interaction two years prior to the extant year (t-2) to the strategic configuration that prevailed one year prior to the extant year (t-1). If the t-2 game was a conflict game (4, 8, 12 and above) and the t-1 game was a non-conflict game, the transition was from conflict to non-conflict. If both the t-2 and the t-1 games were of a non-conflict nature, we designated this as a non-transition even if in fact the games were different. Finally, if the t-2 game was a non-conflict game and the t-1 game was a conflict game, we designated this as a conflict transition. Table 2.4 displays the relationship between game transition and conflict outcomes.

The results show several interesting things. First, as in previous cases, the results are highly significant for conflict. As the m_b scores suggest – for both the rivalry and non-rivalry interactions – the transition from non-conflict game configurations to conflict game configurations has a strong effect on the frequency of conflict. Also, as in previous analyses, the relationship between game transitions and wars is marginally significant but it is in an opposite direction. The reason is that while the observed frequency of transition from non-conflict to conflict games and the actual occurrence of war is considerably higher than the expected one – and thus consistent with the test hypothesis – there is also a

Table 2.4 Relationships between game transitions and conflict

Stratum	Type of transition	Conflict outcome No conflict	Conflict outcome Conflict	War outcome No war	War outcome War
General	Conflict→Non-conflict	182 (59.7)	123 (40.3)	280 (91.8)	25 (8.2)
	No change	9421 (90.9)	939 (9.1)	10169 (98.2)	191 (1.8)
	Non-conflict→Conflict	424 (40.4)	625 (59.6)	986 (94.0)	63 (6.0)
	Total N=11,714	10027 (85.6)	1687 (14.4)	11435 (97.6)	279 (2.4)
		$\chi^2 = 2142.38$; $m_b = 0.73$		$\chi^2 = 116.51$ $m_b = 0.13$	
Non-Rivalry	Conflict→Non-conflict	36 (94.7)	2 (5.3)	37 (97.4)	1 (2.6)
	No change	4857 (99.4)	29 (0.6)	4884 (99.9)	2 (0.1)
	Non-conflict→Conflict	90 (86.5)	14 (13.5)	104 (100.0)	0 (0.0)
	Total N=5,028	4983 (99.1)	55 (0.9)	5025 (99.9)	3 (0.1)
		$\chi^2 = 198.34$; $m_b = 0.92$		$\chi^2 = 42.50$; $m_b = -0.02$	
Rivalry	Conflict→Non-conflict	146 (54.7)	121 (45.3)	243 (91.0)	24 (9.0)
	No change	4564 (83.4)	910 (16.6)	5285 (96.5)	189 (3.5)
	Non-conflict→Conflict	334 (35.3)	611 (64.7)	882 (93.3)	63 (6.7)
	Total N=6,686	5044 (75.4)	1642 (24.6)	6410 (95.9)	276 (4.1)
		$\chi^2 = 1068.19$; $m_b = 0.74$		$\chi^2 = 37.64$; $m_b = -0.17$	

strong tendency of non-conflict transitions to be associated with war outbreaks. This tendency is also present in the case of non-conflict transitions and conflict outbreak, but there it has a marginal effect on the overall relationship.

The effects of game transition on the probability of conflict and war outbreak, controlling for other determinants of conflict, is given in

Table 2.5 Effects of strategic game transitions and control variables on dispute behaviour: an event-history analysis

Variable	Stratum	Param	MID years Std Err.	Δ Prob. disp.	Param	War years Std Err.	Δ Prob. war
N=14,822	General	−2 LL+	999.40		−2 LL	219.27	
Joint dem.		−1.75	0.16**	−43%	−3.55	1.00**	−47%
Alliance		−0.52	0.06**	−40%	−1.42	0.21**	−26%
Contiguity		0.44	0.05**	56%	0.58	0.13**	49%
Cum. Conf.		0.04	0.01**	4%	0.05	0.01**	5%
Conf. Trans		0.68	0.04**	67%	0.06	0.12	6%
N=5,978	Non-Rivalry	−2 LL	70.16		−2 LL	4.53	
Joint dem.		−1.10	0.61*	−51%	NA	NA	NA
Alliance		−0.43	0.37	−22%	NA	NA	NA
Contiguity		0.54	0.37*	63%	NA	NA	NA
Cum. Conf.		0.01	0.02	0%	NA	NA	NA
Conf. +1 → 0		−0.83	0.73	−39%	NA	NA	NA
Trans. 0 → +1		1.49	0.78*	63%			
N=8,711	Rivalry	−2 LL	803.07		−2 LL	131.77	
Joint dem.		−1.32	0.16**	−58%	−3.05	1.00**	91%
Alliance		−0.37	0.06**	−18%	−1.25	0.21**	55%
Contiguity		0.20	0.05**	10%	0.38	0.13**	19%
Cum. Conf.		0.02	0.01**	1%	0.03	0.01**	2%
Conf. +1 → 0		−0.69	0.06**	−33%	−0.60	0.16**	−29%
Trans. 0 → +1		0.45	0.08**	36%	−0.16	0.21	−8%

Table 2.5. The results show that game transition in general, not just transitions from non-conflict to conflict games, causes a significant increase in the probability of conflict. It is evident, and perfectly consistent with our model, that a transition from a non-conflict game to a conflict game would cause a significant increase in the actual probability of conflict. However, it remains to be explained why a transition from a conflict game to a non-conflict game also has an effect of increased probability of conflict and war. This is a puzzle that we do not resolve here. It may well be that it is in these shifts that misperception is likely to set in and affect the judgment of the rivals with respect to the kind of strategic configuration they are playing. Whether or not this is the case, remains to be studied.

VI. SUMMARY

What we can say for now is that, despite the many limitations that are involved in transforming an abstract model that gets much of its conceptual dynamics from analyses involving misperception and incomplete information, the analyses conducted here reveal that actors do behave strategically in enduring rivalries. Moreover, the present examination shows that actors may well change their preferences in accordance with the outcome they obtain in prior confrontations and in response to changes in the balance of capabilities. These preference changes take place alongside other strategic shifts (e.g. alliances, regime structures, etc.), and they have a significant effect on actors' conflict behaviour in subsequent confrontations.

Given the limitations of the test we conducted here, the next stage in the empirical evaluation of the model calls for the relaxation of restrictive assumptions. In particular, if we admit incomplete information, the possibility of misperceptions should be addressed. Indeed, we treat this issue at the theoretical level by incorporating a *learning* component as another process that underlies game transitions. This element of the model was tested in a comparative case study of four enduring rivalries at their early stages; the results indicated that learning is a good predictor of shifts in subjective games, although exogenous changes in capability exert an important influence as well (for details, see Maoz and Mor, 1996a; 1997). Testing the fully-specified model – preference change *and* learning – over the entire duration of EIRs (with both objective and subjective measures of capabilities) is a future objective that will be undertaken once data collection and coding are completed.

At the same time, additional avenues remain for developing the model itself. One intriguing possibility is the association of certain preference structures with certain regime types through the satisfaction parameter. For example, if we can assume that democracies tend to be satisfied (and perceive other democracies as such), then the population of dyadic interactions we analyze at the theoretical level become empirically more meaningful (and relevant to the debate on the democratic peace). Regime *changes* can then be seen as another determinant of preference change, as well as an occasion for learning about the opponent, which affects the nature of subjective games. More generally, because our parameters of preference formation address both values and power – two variables that drive many analyses of international relations – they open up the possibility for applying the model to a diverse set of issues.

NOTES

1. A previous version of this paper was presented at the annual meeting of the American Political Science Association, Chicago, Ill., September 1995. This study was supported by the grant from the Israeli National Science Foundation. We wish to thank Frank Harvey and Bruce Russett for useful comments on previous drafts. We alone are responsible for any errors.
2. For an analysis of the early stages of EIRs and a comparative case study, see Maoz and Mor (1996a; 1997).
3. For a related concept, *protracted conflict*, see Azar, Jureidini, and McLaurin (1978) and Brecher (1993:50). For a dissenting view that criticizes dispute thresholds as operational criteria for enduring rivalries, see Thompson (1995).
4. Maoz and Mor (1996a; 1997) show that even the initial stages of enduring rivalries are characterized by evolving preference structures.
5. As argued below, in this article we ignore differences in game perceptions (such as are implied in Figure 2.1), which are discussed in Maoz and Mor (1996a; 1997).
6. At this point we do not specify the nature of initiation actions. We also treat all escalations to dispute/crisis/war levels as substantively equivalent. Obviously, crisis management makes a great deal of difference. See Lebow (1981); Leng (1993); Brecher (1993); and George (1984). These issues will be explored in subsequent research.
7. These two factors are also based on Leng's (1993) analysis of issues and capabilities as factors that determine bargaining strategies, and thus outcomes, of international crises. See also Hensel (1994a).
8. Figure 2.3 is only an analytic device designed to simplify our presentation of preference formation. We do not imply that actors actually engage in such a decision sequence.
9. The dichotomization of the values of the satisfaction and capabilities parameter may sound overly simplistic, especially when considered from a rational choice perspective. However, we justify this formulation on the ground that we opt for an analysis of strategic structures of EIRs that is relatively simple and, as such, relies on ordinal preferences rather than on cardinal utilities. Since we attempt to do something that most game-theoretic analyses of international politics shy away from – that is, specify how preferences are formed and how they change – we have to start by trying to walk in this field before we begin to run into a more complex process of trying to develop cardinal utility functions. It is also interesting to note that the capability ratio factor is dichotomized in many empirical studies of dyadic interactions. See for example Bremer (1992, 1993); Huth and Russett (1993); Maoz and Russett (1993).
10. In a subsequent study (Mor and Maoz, 1997), we expand the model to include alternate assumptions about the hierarchy between satisfaction and capabilities. We include a possibility that capability-related calculations override satisfaction-related calculations. This makes for a more complex supergame model.
11. The term 'supergame' usually refers to a finite set of identical component games that are tied together by means of transition probabilities. Because we conceptualize a series of non-identical games, a 'stochastic game' is a

more appropriate description (see Shubik, 1982:55). However, contrary to what this term implies, we do not assume that players' strategies determine the probabilities that govern transitions across games (and such probabilities do not exist in our model). Our conception, therefore, is similar to what Snyder and Diesing (1977) call, somewhat imprecisely, a 'supergame.'

12. See Brams (1994:224) for formal definitions of Nash equilibrium and nonmyopic equilibrium and for the analysis of games using these solution concepts.
13. See Brams (1994:1–18) for a more elaborate justification of the use of TOM in modelling international political interactions.
14. For an analysis of the model under incomplete information and learning, see Maoz and Mor (1996a; 1997).
15. See the nonmyopic equilibria for games number i, ii, v, and vi of the supergame. Game vi is the famous Stag Hunt. It contains two Nash equilibria, only one of which (the Pareto-superior outcome) is the status quo outcome. See Maoz (1990a: chap. 2) and Robert Jervis (1978).
16. Admittedly, this is a rather arbitrary way of endogenizing satisfaction, but we offer it as a first cut, to be tested empirically later in the chapter. We should also note that there may be exogenous factors that affect satisfaction – for example, regime change – but we do not address such changes in this paper.
17. The new MID dataset contains many disputes of a lower order, which involve low levels of hostility or minor military acts (e.g. seizure of ships or planes and their release after a short while). These disputes are typically non-reciprocal, that is, one side initiates them and the other side does not respond at a hostility level which qualifies for coding. These disputes are also typically short, lasting one or several days. These contrast with the more 'serious' disputes that – while they may involve little or no violence – are regarded by participants as threatening and dangerous. The latter type are typically of a reciprocated nature, that is, both parties threaten, display, or use military force against each other. Thus we call these 'reciprocated disputes.'
18. We ran all analyses with the alternate assumptions, one that in the 0.825–1.2 capability range both actors perceive lack of capability, and the current assumption. Results differed in terms of parameter values, but not in terms of sign and of significance levels.
19. This is so because the 'objective' version of the supergame predicts that mutual satisfaction is a sufficient condition for no conflict.
20. Several other factors, such as economic interdependence, growth and political stability will not be examined here. They will be included in subsequent investigations.
21. Briefly, for the computation of the m_b statistic, each cell in a contingency table gets an *a priori* designation in terms of the relationship between predicted and observed frequencies. In error cells (that is, cells in which there should be no cases according to the test hypothesis), expected frequencies must be higher than observed frequencies. In non-error cells, expected frequencies must be lower than observed frequencies. In non-prediction cells, that is in cells for which there is no specific prediction,

the relationship between observed and expected frequencies is of no significance. Now, once expected and observed frequencies are obtained, each cell is examined and designated as a consistent cell, that is, a cell in which the relationship between observed and expected frequencies matches the *a priori* expectation, or it is designated as an inconsistent cell, that is, a cell in which the relationship between observed and expected frequencies is inconsistent with the *a priori* specification. The m_b statistic sums across the chi-square scores of the consistent and inconsistent cells, respectively, and subtracts the latter sum from the former. The product is then divided by the total chi-square score for the table. This allows determination of the proportion of the total chi-square score that is accounted for by the test hypothesis. The m_b score varies from -1 to $+1$, with positive scores consistent with the test hypothesis and negative scores showing a negative association between the variables.
22. When these two games are omitted for the war-year analysis, the m_b score goes up to 0.39, which is statistically significant in the direction predicted by the model.
23. The parameter estimate for CONFGAME in an analysis excluding games vii and xv is 0.26, standard error is 0.15, $p < 0.02$, and probability of war increases by 29 per cent when the game is a conflict game.

3 Foreign Policy Choices and Domestic Politics: A Re-examination of the Link Between Domestic and International Conflict

Paul K. Huth and Ellen Lust-Okar

I. INTRODUCTION

A common belief among scholars and policy-makers is that domestic political unrest causes important changes in the foreign policy choices of state leaders. One well-established argument posits that domestic unrest leads to more aggressive and confrontational foreign policy behavior as ruling elites seek to divert political attention at home away from internal problems by rallying nationalist political support behind a policy of conflict and crisis with an external adversary. There are, however, alternative arguments which posit quite different relationships between internal and external conflict. For example, another common hypothesis proposed by analysts is that domestic political instability and turmoil cause state leaders to withdraw from foreign affairs as they focus state resources and their attention on dealing with internal political and economic problems.[1] In this line of argument there is a negative (as opposed to a positive) relationship between domestic unrest and international conflict. This lack of consensus on the theoretical links between internal and external conflict helps to explain the absence of strong and consistent findings in empirical studies on the subject.[2] As a result, while it seems quite intuitive to believe that periods of domestic instability could have profound implications for foreign policy, political scientists clearly disagree about what should be the expected relationship, and the lack of clear empirical results has not been able to help resolve the theoretical debate.

In this chapter we present a new theoretical argument which we believe makes an important contribution to reconciling the opposing arguments in the scholarly literature. Instead of arguing generally that

Foreign Policy Choices and Domestic Politics 63

domestic unrest is either positively or negatively related to international conflict, we hypothesize that only under certain specific conditions should unrest increase the likelihood of international crises and the threat of war. Furthermore, we posit that under a different set of conditions the response of foreign policy leaders to domestic unrest should be to avoid international conflict. Thus, we will show in this chapter that while existing arguments in the literature are not broadly true, they are more compelling when a more restricted and well-defined set of conditions is specified. The contribution of this chapter, then, is to discuss and analyze the more restricted set of conditions which lead to a systematic causal pattern between internal and external conflict.

While we argue that international political and military conditions constrain and shape the foreign policy choices of state leaders, we believe that a critical set of variables to analyze resides at the level of domestic politics. We focus on the decision of state leaders to either repress or accommodate the demands of political opposition, and on how that decision has significant implications for whether state leaders will pursue a more aggressive foreign policy. In particular, we argue that when state leaders favour repressing domestic opposition, the incentives to escalate international disputes are much stronger compared to situations in which leaders feel the need to accommodate the demands of political opposition.

In our theoretical framework we posit a tight connection between state leaders' domestic and foreign policy choices. Ruling elites use foreign policy to support and advance domestic policy initiatives, and conversely those elites also are very sensitive to the threat that foreign policy failures can have on their own domestic political standing. The key to reconciling the existing theoretical disagreements about the link between internal and external conflict is to think carefully about the reciprocal influence of domestic and international politics on each other. We therefore begin our analysis with the theoretical position that to explain foreign policy choices we must model very carefully the domestic policy choices of foreign policy leaders. A major weakness of the existing literature on domestic unrest and international conflict is that international relations scholars typically do not model the domestic political environment within which political unrest has developed, and therefore they do not pay attention to the *type of domestic response* leaders choose to counter the opposition they face. By ignoring these domestic policy choices and the domestic conditions that give rise to such choices, we believe that it is very difficult to predict on a consistent basis whether domestic unrest will produce more or less international conflict since foreign policy choices are tightly linked to domestic policy choices. The model we present focuses on the interactions between two states. The first state is a challenger who seeks to overturn the political and military status quo in its relations with its adversary, a long-standing rival. Within the model we focus our attention on trying to predict how the challenger state's foreign policy behavior will vary in response to periods of domestic political unrest. Thus, the starting point for our model is a period of domestic unrest within the challenger, and then we analyze how the challenger and rival states respond to that unrest.[3] In several ways then we narrow the questions we ask of the model. For example, we do not analyze in detail how the rival state responds to periods of domestic unrest within the challenger state,[4] nor do we consider the foreign policy behavior of the challenger directed towards states that are not long-standing rivals. Finally we restrict our analysis to non-democratic challenger states.[5] Empirically in the post-World War II era, the model is applicable to studying bilateral relations between states with a history of protracted conflict such as Syria–Israel, Egypt–Israel, Iran–Iraq, Pakistan–India, Somalia–Ethiopia, or Ecuador–Peru. Our general arguments and theoretical framework can be extended beyond these rivalries, and in future work such extensions will be developed. Enduring rivalries, however, are a very important subset of dyads to study since they account for a disproportionate amount of interstate conflict in the international system (see Goertz and Diehl, 1992b, 1993). In addition, if domestic unrest is an important cause of international conflict, then enduring rivalries should provide a rich dataset to test for connections between internal and external conflict.

The remainder of this chapter is structured as follows. In section two we present an overview of the model and its basic assumptions. In section three we focus in greater detail on the domestic response of incumbent elites to political unrest, while in section four we analyze how the international context shapes the foreign and domestic policy choices of leaders. In section five we conclude by discussing some issues related to testing our arguments empirically and the contributions of our model to the existing theoretical literature.

II. OVERVIEW OF MODEL

We employ a rational choice framework for analyzing the decisions of the challenger state, and we assume a single unitary actor makes foreign and domestic policy choices. While we model the decisions of a challenger state as being made by a single key individual who must make the final choice about how to respond to domestic political unrest and what type of foreign policy should be adopted to support domestic policy choices,[6] we do not imply that this key decision-maker is isolated from the influence of other political actors within or outside the government. A second assumption we employ is that the unitary actor chooses from alternative policies the option with the greatest expected utility. Finally, in calculating the relative costs and benefits of policy alternatives we assume that the key decision-maker's preferences among alternatives are transitive and stable.

Before turning to the basic structure of our model it is important to state briefly the basic assumptions we make regarding the policy preferences and political environment within which decisions are reached. This model integrates assumptions from traditional realism as well as theoretical works that challenge realism from the perspective of domestic politics. This modified realist model[7] portrays state leaders as foreign policy decision-makers who seek to maximize their chances of staying in power while attempting to promote the military security of their country. Political leaders are very careful to pursue foreign policies that strengthen their domestic political position and are therefore judicious in limiting the threat or use of military power to international disputes where the costs of military conflict are not substantial.

The assumptions of the modified realist model are as follows:

Assumption 1: Due to the anarchical nature of the international system, state leaders cannot depend upon a recognized supranational authority to settle disputes with other countries. As a result, state leaders are ultimately responsible for protecting their country from possible military attack and advancing their country's security interests in conflicts with other states.

Assumption 2: The threat or use of military power is the ultimate recourse for state leaders to resolve disputes with other countries and ensure their security.

One important implication of these first two assumptions is that foreign policy leaders should be selective in resorting to military threats or the use of force because a state's diplomatic position and military capabilities can be overextended in a confrontational and very active foreign policy. Overextension can risk military involvement in peripheral conflicts and compromise a country's diplomatic position and influence.

Assumption 3: A primary goal of state leaders is to maintain their position of domestic political power.

Assumption 4: The ability of state leaders to remain in power is strongly related to generating support among various domestic political constituencies.

Assumptions one, three, and four imply that state leaders must manage two basic political roles: (1) they are held accountable for preserving the national security of their country, and (2) they are politicians who seek to remain in power and thus are concerned with existing or potential political opposition from counter-elites. It follows then that state leaders' foreign policy decisions are examined in terms of the consequences for their domestic political position, and foreign policy may be utilized to advance their domestic political interests.

Assumption 5: Domestic political groups consistently seek to shape the domestic and foreign policy choices of state leaders in order to advance their own political and economic interests. These groups exert pressure and influence on political leaders through a variety of channels – the bureaucracy, the military, legislatures, the media, and elections – and they are most active in pressuring the government when they believe that government policies threaten their interests.

Assumptions four and five recognize that all state leaders rely upon domestic coalitions to maintain their positions in power. Even in non-democratic systems, in which leaders are frequently characterized as using repression solely to maintain power, political elites rely upon some domestic political groups for support. Consequently, various groups continue in their struggle to exert pressures upon state leaders, and state elites constantly balance demands from these various groups in attempting to maintain their position (See Migdal, 1988).

Assumption 6: State leaders must accommodate some demands in order to maintain their position in power. When choosing between policies which would grant them the same level of popular support, incumbent elites prefer to accommodate demands which require fewer concessions over those which require greater concessions.

When state elites are forced to accommodate demands, they prefer to accommodate those demands which require smaller changes from the status quo for two reasons. First, incumbent elites have true policy preferences and prefer policies close to their position. Second, elites have chosen a position which grants sufficient coalition support at the least maintenance cost. In changing their position, state leaders are likely to lose support of some coalition supporters in order to satisfy new demands. The greater the change from the current policy, the more likely that it will disturb the domestic balance of power and threaten the leadership's position.

Assumption 7: State leaders believe that a foreign policy setback for their country stemming from a diplomatic retreat or military defeat will impose high domestic costs on them.

Typically, the public is not very attentive to foreign policy issues, but if their country does become engaged in a crisis or military conflict, foreign policy becomes much more salient, and counter-elites and the public are likely to hold their country's political leadership accountable for the outcome of the international confrontation (see Bueno de Mesquita and Lalman, 1990; Lake, 1992). An implication of this assumption is that state leaders should be sensitive to the potential costs that domestic groups and constituencies might suffer as a result of military conflict with another country.[8] Leaders' estimates of anticipated domestic opposition should influence their foreign policy decisions, and they can generally expect high levels of political support for confrontational policies with other states only if the direct material and human costs of such policies for key political groups are not high.

With the basic assumptions of the model presented, the next step is to summarize the policy choices facing a challenger state confronted with domestic political instability. Faced with a domestic crisis, incumbent elites make two interrelated decisions. They decide whether to repress or to accommodate domestic opposition, and they choose whether to escalate their foreign policy towards a rival state. We argue that the choices made in the domestic arena affect the costs and benefits of foreign policy choices, and conversely choices in the foreign policy arena affect the payoffs for domestic policies. The challenger's decision to accommodate or repress domestic conflict is therefore intricately linked to its decision to escalate or maintain its foreign policy toward a rival state. The policy choices of a challenger and rival are presented in Figure 3.1.[9]

We begin at node 1, where we assume that incumbent elites experience and recognize a manifest domestic threat (i.e. anti-government strikes, protests, and demonstrations, military coup attempts or terrorist attacks). In addition to the steps taken to restore political order, they choose either to repress the opposition's demands or to accommodate them. Both the state undergoing domestic unrest and its rival will then decide whether to escalate their international dispute with

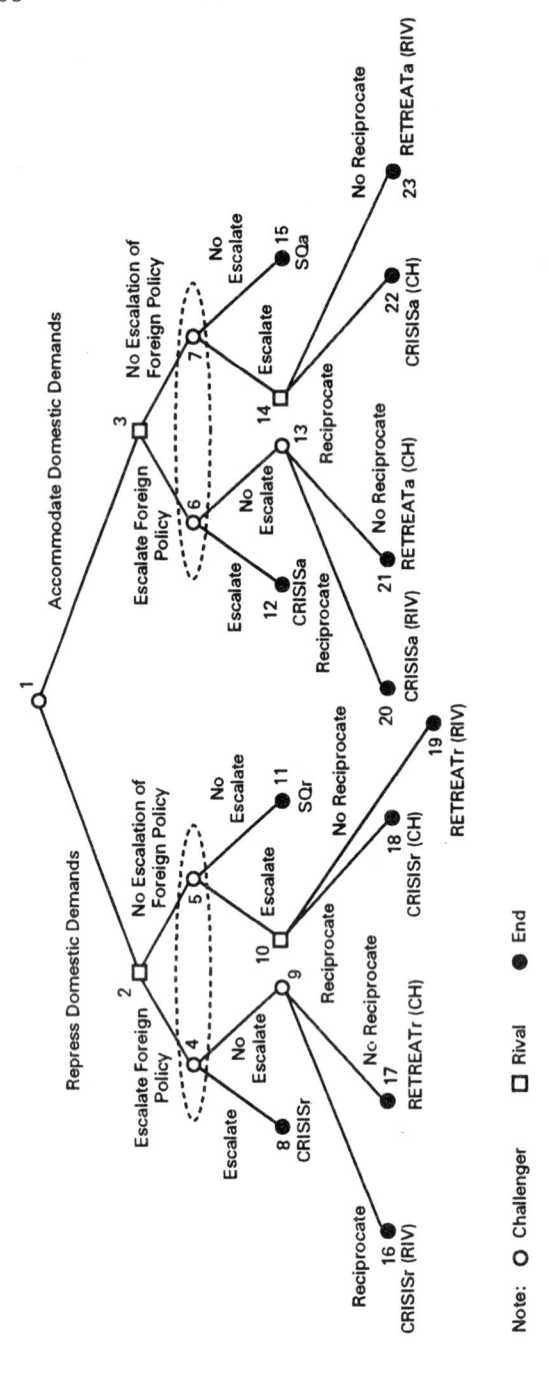

Figure 3.1 The interaction between domestic conflict and foreign policy

Foreign Policy Choices and Domestic Politics 69

each other. They make this decision simultaneously. The rival state, having viewed the challenger's domestic policy decision, knows whether it is at node 2 or node 3. The challenger, however, does not know where it is on the game tree. It can recall its own past history and thus is aware of whether it has repressed or accommodated domestic demands. However, it will choose whether to escalate its foreign policy at the same time as the rival makes its choice. If the challenger has repressed domestic demands, it is at either node 4 or 5. If it has accommodated demands, it is at either node 6 or 7. Because states decide simultaneously whether to escalate the international dispute, they take into account the probability that the rival will escalate the dispute when making their own decisions, but they are not influenced by their opponent's actual choice.

Once both states have made their initial, simultaneous decisions, they are fully aware of the other's choice. The rival knows whether the challenger has escalated its foreign policy stance, and the challenger is aware of whether the rival has increased political and even military pressure against it. As a result, both states know at which of the nodes from 8 to 15 they are located. If both states escalate, they are in an international crisis. This crisis can be accompanied by repression at home (CRISISr at node 8) or accommodation of domestic opposition (CRISISa at node 12). If both states choose not to escalate the international dispute, then the international status quo persists, represented by SQr at node 11 if the challenger has also repressed domestic demands and SQa at node 13 if it has not.

If one state has escalated and the other has not, the game continues. If the rival state has escalated and the challenger has not, the challenger finds itself at either node 9 or node 13. The challenger can reciprocate the escalation, resulting in a crisis initiated by the rival, CRISISr(RIV) at node 16 or CRISISa(RIV) at node 20. It can also choose not to reciprocate, ending in the challenger's retreat, RETREATr(CH) at node 17 or RETREATa(CH) at node 21. If the challenger has escalated and the rival has not, the rival has the same opportunity to reciprocate escalation. Reciprocation results in a crisis initiated by the challenger, either CRISISr(CH) at node 18 or CRISISa(CH) at node 22. Non-reciprocation leads to the rival's retreat, RETREATr(RIV) at node 19 or RETREATa(RIV) at node 23.

We will not fully analyze the game at this time but instead will focus on how changes in the payoffs for the various outcomes affect the challenger's decisions in both the domestic and international arenas. Simplified versions of the outcomes are given in Table 3.1. We assume that the payoffs for crises are equivalent, regardless of which actor initiates them. This assumption is reasonable in the context of rivalries. The challenger state in an enduring rivalry generally has long-standing disputes over specific issues, while the rival seeks to maintain the status quo. Because the demands are well known, there is little advantage to being the demand-maker in initiating the challenge. In addition, since we are examining the initiation of crises and militarized confrontations, not the initiation of full-scale wars, assumptions about first-strike advantages are irrelevant. Finally, we assume that at least in the short term there are no significant differences in the domestic benefits of employing force for offensive vs. defensive purposes for two reasons. First, political leaders consistently legitimize the use of force as a defensive response to external threats even if they are initiating force. As a result, masses and counter-elites are often not in a very good position in closed political systems to assess whether their country's use of force is aggressive or more reactive in nature. Second, the duration and strength of 'rally around the flag' effects are strongly related to how successful the outcome of a military engagement is, regardless of which party initiated the conflict. Given this simplification, we examine the payoffs for four outcomes: a crisis, the challenger's retreat, the rival's retreat, and the status quo.

There are three components for each payoff: stable domestic costs and benefits, stable international costs and benefits, and variable domestic costs and benefits. That is, there are payoffs in the decision to repress or accommodate domestic opposition that remain constant regardless of the foreign policy action. These are represented by DOMESTICrep and DOMESTICacc, respectively, and they include the costs of repressing the opposition plus the benefits of maintaining the status quo domestic policy rather than granting concessions. Some payoffs for the decision to escalate or maintain foreign policy are also constant regardless of the domestic policy chosen. These payoffs for an international crisis, the challenger's retreat, the rival's retreat, and the status quo are symbolized by INTERcrisis, INTERretreat, INTERadvantage, and INTERsq, respectively. They include the likelihood of success in a military confrontation, as well as the foreign policy concessions to be gained or lost, and the costs of escalation, all of which remain constant regardless of the decision to repress or accommodate domestic opposition. There are, however, payoffs that vary depending on whether or not the challenger has chosen to escalate the rivalry or maintain its foreign policy position. A central assumption of the externalization literature is that states experiencing domestic unrest value the 'rally around

Table 3.1 Simplified payoffs for challenger state

Outcome	Challenger if repress domestic demands	Challenger if accommodate domestic demands
CRISIS	DOMESTICrep + INTERcrisis + (DOMESTICrep*INTERcrisis)	DOMESTICacc + INTERcrisis
RETREAT(CH)	DOMESTICrep − INTERretreat − (DOMESTICrep*INTERretreat)	DOMESTICacc − INTERretreat
RETREAT(RIV)	DOMESTICrep + INTERadvantage + (DOMESTICrep*INTERadvantage)	DOMESTICacc + INTERadvantage
SQ	DOMESTICrep + INTERsq + (DOMESTICrep*INTERsq)	DOMESTICacc + INTERsq

the flag' effect more than states which are not experiencing domestic instability. We expand upon this assumption, recognizing that states which are repressing domestic opposition value the 'rally around the flag' effect more than states which are accommodating the opposition's demands. Similarly, states which repress the military's demands benefit more from the diversionary effects of escalation than states which accommodate military demands. To simplify further, we consider only the additional benefits of international escalation that states obtain when they also repress domestic opposition. These are represented by DOMESTICrep*INTER.

Looking at Table 3.1, we can understand how domestic and international factors interact, affecting decision-making in both arenas. Imagine a state in which, isolated from the foreign policy arena, the costs of repressing domestic opposition are greater than the policy concessions necessary for accommodation. That is, DOMESTICacc > DOMESTICrep. Further, assume that the state views the constant expected benefits of foreign policy escalation to be less than the status quo.[10] In this case, the incumbent elites would necessarily choose to maintain the status quo over foreign policy escalation. If incumbent elites made domestic and international decisions independently of each other, the challenger state would then accommodate the domestic opposition and continue a non-escalatory policy towards its international rival.

That states do not make foreign and domestic policy decisions in isolation is well recognized, and it has profound effects in both arenas. A state which previously preferred to accommodate domestic opposition and not initiate foreign policy escalation may choose to repress the domestic demands and escalate against its rival when the interactive effects of foreign policy escalation are sufficiently high.[11] As we will discuss shortly, when 'rally around the flag' effects are great, or when the ability to divert military opposition is extremely valuable, these benefits allow incumbent elites to repress their domestic opposition's demands and give them cause to escalate their international dispute against their long-standing rival. Thus, we cannot consider the apparently sequential decisions of leaders to respond to their domestic opposition and then initiate foreign policy actions to be independent events. We also cannot take domestic responses to internal challenges as a given and look merely at how these responses influence international relations. Leaders, looking ahead to their foreign policy options, make their domestic decisions based upon their own expectations about the outcomes of escalating international disputes. When conditions for escalation are favorable and/or the potential domestic gains from escalation are high, incumbent elites should respond to the political instability through domestic repression and international escalation. When the international conditions for escalation are less favorable and/or domestic gains from escalation are low, incumbent elites are more likely to accommodate their opposition and maintain the international status quo. We will now discuss each of these payoffs in more detail.

III. POLITICAL RESPONSE TO DOMESTIC OPPOSITION

As noted in Assumptions 3–6, the primary goal of state elites is to stay in power, using the support of key constituencies to balance against the demands of domestic political opponents. When faced with domestic political unrest, elites choose either to accommodate or repress the opposition's demands.[12] Elites' decisions to accommodate or repress domestic opposition depend on both domestic and international factors. Here, we will focus on three sets of domestic variables which help to determine the state's response to internal challenges: the nature of the opposition group challenging the incumbent regime, the nature of the state responding to the challenge, and the nature of the society within which the challenge occurs. Some of these factors are associated with constant costs and benefits, making repression or negotiation more or less likely regardless of the international context within which they occur. Other factors affect the regime's ability to gain domestic advantage through foreign policy escalation, and thus the expected utility

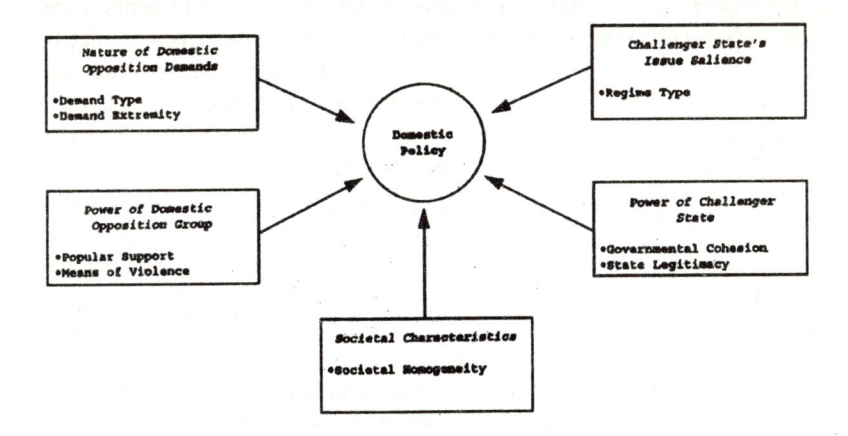

Figure 3.2 Domestic factors influencing response to domestic opposition

of international escalation helps determine the likelihood that the state may gain these benefits. We begin with an examination of domestic factors affecting a state's response regardless of international escalation, and then turn to factors which may alter the state's response when the challenger escalates the international conflict. Figure 3.2 summarizes the factors influencing the decision to repress or accommodate domestic opposition.

Constant Domestic Factors Affecting State Response to Domestic Opposition

The Domestic Opposition

The nature of the domestic opposition is a critical factor in determining how incumbent elites respond to political instability. Political opponents, like all political actors, can be described in terms of the preferences they hold, their salience for these preferences and the power they wield with which to press their demands. We will assume the opposition's salience is high and constant since political opponents consider their demands important enough for them to undertake manifest, often dangerous and illegal, actions in confronting the incumbent elites. We focus, then, on hypotheses about how differences in the opposition's preferences and their ability to challenge the regime affect whether incumbent regimes choose accommodation or repression.

The first set of hypotheses concerns the opposition's demands. Recall from Assumption 5 that state elites prefer to grant fewer concessions in accommodating opposition demands over granting greater concessions. Thus, the greater the concessions required to accommodate opposition demands, the less likely governments are to accommodate these demands (see O'Keefe and Schumaker, 1983; DeNardo, 1985). From this assumption, we derive two hypotheses:

HD1.1 Incumbent elites are more likely to accommodate domestic economic demands than they are to accommodate domestic political demands.

HD1.2 Incumbent elites are also more likely to accommodate moderate than extreme demands.

These hypotheses reflect the two components of demand extremity, the type of demand and the intensity of the demand. First, we hypothesize that the type of opposition demand influences the government's choice to accommodate or repress. In particular, incumbent elites view economic demands as less threatening and more easily reversed than political demands. Thus, *HD1.1* expects that domestic elites are more likely to accommodate economic than political demands. This hypothesis receives some support in a study of African political protest and reform. Examining 30 nations between 1989 and 1991, scholars found that political elites first tried to satisfy economic demands, and only when this failed to weaken the opposition did state elites make political concessions as well (Bratton and van de Walle, 1992).

The second auxiliary hypothesis, *HD1.2*, is based upon the premise that the level of concessions necessary to accommodate political opposition is determined by the distance between the status quo policy and the opposition's demands (see DeNardo, 1985; Hagan, 1993). The extremity of the opposition's initial demands and the extent to which the opposition groups are willing to compromise with incumbent elites over these demands determines how much elites must sacrifice to satisfy the domestic opposition. Since elites prefer small policy changes from the status quo over large ones, they initially try to grant the smallest concessions necessary. When the opposition's demands are moderate or when the opposition is willing to compromise its demands at a moderate position, the government is more likely to accommodate. Empirical studies support this hypothesis, finding for example that political elites first try to satisfy political demands by small changes such as reorganizing the dominant political party, only later granting measures of greater political liberalization (Bratton and van de Walle, 1992; O'Keefe and Schumaker, 1983).

A measure of demand extremity then includes both a representation of the type of demand and a scale of extremity. The type of demand may be represented by a dummy variable for domestic economic and political demands. A scale of extremity may be similar to Hagan's three-level scale of intensity, in which he distinguishes between cases when the opposition challenges the overall policies of the incumbent elites, opposes the maintenance of the regime in power, or challenges the norms and structure upon which the entire political system is based (Hagan, 1993).

Even extreme demands may be accommodated, however, when the opposition is very powerful. As noted in Assumption 3, the primary goal of state elites is to stay in power. Thus, we expect that when governments are unable to remain in power while repressing extreme demands, they will attempt to accommodate these demands. More powerful groups are more likely to gain such accommodation. Simply, the more powerful an opposition group, the more costly it is for the government to repress the opposition demands. The costs of accommodation relative to those of repression decrease, therefore, and government elites become more likely to choose accommodation. This leads us to a second set of hypotheses regarding the resources with which the opposition can press its demands.

HD2.0 Incumbent elites are more likely to accommodate the demands of strong opposition groups than they are to accommodate those of weak opposition groups.

The opposition's strength is a function of the resources it controls. By distinguishing between the types of resources that opposition groups control, we derive three auxiliary hypotheses:

HD2.1 Incumbent elites are more likely to accommodate demands made by large movements than they are to accommodate the demands made by smaller movements.

HD2.2 When the middle class participates in the opposition movement, the government is more likely to accommodate opposition demands.

HD2.3 The greater the opposition's ability to impose anti-state violence, the more likely are incumbent elites to accommodate their demands.

HD2.1 hypothesizes that an opposition movement's strength increases with the number of persons participating in it. There are two reasons for this. First, as DeNardo (1985) notes, there is 'Power in Numbers.'

Large movements are more costly and difficult to repress than small movements and are thus more likely to achieve their demands. The relationship between the number of participants and the likelihood of success need not be linear, however. Initially, larger movements may merely result in greater repression. Once they have reached a threshold, however, state elites may have little choice but to accommodate demands. This was well illustrated by the German Democratic Republic in 1989. At first, the government responded to growing weekly demonstrations with increasingly harsher punishment, but once the crowds had reached 70,000 the security forces no longer attempted to stop the demonstrators, and the East German government was forced to accommodate demands (Francisco, 1993). Similarly, 'the vastness of the movement and the sheer size of public demonstrations' in Brazil's campaign for direct presidential elections frightened both incumbent and opposition elites. It led elite members of the ruling party to break with the military government, forming a coalition with opposition elites which would usher in a conservative governmental transition (Alves, 1989). As mass opposition movements become larger, they are more likely to pass a threshold beyond which governments become willing to accommodate their demands.

Large movements are also stronger because they generally include cross-class coalitions. Cross-class alliances are more difficult to repress and consequently are more likely to have their demands accommodated (Kowalewski and Hoover, 1995; Eckstein, 1989). *HD2.2* predicts that the middle class plays a particularly important role within these class alliances. As noted in Assumption 4, state elites depend upon the support of key domestic constituencies to retain their positions in power. Middle classes are more likely than working or agrarian classes to be constituents supporting the ruling coalition. They also are likely to control greater resources by which to press their demands. Thus, we expect that state leaders will be less willing to repress middle-class opposition than they are to repress other opponents. Empirically, Eckstein (1989) emphasizes this with regard to Latin America. There, only agrarian movements which have benefitted from middle class support have led to regime transitions. Similarly, middle-class involvement has been critical in the success of working-class movements in Mexico, Bolivia, Cuba, Nicaragua and Chile (Garreton, 1989).

Finally, *HD2.3* states that when political opponents are unable to mobilize a mass-based protest movement, they may use violence to gain concessions. As with the relationship between the size of movements and the government's likelihood to accommodate opposition groups, initially governments may respond to more violent movements with repression. However, once violence has reached a level which state elites cannot control, they are likely to accommodate the opposition demands. The greater a movement's ability to use violence to press its demands, the more likely the movement surpasses the threshold beyond which governments are likely to make concessions. Military opponents are likely to control the greatest potential power. With arms at their disposal and troops potentially at their command, military opposition may be the most powerful threats to authoritarian regimes. Consequently, we expect that military demands are more likely to be accommodated than other demands, when the nature of the demands remains equal. Civilian groups unable to mobilize mass support may also use violence to force governments to accommodate their demands. These groups can use terrorism to maintain their organizational cohesion and spur further mobilization, as well as to weaken the state, disable its repressive apparatus and strain government resources (DeNardo, 1985; Chai, 1993). Although the costs of using anti-government violence may be high, eventually the use of violence by civilian groups makes governments more likely to accommodate opposition demands.

It should be noted that there is some evidence contrary to *HD2.3*, but these results may be due to spurious correlations. For example, Kowalewski and Hoover (1995) concluded that increased violence often makes 'officials angrier and more intensely repressive.' A study of 175 protest incidents in Malaysia, the Philippines and Thailand from 1960 to 1978 also found that violent strategies were more likely to result in greater repression and less accommodation than non-violent protests (O'Keefe and Schumaker, 1983). Finally, when violent protest movements do lead to accommodation, it is often the non-violent groups which are appeased (O'Keefe and Schumaker, 1983:383). Yet, these results may be due to several related factors. First, groups which make extreme demands generally are 'highly assertive in challenging the regime, often to the point of violating basic political norms in the system' (Hagan, 1993). Since regimes prefer accommodation of moderate demands over accommodation of extreme demands, it is not surprising that governments would be less likely to accommodate extreme groups using violent means than more moderate groups using less violent means. Second, groups tend to use more violent means in repressive states, since repressive systems make mobilization of peaceful protests difficult, if not impossible, for opposition elites (DeNardo, 1985). In addition, illegal opposition groups can use violent means as a tool to maintain their organizational strength (Chai, 1993). If more violent opposition groups emerge in repressive states, the correlation between the use of violence and repression may also be due to additional factors which have made these states more repressive. That the use of violence may make accommodation more likely *ceteris paribus* remains a reasonable theoretical proposition and deserves to be tested.

The opposition's power, then, is measured in terms of military or civilian power, and within the civilian sector is measured in terms of the level of popular support and the use of violence. There are two measures of opposition popular support for mass-based civilian opposition movements. The first measure should take into account the total number of participants joining the protest movement.[13] We expect that the greater the number of participants, the more likely the government is to accommodate their demands. A second measure of opposition strength is the involvement of middle classes.[14] This should be tested separately, with the expectation that middle-class support makes the government more likely to accommodate the opposition's demands. Finally, when civilian opposition movements rely on violence to make their demands, their strength will also be measured by the level of anti-government violence committed.[15]

The opposition's ability to use their resources also affects the state's decision to repress or accommodate their demands. We expect:

HD3.0 The greater the opposition's organizational strength, the more likely the government will accommodate demands.

The opposition elites' organizational strength helps to determine how efficiently they can use their resources to press demands, and how likely they are to maintain a hard-line negotiating position. Previous work has suggested that greater factionalization among opposition leadership decreases their success (see Kowalewski and Hoover, 1995; DeNardo, 1985; Gamson, 1975). The easier it is for incumbent elites to appease selectively small portions of the opposition while fragmenting and repressing the majority, the less likely they are to accommodate the opposition's demands. Thus, the emergence of a hegemonic leader or group of leaders helps to overcome the problem of fragmentation and thus makes accommodation more likely.

This hypothesis has found some support in the cases of Syria in 1941 and Korea in 1986. In the first case, Syrian nationalists were divided in their struggle against the French mandate until early 1941. In that year, one of the most powerful opposition leaders was murdered, and leaders of most other opposition groups, fearing implication in the affair, fled to Iraq. Only one major opposition leader, Shukri

Quwatli, was left to carry on the struggle. Unrivaled in his position, he was able to lead the country's most successful campaign against the French to that date, beginning a series of strikes which spread throughout the country.[16] Similarly, the emergence of a hegemonic opposition leader in Korea led to the success of the democratic movement in 1986. At this time, Kim Dae Jung was under a political ban and thus carried the 'moral authority' within the opposition. He was also adamant that the opposition be granted direct popular elections. When Lee Min Woo, the official leader of the New Korea Democratic Party, suggested they accept a compromise, the majority of the party members in the National Assembly responded to a call by Kim Dae Jung and his fellow leader, Kim Young Sam, to repudiate Lee and form a new party. Given the hegemonic support of Kim Dae Jung, no opposition leader could suggest a compromise, and the government was forced to provide direct presidential elections (Han, 1988). In both cases, events leading to the emergence of a hegemonic opposition leader made it possible for the movements to achieve goals that had previously been unattainable.

The Challenger State

We also examine factors affecting the state's preferences, salience and power to determine when states are more likely to repress or accommodate domestic opposition. In this case, we assume that all states prefer the status quo over the opposition's demands, or no conflict will result. However, there is considerable variation between incumbent regimes in their salience over the issues at stake and their ability to repress the opposition's demands. Before addressing the hypotheses that we will examine in future work, two theoretical points should be made.

First, regime type affects the degree to which states prefer repression over accommodation. The most obvious distinction is between polyarchies and hegemonies. As Kowalewski and Schumaker explain:

> Polyarchies are open pluralist systems where institutions are structured to facilitate widespread citizen participation in the policy process. Hegemonies are closed, monistic systems, where extensive controls are placed on the organization, representation, and expression of citizen preferences. Unlike pluralist regimes, hegemonic regimes claim a monopoly of political truth and hence are less likely to tolerate dissenting groups. Thus, protest groups are likely to win fewer concessions and suffer more repression when making demands

on hegemonic rather than pluralistic regimes (1981:57–58; see also Muller and Weede, 1990; Gurr,1988).

Put differently, the mobilization of opposition in a hegemonic system challenges the very basis of the regime. Consequently, elites in these states value the maintenance of their status quo position and repression of opposition demands more than elites in polyarchies. Even granting small concessions to opposition groups is costly when concessions suggest the weakness of the hegemonic regime. Thus, non-democratic leaders are more likely to repress demands than democratic leaders, although accommodation remains a viable option.[17] We will not test this hypothesis directly because we are limiting our dataset to hegemonic regimes. However, this theoretical distinction should be recognized.

Second, within regime types, there may be variation in the states' repressive resources by which to control the opposition. Tsebelis and Sprague (1989) argue, for example, that states do not control an unending supply of resources with which to repress the opposition. In addition, Gurr (1988) suggests that leaders who gain power through violent means are more likely to have fostered repressive forces. These leaders are thus more likely to repress the opposition's demands. Unfortunately, there is little empirical support for Gurr's hypothesis (Geller, 1987; Rousseau, 1996: chap. 7). Furthermore, we expect that among non-democratic states there is little variation in the amount of repressive forces which elites can call upon to control internal unrest. The extent to which limitations of repressive forces are important, then, will be reflected in the importance of the opposition's power to make its demands.

Instead, we focus on how variation in a state's power to repress opposition demands is associated with political factors:

HD4.0 The greater the division among government elites over the issues at stake, the more likely that states will respond through accommodation.

HD4 predicts that central elites are less likely to repress opposition demands when some of the elites sympathize with or openly support opposition demands. To repress demands not only incurs costs imposed by the political opponents, but risks the cohesiveness of the central coalition. Some political elites may be disaffected if the ruling coalition represses demands of constituencies which are key to their support. As noted in Assumption 4, since state elites rely upon these key constituencies to remain in power, these elites are more likely to try to strike a deal with the political opponents. Consequently, we include a variable to reflect the presence or absence of division within the elite coalition over the issues at stake and expect that state elites are likely to accommodate opposition demands when there is internal division over the issues at stake.[18]

Factors Affecting the State's Ability to Use International Escalation to Offset Domestic Unrest

We argued in section two that the choice of accommodation or repression may, in part, be determined by the state's ability to use international crises to offset the costs of repressing domestic opposition. Much of the externalization literature assumes that states may use international escalation to offset domestic unrest either through the 'rally around the flag' effects of international crises or through the diversion of military opponents towards crises abroad. In either case, the domestic utility of international escalation is greater for states repressing domestic opposition than for states accommodating this opposition. The extent to which states may benefit from international escalation, however, depends upon domestic factors. We set forth two additional hypotheses, pertaining to the nature of the state and the society experiencing domestic unrest:

HD*I1 When the masses identify strongly with state actions, states will be more likely to repress demands and externalize domestic conflict.

HD*I2 Elites in less homogeneous societies will be more likely to accommodate opposition and less likely to externalize domestic conflict than elites in more homogeneous societies.

HD*I1 addresses the potential benefits of the 'rally around the flag' effect. Where masses believe the ruling coalition reflects their interests, they will identify strongly with the state's international policy goals. Escalation will then bring greater domestic benefits to state elites in legitimate regimes than to state elites in less legitimate regimes. This additional rally effect is more likely to offset the domestic costs of repression and allow regimes to undertake a policy of international escalation and domestic political repression. Where the masses are less likely to support state goals strongly, the 'rally around the flag' effect should be weaker. In this case, states are more likely to accommodate opposition demands.

An interesting sub-hypothesis regarding the relationship between the level of foreign policy escalation and state legitimacy should be noted.

Although we posit that state legitimacy is positively related to the likelihood that states will escalate against international rivals in response to domestic unrest, it may be negatively related to the level of escalation when it occurs. That is, when states choose to escalate their foreign policy in an attempt to offset domestic unrest, those states which have lower levels of legitimacy are likely to escalate to higher levels of conflict within an international crisis. The underlying logic for this is simple. We assume that the 'rally around the flag' effects of international escalation increase as the intensity of an international crisis increases. Thus, for states with low legitimacy to benefit from escalation, they must escalate to higher levels of international crisis than states with high legitimacy.

Unfortunately, measuring the extent that the masses view their governments as legitimate is extremely difficult. To simplify greatly, we will consider how much the ruling coalition reflects the population at large. Specifically, we will determine the percentage of the population from the same ethnic, religious or sectarian group as the majority of the leadership coalition. In a country such as Syria, therefore, where the ruling coalition is under primary control of the Alawites, who make up less than 16 per cent of the population,[19] the state's legitimacy would be relatively low. In such a case, where the state gains less popular support from externalization, it is more likely to accommodate opposition demands. In this particular case, however, we have often seen the logic described in the sub-hypothesis. When faced with demands the regime cannot meet, President Assad adopts a policy of international escalation. Daniel Pipes (1990:160) explains:

> ... for the 'Alawis to have given the Sunnis more would have cut into their own power, and this they could not do out of fear of a Sunni takeover. Gerard Michaud noted that 'Alawis remain persuaded that the slightest concession on their part and they will revert back to their own status of "damned of the earth".' To rid the system of the sectarian bias would be tantamount to destroying the regime.

> [Thus, i]f the Asad regime was to appeal to its people and inspire their loyalty on a nationalist basis, it had to look outward. The rulers needed a mechanism of expansion, preferably with a radical tinge. Laurent and Basbous explained this with regard to Lebanon. 'From 1920 the Sunni Muslims of Syria felt a constant, almost visceral irredentism toward Lebanon. The 'Alawis had to match these or, if possible, do better. This was the main reason why they tried so hard to "recover" Lebanon.' The same applied to the other lost lands of Greater Syria (Pipes, 1990:186–7).

HD*12 notes, similarly, that the potential 'rally around the flag' effects from escalation also depend upon the homogeneity within the society. As Levy (1989a) argues, if the in-group theory is correct, it should be the case that higher levels of ethnic, sectarian or regional cleavages correspond to lower rally effects from escalation. Governments in highly divided societies would expect that they would benefit less from escalation than would governments in less divided societies. Consequently, we include a measure of societal homogeneity, expecting that the greater the homogeneity, the less likely opposition demands are to be accommodated.

Three sets of domestic factors then determine whether state elites repress or accommodate government opposition: the nature of the domestic opposition, the nature of the ruling coalition, and the nature of the society within which the conflict occurs. The less extreme the opposition demands, the more likely that the government will accommodate them. The extremity of demands is a function of the type of demands (i.e. economic vs. political demands) and the extent to which compromise requires a change from the status quo. More powerful opposition groups are also more likely to have their demands accommodated. The opposition's power is positively related to its level of popular support, its ability to inflict violence upon the state, and its organizational cohesion. Finally, the nature of the state affects whether or not demands will be accommodated. Regime type affects the state's salience for maintaining the status quo. Polyarchic regimes are less likely to value maintaining the status quo, and more likely to accommodate opposition demands, than hegemonic regimes. For all regime types, the lower the state's legitimacy and the greater the division among central elites over the issues at stake, the more likely the state is to accommodate opposition demands. In addition, states benefit less from international escalation, and thus are more likely to accommodate domestic opposition demands, when the society is heterogeneous.

As we argued in section two, a state's decision to accommodate or repress domestic opposition depends upon its ability to benefit from international escalation. States which repress opposition demands may choose to escalate against their international rivals, using the benefits of the 'rally around the flag' effect and military diversion to offset the costs of repression at home. States which accommodate demands gain few domestic benefits from international escalation. If a state can benefit from international escalation, offsetting the costs of repression, it will prefer a policy of domestic repression and international escalation. If it cannot benefit from escalating the rivalry, either because the expected utility of international escalation is low or the domestic benefits from escalation do not outweigh the costs of repression, the state will prefer to accommodate domestic opposition and maintain the international status quo. *Thus, there is an important link between the type of domestic response to domestic opposition and changes in foreign policy: domestic repression is likely to be accompanied by international escalation, while domestic accommodation is not likely to be accompanied by a challenge to the international status quo.*

Clearly, the potential gain from the 'rally around the flag' effect depends upon the state's expectation of the outcomes of international escalation. Thus, incumbent elites, deciding whether to repress or accommodate their domestic opposition, also consider the potential costs of international escalation. In doing so, they calculate the expected utility of escalation in a manner which will be described next.

IV. FOREIGN POLICY CHOICES

At the same time that leaders within the challenger state decide what domestic policies they should adopt in response to the opposition they face, they also consider their foreign policy options. More specifically, leaders evaluate whether escalating a dispute with its long-standing rival will serve to support the preferred domestic response to political unrest, or whether it will work at cross-purposes to domestic policy needs. Put differently, political leaders need to calculate the expected utility of escalation against their rival and determine whether a policy of escalation is appropriate given domestic policy preferences. In this section we will focus on how the diplomatic and military position of the challenger state should affect calculations about the costs and benefits of threatening a military confrontation with its rival and thus provoking an international crisis.[20]

Assumptions 2–7 provide the theoretical foundation for a series of hypotheses. The first set of hypotheses are as follows:

HI1.1 There is a positive relationship between the military strength of the challenger and the probability that a challenger will initiate a militarized confrontation with its rival.[21]

HI1.2 There is a positive relationship between the military strength of the challenger and the level of escalation reached by a challenger in a militarized confrontation with its rival.[22]

The logic of these hypotheses is that the stronger the challenger is, the higher the probability that it can overturn the status quo by the use of military force or compel the rival to accept its demands backed by the credible threat of force. Conversely, the weaker the challenger, the greater the risk of a diplomatic or military defeat if the challenger confronts a strong rival. Military weakness increases the risks of a foreign policy defeat which, in turn, is a threat to the domestic political position of leaders within the challenger, particularly when leaders already face considerable domestic unrest. Challenger states with greater relative military capabilities will be more likely to initiate militarized confrontations and more willing to escalate those conflicts based on higher expectations of achieving their political and/or military goals.[23]

The second hypothesis derived from Assumptions 2-7 focuses on the involvement of the challenger in conflicts with other states:

HI2.1 There is an inverse relationship between a challenger's involvement in militarized disputes with other states and the probability that a challenger will initiate a militarized confrontation with its rival.

HI2.2 There is an inverse relationship between a challenger's involvement in militarized disputes with other states and the level of escalation reached by a challenger in a militarized confrontation with its rival.

HI2.3 There is a positive relationship between a rival's involvement in militarized disputes with other states and the probability that a challenger will initiate a militarized confrontation with the rival.

HI2.4 There is a positive relationship between a rival's involvement in militarized disputes with other states and the level of escalation reached by a challenger in a militarized confrontation with the rival.[24]

If the challenger is engaged in militarized conflicts with other states, it is less likely to be in a strong position to apply diplomatic and military pressure against a rival because it intends to commit, or has already committed, some of its available diplomatic and military resources to a dispute with another country. This weakens the bargaining position of the challenger against the rival, and heightens the risk of a foreign policy setback stemming from the unwillingness to risk war with the rival at a time of other more pressing foreign policy commitments. Political leaders within the challenger state should then favor escalation of an ongoing dispute with the rival when disputes with other states are less dangerous and the risks of military conflict with other states are low. Conversely, if the rival is engaged in militarized conflicts with other states, the challenger should believe that the rival is more vulnerable to coercive pressure and even military attack and therefore be more willing to initiate and escalate militarized disputes with its rival.

The final hypotheses derived from Assumptions 2–7 are as follows:

H13.0 There is a positive relationship between a stalemate in prior negotiations between the challenger and rival and the probability that a challenger will initiate a militarized confrontation with its rival.[25]

H14.0 There is a positive relationship between rival actions to change the status quo over a disputed issue and the probability that a challenger will initiate a militarized confrontation with its rival.[26]

H15.1 There is a negative relationship between the number of times a challenger has previously suffered a defeat or stalemate in armed conflict with a rival and the probability that a challenger will initiate a militarized confrontation with its rival.

H15.2 There is a negative relationship between the number of times a challenger has previously suffered a defeat or stalemate in armed conflict with a rival and the level of escalation reached by a challenger in a militarized confrontation with its rival.[27]

The logic of *H13.0* is that increased coercive pressure and threats of force by the challenger should be correlated with periods of active diplomacy and ongoing negotiations between challenger and rival. Challengers should resort to higher levels of coercive pressure in order to back up their diplomatic position in talks. Since military power is the most important component of a state's bargaining power, the timely threat or use of military power should be used by the challenger to communicate to the rival its resolve and the risks of stalemate in current negotiations.

If we extend this logic further, leaders within the challenger state will be more likely to escalate a dispute against the target after the failure of diplomatic efforts and negotiations for three reasons. First, the challenger may resort to increased coercive pressure in order to convince the rival that a continued stalemate in negotiations carries with it a heightened risk of armed conflict. Thus, political and military pressure would be designed to compel the rival to be more accommodative in future talks. Second, the challenger may turn to coercive pressure and military force as the only viable alternative, having lost confidence in the use of diplomacy and negotiations to change the status quo. Finally, an additional incentive for the challenger to escalate a dispute after a stalemate in negotiations is that a stalemate can be

Foreign Policy Choices and Domestic Politics 87

portrayed by domestic political opposition as a foreign policy setback for the current leadership. As a result, the challenger may utilize a more confrontational policy to counter mounting domestic political discontent about the state of relations with the rival or to prevent such opposition from arising.

The challenger should also respond to actions taken by the rival to establish and/or consolidate its control over the issues at stake by escalating the dispute to higher levels of diplomatic and military conflict. There are three reasons for this. First, increasing coercive pressure could signal to the rival that its actions are unacceptable and will be costly to continue, and therefore the rival should enter into negotiations. Second, challengers can initiate military actions in an attempt to prevent the rival from establishing a new and unfavorable status quo. Third, the challenger could resort to military force in an attempt to resolve the dispute by means of a *fait accompli* based on the belief that the further passage of time would only benefit the target. In sum, *HI4.0* posits that when the past policies of the challenger have failed to prevent the rival from initiating actions that threaten its position in the dispute, the challenger should turn to more coercive policies based on the belief that the threat or use of force is the most important means by which to protect its interests. In addition, as with *HI3.0*, domestic political concerns could also pressure leaders within the challenger state to respond to the actions of the rival. In this case, the failure to respond would open the leadership of the challenger to charges of weakness and a foreign policy defeat, which the leaders could seek to undercut by confronting the rival target openly and more aggressively.

The logic supporting *HI5.1* and *HI5.2* is that the repeated demonstration of military strength by the rival should lead a challenger to avoid high levels of escalation in the future. The initial response of the challenger to a military defeat may be to build up its military strength further and attack once again in an attempt to reverse previous losses. If the rival, however, continues to inflict substantial costs on the challenger in subsequent confrontations, then leaders within the challenger state should acknowledge the stronger military capabilities of the rival and be less willing to initiate and escalate to high-level militarized confrontations. Leaders within the challenger state should learn then from their country's past failure in military encounters to respect the military strength of their rival and to avoid escalation against a superior opponent.

The final issue to consider is how leaders within the challenger state integrate their calculations about the utility of a domestic response to political unrest with the expected payoff of escalation against an enduring rival. Up until this point we have discussed the payoffs for domestic and foreign policy options in isolation from one another. We argued, however, at the outset that the two sets of policy choices need to be considered in combination to understand fully whether domestic unrest will cause increased international conflict.

In Table 3.2 we present four different combinations of domestic and foreign policy options for the challenger which nicely capture the range of likely policy pairings. As we argued above, if ruling elites are considering repressing the domestic opposition they face, then the option of foreign policy escalation is going to be more attractive from a domestic political perspective. External conflict can be utilized to mobilize nationalist support and generate 'rally around the flag' effects to help offset the discontent produced by a domestic policy of repression. Thus, foreign policy escalation is expected to be most likely when ruling elites have high expected utilities for both domestic repression and international conflict with a rival (cell 1). A good example is Iraq's invasion of Kuwait in 1990. Following the end of the war with Iran in 1988, Iraq faced serious economic problems as it attempted to recover from the war. Discontent within the military was particularly acute as soldiers returning from the battlefield were unable to find well-paying jobs. Saddam Hussein survived multiple coup attempts during the period from late 1988 until early 1990 and ruthlessly dealt with those groups and factions that were behind the attempted coups. Analysts have argued that by early 1990 the option of invading Kuwait was under consideration as a way for Hussein to divert the military away from further involvement in domestic politics and to address some of his pressing economic problems. For Hussein the expected military and political costs of invading Kuwait seemed minimal as the United States did not clearly threaten to intervene against Iraq, and Hussein believed that other Arab states would protest but eventually accept the occupation and overthrow of the existing Kuwaiti regime (see Freedman and Karsh, 1993: chapters 2-3; Miller and Mylroie, 1990).

In contrast, foreign policy escalation is expected to be less likely when leaders strongly favor some form of accommodation to the demands of the political opposition, and the expected payoff of confronting a rival in an international crisis is low (cell 4). In such a situation the domestic political incentives to escalate are weak and the expected foreign policy gains of a militarized confrontation with the rival are minimal as well. Analysts have argued for example that Syrian President Asad in the 1990s has adopted some limited accommodative policies

Table 3.2 Influence of domestic and foreign policy variables on the likelihood of international conflict

		Foreign policy	
		High utility of escalation	Low utility of escalation
Domestic policy	High utility of repression	Very high likelihood of international conflict	Low likelihood of international conflict
	Low utility of repression	Moderate likelihood of international conflict	Very low likelihood of international conflict

towards various political opponents, such as releasing some political prisoners, negotiating with exiled opposition leaders and permitting the return of political exiles, and enlarging parliament by allowing more independent members (see Lobmeyer, 1994; Kienle, 1994). At the same time, Asad's utility for escalation towards Israel is low even though he strongly desires the return of the Golan Heights from Israel. Asad has not engaged his country's armed forces in military confrontations with Israel in the disputed territory due to Israeli military superiority (see Lawson, 1994; Ma'oz, 1995: chapters 9–12). Cells 1 and 4 in Table 3.2 then generate clear and opposite predictions about the likelihood of foreign policy escalation.

In cell 3 the situation is more complex as leaders tend to favor domestic accommodation which does not generate political incentives to escalate against an international rival. However, the expected utility of escalation from the perspective of foreign policy gains looks favorable and thus escalation is expected to be likely but domestic politics should play no significant role in explaining why escalation would take place. The Green March by Morocco against Spain in the Western Sahara during 1975 would seem to fit this pattern. King Hassan in the face of increased domestic pressure and opposition during the period 1973–5 had opened up the political system by negotiating with political parties and preparing them to compete in elections. At the same time, the policy of increasing support for Polasario attacks against the Spanish and then threatening Moroccan armed intervention if Spain countered a march by Moroccan civilians into Spanish Sahara was driven largely by the growing perception that Spain lacked the resolve to hold onto the territory and that Morocco had diplomatic support from neighboring countries like Mauritania and Algeria (see Hodges, 1983: chapters 26–8).

Finally, the likelihood of escalation should be low in cell 2 because even though a high value for domestic repression should lead ruling elites to turn to foreign policy escalation, the unfavorable prospects for confronting a rival in a militarized dispute should discourage elites from consistently escalating. Again, the case of Syria vs. Israel under Asad is illustrative. Throughout the 1970s and 1980s Asad often repressed domestic political opposition and unrest but Asad did not frequently initiate militarized conflicts with Israel during these periods of repression. The risks of armed conflict with Israel were simply too high. Instead, scholars have argued that when Asad turned to escalatory actions to divert attention away from internal unrest and repression, the typical target was the far weaker and divided country of Lebanon (see Lawson, 1984; McLaurin, Mughisuddin and Wagner, 1977; Evron, 1987). Thus, we see that for Syria the driving force in explaining the different policies of escalation in Lebanon vs. Israel is not differences in domestic responses to political unrest but the expected costs and benefits of military conflict against each state.

In sum, in Table 3.2 we see that the common characteristic of domestic unrest in four situations does not lead to similar predictions about foreign policy escalation. Instead, we find that the likelihood of escalation ranges from very low to very high depending upon the combination of payoffs for domestic responses to opposition and international conflict with a rival. Thus, even though domestic unrest by itself cannot be utilized as a variable to generate clear predictions about foreign policy escalation, we have shown that consistent and more subtle predictions can be made if a more detailed and integrated approach to specifying the domestic and international context of decisions faced by ruling elites is developed.

V. CONCLUSION

The hypotheses set forth in this paper can be tested in two steps. First, an empirical test of the primary hypotheses presented in the sections on domestic and foreign policy choices could be set up as a pair of hierarchical simultaneous equations with the ruling elite's domestic response to unrest the endogenous variable in the first equation and the elite's decision whether to escalate its dispute with an international rival the endogenous variable in the second equation. In summary form:

> domestic response = f(demand type, demand intensity, opposition popular support, opposition level of violence, opposition middle class support, societal homogeneity, regime legitimacy, government cohesion, and international expected utility of escalation).

> foreign policy escalation = f(military balance, challenger and rival dispute involvement, prior military defeats, stalemate in negotiations, rival challenge to status quo, domestic response).

A third multilevel probit equation can be used to test the auxiliary hypotheses regarding the level to which states escalate conflict. This equation remains identical to the first equation modelling domestic response, but with two exceptions. First, the dependent variable will be the level of escalation, coded across multiple levels. Second, and more importantly, we expect that the impact of societal homogeneity and regime legitimacy on the level of escalation is inverse to that found in the first equation. Finally, we should note that variables from the domestic and international context are in all equations, representing the reciprocal influence of each on the other. Given our focus on challenger relations with long-standing rivals we propose to test these equations on a dataset which consists of all post-World War enduring rivalries.[28] Within each enduring rivalry we propose to examine all years in which challenger states experienced heightened levels of domestic unrest.[29] All cases will be included in the estimation of the first two equations, and those cases in which escalation occurs will be used to estimate the final model.

One of the central developments in the theoretical literature on international relations over the past decade has been the argument that domestic politics must be incorporated into theories in a systematic way (Bueno de Mesquita and Lalman, 1992; Huth, 1996; Snyder, 1991; Rosecrance and Stein, 1993; Evans, Jacobson and Putnam, 1993; Peterson, 1996; Russett, 1993). Our work in this project fits squarely within this developing literature. By bringing in domestic politics and according it a central theoretical role, we believe that we have helped to bring logical order and structure to an area of the international conflict literature which is marked by multiple and even contradictory hypotheses. Our model nicely illustrates the advantages and new insights that can be gained by examining domestic politics quite closely when trying to make predictions and causal statements about the conditions which promote international conflict. Indeed, the much larger literature on the causes of war and crises needs to be reexamined from the theoretical perspective of integrating domestic and international levels of analysis. Long-standing questions about alliances, arms races, deterrence, and crisis bargaining can all be reconsidered in this light. We suspect that more rigorous attention to modeling the interplay between domestic and international politics will result in clarification of many theoretical debates and disjunctures in the literature and produce new hypotheses as well. Far too much of the international relations literature has been devoted to demonstrating the weaknesses of a realist approach by arguing that domestic politics can play an important role in explaining behavior. While useful as a means of critiquing realism, the more important task of theoretical work is to start with the premise that both levels of analysis must be examined within an integrated approach to understood policy choices at either level.

NOTES

1. For a summary and overview of much of the theoretical literature on the domestic causes of international conflict see Levy (1989a).
2. See Levy (1989a) for a review of the empirical literature. More recent empirical studies would include Mansfield and Snyder (1995); Lian and Oneal (1993); Ostrom and Job (1986); James (1988: chap. 5); James and Oneal (1991); Russett (1990: chap. 2); Morgan and Bickers (1992); DeRouen (1995); Meernik (1994); Wang (1996); Walt (1992).
3. It is possible then that we would include in our analysis cases where the challenger's ongoing involvement in a militarized conflict or war produces manifest political unrest at home for the challenger. However, if international escalation does not trigger domestic unrest, then the case would not be included in our data set. We make no specific assumptions about the initial cause(s) of domestic unrest within the challenger. Those causes may be driven by domestic factors and/or related to international conflicts.
4. While our theoretical focus is on explaining the behavior of the challenger state, the anticipated reactions of the rival are of direct concern to the challenger and therefore the logic of strategic thinking is incorporated into many of the hypotheses concerning the decisions of the challenger. The primary reason for the focus on the challenger is that it is the actions and decisions of the challenger that are the fundamental causes of conflict and accommodation over disputed issues in an enduring rivalry. It is the challenger that seeks to change the status quo and decides whether to pursue its claims aggressively or to seek a settlement, while the rival generally responds to these actions.

5. We exclude democratic states as challengers in the model for two reasons. First, since we employ the unitary actor assumption (see below) we believe that such an assumption is more reasonable for non-democratic states in which powerful leaders often do exercise dominant political power. Second, democratic leaders' options for violent repression of domestic political opposition are sufficiently constrained in comparison to most non-democratic leaders that we prefer to separate the two groups of leaders for purposes of analysis.
6. See Bueno de Mesquita (1981: chap. 2) and Bueno de Mesquita and Lalman (1992: chap. 1) for a discussion of how the unitary actor assumption deals with the problem of Arrow's Paradox.
7. See Huth (1996: chap. 3) for a more detailed discussion of the basic assumptions and logic supporting the modified realist model.
8. Empirical studies indicate that political leaders can mobilize public support for a wide range of confrontational foreign policy actions, but this 'rally around the flag' effect can be quite limited in duration, particularly in situations in which military force is employed by state leaders. For a good summary of the literature see Russett (1990: chap. 2). Empirical studies which identify a clear relationship between the costs and/or defeat in war and the political stability of regimes are Bueno de Mesquita, Siverson and Woller (1992); Bueno de Mesquita and Siverson (1995); and Cotton (1986).
9. This model is similar to the model of deterrence, presented by Kilgour and Zagare (1991).
10. The expected utility of escalation is the probability that the rival reciprocates (Πr) times the utility of a crisis (INTERcrisis) and the probability that the rival retreats ($1-\Pi r$) times the utility of reciprocation (INTERadvantage): EU(escalation) = Πr*INTERcrisis + $(1-\Pi r)$*INTERadvantage. Thus, the state will choose not to escalate as long as INTERsq > Πr*INTERcrisis + $(1-\Pi r)$*INTERadvantage.
11. This will occur when the interactive effects of escalation are greater than the difference between the value of accommodation and repression, and when the expected utility of escalation with interactive effects is greater than the difference between the expected utility of the status quo and the expected utility of escalation without interactive effects. That is, Πr(DOMESTICrep*INTERcrisis) + $(1-\Pi r)$ * (DOMESTICrep*INTERadvantage) > (DOMESTICacc − DOMESTICrep) and Πr*(DOMESTICrep*INTERcrisis) + $(1-\Pi r)$ * (DOMESTICrep*INTERadvantage) > INTERsq − [Πr*INTERcrisis − $(1-\Pi r)$ * INTERadvantage].
12. In many cases, governments respond to political opposition through a combination or repressive and accommodative policies. They may accommodate the demands of some political opponents in order to weaken the opposition movement, and thus repress the remaining demands. We will consider state elites' policies accommodative when more than half of the opposition's demands have been met. The response will be coded as repressive otherwise.
13. The measure may be similar to the seven-point scale which Taylor and Jodice (1983) adopt. However, this scale is implicitly log-linear, and would not pick up potential threshold effects. A more useful and efficient measure

may be constructed from the average number of recorded participants for demonstrations.
14. This measure would be a dichotomous dummy variable of no middle-class involvement/middle-class involvement.
15. This measure would include the number of deaths from opposition-initiated actions, from the beginning of the crisis until the end of the unrest, and the number of terrorist incidents in the same time period.
16. For similar theoretical remarks, see Maxwell and Oliver (1993). For a full discussion of this argument with respect to the Syrian Nationalists' strike in 1941, see Lust-Okar (1993). See also Khoury (1987); Longrigg (1978); and Warner (1974) for analyses of the politics surrounding the strikes.
17. Empirical examples of non-democratic leaders accommodating demands include the Syrian response to the Constitutional Riots in 1973, the Moroccan response to popular unrest in 1984, and the Jordanian response to bread riots in 1989. Furthermore, cases which have led to various degrees of political and economic liberalization in Eastern Europe, the former Soviet Union and much of the Third World are cases in which economic and political demands are accommodated by non-democratic political elites.
18. Since data regarding the presence or absence of elite divisions in non-democratic regimes is difficult to obtain on a systematic basis, the nature of the ruling coalition may provide a useful proxy. Several studies suggest a relationship between the likelihood of intergovernmental divisions and the nature of the ruling coalition. For example, Barbara Geddes (1995) found that military juntas are more likely to fragment than military dictatorships. Given the greater propensity of these regimes for internal division, we may expect that juntas are more likely to accommodate opposition demands than dictatorships. Similarly, Daniel Geller (1987) concludes that centrist nations dissolve internal unrest more quickly than polyarchies or personalist nations. Unfortunately, the mechanism by which they reduce domestic opposition is unclear. However, the study points to the possibility of similar dynamics, that centrist nations may experience internal divisions and accommodate unrest more quickly than personalist nations. Thus, we should examine how the likelihood that centrist regimes accommodate opposition demands differs from the likelihood that personalist regimes do so.
19. Alawite, Druze and other Muslim sects together total 16 per cent of the Syrian population (Central Intelligence Agency, 1992:330).
20. We are defining escalation by the challenger state as actions directed at the rival state which entail the threat of and/or resort to the use of military force. If we think of escalatory actions on a scale ranging from low to high militarized behavior, then verbal threats and warnings would anchor the low end, initiating the large-scale use of military force would define the upper end, and alerts and shows of military force would define the intermediate positions on the scale.
21. This positive relationship between the challenger's military advantage and the initiation of militarized conflicts could be attenuated due to situations where the challenger enjoyed such a decisive advantage that the much weaker rival made critical concessions to avoid military conflict. The

selection process for enduring rivalries, however, reduces this potential problem because few international disputes which become enduring rivalries are characterized by a very lopsided balance of military forces. In addition, even much weaker states will typically not make major concessions to settle a dispute unless they are at least faced with coercive threats and military actions threatening war by a much stronger state.

22. Relative military capabilities could be measured as the summed average ratio of challenger to rival military expenditures, number of armed forces, and expenditures per soldier. See Huth (1996: appendix C) for a more detailed discussion of this measure.

23. A number of studies have found that relative military capabilities are an important explanatory variable in predicting the initiation and escalation of militarized confrontations. See, for example, Rousseau, Gelpi, Reiter and Huth (1996); Huth (1996); Huth, Gelpi and Bennett (1993); Huth, Bennett and Gelpi (1992); Huth (1988a).

24. Militarized dispute involvement with other states could be measured as what percentage of the months that a case of domestic unrest persisted was the challenger/rival involved in an international dispute with other states in which the challenger/rival threatened or resorted to the use of military force. Several previous studies have found that the involvement of states in multiple disputes at the same time affects patterns of militarized conflict initiation and escalation. See Rousseau, Gelpi, Reiter and Huth (1996); Huth (1996); Huth, Gelpi and Bennett (1993); Huth, Bennett and Gelpi (1992).

25. This variable could be measured by coding the outcome of the most recent round of negotiations between the challenger and rival prior to the case of domestic unrest within the challenger. If the outcome was the failure of the rival to make concessions on the issues in dispute then a value of 1 could be coded and 0 otherwise. See Huth (1996) for more details on the measurement of this variable and empirical findings linking prior stalemates in negotiations in territorial disputes with subsequent military escalation. Also see Leng (1983) for results which relate prior stalemates and unfavorable crisis bargaining outcomes between rivals to higher levels of escalation between the same states in subsequent confrontations.

26. This variable could be coded a value of 1 if the rival within six months prior to the case of domestic unrest within the challenger had undertaken actions to alter the prevailing economic, political, or military status quo over the issue at stake in their dispute, and 0 otherwise.

27. The number of past defeats could be measured as how many times had the challenger suffered a defeat in a war or militarized conflict short of war with the rival. See Huth (1996) for more details on the measurement of this variable and findings which link prior military defeats for challenger states to lower probabilities of military escalation in territorial disputes.

28. See Goertz and Diehl (1992b) for a discussion of coding rules for identifying enduring rivals.

29. A promising dataset for identifying cases of domestic unrest would be the SHERFACS dataset created by Frank Sherman which includes approximately 1000 domestic 'quarrels' between 1945 and 1985. For a general description of the dataset see Sherman (1994).

4 Loss Aversion, Framing, and Bargaining: The Implications of Prospect Theory for International Conflict

Jack S. Levy

Prospect theory was developed in the late 1970s by Kahneman and Tversky (1979) in response to cumulating evidence of systematic behavioral violations of expected-utility theory. It is now a leading alternative to expected utility as a theory of choice under conditions of risk.[1] Prospect theory is best known for its claims that people tend to over-weight losses with respect to comparable gains, that they are generally risk-averse with respect to gains and risk-acceptant with respect to losses, that they respond to probabilities in a non-linear manner, and that how they frame a problem around a reference point has a critical influence on their choices. The theory generates a rich and intriguing set of hypotheses about international relations, but attempts to apply the theory outside the highly controlled environment of the experimental laboratory are plagued by a number of difficult methodological problems (Jervis, 1992; Levy 1992b; Stein, 1992).

In this study I examine some of the primary anomalies in expected-utility theory that emerge from experimental research in social psychology, summarize how prospect theory incorporates these anomalies, and explore some of the implications of prospect theory for international conflict in general and for bargaining and coercion in particular. One important theme is that the bargaining behavior of political leaders is different when the issue is the distribution of losses from that when the issue is the distribution of gains. Another is that crisis bargaining behavior is more destabilizing than rational choice theories predict, because political leaders are less likely to make concessions and more likely to gamble and risk large losses in the hope of eliminating smaller losses altogether.

DESCRIPTIVE ANOMALIES IN EXPECTED-UTILITY THEORY

The expected-utility principle posits that actors aim to maximize their expected utility by weighting the utility of each possible outcome of a given course of action by the probability of its occurrence, summing over all possible outcomes for each strategy, and selecting the strategy with the highest expected utility. Expected-utility theory assumes that an actor's utility for a particular good is a function of net asset levels of that good, so that the marginal utility of changes in assets is a function of existing levels of assets. Most applications of the theory in the social sciences add the auxiliary assumption (Simon, 1984) that individuals have diminishing marginal utility for most goods, which is reflected by a concave utility function. This assumption is descriptively accurate for many types of behavior and enhances the analytical power and elegance of the theory, but diminishing marginal utility is not an essential component of expected-utility theory and violations of the former are not necessarily inconsistent with the latter.

An actor's attitude or orientation towards risk is defined in terms of the shape of an actor's utility function. An actor is risk-averse if his utility function is concave, risk-neutral if his utility function is linear, and risk-acceptant if his utility function is convex. Given a choice between two options, one involving a certain outcome of utility x and the other involving a lottery or gamble with the equivalent expected utility x, a risk-averse actor will prefer the certain outcome, a risk-acceptant actor will prefer the gamble, and a risk-neutral actor will be indifferent between the two.

I now turn to experimental evidence of the various ways in which individual behavior deviates from the predictions of expected-utility theory.[2]

Reference Dependence

One finding is that people are more sensitive to changes in assets than to net asset levels. They think in terms of *gains* and *losses* rather than levels of wealth and welfare. Thus Kahneman and Tversky (1979:273) argue that 'the carriers of value or utility are changes of wealth, rather than final asset positions that include current wealth.' These changes in assets are defined around a reference point (which is usually but not always identified with current assets). This *reference dependence* (Tversky and Kahneman, 1991:1039) runs contrary to the standard expected-utility postulate of an individual utility function that is defined over levels of wealth and draws support from a variety of experimental studies (Tversky and Kahneman, 1986:S258; 1991). There is also evidence that the marginal value of both gains and losses is a decreasing function of their magnitude, which Tversky and Kahneman (1991:1048–1050) refer to as *diminishing sensitivity*. Kahneman and Tversky (1979:277) concede that individual evaluations of changes in wealth or assets are not entirely independent of net asset levels, and that a more accurate representation would specify value as a function of both net asset position and the magnitude and direction of the deviation from a reference point. But they argue that evaluations of value are much more sensitive to the latter than to the former and that for the purposes of constructing a parsimonious theory of choice the impact of net asset levels can be ignored. They find, for example, that when people are faced with the choice between a lottery that involves a 50 per cent chance of nothing and a 50 per cent chance of winning $1000[3] and the certainty of receiving a given amount of money (the *certainty equivalent*), the approximate amount which leaves most people indifferent between the gamble and the certainty equivalent (generally $300–$400) does not vary significantly as a function of the wealth of the subjects (Kahneman and Tversky, 1979:277).

The notion that the primary carriers of value are changes in assets rather than net asset positions is the central analytic assumption of prospect theory. It leads Kahneman and Tversky to replace the utility function defined over asset levels to a *value function* defined over deviations from a reference point. A typical value function is displayed in Figure 4.1. The S-shape of the value function reflects diminishing sensitivity and has important implications for risk orientation, as we shall see.[4]

Loss Aversion

The assumption that people are more sensitive to changes in assets than to net asset levels is also indirectly reflected by the fact that people respond differently to losses than to gains. They overvalue losses relative to 'comparable' gains (*loss aversion*) and they have different *risk orientations* for losses than they do for gains.

Both experimental evidence from the laboratory and empirical evidence from natural settings clearly demonstrate the asymmetry in peoples' evaluations of losses and gains. The basic finding is that losses hurt more than gains gratify. The pleasure people get from unexpectedly finding $10 is less than the pain they suffer from losing $10.

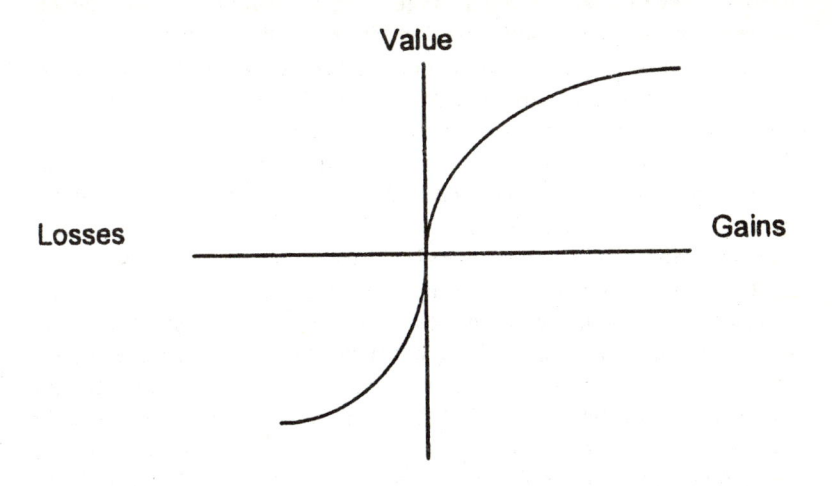

Figure 4.1 A value function

Most people are disinclined to accept symmetric bets involving a fifty-fifty chance of winning or losing a given amount. As Jimmy Conners exclaimed, 'I hate to lose more than I like to win' (Levy, 1992a:175).

Loss aversion is reflected by the greater steepness of the value function on the loss side and is analytically distinct from risk orientation, which refers to the curvature of the value function. One can speak of loss aversion in choices among certain outcomes, as demonstrated by Tversky and Kahneman's (1991) recent reference-dependent model of loss aversion in riskless choice.

Loss aversion leads people to value what they have more than comparable things that they do not have. The pleasure of acquiring something new is less than the pain of losing current possessions of comparable value, and the very process of acquiring an object enhances the value of that object. People who acquire an item, even a fairly trivial item such as a school coffee mug, often refuse to sell it at prices they would not even consider paying for it in the first place. This over-evaluation of current possessions is the *endowment effect* (Thaler, 1980:43–7). Loss aversion and the endowment effect also help to explain why people over-weight out-of-pocket costs (losses) relative to opportunity costs (foregone gains). People tend to get more upset when they buy a stock which then drops in price than when they fail to buy a stock which then goes up.

There is substantial experimental evidence in support of the hypothesized endowment effect. In one experiment Kahneman, Knetsch and

Thaler (1990) found that the average price at which randomly selected students are willing to sell school coffee mugs that they had just been given is twice as high as the average price at which other randomly selected students are willing to buy a mug.[5] These experiments were designed to control for other possible explanations for the observed discrepancy between buying and selling prices, including strategic bargaining, learning through repeated trials or market experience, and transactions costs (Knez and Smith, 1987; Brookshire and Coursey, 1987; Coursey, Hovis and Schulze, 1987; Knetsch and Sinden, 1987).

If tokens are substituted for mugs, however, and subjects are allowed to sell tokens for cash, selling prices and buying prices were nearly identical. This and related experiments suggest that the endowment effect does not apply to normal commercial transactions. Money expended on an item is not treated as a loss, and goods purchased for eventual sale or barter – as opposed to use – generally do not generate an endowment effect (Kahneman, Knetsch and Thaler, 1991:200). This has important implications for 'bargaining chips' in negotiations. The experimental evidence, though tentative, suggests that endowment effects are stronger and more consistent if one is given physical possession of a good, as opposed to a property right to receive the good at some point in the future, or a chance to receive such a good (Kahneman, Knetsch and Thaler, 1990:1342).

These findings are particularly significant given the relatively trivial items used in the experiments and the fact that the endowments are windfalls and therefore somewhat artificial. In natural settings, where individuals often go to considerable efforts to acquire endowments in the first place and where the symbolic value of endowments may be quite high, we would expect the magnitude of the endowment effect to be even greater (Knetsch, 1989:1282).

Risk Orientation

People also treat losses differently than gains in their attitudes toward risk: there is a tendency for people to be risk-averse with respect to gains and risk-acceptant with respect to losses. This means that individual utility functions are concave in the domain of gains and convex in the domain of losses and thus have a *reflection effect* around the reference point (Kahneman and Tversky, 1979:268). This pattern has been found repeatedly for a variety of individuals and situations (Fishburn and Kochenberger, 1979), but it may break down for very small probabilities or for catastrophic losses.

In a typical experiment 80 per cent of respondents prefer a certain outcome of $3000 to an 80 per cent chance of $4000 and 20 per cent chance of nothing. If faced with the same two negative prospects, however, 92 per cent of respondents prefer to gamble on an 80 per cent chance of losing $4000 and 20 per cent chance of losing nothing to a certain loss of $3000. In both cases respondents chose the option with the lower expected value, and the combination of these two patterns is inconsistent with expected utility theory. This experimental design has been repeated over and over with different sets of numbers, and the results are quite robust (Kahneman and Tversky, 1979:268; Tversky and Kahneman, 1986; Quattrone and Tversky, 1988; Slovic and Lichtenstein, 1983).

FRAMING EFFECTS

Because of the asymmetrical treatment of gains and losses and the importance of the reference point in defining these distinct domains, the identification of the reference point or *framing* of a choice problem becomes critical. One striking example of framing effects can be found in the medical example offered by Tversky and Kahneman (1986:S260):

> Imagine that the US is preparing for the outbreak of an unusual Asian disease, which is expected to kill 600 people. Two alternative programs to combat the disease have been proposed. Assume that the exact scientific estimates of the consequences of the programs are as follows:
>
> (*Survival frame*) If Program A is adopted, 200 people will be saved. If Program B is adopted, there is 1/3 probability that 600 people will be saved, and 2/3 probability that no people will be saved.
>
> The identical description of the situation is given to a second group of subjects, but the same information about the alternative treatment programs is framed differently.
>
> (*Mortality frame*) If Program C is adopted 400 people will die. If Program D is adopted there is a 1/3 probability that nobody will die, and 2/3 probability that 600 people will die.
>
> In the survival frame 72 per cent (N = 152) of the subjects preferred Program A, indicating a risk-averse preference for saving 200

with certainty over a gamble with the same expected value. In the mortality frame (N = 155), however, 78 per cent preferred Program D, indicating a risk-acceptant preference for a gamble in the hope of preventing 400 people from certain death. The only difference in the choice problems faced by the two groups is the framing of the outcomes in terms of the number of lives saved or lost.

These results have been duplicated in many other experimental studies (McNeil et al., 1982; Tversky and Kahneman, 1986). They demonstrate that a change in frame can result in a change in preferences in spite of the fact that all of the key parameters of the choice problem remain the same. These *preference reversals* are inconsistent with the invariance axiom of expected-utility theory, which requires that logically identical choice problems should yield identical results (Kahneman and Tversky, 1979; Grether and Plott, 1979; Slovic and Lichtenstein, 1983; Goldstein and Einhorn, 1987; Segal, 1988; Tversky, Slovic and Kahneman, 1990). Although it might be possible for expected-utility theory to incorporate loss aversion, the reflection effect, and changing risk orientations over different domains, framing effects are much more difficult if not impossible to incorporate into expected-utility theory.

Framing effects are not always this strong. Their magnitude is a function of the *transparency* of the choice problem. If the similarities between two choice problems are quite obvious, behavior is more likely to be consistent with expected-utility theory. But in non-transparent situations where the similarities between two different representations of the problem are partially concealed, behavior is likely to deviate significantly from expected-utility theory (Kahneman and Tversky, 1979; Arrow, 1982). The medical example demonstrates that it does not take too much complexity to make a choice problem opaque.

In many simple choice problems the framing of the problem is largely predetermined by the situation (or the experimental design). In a static situation which involves a well-defined and salient status quo, for example, the status quo is likely to serve as the reference point. In other situations, however, the framing of a choice problem is more subjective and sensitive to how the individual responds to a situation and encodes a decision. This is particularly likely when the situation is changing, when there is no salient status quo, or where there is a sequence of successive choices rather than a single choice.

With respect to the latter situation, an important question is whether the reference point is defined in terms of one's asset position at the beginning of the series of choices (the cumulative frame) or with respect to one's current asset position after a series of actions have already been taken. If a gambler who suffers a series of losses adopts the cumulative frame of her asset position at the beginning of the evening, she will be more inclined to be risk-acceptant and attempt to recover her losses, whereas if she frames around current assets after the losses she will tend to be more risk-averse. Someone on a winning streak, however, will be more risk-averse if she frames her choice in terms of her initial assets rather than their total assets at the time of each new bet.

This example illustrates the importance of how individuals *accommodate* to gains or losses. Accommodation to losses induces a tendency towards risk aversion because any improvement in one's new position will be treated as a gain rather than as a recovery of losses; accommodation to gains induces risk seeking because any retreat from one's new position will be framed as a loss rather than a forgone gain. This leads to the questions of whether people accommodate to change, in what direction, how quickly, and under what conditions. The literature provides few answers to this question – other than to say that framing is highly subjective, poorly understood, and basically unexplored. In nearly all laboratory studies the reference point is inherent in the structure of the problem given to the subject rather than a variable which is manipulated in order to examine its effects.

One hypothesis that emerges from the literature, however, derives from the tendency toward an *instant endowment effect* which applies to new acquisitions but not to new losses (Kahneman, Knetsch, and Thaler, 1990:1342). This implies that people accommodate or *renormalize* (Jervis, 1992) to gains more quickly than to losses. One implication is that under conditions of change there is a tendency for actors to shift towards a more risk-acceptant orientation more quickly than towards a more risk-averse orientation. If this is true, we would expect that a gambler on a losing streak will be more willing to take excessive risks than one on a winning streak, even though in strict monetary terms the latter can better afford any further losses.

The hypothesis of an instant endowment effect has important consequences for strategic interaction in dynamic situations. If A has just made a gain at the expense of B, B's attempt to recover his losses (from the old status quo) will be perceived as a potential loss by A (from the new status quo), so that both parties will be in the domain of losses and be more risk seeking.

Response to Probabilities

Whereas the expected-utility principle posits that the utilities of outcomes are weighted by their probabilities in a linear combination, experimental evidence suggests that people systematically deviate from this principle. First of all, a number of studies (for example, Allais, 1953) have shown that individuals over-weight outcomes which are certain relative to outcomes which are merely probable. Because of this *certainty effect* (Kahneman and Tversky, 1979:265) people attach greater value to the complete elimination of risk than to the reduction of risk by a comparable amount. This is graphically illustrated in an experiment involving a hypothetical game of Russian roulette, where people are willing to pay far more to reduce the number of bullets in a revolver from 1 to 0 than from 4 to 3 (Quattrone and Tversky, 1988:730), even though the changes in expected utility are equivalent.

The certainty effect also interacts with the reflection effect in the value function to reinforce tendencies toward risk aversion for gains and risk seeking for losses for choices between a certain outcome and a lottery. The over-weighting of certain gains induces greater caution while the over-weighting of certain losses encourages the gamble. This helps to explain the tendency to sell winners too early (to lock in a certain gain) and hold losers too long (and thus risk a larger loss in the hope of avoiding a certain loss) (Shefrin and Statman, 1985).

People also over-weight small probabilities, though if probabilities are extremely small behavior is unpredictable.[6] Although extremely unlikely events are sometimes treated as if they were impossible, at other times they are over-weighted. This unpredictability of response is reflected by behavior with respect to AIDS or to insurance against rare catastrophes. Thus Kahneman and Tversky (1979:282-3) argue that 'Because people are limited in their ability to comprehend and evaluate extreme probabilities, highly unlikely events are either ignored or over-weighted, and the difference between high probability and certainty is either neglected or exaggerated.'

In contrast to their response to small or extremely small probabilities, people tend to under-weight moderate and high probabilities. This means that except for small probabilities people tend to give more weight to the utility of a possible outcome than to its probability of occurrence rather than giving them equal weight as posited by expected-utility theory.

SUMMARY OF PROSPECT THEORY

Prospect theory integrates these observed behavioral patterns into a theory of risky choice. Kahneman and Tversky (1979) distinguish two phases in the choice process. In the *editing phase* the actor identifies the reference point, the available options, the possible outcomes and the value and probability of each (Tversky and Kahneman, 1981:453; Kahneman and Tversky, 1979:274, 284–5). In the *evaluation phase* he combines the values of possible outcomes with their weighted probabilities to determine the preferred prospect or choice.

Kahneman and Tversky (1979) have developed a formal (but not axiomatically based) model of the evaluation of prospects but not a theory of editing or framing. Because of the subjectivity and unpredictability of framing, particularly in complex situations, they restrict themselves to choice problems 'where it is reasonable to assume either that the original formulation of the prospects leaves no room for further editing or that the edited prospects can be specified without ambiguity' (Kahneman and Tversky, 1979:275). That is, they focus on the evaluation of prospects rather than the editing of choices and treat framing as an exogenous rather than endogenous variable. A knowledge of the actor's reference point is absolutely essential for any empirical application of prospect theory, however, and the absence of a theory of framing is the single most serious limitation of prospect theory and the most important task for future research.[7]

A detailed summary of prospect theory is not necessary here (see Kahneman and Tversky, 1979), but I want to note that attitudes towards risk are determined by the combination of the S-shaped value function and the probability weighting function and not by the value function alone. Although this combination usually generates risk aversion with respect to gains and risk acceptance with respect to losses, the overweighting of small probabilities can trigger a reversal of risk propensities under certain conditions, depending on the precise shapes of the two functions (Kahneman and Tversky, 1979; Levy, 1992a:183–4).[8] Thus the existence of small probabilities is a necessary but not sufficient condition for risk aversion in the domain of losses and risk acceptance in the domain of gains.[9]

IMPLICATIONS FOR NEGOTIATION AND BARGAINING

The most common reference point is the status quo, and most changes in the status quo are advantageous in some respects and disadvantageous in other respects. The endowment effect and the loss aversion properties of the value function imply that the latter are over-weighted relative to the former, so that if the benefits and costs of departures from the status quo are equal in 'objective' terms the losses will dominate in the evaluation of alternatives. The result is a tendency towards status quo choices more frequently than expected-utility theory would predict. This *status quo bias* (Samuelson and Zeckhauser, 1988) is reflected in the tendencies for selling prices to exceed buying prices and for undertrading, as demonstrated in a number of experimental and field studies of consumer and investment behavior (Knetsch and Sinden, 1984; Hartman, Doane and Woo, 1991).

The status quo bias conforms to our intuitive sense of international politics: states generally seem to make greater efforts to preserve the status quo against a threatened loss than to improve their position by a comparable amount. They are sometimes willing to fight to defend the same territory that they would not have been willing to fight to acquire, or to accept greater costs in order to maintain an international regime than to create it in the first place (Keohane, 1984). Admittedly, it may not be easy to demonstrate this empirically or to measure the magnitude of the hypothesized effects, and there are some notable exceptions to the hypothesized pattern. There are also reputational considerations and other factors which might provide states with an incentive to remain at the status quo (Jervis, 1989:29–35; Levy, 1992b:284–5).

In fact, loss aversion may interact with some of these other factors in important ways. States may be more concerned to prevent a decline in their reputation or credibility than to increase it by a comparable amount, more worried by the costs of falling dominoes than optimistic about the gains from others bandwagoning in their favor (Jervis, 1991), so that loss aversion helps to explain asymmetries in reputational interests. There may also be domestic political reasons why decision-making elites go to considerable efforts to avoid losses. The apparent tendency for domestic publics to punish their political leaders more for strategic or economic losses than to reward them for comparable gains may itself be a function of loss aversion operating at the level of public opinion. Loss avoidance by political leaders may be a rational response to these domestic constraints.

The status quo bias is closely related to a *concession aversion* (Kahneman, Knetsch, and Thaler, 1990:1345) in a bargaining situation. Bargaining involves making concessions on some issues in return for compensation on others. Loss aversion and the endowment effect imply that actors have a tendency to treat the concessions they give up as losses and the compensation they receive from the other actor as gains and to overvalue what they give relative to what they get. As a result, there is a shrinkage in the size of the bargaining space of mutually beneficial exchanges, a greater tendency to risk the consequences of a non-agreement or deadlock in an attempt to minimize one's concessions, and a lower probability of a negotiated agreement than utility-based bargaining theory might predict.

This concession aversion is even more pronounced if an actor has additional reasons for perceiving a negotiated agreement as a loss, such as the perception that the current status quo is unacceptable. Then a negotiated settlement that is close to the status quo and that each side knew was acceptable to the other (and therefore an option with a certain outcome) would be seen as a certain loss and thus be over-weighted, which would further increase the incentive to undertake excessive risks in order to avoid that loss. More generally, whenever we find perceptions of certain losses, whether defined in terms of the status quo or alternative aspiration point, prospect theory hypotheses predict particularly risky behaviour in order to avoid those losses.

There is a potentially important qualification to this asymmetry in bargaining over gains and losses. As noted earlier, loss aversion and the endowment effect are likely to be minimal in routine economic transactions or where goods are acquired for later sale rather than use (Kahneman and Tversky, 1984:348–49; Kahneman, Knetsch, and Thaler, 1991:200). This implies that if concessions involve a 'bargaining chip' and especially if the 'chip' was acquired or created with that purpose in mind, the asymmetry of value attached to concessions given and compensation received is likely to be much less, so that the likelihood of a successful compromise would be larger.

On the other hand, the longer one possesses a good and the greater the effort and resources expended to acquire it, the greater its perceived value, as cognitive dissonance theory would suggest (Jervis, 1989:169). This point may be particularly important with respect to the territorial acquisitions which result from wars. The more costly the war in human and economic terms, the greater the perceived value of the new possessions.

The underlying hypothesis running throughout this analysis is that people behave differently when the issue is the distribution of losses rather than the distribution of gains, so that how the bargainers frame the problem in terms of gains and losses is itself a critical variable. Consider a bargaining situation in which each side makes an initial offer and then is given the choice between accepting a compromise agreement halfway between the two offers or accepting an arbitrated solution. The contrast here is between the certainty of the negotiated compromise agreement and the uncertainty of the arbitrated agreement. Our theoretical discussion implies that the likelihood of the compromise agreement being accepted depends in part on whether the two negotiators perceive it as a gain from their adversary's initial offer or a loss from their own initial offer. To the extent that they frame the compromise as a retreat from their initial offer and thus define it as a loss, they will be more willing to reject the certain loss that would result from the negotiated agreement and accept the riskier outcome of arbitration.[10]

Although less experimental work has been done on the impact of framing on bargaining behavior than on individual choice, what evidence exists provides some support for this hypothesis (Tversky and Kahneman, 1986:S262; Bazerman, 1983). Neale and Bazerman (1985) conduct an experiment in which subjects are assigned the role of management negotiators. One group of subjects is given a negative frame ('Any concessions beyond those granted will represent serious financial losses to the company') and another is given a positive frame ('Any union concessions from their current position will result in gains for the company'), but the choice problems facing each group is mathematically equivalent. Neale and Bazerman find as predicted that subjects in the negative frame (as compared to those in the positive frame) are less likely to settle for the certainty of the negotiated agreement, more likely to accept the riskier gamble of arbitration, and more likely to end up with less successful outcomes.[11] Morgan and Wilson (1989) find a similar pattern in their experimental test of a spatial model of crisis bargaining in international relations.[12]

There has been a great deal of theoretical and empirical research on the conditions under which cooperation is most likely in international politics (Jervis, 1978; Keohane, 1984; Grieco, 1990). Most of the empirical work has focused on issues related to international political economy, where the assumption that states act to maximize absolute gains is a plausible one and where the problem can often be framed in terms of the distribution of gains from greater cooperation. As Stein and Pauly (1993) suggest, however, cooperation should be more difficult when the issue involves the distribution of losses rather than gains.

The empirical case studies in Stein and Pauly (1993) generally support this hypothesis. Richardson (1992), for example, argues that in the Suez crisis British leaders defined their reference point as the status quo ante, treated Egypt's nationalization of the canal as a certain loss, and consequently were willing to undertake military action that risked larger losses in order to restore the status quo ante and avoid the certain loss.[13]

Stein (1992:223) briefly examines the Israeli decision to attend the regional peace conference proposed by the United States and the Soviet

Union in October 1991. Israeli leaders believed that their failure to agree to attend the conference would result in the loss of badly needed loan guarantees and a severe strain in their overall relationship with the United States. A 'successful' conference might also involve losses, including some revision of the territorial status quo, but Stein argues that the Israelis chose to gamble on the uncertain outcomes of the conference rather than to suffer the certain loss of rejecting the US initiative.[14]

If all states defined their reference point in terms of the status quo and if the status quo was basically acceptable and unchanging, then loss aversion, the status quo bias and concession aversion should reinforce stability in international politics. If all states were excessively cautious in attempting to improve their positions, there should be fewer challenges to the status quo than we might expect on the basis of an expected-value maximization hypothesis.

The problem is that political leaders do not always perceive the status quo to be satisfactory. In those situations the framing of a choice problem around an expectation or aspiration level or other more positive reference point leaves the status quo as a certain loss that actors try to avoid through excessively risky gambles. The result is that challenges to the status quo are more common than a straightforward cost–benefit calculus might predict.

The fact that people sometimes frame around an expectation level, aspiration level, or some other point rather than the status quo suggests that the concept of the status quo bias is misspecified. The bias is really a *reference point bias*, a greater tendency to move toward the reference point than predicted by expected-utility theory. Whereas the hypothesized status quo bias is generally stabilizing in the sense that it reinforces the status quo, the reference point bias may be destabilizing whenever the reference point deviates from the status quo. This is particularly likely to occur if one or more actors perceives that its current position is deteriorating.

Perceptions of Decline[15]

If a state perceives itself to be in a deteriorating situation it may see the status quo as a certain loss, over-weight that loss, and therefore be willing to take excessively risky actions in order to maintain that status quo against further deterioration or perhaps to recover recent losses. This problem gets little attention in the experimental literature, which deals almost exclusively with static choice problems, but it is a common and important phenomenon in international relations.

In a crisis situation loss aversion may lead states to take preemptive action and accept the risks inherent in initiating war if they are certain that the adversary is about to initiate a first strike, even though a standard cost–benefit calculus might call for restraint (Jervis, 1989:171). Or states may prefer to take a risky action than to suffer the loss of credibility that they expect to follow a policy of inaction. Loss aversion and risk-seeking to recover sunk costs helps to explain why states continue to follow failing policies far longer than a standard cost-benefit calculus might predict (Jervis, 1992), as illustrated by the American intervention in Vietnam and the Soviet intervention in Afghanistan. States may also take disproportionately risky action short of war. Ross (1984:247) concludes that although Soviet leaders tended to be risk averse, they were willing to engage in the 'use of decisive and perhaps risky action far more readily for *defending* as opposed to *extending* Soviet gains.'

Gains and losses need not be defined exclusively or even primarily in terms of a state's international security and influence, for state officials are also concerned about their domestic political positions. They may take forceful action against external enemies in order to secure a diplomatic or military victory that might pacify their domestic critics or otherwise distract attention from domestic problems. The temptation towards such diversionary action may be enhanced by risk-acceptant attitudes in the domain of losses created by a deteriorating domestic situation (Levy, 1989a:274). The combination of perceived external decline and internal insecurity may be particularly conducive to risk-seeking, as McDermott (1992) shows in her case study of the US decision to attempt a hostage rescue mission in Iran in 1979.

The prospect of even small losses may be sufficient to induce risk-seeking behavior, particularly if the losses are perceived to be certain. A setback might be minor compared to a state's overall position, but because it is evaluated in terms of deviations from a reference point rather than one's net asset position its effects can be quite substantial. Moreover, because of the anticipation that any such setback will involve significant reputational costs, falling dominoes, and a disproportionate domestic political reaction, even small losses appear to have significant consequences. Consequently, political leaders may be inclined to engage in relatively risky behavior in order to avoid or recoup even small losses or retreats from the status quo (Jervis, 1989:170).

The destabilizing tendencies of loss aversion might be particularly great if two adversaries both perceived themselves to be in a deteriorating situation. This could occur because the opposing political leaders perceived the situation differently; because they focused on different dimensions of power, geographical systems, or time frames; or because one set of political leaders focused on their state's relative external decline while the other focused on its deteriorating domestic situation. If mutual perceptions of losses occurred, loss aversion might drive both towards riskier strategies than warranted by straightforward cost–benefit calculations. I have suggested that this may have been the situation for France and Germany in 1870 and perhaps also for the United States and Japan in 1941 (Levy, 1987:93). It might also have been true for the United States and Iraq in 1990–91: the US feared Iraq's acquisition of nuclear and biological weapons, and Iraq may have feared a deterioration of its position in the context of Soviet decline, unconstrained American hegemony and its hostility toward Iraq, and the possibility of a diplomatic realignment in the Middle East.

Actors' simultaneous representations of their respective choice problems as ones involving the domain of losses and the mutual risk-seeking tendencies associated with it can also be induced by the effects of framing in a changing situation. States might identify different reference points to frame their respective decisions and this might lead both to perceive that they were defending the status quo. Consider a situation in which state A has just made a tangible gain at state B's expense, say through the seizure of territory. The endowment effect suggests that A will accommodate to its gains much more quickly than B will accommodate to its losses. Consequently, B will attempt to recover its losses and restore the old status quo and A will attempt to maintain the new status quo against B's encroachments. Each will accept larger than normal risks in order to maintain its version of the status quo.

This behavior leads Jervis (1989:171) to suggest that a *fait accompli* strategy is more dangerous than George and Smoke (1974:536–40) imply because the target will make a greater effort to recover its loss than one might expect on the basis of a straightforward calculation of costs and benefits. Possible illustrations of this might include Britain's resolve to recover the Falklands after their seizure by Argentina in 1982 and the American/Allied determination to roll back Iraq's invasion of Kuwait in 1990–91. It is interesting in this regard to consider whether Khrushchev and the rest of the Soviet leadership viewed their withdrawal of missiles from Cuba as a return to the status quo or a retreat from it. The former would have been easier in psychological terms. Of course, if the initiator conceives of its *fait accompli* as an attempt to recover old possessions rather than make new acquisitions, its resistance will be all the greater, as evidenced by Argentina's determination to recover the Malvinas in 1982.

The changes which induce these framing effects may be gradual rather than sudden. Consider a situation in which A is slowly gaining in power at the expense of B and the two states try to negotiate a settlement over a conflict between them. It is possible that A may frame his reference point at some future asset level based on the assumption of the continued improvement in his position, treat any point short of that aspiration level as a loss, and be willing to undertake inordinately risky actions to reach his target position. Meanwhile, B is likely to use the current status quo as the reference point and to be risk seeking in order to maintain it.

Deterrence and Compellence

The framing of a decision problem can also affect behavior with respect to deterrence and other forms of bargaining. Loss aversion helps to explain why influence attempts based on coercion are more likely to be successful if the target sees itself in the domain of gains and is contemplating an effort to improve its position, than if it sees itself in the domain of losses and is considering how to prevent its position from deteriorating further (Lebow and Stein, 1987). That is, it is easier to deny the adversary a gain rather than to force the adversary to suffer a loss. It is also easier to deter an adversary from initiating an action she has not yet taken (and thus deny her a gain) than to compel her to do something she does not want to do, to stop doing something she is already doing, or to undo something she has already done (each of which is likely to be framed as a loss) (Schelling, 1966:69-91; Jervis, 1989:29n).

The issue of deterrence leads to another interesting question relating to framing. When states issue deterrent threats, it is often in response to prior threats by a potential initiator. The initial threat of military action in itself changes the status quo in terms of utilities because of the reputational and perhaps domestic political costs involved. What happens if the state making the threat is then confronted by a counter-threat from the target or the target's protector? Does the first state frame a possible withdrawal of the threat (or failure to implement it) as a retreat *to* the old status quo or a retreat *from* the new status quo? (Levy, 1989b:126–7) The second frame is more likely to induce risk-seeking behavior and the escalation of the conflict along the lines that Brecher suggests in his introductory essay.

CONCLUSION

Prospect theory is a significant theoretical innovation that was developed to account for behavior that repeatedly and systematically deviates from expected-utility theory. It is based on a different set of assumptions and generates a different set of hypotheses about conflict, crisis, and war than do rational choice theories. Prospect theory provides different answers to some of the same questions and in addition suggests a new set of questions to investigate, such as the impact of framing on state foreign policy choices.

Although prospect theory advances plausible interpretations of a number of significant patterns of behavior in international relations, a great deal of theoretical and empirical research needs to be done before we can be confident that prospect theory constitutes a generalizable and empirically valid theory of behavior. On the theoretical level a critical task is to specify the individual, institutional, and environmental factors which influence how individuals identify the reference point around which they frame their choice problems. As emphasized above, prospect theory offers no theory of framing. On the empirical level the primary task is to develop research designs that facilitate the determination of how an actor frames a choice problem. Unless actors' reference points can be empirically identified independently of the choices which are hypothesized to follow from framing, loss aversion, and risk orientation, prospect theory can provide little explanatory power.

It is important to emphasize that prospect theory is a theory of *individual decision* and that consequently it is incomplete as a theory of international politics. What we ultimately need are theories that explain how individual decisions driven by framing, loss aversion, and probability weighting get aggregated into collective decisions for the state through the foreign policy process, and how the decisions of strategically interdependent states interact within the larger international system. That is, the insights of prospect theory need to be subsumed within a larger theory of foreign policy and also within a larger theory of strategic interaction and international politics.

NOTES

1. The probabilities of all possible outcomes are known under conditions of risk, not completely known under conditions of uncertainty, and known to be either zero or one under conditions of certainty.
2. The following discussion builds on my more extensive summary of prospect theory (Levy, 1992a). See also Tversky and Kahneman (1986) and Kahneman and Tversky (1979).
3. I will subsequently represent gambles of this sort as (0, .50; 1000, .50), or, more generally, (x, p; y, 1-p).
4. The assumption that the impact of deviations from a reference point is relatively insensitive to the level of wealth or assets is probably not valid for 'ruinous' losses or for other threshold effects that reflect special circumstances (Kahneman and Tversky, 1979:278–9).
5. The sellers have the option of keeping the mug and the buyers have the option of keeping an equivalent amount of money. This two-to-one ratio of selling prices to buying prices is typical, though sometimes it is as high as three or four to one (Knetsch and Sinden, 1984; Knetsch, 1989; Kahneman, Knetsch, and Thaler, 1990:1336; Hartman, Doane and Woo, 1991:142).
6. Although there is no conclusive evidence as to the specific point at which over-weighting shifts to under-weighting or whether this point varies significantly across individuals or conditions, preliminary evidence suggests that it falls in the .10 to .15 range (Hershey and Schoemaker, 1980).
7. Potentially important sources of framing in international relations include emotional states (Farnham, 1992) and historical analogies (McDermott, 1992; Levy, 1994; Taliaferro, 1994).
8. This possibility is frequently ignored in recent discussions of prospect theory in political science. This is particularly serious in international relations, where choices involving possible outcomes with small probabilities but large consequences arise fairly often.
9. Note that these are precisely the conditions under which people engage in gambling and buy insurance. Prospect theory provides a straightforward explanation of both of these phenomena, whereas expected-utility theory cannot easily explain both gambling and the purchase of insurance by the same person.
10. Important here is the assumption that the expected value of the arbitrated outcome is lower than that of the negotiated outcome, due to such arbitration costs as time delays, arbitration fees, loss of control over the outcome, etc. (Crawford, 1979; Neale and Bazerman, 1985:37). One parallel to arbitration in international crisis bargaining is war, which is more costly than a negotiated agreement that produces the same political settlement.
11. Neale and Bazerman (1985) also show that the likelihood of a subject selecting the riskier arbitrated settlement depends also on her degree of confidence in being able to predict the outcome of arbitration. This parallels the tendency among political leaders to overestimate the probability that their own coercive threats will induce compliance by the adversary or that they can defeat the adversary in war if the crisis escalates.
12. Subjects sought agreements when the payoffs were positive but were more

likely to risk war when the payoffs were negative, although in each case the preferred outcome had a lower expected value than the alternative. For an interesting experimental study of Israeli attitudes about giving up the Golan Heights (a loss), as opposed to returning them to their Syrian owners (a forgone gain), see Mintz and Geva (1994).
13. Richardson (1992) concedes that the British greatly underestimated the probability that the US would oppose the operation and thus 'dismissed the risks of using force.' This appears to fit an expected-utility hypothesis based on the minimization of losses as well as a loss aversion hypothesis.
14. Note that Stein's argument, along with some others in the Stein and Pauly collection, differs in an important respect from the Neale and Bazerman (1985) and Morgan and Wilson (1989) studies. In the Stein/Pauly studies it is the absence of agreement that is defined as the certain outcome. In the Neale and Bazerman (1985) studies it is the agreement the bargainers know they can reach with each other that provides the certain outcome, so that the combination of loss aversion and the over-weighting of certain outcomes leads actors to try to avoid the certain loss inherent in agreement by opting for the risky alternative instead.
15. This section builds on Levy (1992b).

Part Two
Crisis

5 Crisis Escalation: A New Model and Findings
Michael Brecher

Escalation has several meanings in the context of crisis, conflict and war. For some it is a *pre-war* process that leads to war. For others it is an *intra-war* process that enlarges the scope, increases the intensity, or crosses a limit, of an ongoing war. And for a few the concept has even broader application, extending across the spectrum from *non-violent* crisis, through *conventional war*, to total *nuclear war*. In short, escalation refers to three distinct processes:

(a) change from *embryonic* to *full-scale* crisis; in terms of stress, from low to peak stress;
(b) change from *non-violent* to *violent* crisis; and
(c) change from *no/low violence* to *severe violence*.

These processes unfold at both levels of analysis, as the *escalation phase* of an international crisis, and the *crisis period* of a foreign policy crisis. Each connotes qualitative change in an interstate crisis. Each taps a distinct dimension of escalation.

This inquiry is guided by a set of research questions at both levels of analysis:

1. When can a low-stress onset phase be expected to escalate to a full-scale international crisis?
2. Under what conditions is international crisis escalation most likely to be violent?
3. What conditions are most likely to lead to severe violence during an international crisis?
4. What are the conditions in which a state is most likely to be prone to a full-scale crisis?
5. When will a state be most vulnerable to violent crisis escalation?
6. How do states cope with the high stress of the escalation phase/crisis period, whether it is characterized by no, low, or severe violence?

To answer these questions, a model of crisis escalation will be specified; hypotheses that derive from the model will be framed; these will be tested with multiple strands of evidence from crises during the period from the end of 1918 to the end of 1988; and the findings on coping with escalation by ten states in crises will be presented.

I. MODEL OF CRISIS ESCALATION

A model to explain crisis escalation is inherently complex, for the phenomenon is multi-faceted; that is, the conditions that make change from onset (pre-crisis) to escalation (crisis period) most likely are not necessarily the same as those that best account for change from no violence to violence and change from low violence to war; or, at the state level, the use of violence to initiate escalation, and vulnerability to violent escalation. Thus all variables that help to explain each of these aspects of escalation must be included in the model.

The fundamental postulate of the escalation model is that the dependent variables, escalation, violence, and vulnerability to violence, require the prior presence of three perceptual attributes: more acute value threat, awareness of time pressure and heightened war likelihood; and, at the system level, more intense disruptive interaction between the crisis adversaries than in the onset phase. These are, in short, the defining conditions.

The escalation model is parsimonious in its initial formulation: two explanatory variables – perceptually-generated stress and more intense disruption – are causally linked to the changes that constitute escalation. The model must be enlarged, however. For, while it is logically and empirically correct that the specified conditions lead to escalation, there remains a crucial 'black hole' in the explanation of escalation: what generates these conditions? Or, in operational terms, what makes it most likely that perceived acute threat, time pressure, and heightened war likelihood, and more intense disruption, will emerge and escalate an incipient pre-crisis to a full-scale crisis, often with violence and even war? In formal terms: the composite perceptual attribute and disruptive interaction serve as the model's *intervening* variables, and escalation is the dependent variable. But what are the prior *independent* variables?

This question leads to a second postulate of the escalation model, namely, that the process of escalation is most likely to occur when a particular set of *system, interactor, actor* and *situational* attributes is present. The first cluster comprises relatively static contextual conditions – structure/polarity and system level. Interactor variables are conflict setting, capability, regime pair, and geographic distance. The actor group

Crisis Escalation: A New Model and Findings

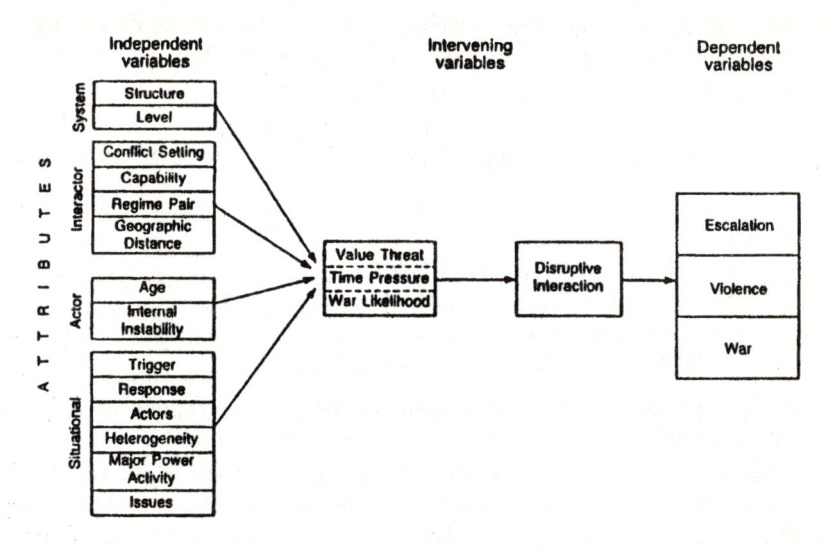

Figure 5.1 Crisis escalation model

consists of age and domestic instability. And there are many situational attributes: triggering act/event/change, response, major power activity, number of actors, extent of heterogeneity, and range of issues.

The links among the explanatory, intervening and dependent variables in the escalation model are presented in Figure 5.1.

The operational categories are as follows:

system
    structure – multipolarity, bipolarity, polycentrism;
    level – dominant system, subsystem;

interactor
    conflict setting – non-protracted conflict (non-PC), PC, long-war PC;
    capability – positive, negative;
    regime pair – democracy, civil authoritarian, military;
    geographic distance – contiguous, proximate, remote;

actor
    age – new, modern, old;
    internal instability – low, medium, high;

situational
    trigger – non-violent, violent, environmental change;

response – non-violent, violent;
number of actors – one, two, three or more;
heterogeneity – none, one, two, three, four;
major power activity – no/low, high;
issues – one, two non-military, military, two including military, three;

intervening
value threat – low, medium, high;
time pressure – moderate, intense;
war likelihood – lower, higher;
disruptive interaction – moderate, intense.

I begin with system *structure*. Among the three configurations of world politics from the end of World War I to the end of 1988, polycentrism – a hybrid of two power centres and many autonomous decision-making actors – is the most likely to escalate an incipient crisis and to generate violence, for several reasons. First, polycentrism imposes fewer constraints on state behavior, including resort to violence. Moreover, all crisis actors in this structure confront more uncertainty about hostile coalitions, given the large number of unaligned states in the global system. And third, the lack of a universally recognized authority in the system means a greater likelihood that, once a crisis is in motion, adversaries will escalate its intensity and use violence to ensure their share of scarce resources.

Since polycentrism is most permissive of violent catalysts to escalation, it is most likely to intensify perceptions of value threat, time pressure, and war likelihood, as well as intensifying disruptive interaction between the adversaries. Bipolarity, in contrast, tends to induce non-violent escalation: because its major powers are acutely conscious of their role as security managers, the likelihood of escalation or of violent change is therefore reduced. These arguments merit elaboration.

In a bipolar structure the two major powers possess the interest, as well as the power, to extend their reach to the peripheries of their respective bloc, controlling most of the disruptive interaction between its members and those of the competing bloc. In other system structures, especially multipolarity, the flexible alliance pattern among the major powers reduces the scope and effectiveness of their control over the behavior of lesser powers. For this reason, too, violence is least likely in bipolarity.

System structures also vary in the relative power of potential adversaries. There is more uncertainty and, therefore, a tendency to underestimate one's relative power in multipolarity and polycentrism, because of flexible alignments. The opposite is true of bipolarity, due to a rigid alliance pattern. This means, all other things being equal, a greater likelihood of uncontrollable arms races – and greater proneness to crisis escalation and violence – in polycentrism and multipolarity; for, while arms races also occur in bipolarity – they may even be more intense and prolonged – they will be fewer in number and more easily limited in scope and damage, since fewer actors are effectively involved in the arms control negotiating process.

System *level*, too, contributes to the escalation process. For the period under inquiry the dominant system comprised: from the end of 1918 to the end of August 1939, the seven great powers of the inter-World War period, France, Germany, Italy, Japan, the UK, the US, and the USSR; and, for 1945–88, the two superpowers, the United States and the Soviet Union, along with their blocs of allies and clients, organized in NATO and the Warsaw Pact, respectively.

'A subsystem, or subordinate system, shares the same attributes as the dominant system; that is, it comprises a set of actors who are situated in a configuration of power *(structure)*, are involved in regular patterns of interaction *(process)*, are separated from other units by *boundaries* set by a given *issue*, and are constrained in their behavior from within *(context)* and from outside the system *(environment)*' (Brecher and Ben Yehuda, 1985:17). Its members are weaker than their capability counterparts in the dominant system; that is, major powers in both, and minor powers in both. Moreover, events in the dominant system have a potential for greater impact on the subsystem than the reverse; that is, the former has the power to penetrate the latter more frequently, intensely, and effectively.

The link of system level to crisis derives from the major powers' interest in system stability. Thus, they tend to act so as to reduce the incidence of crises, especially in the dominant system. One reason is their shared function as 'security managers' of world politics. Another is that, especially in the nuclear era, they are the repositories of 'state of the art' technology, and are therefore conscious of the damage that crises can cause for participants and systems alike. At the subsystem level, by contrast, the major powers of the dominant system prefer to remain aloof, lest crises on the periphery feed back and undermine their relations, destabilizing the dominant system itself. They tend, therefore, to be permissive about interstate politics in subsystems, providing the setting for more, and more disruptive, crises on the peripheries of the global system. At the same time, their power to intervene is omnipresent. Thus the outcome of subsystem crises and, often, the survival of subsystem actors depend ultimately upon their goodwill.

Dominant system crises are expected to be less intense and less violent than those in subsystems. One reason, as noted, is the major powers' primary interest in system stability. The other is their more acute awareness of the cost of violence: it can undermine their individual status in the power hierarchy, as well as the structure of the system. Thus violence in crises is to be avoided or controlled through major power crisis management. And the powers tend to limit their resort to violence to those crises which threaten their most fundamental values – existence, influence or core material interests.

In subsystem crises, the use of violence is more likely for these and several other reasons. One is that the major dominant system powers are reluctant to assume additional responsibilities as crisis managers and tend to acquiesce in the regional hegemony of major subsystem powers, provided that this contributes to global stability and does not undermine their primacy in world politics. The risk of spillover to the dominant system will vary greatly, from a highly penetrated Middle East subsystem since 1948, with valuable resources and a geostrategic location perceived to be vital by the major powers, to most subsystems in Africa and Latin America, where neither of these conditions exist. (The Cuban Missile Crisis was an aberration in this respect.) All this strengthens the disposition of major subsystem powers to escalate violence in the crisis period, in order to protect threatened values or to advance interests. They can do so because of their greater freedom of action in their own regional domain.

In subsystem crises, violence, including war, is a more acceptable technique of crisis management and a more widely used method of behavior to protect basic values. The relative absence of external constraint, pervasiveness in past experience, and the expectation that violence will be used in crises, if necessary, make it much more likely that subsystem crises will exhibit more intense violence as a crisis evolves. Finally, adversaries in subsystem crises are also more likely to be geographically close to each other. This is so because their ability to project power abroad is less than that of their dominant system counterparts. One effect of physical proximity is to facilitate the resort to violence in crisis management.

Interstate crises that occur during a *protracted conflict* (PC) are more prone than others to escalation, including violence and war. For one thing, an issue in a PC crisis may be limited but it is linked to values in dispute over a prolonged period. Threatened values in non-PC crises, by contrast, are free from the psychological legacy of an ongoing conflict. Thus PC crises generate more basic value threats. And these are more likely than low values under threat to induce violence by one or more crisis adversaries. Such a conflict, over time, also generates more issues in dispute, for mistrust spills over to all domains of interaction. The result is that virtually any issue over which there is less than total understanding becomes a source of friction, hostility and mutual threat.

Protracted conflict also provides more inducement to violent escalation because of the cumulative effects of such a conflict. Put simply, prolonged, acute and widespread hostility between the same adversaries creates an anticipation of violent behavior in the future. Moreover, frequent resort to violence accentuates the image of violence as a protracted conflict norm. And further, the importance of values threatened in a protracted conflict creates a disposition for all contending actors to employ violence, especially because preemptive violence from a long-term adversary is expected. All this puts a premium on violent escalation in a PC crisis and violence in crisis management by the target state.

In crises outside a protracted conflict, adversaries may or may not employ violence: there is no more reason to anticipate a violent escalation than a non-violent one. The type of trigger will depend upon the constellation of a specific crisis, such as the power balance, issues in dispute, geographic distance, regime type, etc. Moreover, even when violence is used, there is no *a priori* disposition to resort to full-scale war. In sum, past experience and anticipated future behavior strengthen the likelihood of extreme violence in a crisis during a protracted conflict; they do not in non-PC crises.

A protracted conflict also accentuates the quest for a favorable balance of power. Violence must always be anticipated by a rival state, and weaker military capability will stimulate an effort to correct the imbalance. The result is usually an arms race that enhances value threat perception and disruptive interaction. The spiral, in turn, increases the likelihood of escalation, often with violence.

Capability has varying consequences for the use of violence in crises. If power discrepancy is high, a stronger adversary need not trigger a crisis by violence. This is so because the stronger state expects victory without violence, while deterring the weaker adversary from employing violence, unless a fundamental value, notably existence, is at stake. By contrast, a condition of no or low power discrepancy reduces the credibility of a threat to use force. Further, in a situation of low credibility a state will be more inclined to employ violence in order to demonstrate the credibility of its resolve. In sum, no/low power discrepancy increases the likelihood of violent eruption.

In the escalation phase, when adversaries are equal in power and the military balance is so perceived, resort to war is unlikely, because of an uncertain outcome and high cost. But when a large power gap is perceived, the stronger actor will be more inclined to use its superior capability in the expectation that violence/war will result in goal achievement. Conversely, negative power discrepancy, that is, weakness, will likely lead to non-violent escalation if, in fact, the weaker party escalates at all. The same logic applies to the most likely response to crisis escalation. Positive power discrepancy (relative strength) will induce a violent response, while negative power discrepancy will generate a non-violent response.

Regime pairs are expected to vary in their use of violence during interstate crises. The leaders of military regimes are the most likely to rely on violence, whatever the nature of the initial catalyst. Violence is normal behavior for the military in power, for the military generally achieve and sustain power through violence and tend to use this technique in all situations of stress, internal and external. Violence is also legitimate and effective. As a threat becomes more acute, in the crisis period, with the addition of perceived time pressure for decision and increasing probability of military hostilities, soldiers in power are likely to employ violence or more severe violence, even if alternative techniques of crisis management are available.[1]

Disputes between democratic regimes are unlikely to lead to violence in crisis management: their ideological dispositions, past experience and societal constraints make violence, especially war, an option of last resort, even in a phase of rising stress. Along a scale of disposition to violence, a military regime pair will be closely followed by a mixed authoritarian regime pair and civil authoritarian crisis adversaries in the likelihood of resort to violence/war to manage a crisis at its peak (Schweller, 1992).

Geographic distance between adversaries is another source of crisis escalation. At the extreme, contiguity will increase A's perceptions of a more acute threat, time pressure, and the heightened likelihood of military hostilities with B – and vice versa. Proximity, in turn, makes more likely the use of violence by one or more adversaries. First, it is readily available. Secondly, distrust, created or intensified by a crisis, makes both parties more willing to test the other's resolve. Thirdly, the lack of effective system constraints on interstate violence facilitates the choice of violence to protect or enhance values that are threatened in a crisis. Finally, mutual fear of possible invasion puts a premium on violence lest the adversary gain an advantage through violent preemption.

Age is one of the actor attributes that is salient to the use of violence in crises. Generally, states that attain independence through violence, that is, new states, are likely to persist in violent behavior thereafter. The process merits attention because it applies to so many members of the twentieth-century global system. Violent struggle for independence has been a widespread pattern in the Third World since the end of World War II, though some states were recipients of independence through a relatively peaceful transfer of power (for example, India, Pakistan, Burma and Ceylon in 1947–48, French colonies in North and Equatorial Africa from 1956 onwards, with the notable exception of Algeria). When used for the supreme nationalist goal, violence often acquires an aura of legitimacy. This spills over to a disposition to employ violence after independence. In short, all other things being equal, older states are less likely to rely on violence.

Escalation to war is more likely when crisis actors are confronted with *internal instability*. The more intense the internal turmoil, the greater the disposition to war. Reciprocity by the adversary provides another incentive to violence. And when both actors are afflicted with domestic turmoil, war is even more likely. Either may set the escalation process in motion. And the externalization of internal turmoil may not be successful. But it is an attractive way of coping with domestic opposition to leaders, their policy, or both. For the same reason, instability will predispose target states to employ violence in responding to crisis escalation.

Among the attributes of a crisis that affect escalation the first in time is *breakpoint/trigger*. A violent trigger is more likely than non-violence to generate perceptions of threatened values, time pressure, and heightened war likelihood. The more intense the violence the more acute will be those perceptions. Moreover, when a catalyst is violent the target is likely to respond in kind. The initiator is likely to reciprocate, in accordance with the 'conflict-begets-conflict' syndrome. The ensuing spiral of disruptive interaction is much more likely than non-violent triggers to escalate to the most intense form of violence, namely, war. Conversely, if escalation begins with a non-violent act, the target is more likely to eschew violence, in accord with a tit-for-tat strategy.

The *response* of a target state will also impinge upon the escalation process. If its response to a non-violent trigger is moderate violence, the crisis initiator will perceive a higher-than-normal likelihood of war and, therefore, will be likely to counter-respond with equal or more intense violence. If a target's response is war, the initiator will perceive acute hostility and react accordingly. If a target's response is more violent than the trigger, this may create a perception of military weakness on the part of the initial escalating actor. And that perception, in turn, will affect its subsequent behavior. If it perceives the target to be stronger, the actor that set escalation in motion will be less inclined to counter-respond with further violence, lest the upward spiral continue unabated and lead to defeat, with an accompanying high cost in terms of unattained crisis goals. In short, all other things being equal, the type of response by a crisis target will likely shape the course of escalation and, if violence is used, its intensity.

The introduction of violence into a crisis at any time has other consequences. Violence threatens more interests of more states, directly or indirectly, than does non-violence. It raises the tension level. States that are geographically close to the adversaries and/or have alliance commitments are much more likely to enter a crisis when violence is present because of the assumption that this poses a more serious danger to their interests and cannot be ignored.

The *number of actors* in an interstate crisis, too, affects the escalation process. First, in the absence of countervailing influences, more actors will lead to more, more diverse, and probably more basic values at risk, in the combined perceptions of adversaries. Second, more actors in an international system generate more dyads (pairs), creating a larger potential of adversarial competition. Similarly, more actors in a crisis lead to more disruptive interaction, with a consequent greater likelihood of violence including escalation to war.

The thrust to violent escalation also has consequences for bargaining strategy and choices at key decision points during a crisis. More precisely, the larger the number of parties in a bargaining sequence, the more difficult it is to attain a solution that will satisfy all concerned. Under such circumstances there is reason to expect that one or more actors will resort to violence in the escalation phase.

This reasoning also applies to the extent of *heterogeneity* among crisis adversaries. The wider their divergence in military capability, economic development, political regime, and culture, the more difficult it is to achieve accommodation, leaving a larger residue of unresolved disputes. That, in turn, creates a larger scope for mistrust and perceived value threat that are more likely to be expressed in violent behavior. Heterogeneous adversaries are also less likely to communicate effectively their intentions and terms of settlement. This too will increase hostility and a greater disposition to violence. Stated differently, more heterogeneity leads to more misperception and, as a consequence, a more likely resort to violence.

Major power activity in other states' crises almost always occurs after they have become full-scale crises. The more active the major powers in an interstate crisis the more likely it is that both initiator and target will perceive a more basic value threat – because of the potential damage that can be inflicted by the adversary as a result of aid provided by a patron.

A paradox of major power activity in crises is evident with respect to the likelihood of violence. On the one hand, major powers, as noted, tend to act so as to reduce the likelihood of violence or to limit its intensity, duration and scope. This takes the form of withholding aid to a client. On the other hand, major powers have commitments to allies and clients that call for and expect support in the form of military aid and, if necessary, direct intervention. This second strand of the paradox strengthens the process of escalation to violence or, if it already exists, to war.

A closely related situational attribute is *issues*. The larger the number of disputed issues in a crisis, the more acute will be the perceived threat to values on the part of all adversaries. Each issue poses a threat to some value and reinforces the negative effect of all other contested issues. That, in turn, contributes to a perception of increasing danger, the need for vigilance and, in general, a conflict spiral between adversaries. The same process, from issues to more mistrust to conflict spiral, generates a greater disposition to violence. Moreover, the larger the number of unresolved issues the more uncertain will be the environment for bargaining and non-violent accommodation by the crisis actors. This will occur unless a difference in preference orderings facilitates a mutually satisfying trade-off. In that setting of instability and disruptive interaction, adversaries will be more disposed to resolve the disputes by violent escalation – begetting a violent response.

Finally, multiple-issue crises have more potential than single-issue cases to produce change in the international system(s) of which they are members. Thus they are more likely to attract the attention of major powers. That interest will be reinforced if the adversaries resort to violence, for violent interactions are destabilizing.

Of the threefold perceptual condition, *value threat* is the first to emerge in a conflict and marks the outbreak of a foreign policy crisis. Moreover, threat generates an awareness of a higher-than-normal likelihood of military hostilities before the threat is overcome. And both of these create time pressure for response to the value threat and the threat of violence.

The more basic the value(s) at risk, the higher the cost crisis actors are willing to incur to protect them, and the more extreme will be their crisis management (value-protecting) technique. Violence is the most extreme method to manage a crisis, and war is the most intense form of violence. Thus, if existence or some other core value is perceived to be at stake, the likelihood is very high that violence will be employed, or intensified, to prevent the loss or weakening of that value. In sum, heightened threat is a major source of the peak stress period. And it increases the likelihood of violence during crisis escalation.

Time pressure refers to available time for decision in relation to the deadline for choice. When decision-makers are uncertain about the adversary's intention and capability, as they usually are in a crisis, time pressure is likely to increase. So too will the perceived *probability of war*.

The three perceptual conditions are closely linked. The higher the threat and the more basic the threatened value, the higher will be the perception of war likelihood. Acute threat will also increase the sense of time pressure to respond. And more intense time constraint will increase the perception of war likelihood and the awareness of value threat. Finally, the higher the expectation of war, the more active and basic will be the value threat and the perceived response time. These mutually reinforcing perceptions induce a feeling of stress, thereby providing the logical basis for treating them as a composite intervening variable.

II. HYPOTHESIS AND FINDINGS ON ESCALATION

The first question on crisis escalation posed early in this paper focused on change from an incipient to a fully crystallized crisis, a situation characterized by acute value threat, time pressure for choice, and heightened war likelihood, perceived by at least one actor, and more disruptive interaction that poses a challenge to the structure of the system(s) in which disruption is occurring. Empirically, these defining conditions were present in all cases from the end of 1918 to the end of 1988 – 829 foreign policy crises and 388 international crises. A more basic question is why this process occurs. Stated in terms of the escalation model, under what conditions is an embryonic crisis most likely to develop into a full-scale crisis? The answer is that a conflict spiral is most likely to be set in motion when a cluster of other factors is present. Three of them are system or interactor attributes: *a polycentric structure*, which permits more freedom of action by its autonomous actors; *a protracted conflict*, which generates long-term mutual mistrust and a mutual expectation of violence, tending to induce more hostile behavior; and geographic proximity, which facilitates more hostile behavior between crisis adversaries.

Their effects are strengthened by the role of several situational attributes: when more than two actors are engaged in higher-than-normal hostility, conciliation, compromise and dispute settlement become more difficult, as distrust and uncertainty generate increasing reluctance by all participants to yield to the adversary's demands; the more heterogeneous the crisis adversaries, with respect to military capability, economic development, political regime and culture, the more likely will hostility escalate between them; and if multiple issues are at stake, cutting across simple coalitions of actors, the task of preventing crisis escalation is rendered even more difficult.

From the escalation model several propositions are derived at the system/interactor level.

Hypothesis 1. An incipient international crisis is most likely to develop into a fully-crystallized crisis when:
- a crisis occurs within a polycentric structure;
- it takes place outside the dominant system;
- it is part of a protracted conflict;
- the main adversaries are geographically proximate to each other;
- there are more than two adversarial actors;
- they are heterogeneous in military, economic, political and/or cultural terms; and there are several cross-cutting issues in dispute.[2]

Two precipitating conditions, type of trigger and response by the adversaries, apply to escalation from no violence to violence, and from no/low violence to war, the second and third meanings of this concept. Both violent and non-violent triggers generate perceptions of threat. However, a violent trigger is not essential to escalation. The 'conflict spiral' is reinforced by a tendency to reciprocal response by the target: violent or non-violent triggers tend to beget violent or non-violent responses; and the spiral effect becomes self-sustaining. The outbreak of violence as the catalyst to escalation is logically possible and empirically discernible in many combinations of system, interactor, actor and situational attributes. However, violence is most likely when a particular set of factors from all four clusters is present at the beginning of the escalation phase. These include all of the factors noted in H.1.

Two additional interactor attributes help to explain the escalation dynamic to violence. One is relative capability; the other is regime pair. When a crisis actor is stronger than its adversary, it is more disposed to introduce violence into a crisis, in the expectation that resort to violence will achieve its objectives. Moreover, if both adversaries are governed by a military regime or they are mixed authoritarian (military/civil), violence is much more likely: as noted, decision-makers of such regimes achieved and/or sustained power by violence; it is familiar, legitimate and the preferred technique for coping with crises as well.

Several situational attributes also serve as explanatory variables. If the type of trigger to escalation is low-intensity violence, and the target's response is tit-for-tat, the spiral to violence or more intense violence is very likely. Moreover, major power activity tends to exacerbate tension between clients engaged in a crisis; military aid facilitates the use of violence by one or both adversaries, and a spiral effect culminating in violence or more intense violence is most likely to ensue.

Two hypotheses on violence are derived from the escalation model:

Hypothesis 2. An international crisis is most likely to escalate through violence when:
- all of the conditions specified in H.1 operate;
- there is considerable power discrepancy between the adversaries; they are ruled by military or other types of authoritarian regime; and
- major powers are active in supporting clients in the crisis with military aid.

Hypothesis 3. An international crisis is most likely to escalate to *severe* violence when:
- all of the conditions specified in H.1 and 2 operate;
- the breakpoint (trigger) to escalation takes the form of a violent act; and
- the target responds with equal severity or stronger acts.

The substantive redundancy in H.2 and 3 derives from the fact that escalation to serious clashes or war is, in essence, an extension of escalation to any form of violence. This is certainly true of the system and interactor attributes – polycentric structure, protracted conflict setting, geographic proximity and regime pair. As for actor attributes, the more heterogeneous the adversaries the more they will be prepared to employ severe violence in order to triumph in an external crisis. Similarly, the more active the major powers the more likely will a crisis escalate to severe violence.

What does the evidence from twentieth-century crises reveal about these expectations? The major findings on escalation (H.1) are set out in Table 5.1.

As evident, four of the expectations are *very strongly* or *strongly* supported, those relating to structure, system level, geographic distance, and heterogeneity. There is moderate support regarding conflict setting. The finding for number of actors is mixed. And the postulate regarding issues is not supported.[3]

Turning to H.2, nine types of crisis trigger were operationalized in the International Crisis Behavior (ICB) Project. These were grouped into three categories: *non-violent*, including external verbal, political, economic, and non-violent military acts, external change, and internal verbal challenge to a regime; *direct violent*, including internal physical violent challenges to a regime; and *indirect violent*, that is, violence directed to an ally or client state.

The aggregate findings on *violence in international crisis escalation* (H.2 and 3) are presented in terms of the proportionate frequency or direct violent triggers, or of severe violence (war and serious clashes) in the escalation phase. These are reported in Tables 5.2 and 5.3.

In sum, the data on 70 years of crisis provide *very strong* or *strong* support for four elements of H.2 – structure, system level, geographic distance, and regime type (pair), moderate support regarding conflict setting, and mixed support for major power activity.

As for H.3 (Table 5.3), the evidence on severe violence in international crises is pervasive. There is *very strong* or *strong* support for six of the 12 postulated linkages: number of actors, issues, regime type (pair), major power activity, trigger and response. There is also *moderate* support for heterogeneity, and for structure (polycentrism compared to bipolarity) as explanatory variables; and modest support regarding system level, conflict setting, and geographic distance. Thus the model has much greater explanatory power for the change from no/low violence to severe violence *during* the escalation phase than for the likelihood of a violent trigger to escalation.

The findings on trigger and response (Table 5.3) shed light on crucial conditions of severe violence in an international crisis.[4] Just as change from an incipient to a full-scale crisis and to violence/war merits analysis at the international level, so too these processes at the state/actor level require attention.

Table 5.1 International crises: findings on Hypothesis 1

Number and distribution of cases that escalated to full-scale crisis

Independent variable	Category	No.	%	Category	No.	%
Structure	Crises per year, polycentrism	7.42		crises per year, multipolarity	3.95	
				crises per year, bipolarity	5.14	
System level	subsystem		82	dominant system		18
Conflict setting	PC*		59	non-PC		41
Geographic distance	contiguous		69	non-contiguous[a]		27
Number of actors	one crisis actor		35	two crisis actors		44
				three or more crisis actors		21
Heterogeneity	low: no differences/1 difference		21	high: 3 or 4 differences		53
	two differences		26			
Issues	m-s issue alone		40	m-s and another issue		32
	non-m-s issue		12	2 non-m-s issues		3
				non-m-s issues		4

N = 388 international crises (except for Geographic Distance[a])
* PC, in all tables where it appears = protracted conflict.
a. International crises with more than 2 crisis actors were excluded from this element because of the assumption that multi-actor crises would mask the effect of geographic distance. For this variable, n = 306; 4 per cent = missing data.

Table 5.2 Violence in escalation of international crises: findings on Hypothesis 2

*Proportion of direct violent triggers**

Independent variable	Category	%	Category	%
Structure**	polycentrism	47	multipolarity	25
			bipolarity	20
System level	subsystem	38	dominant system	15
Conflict setting	PC	47	non-PC	29
Geographic distance	contiguous	42	non-contiguous	24
Number of actors	one crisis actor	36	three	36
	two adversaries	38	four or more	23
Heterogeneity	no differences/one difference	42	three or four differences	33
Issues	m-s issue alone	48	m-s and another issue	27
	three issues	29	non-m-s issue	13
			two non-m-s issues	18
Regime type (pair)	democratic	27	authoritarian	44
Capability	no/low PD***	48	high PD	25
Major power activity	great powers (1918–39) low	29	great powers (1918–39) high	59
	superpowers (1945–88) low	60	superpowers (1945–88) high	41

N = 311 cases (388 minus 77 IWCs); of the 311 cases, direct violent triggers = 104.
* The proportion of international crises triggered by direct violence was 35 per cent, by indirect violence, 6 per cent, and by nonviolent military acts, 17 per cent. For the other 42 per cent, the catalyst was non-violent and non-military.
** The reported distributions in this table and all others relating to the 5 tested hypotheses are derived from standard contingency table analysis: the categories of the independent variable are interpreted in relation to one value of the dependent variable. Percentages are calculated along the column (dependent variable) scores of a two-by-two contingency table, for both categories of the independent variable.
*** PD, in all tables where it appears = power discrepancy.

Table 5.3 Severe violence in international crises: findings on Hypothesis 3

Proportion of crises with severe violence (serious clashes, full-scale war)

Independent variable	Category	%	Category	%
Structure*	polycentrism	42	multipolarity	41
			bipolarity	32
System level	subsystem	40	dominant system	33
Conflict setting	PC	46	non-PC	32
Geographic distance	contiguous	40	non-contiguous	29
Number of crisis actors	single actor	23	three actors	39
	two actors	46	four or more actors	60
Heterogeneity	no differences/one difference	31	two or more differences	43
Issues	one non-m-s issue	26	two or more issues, incl. mil-sec	45
Regime type	democratic	18	authoritarian	33
Capability	no/low PD	48	high PD	41
Major power activity	great powers (1918–39) low/no	30	great powers (1918–39) high	45
	superpowers (1945–88) low/no	32	superpowers (1945–88) high	49
Trigger	non-violent	28	violent	56
Response	weaker	7	equal/stronger	77

N = 311 cases (388 minus 77 IWCs).
* See note a to Table 5.1. For this variable, n = 253; 4% = missing data.

Based upon the reasoning set out in the escalation model, two propositions at the actor level are presented here:

Hypothesis 4. A state will be most prone to crisis escalation when:
- it is not an actor in the dominant system;
- it is ruled by a non-democratic regime;
- it is engaged in a protracted conflict with one or more other states;
- it has an unfavorable power relationship with its adversary;
- it is geographically contiguous to its adversary;
- it is a young or new state; and
- it is experiencing acute internal instability.

As for the dimension of violence:

Hypothesis 5. A state is most likely to be vulnerable to violent crisis escalation when all of the conditions specified in H.4 operate in its foreign policy crisis;
- its regime is of short duration; and
- its territory is small.

The aggregate findings on vulnerability to escalation are set out in Table 5.4.

In sum, the data on interstate crises from the end of 1918 to the end of 1988 exhibit *very strong* or *strong* support for four of the seven elements in H.4, system level, regime type, geographic distance, and internal instability. There is also moderate support for the postulate regarding conflict setting. Proneness to foreign policy crises does not, however, seem to be related to power discrepancy or age. The finding for capability is, in fact, counter-intuitive – stronger states seem to be more vulnerable than weaker states to a foreign policy crisis. Parenthetically, this finding is consistent with power transition theory.

The findings on proneness to direct violent crisis escalation (H.5) are derived from the data on the total number of 829 foreign policy crises minus intra-war crises (IWCs) and missing data, that is, 593 cases (Table 5.5).

Overall, the evidence on foreign policy crises during most of the twentieth century supports eight of the nine postulated linkages in H.5: three *very strongly* – system level, geographic distance, and regime duration; three *strongly* – age, capability, and regime type; and two *moderately* – conflict setting and size of territory.

The evidence from qualitative research is even stronger: ten in-depth case studies on behavior under stress reveal a widely shared pattern of coping during the crisis period, despite notable diversity in *actor* and

Table 5.4 Proneness to foreign policy crisis: findings on Hypothesis 4

Independent variable	Distribution of foreign policy crises by vulnerability			
	Category	%	Category	%
System level	subsystem	74	dominant system	26
Regime type	democratic	37	authoritarian	63
Conflict setting	PC	57	non-PC	43
Capability	negative PD	36	positive PD	56
Geographic distance	'close to home'	79	'more distant'	21
Age	old states (pre-1815)	34	modern states (1815–1945)	34
			new states (post-WWII)	32
Internal instability	increasing	26	decreasing[a]	2

N = 829 cases
a. The other 72 per cent of the cases showed 'normal' instability (69 per cent) or newly-independent states for which government instability could not be assessed (3 per cent).

Table 5.5 Proneness to violent crisis escalation: findings on Hypothesis 5

Distribution of foreign policy crises by vulnerability

Independent variable	Category	%	Category	%
System level	subsystem	35	dominant system	7
Conflict setting	PC	37	non-PC	27
Geographic distance	'close to home'	34	'more distant'	7
Age	old states	24	new states	46
Regime type	democratic	22	authoritarian	37
Capability	negative/no PD	34	positive PD	18
Internal instability	increasing	25	decreasing	58
Regime duration	short	35	long	16
Territory size	small	30	large	23

N = 593 cases (829 minus 236 IWCs)

situational attributes, that is, the crisis configuration.[5]

In the context of this inquiry, the discovery of a widely shared pattern of coping with stress is one expression of a *universal strand* in interstate politics. Stress is a universal phenomenon, experienced by decision-makers, as indeed by humans in all civilizations, under certain conditions. So, too, the challenge of coping with stress is a universal challenge. Decision-makers of all states need to make choices in situations of complexity and incomplete information. They all attempt to maximize gains and minimize losses, though different cultures may define gains and losses differently. They all seek to enhance 'national interests,' though its content may vary.

Theoretically, of course, their coping strategy and behavior could vary greatly. And those who assume or expect such diversity will term the finding of common coping with crisis 'counter-intuitive' for it has long been regarded as axiomatic that cultural, racial, historical, political, ideological, and socio-economic differences must result in different behavior. Others who perceive the universal strand in world politics as more significant than the diversity among the members of the global system, are not surprised by the finding of a pattern of common coping on the part of decision-makers of states in crises.

The explanation can be summed up in the concept of *commonality*. Stress is a shared challenge, an indicator of impending harm and danger.

States have common traits that outweigh their diversity, especially the need to survive and to minimize harm from external foes. And foreign policy decision-makers, in coping with crisis-generated stress, act as humans do in all comparable situations of impending harm. In essence, the commonality of statehood, stress and human response to expected harm, or gain, overrides all variations among specific states and generates a near identical pattern of coping in an external crisis. This central finding from the ten case studies, whether regarded as 'intuitive' or 'counter-intuitive,' challenges conventional wisdom and *compels fundamental rethinking about how states cope with interstate crises*, that is, about *crisis management* in world politics.

NOTES

1. It has been argued (Betts [1977], 1991) that soldiers in a democratic regime are more reluctant than civilian leaders to employ force. However, once force is used, the military is unlikely to be interested in limits – they seek victory, as did US General Schwarzkopf in the Gulf War of 1991 (Brecher, 1993: chap. 7).
2. All the hypotheses in this paper are framed in a multi-faceted form. In fact, each of the individual elements within an overarching hypothesis is distinctive and autonomous. Testing will relate each element to one of the dependent variables in the model. The assumption is that the larger the number of constituent parts that is supported the greater the likelihood that the overarching hypothesis is valid.
3. The categories for extent of support are as follows:
very strong = at least twice as much support for the postulated linkage as for the alternative 'value,' e.g., 69 per cent of the cases that escalated to full-scale international crises were contiguous, compared to 27 per cent non-contiguous cases (H.1), in Table 5.1; thus the geographic distance postulate is very strongly supported; *strong* = 50 per cent – 99 per cent higher support for the postulated linkage, e.g., the finding on regime type (H.2), in Table 5.2; *moderate* = 25 per cent – 49 per cent higher support for the postulated linkage, e.g., the finding on conflict-setting (H.5), in Table 5.5; *modest* = 10 per cent – 24 per cent higher support for the postulated linkage, e.g., the finding on capability (H.3), in Table 5.3.
4. They are also related to the perennial 'behavior-begets-behavior' thesis, on which Wilkenfeld (1991) found that crises, like conflicts in general, 'exhibit a very high degree of matching behavior' with respect to trigger-crisis management technique and trigger-violence links: 75 per cent in the former, and 79 per cent in the latter, when the trigger was non-violent.

5. The ten case studies were: the US (Berlin Blockade, 1948-9); the USSR ('Prague Spring,' 1968); the UK (the Munich Crisis, 1938); Germany (at Stalingrad, 1942-3); Israel (October/Yom Kippur War, 1973-4); Syria (Lebanon Civil War, 1975-6); India (India/China Border Crisis, 1962); Hungary (Hungarian Uprising, 1956); Zambia (Rhodesia UDI, 1965-6); Argentina (Falklands/Malvinas War, 1982). The findings from these ten case studies are presented in Brecher (1993).

6 Nuclear Crisis as a Multi-Stage Threat Game: Toward an Agenda for Comparative Research*

Frank P. Harvey and Patrick James

What is the legacy of superpower crisis interactions during the Cold War? Over the course of four decades, the Soviet Union and the United States experienced a number of frightening confrontations, with the entire world as an audience. Now that the rivalry is over, it is appropriate to reflect on the experiences of the superpowers during the bipolar era. The most notable and controversial events are crises, which stand out as exclamation points in the superpower conflict.

This investigation focuses on whether superpower crises – and, by implication, those that involve other nuclear rivals – can be represented as a series of interactions with an essentially similar structure. Although the Berlin Blockade, Cuban Missiles and other confrontations are unique in some obvious ways, it is important for both theoretical and practical reasons to identify and probe any underlying similarities that may exist. In the abstract it is interesting to find out whether superpower crises exhibit some common features with regard to preferences for potential outcomes, which range from victory through compromise and defeat to nuclear annihilation. At a practical level, it is reasonable to be concerned about future – and possibly ongoing, but still unrecognized – cases of nuclear rivalry. Given the economic condition of the former Soviet Union, financially motivated nuclear proliferation is a clear and present danger. Common traits among superpower crises may reappear in other dyads that feature nuclear weapons, so there is more than theoretical and historical interest in these confrontations.

Analysis of superpower crisis interactions, which provides a point of departure for development of a general model, unfolds in four stages. First, literature on deterrence is used to identify problems encountered in previous efforts to obtain cumulative knowledge about deterrence in both the superpower and other rivalries. The second phase introduces the Multi-Stage Threat Game (MTG), which achieves progress in two ways: the MTG overcomes the obstacles encountered by studies of deterrence and is more realistic than existing, single-phase models of superpower rivalry in crises. Third, propositions about the relative consistency of payoffs in the MTG are derived and possibilities for testing are identified. The fourth and final task is to assess the MTG's potential contribution to knowledge about crisis interactions.

Two important qualifications will prevent confusion about the purpose of this study. First, it takes the form of an argument in favor of a particular research agenda, as opposed to a completed project. Second, the evidence provided is logical rather than empirical. The objective is to offer an alternative approach toward assessment of nuclear deterrence theory using US-Soviet rivalry as an empirical base. Testing of propositions derived from the game-theoretic framework will take place at the next stage of this project.

I. DETERRENCE, NUCLEAR WEAPONS AND SUPERPOWER RIVALRY

Literature on nuclear deterrence is primarily speculative and focuses on the behavior expected from nuclear antagonists faced with the prospect of mutual annihilation. By comparison, the relationship between anticipated and observed conduct receives insufficient attention. It still is unclear, for example, whether US and Soviet leaders acted according to the logic derived from standard application of deterrence theory to crises. Since this ambiguity pertains to the longest nuclear rivalry in history, it is reasonable to infer that authoritative knowledge will be even more lacking elsewhere. Given the likely proliferation of weapons of mass destruction in the future, and the failure of non-proliferation regimes in the past, greater understanding of deterrence in nuclear-type crises is essential.

Accumulation of knowledge about the theory of deterrence, conventionally articulated in terms of rational choice (Achen and Snidal, 1989), continues to face many barriers. In the empirical domain, lack of correspondence in case selection represents the most significant problem for the scientific research enterprise. In a comprehensive review of the dominant testing strategy utilized by Huth and Russett (1984, 1990, 1993) and Lebow and Stein (1987, 1989a, 1989b, 1990), Harvey and James (1992) identified both concept formation and measurement as key areas of difficulty, which helped to explain many of the discrepancies across case listings. Among other problems, accurate assessment of rational deterrence theory, within the context of the Huth-Russett/ Lebow-Stein-success-failure framework, requires specification of the attacker and defender in each case. But military-security crises often involve a series of interactions and deterrence episodes, with each side acquiring and playing both roles at various stages. Distinguishing cases of deterrence from compellence also is crucial, because crises frequently encompass both types of threats. The problem is that isolating actions that conform to a deterrence and/or compellence encounter often is difficult to accomplish with any degree of accuracy. In addition to these coding decisions one would have to specify the type of deterrent/ compellent threat being used (for example, nuclear; large scale conventional war; economic; political; etc.), whether the crisis was an immediate or general deterrence/compellence encounter (or some combination), and finally whether the particular interaction constituted a deterrence success or failure.[1] Obviously, with over one thousand possible combinations, case selection and coding would be difficult. As revealed by the ongoing debates, these obstacles cannot be overcome through reference to the historical record. Moreover, each research enterprise (James, 1993) – aggregate data analysis, as applied by Huth and Russett, or structured, focused comparison (George 1979a), as used by Lebow and Stein – manifests the problems that will face any framework that focuses on success versus failure.

An alternative, game-theoretic approach (outlined below) focuses on strategic interaction in crises as discrete events, thus expanding the empirical domain of the inquiry and facilitating better, albeit indirect, judgment of the rationality underlying nuclear and conventional deterrence theory. Briefly, the objective is to determine whether US–Soviet crises during the Cold War had an essentially similar structure in terms of payoffs. Knowledge of the degree of consistency is important to the debate over rational deterrence because advocates of the theory argue that cases are comparable. To the extent that it is possible to identify consistent and compatible payoffs across crises, that account becomes more believable. If instead the cases appear to be rather different in structure, then that would support criticism of efforts to generalize. While this is not a direct test of rational deterrence theory, the proposed crisis-based approach offers some promise in this regard.

The most important advantage is that each of the following issues becomes peripheral: coding of failed versus successful deterrence, identifying attackers and defenders, differentiating deterrence from compellence, and distinguishing immediate, general and extended dimensions. The emphasis shifts to provocation and retaliation by leaders of nuclear states facing (a) direct threats to fundamental values, (b) finite time for response, and (c) high probability of involvement in military hostilities. These are the defining conditions of a foreign policy crisis (Wilkenfeld, Brecher and Moser, 1988), as distinct from an immediate deterrence encounter. A crisis-based approach entails a less rigid, although no less valid, set of criteria for selecting cases appropriate for testing a set of alternative propositions, derived from either conventional or nuclear deterrence and related to rational choice and coercive diplomacy more generally, that lie outside the success/failure framework. A more detailed defence of the approach appears in the fourth and final section.

II. A MULTI-STAGE MODEL OF NUCLEAR CRISES

When game theory focuses on deterrence in the nuclear realm, Chicken is the conventional basis for models of crisis interaction. Brams (1994:130–8), however, used the Cuban Missile Crisis to draw attention to the important issue of whether the preference-ordering from Chicken is consistent with observed behavior. He demonstrated that 'standard' game-theoretic interpretations offer 'little in the way of explanation' of how a compromise 'was achieved and rendered stable in either game [Chicken or Brams' specification].' The matrix suggested by Brams reduces the emphasis on nuclear weapons and stresses tactical superiority of the US in explaining the outcome. The most notable change with respect to preferences is that Soviet maintenance of the missiles, coupled with an air strike by the US, is best for the US and worst for the USSR.[2]

While the alternative vision of Cuban Missiles is compelling, Brams indirectly draws attention to an even more basic obstacle to cumulative knowledge about superpower crises: the uncertainty of measurement. In particular, the nature of payoffs is troubling, regardless of the model at issue. Are the values attached to victory, compromise, stalemate and defeat – the generic outcomes of any conflict – comparable from one case to the next? How are these values to be derived or at least estimated within certain boundaries? Without a systematic approach toward this problem, models of superpower rivalry in crisis must remain mostly speculative.

Analysis of superpower crisis interaction as a single-stage game is typical of the literature on deterrence in at least one sense: it operates on assumptions rather than evidence with respect to payoffs (Brams and Kilgour, 1987b; James, 1991, 1993; James and Harvey, 1992). Of course, some of the existing studies have experimented with different functions, such as linear versus exponential, to represent hypothetical differences between the pure payoffs within the game of Chicken. An example of a linear payoff function would be 0, 1/3, 2/3 and 1 for the crisis outcomes of nuclear annihilation, defeat, compromise and victory, respectively (James and Harvey, 1992). Estimation of payoffs, however, remains extremely underdeveloped in comparison to equilibrium concepts and other aspects of the game-theoretic models.

With a more realistic representation of crisis interactions in multiple stages, knowledge about the specific versus general character of payoffs comes within reach. More precisely, if actions and reactions, along with crisis outcomes, are known, it should be possible to estimate a range of payoff values that is consistent with the behavior observed. If no such range exists, then either the payoffs must fluctuate considerably in relative value across cases or there is a weakness elsewhere in the model that produces inconsistency. Thus the MTG is intended as a step forward in two ways: (1) rather than assuming only one action per player, it allows for two; and (2) eventual intra- and inter-case analysis will permit assessment of consistency in payoffs, which represents a new way of testing whether Chicken is the appropriate metaphor with respect to nuclear rivalry.

Relative simplicity and a greater sense of reality are the dual purposes behind the rules of the MTG:

1. The game begins with a move by Row (R), followed by Column (C); each player is permitted one further move, in that order. The moves are labelled s_1, t_1, s_2 and t_2.
2. Strategies range from cooperation (s_i, $t_j = 1$) to a nuclear strike (s_i, $t_j = 0$).
3. The game may end sooner than two moves by each player, but only if one chooses to cooperate with the other (i.e., $s_i = 1$; $t_j = 1$).
4. Corner payoffs are the same as in the game of Chicken on the unit square: $r_1 < r_2 < r_3 < r_4$; $c_1 < c_2 < c_3 < c_4$.
5. Payoffs for a given point (x,y) within the unit square are a weighted linear combination of the pure payoffs in the corners.
6. The predicted outcome of the game is the subgame perfect equilibrium.[3]

More detailed treatments of the single-stage game of Chicken on the unit square appear in Brams and Kilgour (1987b), James (1991, 1993) and James and Harvey (1992). From this point onward the focus will

Nuclear Crisis as a Multi-Stage Threat Game

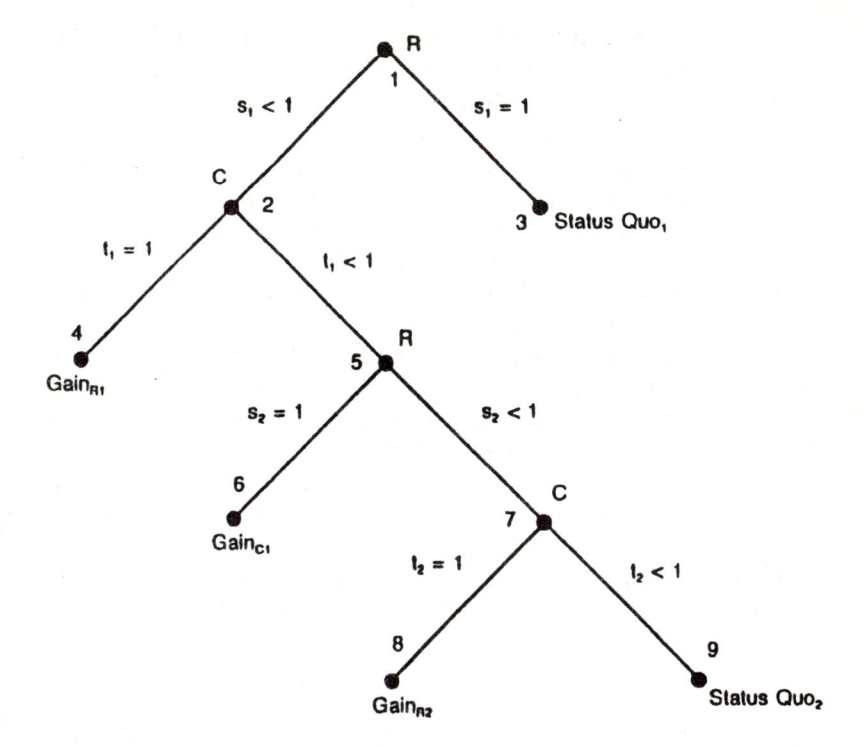

Figure 6.1 The multi-stage threat game

be on how the MTG adapts the previous frameworks to deal with multiple stages of play.

Figure 6.1 shows the MTG in extensive form. The game always begins with a move by Row (R). At node one, R can remain at the status quo ante or seek change, with these choices represented by $s_1 = 1$ and $s_1 < 1$, respectively. This produces either a choice for Column (C) at node two or continuation of the status quo at node three (Status Quo$_1$). At the second node, C can either permit R to make its gain or respond in some way, represented in turn by $t_1 = 1$ and $t_1 < 1$. If C cooperates, the game concludes at node four, with a gain for R (Gain$_{R1}$) as the result. At node five R can cooperate ($s_2 = 1$) or take some other action ($s_2 < 1$). If R chooses cooperation, the game ends at node six with a gain for C (Gain$_{C1}$). At node seven, C can move back to cooperation ($t_2 = 1$) or take further action ($t_2 < 1$).[4] Cooperation means the end of the game at node eight, with a gain for R (Gain$_{R2}$); any other choice produces a new status quo at node nine

(Status Quo$_2$). Note that each player is permitted to move twice, which reflects partial relaxation of the telescoping assumption from the one-stage model of crisis interaction.

More specific attention to the choices of R and C, at nodes five and seven respectively, brings out a principal advantage of the MTG as a model of crisis interactions. Note that R, which previously had selected $s_1 < 1$, is permitted to move back from its act of coercion. The same is true of C, which started off with $t_1 < 1$. This flexibility counteracts the determinism of the single-stage telescoping assumption, which always produces an interior point of the unit square (i.e., $x < 1$, $y < 1$) as the outcome. The MTG, by contrast, allows for a sequence like this: non-violent military action (s_1), indirect military action (t_1), verbal action (s_2), cooperation (t_2). Based on the scale for intensity of bargaining techniques (which will be introduced later), $t_1 < s_1 < s_2 < t_2$. The new status quo (t_2, s_2) reflects C's ultimate choice of cooperation, even though, at one point, it engaged in the most coercive behavior attributed to either player (i.e., t_1).

Payoffs for R and C from a given point (x, y) on the unit square are calculated as follows:

$$P_R(x, y) = (1 - x)(1 - y)r_1 + (1 - x)yr_2 + xyr_3 + x(1 - y)r_4 \quad (1)$$

$$P_C(x, y) = (1 - x)(1 - y)c_1 + (1 - y)xc_2 + xyc_3 + y(1 - x)r_4 \quad (2)$$

These payoff functions are bilinear, meaning linear in each coordinate. The payoffs at each corner (i.e., $r_1, \ldots, r_4$ for R) are 'weighted by the product of the distances, parallel to the axes, from (x, y) to the opposite corner' (Brams and Kilgour, 1987b:837).

Table 6.1 shows the payoffs for R and C at each outcome within Figure 6.1. This permits identification of a preference ordering for each player. Some of the comparisons are determinate. For R, either Gain$_{R1}$ or Gain$_{R2}$ is preferred to Status Quo$_1$, which in turn is better than Gain$_{C1}$. Similarly, Gain$_{C1}$ is preferred to Status Quo$_1$, which is better than Gain$_{R1}$ or Gain$_{R2}$, for C.

Table 6.2 lists the threshold conditions for the pairs of outcomes that are indeterminate in ordering. The expressions are simpler than might be expected on the basis of Table 6.1 because the minimum (r_1 and c_1) and maximum (r_4 and c_4) payoffs are assumed to be 0 and 1, respectively, for each player. Since only relative distances between the pure payoffs (i.e., $r_1, \ldots, r_4$ and $c_1, \ldots, c_4$) are significant, 0 and 1 are convenient values to use for the boundaries of nuclear annihilation

Table 6.1 Outcomes and payoffs in the multi-stage threat game

Outcome and position on unit square		Payoffs for Row (P_R) and Column (P_C)
Status Quo$_1$	(1,1)	$P_R = r_3$ $P_C = c_3$
Gain$_{R1}$	(1,s$_1$)	$P_R = s_1 r_3 + (1 - s_1) r_4$ $P_C = (1 - s_1) c_2 + s_1 c_3$
Gain$_{C1}$	(t$_1$,1)	$P_R = (1 - t_1) r_2 + t_1 r_3$ $P_C = (t_1 c_3) + (1 - t_1) c_4$
Gain$_{R2}$	(1,s$_2$)	$P_R = s_2 r_3 + (1 - s_2) r_4$ $P_C = (1 - s_2) c_2 + s_2 c_3$
Status Quo$_2$	(t$_2$,s$_2$)	$P_R = (1 - t_2)(1 - s_2) r_1 + (1 - t_2) s_2 r_2$ $\quad + t_2 s_2 r_2 + t_2 (1 - s_2) r_4$ $P_C = (1 - t_2)(1 - s_2) c_1 + (1 - s_2) t_2 c_2$ $\quad + t_2 s_2 c_3 + s_2 (1 - t_2) c_4$

Table 6.2 Threshold conditions for preference orderings

Preference ordering	Threshold conditions
Row player:	
Gain$_{R2}$ > Gain$_{R1}$	$s_1 - s_2 > 0$
Status Quo$_2$ > Status Quo$_1$	$(1 - t_2) s_2 r_2 + (t_2 s_2 - 1) r_3 + t_2 (1 - s_2) > 0$
Gain$_{C1}$ > Status Quo$_2$	$[1 - t_1 + t_2 (1 - s_2)] r_2 + (t_1 - t_2 s_2) r_3$ $\quad + t_2 (s_2 - 1) > 0$
Gain$_{R1}$ > Status Quo$_2$	$(t_2 - 1) s_2 r_2 + (s_1 - t_2 s_2) r_3 + (1 - s_1 + t_2 s_2)$ $\quad > 0$
Gain$_{R2}$ > Status Quo$_2$	$(t_2 - 1) s_2 r_2 + (1 - t_2) s_2 r_3 + (1 - t_2)(1 - s_2)$ $\quad > 0$
Column Player	
Gain$_{R2}$ > Gain$_{R1}$	$s_2 - s_1 > 0$
Status Quo$_2$ > Status Quo$_1$	$(1 - s_2) t_2 c_2 + (t_2 s_2 - 1) c_3 + s_2 (1 - t_2) > 0$
Status Quo$_2$ > Gain$_{R1}$	$[(1 - s_2) t_2 + (s_1 - 1)] c_2 + (t_2 s_2 - s_1) c_3$ $\quad + s_2 (1 - t_2) > 0$
Status Quo$_2$ > Gain$_{R2}$	$(1 - s_2)(t_2 - 1) c_2 + (t_2 - 1) s_2 c_3$ $\quad + s_2 (1 - t_2) > 0$
Gain$_{C1}$ > Status Quo$_2$	$(s_2 - 1) t_2 c_2 + (t_1 - t_2 s_2) c_3 + (1 - t_1 - s_2$ $\quad + t_2 s_2) > 0$

and victory (James and Harvey, 1992; Brams and Kilgour, 1987b). The crucial issue with respect to consistency will be whether ranges for r_2, r_3, c_2 and c_3 can be derived in a manner that preserves the ordering from Chicken.

Tables 6.3 and 6.4 list the potential preference orderings for R and

Table 6.3 Possible preference orderings for row player

Type	Preference ordering
I_R	$Gain_{R1} > Gain_{R2} > Status\ Quo_1 > Status\ Quo_2 > Gain_{C1}$
II_R	$Gain_{R1} > Gain_{R2} > Status\ Quo_2 > Status\ Quo_1 > Gain_{C1}$
III_R	$Gain_{R1} > Gain_{R2} > Status\ Quo_1 > Gain_{C1} > Status\ Quo_2$
IV_R	$Gain_{R2} > Gain_{R1} > Status\ Quo_1 > Status\ Quo_2 > Gain_{C1}$
V_R	$Gain_{R2} > Gain_{R1} > Status\ Quo_2 > Status\ Quo_1 > Gain_{C1}$
VI_R	$Gain_{R2} > Gain_{R1} > Status\ Quo_1 > Gain_{C1} > Status\ Quo_2$
VII_R	$Status\ Quo_2 > Gain_{R1} > Gain_{R2} > Status\ Quo_1 > Gain_{C1}$
VIII_R	$Status\ Quo_2 > Gain_{R2} > Gain_{R1} > Status\ Quo_1 > Gain_{C1}$
IX_R	$Gain_{R2} > Status\ Quo_2 > Gain_{R1} > Status\ Quo_1 > Gain_{C1}$
X_R	$Gain_{R2} > Gain_{R1} > Status\ Quo_2 > Status\ Quo_1 > Gain_{C1}$
XI_R	$Gain_{R1} > Status\ Quo_2 > Gain_{R2} > Status\ Quo_1 > Gain_{C1}$
XII_R	$Gain_{R1} > Gain_{R2} > Status\ Quo_2 > Status\ Quo_1 > Gain_{C1}$

Table 6.4 Possible preference orderings for column player

Type	Preference ordering
I_C	$Gain_{C1} > Status\ Quo_1 > Status\ Quo_2 > Gain_{R1} > Gain_{R2}$
II_C	$Gain_{C1} > Status\ Quo_1 > Status\ Quo_2 > Gain_{R2} > Gain_{R1}$
III_C	$Gain_{C1} > Status\ Quo_1 > Gain_{R1} > Status\ Quo_2 > Gain_{R2}$
IV_C	$Gain_{C1} > Status\ Quo_1 > Gain_{R2} > Status\ Quo_2 > Gain_{R1}$
V_C	$Gain_{C1} > Status\ Quo_1 > Gain_{R1} > Gain_{R2} > Status\ Quo_2$
VI_C	$Gain_{C1} > Status\ Quo_1 > Gain_{R2} > Gain_{R1} > Status\ Quo_2$
VII_C	$Status\ Quo_2 > Gain_{C1} > Status\ Quo_1 > Gain_{R1} > Gain_{R2}$
VIII_C	$Status\ Quo_2 > Gain_{C1} > Status\ Quo_1 > Gain_{R2} > Gain_{R1}$

C respectively, given the combinations among the outcomes that can be derived from Table 6.2.[5] As a result there are 96 possible dyads. The subgame perfect equilibrium for each scenario appears in Table 6.5. Since it is very unlikely that preferences in real cases would be distributed evenly among the categories, the relative frequency of outcomes is strictly hypothetical. The percentages are as follows: Status Quo_1 – 18.8 per cent, Status Quo_2 – 33.3 per cent, $Gain_{R1}$ – 22.9 per cent, $Gain_{R2}$ – 25 per cent and $Gain_{C1}$ – 0 per cent. With perfect and complete information, it makes sense that outcomes that produce a gain for the Column player are ruled out; Row would not start the game in the first place. Thus any case in which $Gain_{C1}$ is the result must be explained by incomplete or imperfect information. For now the analysis will be restricted to complete and perfect information, in

Table 6.5 Profile of outcomes

Type of row player	I_C	II_C	III_C	IV_C	V_C	VI_C	VII_C	VIII_C
I_R	Status Quo$_1$	Status Quo$_1$	Gain$_{R1}$	Gain$_{R2}$	Gain$_{R1}$	Gain$_{R2}$	Status Quo$_1$	Status Quo$_1$
II_R	Status Quo$_2$	Status Quo$_2$	Gain$_{R1}$	Gain$_{R2}$	Gain$_{R1}$	Gain$_{R2}$	Status Quo$_2$	Status Quo$_2$
III_R	Status Quo$_1$	Status Quo$_1$	Status Quo$_1$	Gain$_{R2}$	Gain$_{R1}$	Gain$_{R2}$	Status Quo$_1$	Status Quo$_1$
IV_R	Status Quo$_1$	Status Quo$_1$	Gain$_{R1}$	Gain$_{R2}$	Gain$_{R1}$	Gain$_{R2}$	Status Quo$_1$	Status Quo$_1$
V_R	Status Quo$_2$	Status Quo$_2$	Gain$_{R1}$	Gain$_{R2}$	Gain$_{R1}$	Gain$_{R2}$	Status Quo$_2$	Status Quo$_2$
VI_R	Status Quo$_1$	Status Quo$_1$	Status Quo$_1$	Gain$_{R2}$	Gain$_{R1}$	Gain$_{R2}$	Status Quo$_1$	Status Quo$_1$
VII_R	Status Quo$_2$	Status Quo$_2$	Gain$_{R1}$	Gain$_{R2}$	Gain$_{R1}$	Gain$_{R2}$	Status Quo$_2$	Status Quo$_2$
VIII_R	Status Quo$_2$	Status Quo$_2$	Gain$_{R1}$	Gain$_{R2}$	Gain$_{R1}$	Gain$_{R2}$	Status Quo$_2$	Status Quo$_2$
IX_R	Status Quo$_2$	Status Quo$_2$	Gain$_{R1}$	Gain$_{R2}$	Gain$_{R1}$	Gain$_{R2}$	Status Quo$_2$	Status Quo$_2$
X_R	Status Quo$_2$	Status Quo$_2$	Gain$_{R1}$	Gain$_{R2}$	Gain$_{R1}$	Gain$_{R2}$	Status Quo$_2$	Status Quo$_2$
XI_R	Status Quo$_2$	Status Quo$_2$	Gain$_{R1}$	Gain$_{R2}$	Gain$_{R1}$	Gain$_{R2}$	Status Quo$_2$	Status Quo$_2$
XII_R	Status Quo$_2$	Status Quo$_2$	Gain$_{R1}$	Gain$_{R2}$	Gain$_{R1}$	Gain$_{R2}$	Status Quo$_2$	Status Quo$_2$

order to bring out some basic properties of the MTG as a vision of nuclear crisis.

Propositions and Possibilities for Testing

Suppose that Types I_R and VIII_C, from Tables 6.3 and 6.4, respectively, are players in the MTG. The subgame perfect equilibrium can be derived through backward induction. At node seven, C prefers the new status quo (node nine) to a gain for R (node eight), so Status Quo$_2$ is the choice. At node five, R (effectively) selects from the new status quo or a gain for C (node six), so Status Quo$_2$ remains the outcome. At node two, C can choose either the new status quo or a gain for R (node four): once again, Status Quo$_2$ is the result. Finally, at the outset of the game, R can select either the present (node three) status quo or the new one: given its preferences, the outcome is Status Quo$_1$. In other words, superpowers with the above-noted preferences would not experience crises. Instead, they would stay at the status quo. Thus the combination of profiles designated as I_R and VIII_C, if present at all during the Cold War, must have existed during non-crisis periods. Of course, 17 other combinations of player types in Table 6.5 also produce Status Quo$_1$ as the outcome, which serves as a reminder of how much remains to be learned about preferences and payoffs. In sum, it is not enough to assert that superpower crises (and nuclear confrontations in general) feature a common payoff configuration and proceed from there.

More immediately interesting is another instance, which produces an outcome different than the status quo: V_R versus I_C. The subgame perfect equilibrium in this case is Status Quo$_2$. There are a series of inequalities that must be satisfied by players of the types assumed in this game. The expressions appear in Table 6.2, with three being reversed in this instance (Status Quo$_2$ > Gain$_{C1}$ for V_R and Gain$_{R1}$ > Gain$_{R2}$ and Status Quo$_1$ > Status Quo$_2$ for I_C). Given the actions and outcome observed (Status Quo$_2$), r_2, r_3, c_2 and c_3 must meet the overdetermined conditions represented by the series of inequalities. Otherwise, the preference orderings for R and C would change, which in turn alters the process of backward induction. It is necessary, given observed data for s_1, t_1, s_2 and t_2, to produce values of r_2, r_3, c_2 and c_3 that satisfy the threshold conditions for the preference orderings.

Consider the implications for the debate over superpower rivalry. What position would advocates of rational choice and political psychology adopt on the issue of payoffs within the MTG? The concepts of existence and compatibility will be useful in bringing out crucial, and as yet unexamined, differences between these schools of thought.

Existence means that, for a given case, data on superpower actions and reactions, along with the resulting outcome, are consistent with ranges of values for the r_i and c_j that satisfy the requirements just noted. If the ranges of acceptable values hold up from one case to the next, then those crises are said to be compatible. The two general propositions that follow are derived, respectively, from weak and strong interpretations of rational choice. For any given superpower crisis,

P_1: it is possible to identify values for the r_i and c_j that satisfy the conditions implied by superpower actions and the outcome observed.

P_2: the ranges of values identified for the r_i and c_j will be compatible with those of other cases.

Since the values of the r_i and c_j are over-determined, P_1 issues a challenge: What if there is no combination of R and C from Tables 6.3 and 6.4 that is consistent with the behavior and outcome observed? If so, basic questions are raised about the relevance of the MTG – and Chicken in general – as a way of thinking about superpower rivalry. Existence of one or more feasible combinations is a relatively weak requirement to place on a model grounded in rational choice.

More demanding is the test represented by P_2. It is possible that the MTG is a worthy representation of superpower crises but that the relative magnitudes of the payoffs might vary considerably across cases.[6] If so, that would suggest a lower degree of comparability among cases than implied by rational choice, although the Chicken-based MTG might remain a fair representation of the overall process of superpower rivalry in crises.

With respect to case selection and eventual testing of P_1, P_2 and other propositions that might be derived from the MTG, identification of cases and coding relies upon the International Crisis Behavior (ICB) Project (Wilkenfeld, Brecher and Moser, 1988; Brecher, Wilkenfeld and Moser, 1988) and a series of data-based studies that focus on the single-stage model (James, 1991, James and Harvey, 1992).[7] For a given state, a foreign policy crisis arises when central decision makers perceive three interrelated conditions: (1) a threat to basic values, with a simultaneous or subsequent awareness of (2) finite time for response, and (3) high probability of involvement in military hostilities (Wilkenfeld, Brecher and Moser, 1988:2). In all cases a specific danger is experienced by an actor seeking to respond to some change in the status quo.[8]

Table 6.6 Intensity of superpower bargaining techniques

Technique	Intensity	Technique	Intensity
1. Nuclear strike	0.000	9. Non-violent military	0.654
2. Full-scale conventional war	0.098	10. Multiple, including non-violent military	0.720
3. Indirect, full-scale conventional war	0.189	11. Economic act	0.781
4. Serious clashes	0.275	12. Political act	0.841
5. Indirect serious clashes	0.360	13. Verbal act	0.896
6. Minor clashes	0.438	14. No action	0.950
7. Indirect minor clashes	0.514	15. Cooperation	1.000
8. Multiple, including violent military	0.585		

Source: James and Harvey (1992:47).

James and Harvey (1992) and Harvey (1995, 1997) use the ICB data to obtain an initial set of superpower crises (from 1949 onward) which, in principle, is appropriate for testing the deterrence-related propositions derived from the MTG.[9] Only cases that involved the US and the USSR as adversaries, with one superpower threatened directly (or indirectly) by the other, are relevant.[10] Intra-bloc crises (e.g. Hungary 1956, Czechoslovakia 1968), where one superpower threatened a client state and not the more immediate interests of its rival, are excluded. To ensure that nuclear weapons played some potential role in the crisis, conflicts in which clients of one superpower threatened their counterparts are left out; it is virtually impossible in these cases to attribute responsibility to the superpower.[11]

Measurement of s_i and t_j follows the approach developed by James and Harvey (1992). The scale values for the polar points of cooperation and non-cooperation are 1 and 0, respectively. The basic property of that scale is an exponential decrease in values; in other words, as the intensity of an action increases, its score approaches 0 – meaning nuclear attack – more quickly. Table 6.6 displays the 15-point scale of superpower bargaining techniques.[12] The points on the scale combine the coding of the relevant ICB variables, 'triggering action' and 'major response,' and are generated by the following expression:

$$s'_k = 2 - e^{0.693(sk)} \qquad (3)$$

where

s'_k = transformed (exponential) scale point ($k = 1, \ldots, 15$).
s_k = linear scale point.

Each s_k has the value $(k-1)/14$, meaning that $s_1 = 0$, $s_2 = 1/14,...,s_{15} = 1$. The value for the exponent, 0.693, is appropriate given the boundaries intended for s'_k. When $s_k = 0$, the transformation results in $s'_k = 1$; with $s_k = 1$, $s'_k = 0$. The scale in Table 6.6 covers the full range of potential values for cooperation and non-cooperation. There is a fixed zero point, nuclear strike, which represents the absence of cooperation. At the other extreme lies cooperation itself.[13] Although the largest interval on the scale is the one separating a nuclear strike from full-scale conventional war, no qualitative difference in the range of values is assumed.[14]

Some specific, measurement-related advantages of the ICB data should be noted. First, every foreign policy crisis has an explicitly designated triggering act and major response, making it possible to identify circumstances in which one superpower caused the other to experience and cope with crisis conditions. Second, datasets that focus on war are less suitable for testing models like the MTG because the coding does not always distinguish the behavior of the superpowers on an individual basis. Third, and most essential, the ICB listings include case histories and bibliographies, which make it possible to probe for potential inaccuracies prior to coding decisions. Specification of the full set of moves in each crisis ultimately will rely on at least two other sources: the Militarized Interstate Crises data set (Leng, 1993) and the series of case studies from Harvard's Pew Program. The ICB data are ideal for assessment of s_1 and t_1 but further research will be required in some cases to obtain a complete record of actions.

Since it currently is beyond the scope of this project to proceed with a data-based assessment of P_1 and P_2, a few cases will be explored briefly as an alternative. The Suez-Sinai Campaign and Cuban Missile Crises bring out some basic points related to the MTG.

Suez-Sinai produces Status Quo$_1$ as the outcome. Fry (1989:19, 22) describes the most basic policy assumptions of the USSR and US, respectively, in this intense conflict:

1. USSR: do not rule out the need for and possibility of cooperation with the United States on certain issues.
2. US: cooperation with the Soviet Union is possible.

The superpowers acted as reluctant partners during the crisis, dampening escalation while seeking to limit each other's influence. This activity included Security Council resolutions on 30 and 31 October 1956 that called for a ceasefire.

Table 6.5 contains 18 combinations of player profiles that are consistent with the sustained cooperation between the superpowers during

Suez-Sinai. It is essential to look at cases like this one – that is, ICB cases in which the US and USSR are involved but neither threatens the other – when probing for existence and compatibility. Case records will reveal whether one or more of the presumed player types from Table 6.5 (given the observed outcome of Status Quo$_1$) are credible and if the same preference orderings appear to be supported by the evidence from one instance to the next.

Opposite to the outcome of the preceding case is the intense confrontation over missiles in Cuba. The US perceived Soviet deployment of missiles in the Caribbean as a threat to political influence (Brussel, 1989:11). Based on the coding from Harvey and James (1992), R = USSR, C = US and the sequence of actions is as follows: s_1 = 0.654, t_1 = 0.654, s_2 = 1.000, t_2 = 0.654.[15] Thus the outcome is Gain$_{C1}$, which (as noted earlier) is ruled out under conditions of complete and perfect information. This case, in which R initiates a crisis and C ends up gaining, may turn out to be quite exceptional when all data are available. However, at the very least the result points to the value of exploring the MTG both with and without the assumption of complete and perfect information.

Although the MTG goes a step beyond single-stage models of superpower bargaining, it is possible that the telescoping of actions still is too extreme. The MTG allows for only two stages of bargaining. Closer examination of superpower and other nuclear crises may suggest that it is useful to create a more nuanced version of the MTG that can account for reputations and images in enduring rivalries. In its present form, the game assumes that R's leaders would gain (Gain$_{R2}$ at node eight) if C returned to cooperation (t_2 =1) at node seven, following R's second act of aggression (s_2 < 1) at node five. However, if t_1 < s_2 (i.e., if C's initial act of aggression was more hostile than R's response) it is not clear that R's officials would be satisfied with the outcome. After all, US and Soviet leaders became virtually obsessed with image-related issues over the course of the Cold War, as clearly demonstrated in the Cuban Missile Crisis. With these considerations in mind, R would be expected to prefer a more aggressive stance in response to t_1 < 1 for the outcome at node eight to be considered a success. A third option for R at node five, which allows for consideration of retaliation levels, could account for such preferences while adding a new and potentially interesting twist to the extended form game. It also would allow for testing of propositions about reputation and images derived from political psychology.

III. THE MTG, DETERRENCE THEORY, AND THE LEGACY OF SUPERPOWER CRISES

Creation of the MTG permits, at least in principle, more rigorous assessment of whether superpower crises during the Cold War had an essentially similar payoff structure. As previously noted, consistency is important to the debate over rational deterrence because advocates of the theory claim that cases are comparable. If cases are different in structure, then that would undermine the utility of deterrence as a theory or strategy. Critics might raise several questions about whether, in principle, the proposed alternative can be expected to outperform the dominant testing strategy. After all, how can propositions about deterrence be tested if the issues dividing the main testing programs are avoided? The more interesting (and relevant) question, however, is this one: Will propositions from deterrence theory ever be evaluated effectively if coding controversies and related issues continue to divert creative energies? Most of the disputes over case listings of deterrence encounters do not apply to identification of superpower crises; far fewer potentially controversial judgments are required about if and when officials perceived a threat to values, finite time for response, and a high probability of military hostilities. While any immediate deterrence confrontation would constitute an international crisis almost by definition, it is much more difficult to establish the identity of a specific crisis in foreign policy along dimensions such as immediate or general deterrence, and deterrence versus compellence, given previously noted difficulties with coding.

Other skeptics might question whether the new approach can account for subjective costs, benefits and probabilities on behalf of challengers and defenders. A focus on strategic interaction, especially in terms of the payoffs associated with provocation and retaliation levels, can tap into factors that influence decisions about the consequences of crisis escalation in a nuclear dyad. To imply otherwise entails the assumption that decisions are a product of internal psychological beliefs and intuition alone, with little connection, if any, to objective reality. If that is true, then no model (or theory) of nuclear crises should be expected to issue predictions more effectively than another. In fact, an authoritative review of crises in the twentieth century refutes the notion of idiosyncratic decision-making across cases (Brecher, 1993).

Finally, previous studies of deterrence attempt to identify the subjective costs, benefits and probability estimates of defenders and attackers through information obtained (in one form or another) from primary materials. Yet even this knowledge produces divergent interpretations of case histories, disagreement over decision-makers' motives, perceptions and intentions, and different conclusions about deterrence as both a theory and a strategy. Although decision-making processes of the superpowers are important, observable behavior is equally significant when evaluating deterrence or any other related theory. This is precisely why testing strategies that utilize a less rigid set of operational criteria are essential to cumulative understanding.[16]

Efforts to explore the nature of US–Soviet rivalry remain important for several reasons. First, demonstrating that the record of superpower activity generally supports the presence of certain strategies, and not a random distribution of actions (as implied by political psychologists), would lend credibility to the perspective of rational choice. Notwithstanding differences in culture, ideology, political system, religion, history, leadership skills, belief structures, idiosyncrasies, and changes in the distribution of nuclear capabilities, it may be possible to identify a strategic rationale that guided superpower relations throughout their foreign policy crises.

Preliminary evidence, from a one-stage model (James and Harvey, 1992), suggests that the superpowers responded to provocation with threats and counter-threats that actually de-escalated tensions and promoted crisis stability. This result is consistent with expectations from rational choice and nuclear deterrence theory (James and Harvey, 1989; Harvey and James, 1992; Harvey, 1995). Each side seemed to grasp the general requirements for crisis stability and learned vital rules of prudence.[17] Despite high stress, powerful political and psychological pressures to prevail, mutual distrust and many other obstacles to cooperation in security matters, the superpowers developed patterns of restraint to manage the rivalry without crossing the threshold to war.[18] They became motivated by a series of 'disaster avoidance' constraints, embedded within the logic of Mutual Assured Destruction (MAD). The gap between the value of the interests they disputed and the possible cost of war widened. This, in turn, increased the 'range of manoeuvring' that promoted crisis management and de-escalation (Dougherty and Pfaltgraff, 1990:491). Contrary to the image of the 'pathological leader,' routinely depicted by political psychologists and classic pessimists like Kahn (1961) and Wohlstetter (1959), more than just luck prevented hostilities from breaking out between the US and USSR. Opportunities and constraints within superpower rivalry and nuclear deterrence produced long-term stabilization.[19]

Another important objective within this research agenda is to assess whether nuclear rivals are indeed more prone than others to exhibit patterns of rational choice and restraint. If it could be demonstrated that the threat posed by escalation causes nuclear rivals to manage crises better, and prevents disputes from spiralling out of control, those would be important discoveries, especially in the context of nuclear proliferation. Obviously the acquisition of nuclear weapons by non-nuclear powers would not in and of itself satisfy the conditions for nuclear deterrence that prevented the superpowers from crossing the brink. Deterrence would hold only if new nuclear powers could deploy forces in a manner that satisfies the conditions stipulated by Wohlstetter (1959).[20] (Also, the destructive capability of a new nuclear power would have to be large enough to generate rules of prudence.) If a state's deployment fails to meet those criteria, then nuclear deterrence, which traditionally depends on a credible and effective second strike, would not apply. In fact, preemption in a crisis involving two new nuclear rivals would become more likely, given the incentives to launch on warning.

Although US–Soviet nuclear deterrence may appear to have functioned according to the logic derived from rational choice in general and the game of Chicken in particular, it is not obvious that proliferation would contribute to crisis stabilization in every case. Each new nuclear state would need a sophisticated C^3I network, an essential component of the relatively stable superpower relationship. Until such systems are developed to accommodate prospective nuclear rivalries, the post-Cold War system is likely to become less stable as a consequence of proliferation. It appears, at least on the surface, that the only practical solution is to continue strengthening non-proliferation regimes by placing strict limits on the distribution of nuclear materials. The less appealing alternative would be to ensure that states with nuclear weapons (or those in the process of acquiring them) are provided with the right kind of weapons technology (C^3I) to meet the conditions for a stable and effective deterrent. Since the superpower rivalry is the best historical guide to policy, further development and testing of the MTG is justified on both theoretical and practical grounds.

NOTES

* We are grateful to Michael Brecher, Ben Mor, Mats Hammerstrom and Kevin Wang for helpful commentaries.
1. For an excellent discussion of these and other problems with aggregate tests of deterrence theory, see Levy (1988), Jervis (1979) and Morgan (1977).
2. The outcome is described as 'Honorable US action, Soviets thwarted' (Brams, 1994:134).
3. This equilibrium concept originates with Selten (1975). A subgame perfect equilibrium 'is an equilibrium for every part of the game from that node forward' (Bueno de Mesquita and Lalman, 1992:36).
4. There is no requirement that $t_2 < t_1$, s_1 or $s_2 < s_1$, t_1 (bearing in mind that lower values for t_j, s_i mean more intense actions). It is permissible for the second threat or action to be less assertive than the first by either player.
5. Since there are two outcomes in which R strictly gains ($Gain_{R1}$, $Gain_{R2}$) and only one for C ($Gain_{C1}$), more combinations are produced. This difference explains the four additional orderings for R even though the game is symmetric in the sense that each player moves twice.
6. One example of systematic variation would be higher values for r_3 (c_3) when the US assumes the role of R (C). Since the US normally is regarded as the more status-quo-oriented power, with the USSR as its challenger for supremacy, this type of difference in payoff magnitudes might be expected.
7. Initial case selection (by two coders) relied upon the *New York Times Index* and *Keesing's Contemporary Archives*. Area experts and compilations of 'related phenomena' also played significant roles in the process of deriving the case list.
8. Emphasis on crisis interaction rather than immediate deterrence effectively bypasses the need to distinguish different forms of coercive interaction (i.e., compellence versus deterrence).
9. The proposed case listing begins with crises underway in 1949, the first year in which both the USA and USSR could have issued nuclear-based threats.
10. The purpose is to distinguish these encounters from situations of general deterrence. Tests of general deterrence include George and Smoke (1974) and Huth and Russett (1993).
11. The case of Israel and Egypt in 1973 provides an excellent example of this problem; for a more detailed treatment see James and Harvey (1992).
12. For speculation about a more general form of this scale, which would apply to states below the nuclear level, consult James and Harvey (1992).
13. It might be suggested that identifying the act of non-cooperation that initiates a crisis requires problematic values judgments. However, the ICB Project coding procedures, described in Brecher, Wilkenfeld and Moser (1988), minimize problems of reliability. With respect to triggering acts, it is obvious that neither cooperation nor a lack of action (the final two scale points) can trigger a crisis. However, superpower rivalry is assumed to be in progress at all times during the Cold War. Thus each of these non-threatening forms of behaviour may be regarded as a choice available to the players at any given moment.
14. Houweling and Siccama (1988a:48) raise the possibility of a step-level

effect leading to 'compulsory escalation.' Alternative functional forms for the scale of superpower bargaining techniques, which would reflect threshold effects and other theoretical possibilities, become relevant when aggregate data is used to test propositions.

15. Since the USSR reverts to cooperation, with the US sustaining its blockade, the coding stops at that point. Of course, after the USSR announces that it will withdraw the missiles and the crisis terminates, coercion by the US comes to an end.

16. This argument does not repudiate the use of historical materials for the coding purposes that underlie aggregate data analysis. Instead, it is crucial to point out that the foundation for quantitative analysis must not include inherently inconsistent concept formation.

17. For a discussion of 'rules of prudence' and 'rules of the game' see Craig and George (1990).

18. Examples of these 'unwritten rules' received detailed treatment by Zacher (1992:72): 1. Do not threaten second strike capability of opponent (i.e., support, and seek to enhance, mutual deterrence) – e.g., ABM treaty, 1972); 2. Threaten the use of nuclear weapons only as a last resort – when one's territory (or territory of core allies) is threatened; 3. Avoid direct military conflict with military forces of other great powers; 4. Do not militarily threaten core allies of other great powers; 5. Do not undermine the ability of other great powers to monitor major military activities (i.e., enhance C^3I capabilities); etc.

19. For a comprehensive critique of literature on the 'Long Peace' and an important refinement of the concept of 'global instability,' see Brecher and Wilkenfeld (1991). Mueller (1988) and others claim that nuclear weapons did not sustain the 'Long post-WWII Peace' – they 'neither crucially define[d] a fundamental stability nor threaten[ed] severely to disturb it.' The stable relationship among major powers since 1945 would have developed regardless of the bomb, because the horror associated with even conventional warfare served as the real deterrent. In any case, as Mueller argues, the utility of nuclear weapons cannot be assessed in the absence of nuclear war. There is no way to demonstrate that Intercontinental Ballistic Missiles (ICBMs) actually prevented the Soviets from invading Western Europe or deterred the US from attacking during the Cuban Missile Crisis. Consequently, Mueller's claims regarding the irrelevance of nuclear weapons are as valid (and defensible) as the alternative position that they did contribute to international peace and stability. However, as the present study attempts to demonstrate, it is possible to assess the role of these weapons by focusing on superpower rivalry in crises and by evaluating central propositions underlying the theory.

20. These requirements include (a) maintenance of a standing army and a reliable deterrent force in peacetime; (b) the ability of this force to survive a preemptive first strike; (c) the ability of national leaders to make the decision to retaliate and then transmit this command to the military forces (i.e., a reliable Command, Control, Communication and Intelligence network – C^3I); (d) the ability to penetrate enemy active defenses (e.g., anti-aircraft missiles, interceptors, etc.); and (e) the ability to overcome enemy passive defenses (e.g., bomb shelters, civil defence).

7 Interstate Rivalry and the Study of Militarized Conflict
Paul R. Hensel

The concept of interstate rivalry has recently been used to suggest some new directions for the scientific study of militarized conflict. The scholarly literature on rivalry, which was initiated in the mid-1980s and has only begun in earnest in the past five years, has suggested some important advancements in research on interstate conflict. Even more recently, several scholars have begun to advance this rivalry literature even further by focusing on the evolution of interstate rivalries. Taken together, the concepts of rivalry and evolution have already changed the way that many scholars study interstate conflict, and these concepts are likely to continue to affect the way that conflict is studied for many years to come. The first section of this chapter reviews a number of theoretical contributions that have resulted from the concepts of rivalry and evolution.

The second section of this chapter offers a series of original analyses to assess the empirical contributions of rivalry, by comparing a rivalry-based approach and an evolutionary perspective to the more traditional approaches to interstate conflict. These analyses employ the recently updated Correlates of War (COW) Project data on militarized interstate disputes from 1816 to 1992, which covers sixteen more years than the previous data used by most published studies of rivalry (Goertz and Diehl, 1992b, 1993, 1995a) and includes roughly twice as many militarized disputes. As will be seen, the present chapter's analyses also extend the existing literature by controlling for the effects of the issues at stake between two rivals and the outcomes of their confrontations as well as the history of past conflict between them. These analyses thus offer a number of potential contributions to the existing research on interstate rivalry. This chapter concludes by summarizing the impact of the concepts of rivalry and evolution on research to date, and by suggesting how these concepts can help to shape conflict research in the future.

THE CONCEPT OF RIVALRY

Before examining the contributions of rivalry to the study of interstate conflict, we must consider the meaning of rivalry. A number of scholars have discussed rivalry and related concepts in international relations, including 'enmity' (Finlay, et al., 1967; Feste, 1982), 'protracted conflict' (Azar et al., 1978; Brecher, 1984), and 'enduring rivalry' (Wayman, 1989; Goertz and Diehl, 1992b, 1993; Vasquez, 1993; Bennett, 1993). Each of these concepts refers in the general sense to a long-standing, competitive relationship between two or more adversaries. Drawing from the above scholars' work, enduring rivals can be described as two or more 'actors whose relations are characterized by disagreement or competition over some stakes that are viewed as important, where each perceives that the other poses a significant security threat, and where this competition and threat perception last for substantial periods of time' (Hensel, 1994b:2). Furthermore, enduring rivals are often characterized as being involved in repeated confrontations or crises, which helps to highlight the rivals' disagreement over important stakes and which contributes to each rival's perception of a security threat from the other; 'enduring rivalry' in empirical research has become synonymous with 'enduring militarized rivalry' (Wayman, 1989; Goertz and Diehl, 1993; Hensel, 1996a). Examples of states that are commonly described as enduring rivals include France and Germany through much of the nineteenth and twentieth centuries, the United States and Soviet Union during the Cold War, India and Pakistan since 1947, and Israel and Syria since 1948.

Rivalry can also be considered in a broader and more continuous fashion. Many adversaries do not engage in enough confrontations to build up the history of disagreement or the level of threat perception that characterize full-fledged enduring rivalry. Even if such adversaries never become full enduring rivals, though, some scholars (e.g. Wayman and Jones, 1991; Goertz and Diehl, 1993) consider the possibility of 'lesser' forms of rivalry between non-militarized interstate relations and full enduring rivalry.

Adversaries whose disagreements remain confined to the diplomatic, political, or economic realms are typically described as being involved in 'non-militarized interstate relations' (Hensel, 1996a). Adversaries that turn to militarized means of settling their disagreements begin to risk potential escalation to rivalry, and – depending on the frequency or severity of the militarized conflict between them – can be characterized as 'isolated conflict' (Goertz and Diehl, 1993) or 'short-term militarized rivalry' (Wayman and Jones, 1991). Adversaries that confront each other repeatedly can approach enduring rivalry on one or more dimensions, although not qualifying fully: such dyads have been termed 'proto-rivalry' (Goertz and Diehl, 1993) or 'medium-term militarized rivalry' (Wayman and Jones, 1991).

These lesser forms of conflictual relationships may not be as severe or as protracted as full enduring rivalries, but they highlight the continuous nature of rivalry. 'Isolated conflict' adversaries that never go beyond one or two border incidents certainly appear to differ from enduring rivals that engage in numerous crises and wars, but such adversaries also appear to be very different from those that have no disputed issues at stake or those that always resolve their disputed differences peacefully. Similarly, 'proto-rivals' or 'medium-term militarized rivals' that engage in numerous confrontations over time may not reach the levels of tension or hostility that characterize full enduring rivalry, but such relationships would seem difficult to classify in the same category as 'isolated conflict' or 'non-militarized relations.' From this perspective, the concept of rivalry is best viewed as a continuum, with enduring rivalry at one extreme end of the continuum, non-militarized relations at the other extreme, and these other forms of conflict (or lesser forms of rivalry) in the middle. Although some scholars treat 'interstate rivalry' as synonymous with 'enduring interstate rivalry,' the present chapter employs the term 'rivalry' in a more continuous sense, allowing for different types or levels of rivalry. 'Enduring rivalry' represents the high end of this continuum, and hereafter will specifically be called *enduring* rivalry.

As will be seen later, a continuous conception of rivalry is also central to an evolutionary perspective on interstate rivalry. An evolutionary perspective suggests that even enduring rivals rarely begin by recognizing the protracted, hostile nature of their eventual relationship. Instead, most enduring rivals begin much like other adversaries, and evolve through several lesser phases into full-fledged enduring rivalry (Hensel, 1996a). In the early and intermediate stages of a conflictual relationship, the fact that at least one of the adversaries has resorted to militarized methods marks the relationship as a potential rivalry, although whether or not the adversaries will be able to manage their relationship short of true enduring rivalry will depend on future events. If the two adversaries in such a potential rivalry relationship continue to confront each other over time, their relationship may eventually reach the advanced stage of rivalry, at which point the relationship would be classified as a full enduring rivalry.

Having discussed the conceptual meaning of 'rivalry,' I now consider the theoretical and empirical contributions of this concept to the study of interstate conflict. I begin with the contributions of the rivalry concept, both as a case selection mechanism and as a separate phenomenon to be studied. I then examine recent attempts to broaden the study of rivalry by examining the evolution of rivalry.

CONTRIBUTIONS OF THE RIVALRY CONCEPT

The existing literature about rivalry and the evolution of rivalry has made a number of scholarly contributions. Perhaps most important has been a renewed focus on the context in which interstate interactions take place. As Goertz and Diehl (1996) point out, the notion of rivalry has led to the development of the 'rivalry approach' to war and peace, which focuses scholarly attention on contextual issues that are typically overlooked in traditional research on interstate conflict.

Research on rivalry emphasizes the differences between contexts of enduring rivalry, proto-rivalry, and isolated conflict. Research on the evolution of rivalry further emphasizes the changing context of relations between rivals, highlighting the differences in relations between rivals in the earlier and later phases of their rivalry relationship. In each case, the study of rivalry and evolution has identified contexts or settings in which we would expect to observe different patterns of interstate behaviour or conflict. By leading us to expect different patterns or outcomes in different contexts, the study of rivalry and evolution allows us to generate and test more refined theories, and offers the possibility of more meaningful results than more general studies that do not distinguish between different types of contexts.

In this chapter I distinguish three different uses of the concept of rivalry in recent international conflict research. Perhaps the most common use of the rivalry concept employs rivalry as a case selection mechanism to help in testing other, non-rivalry propositions about interstate conflict. A second use of the concept of rivalry employs rivalry as an independent variable, examining the impact of rivalry on other phenomena to see whether conflict behavior differs across rivalry and non-rivalry contexts. The third use treats rivalry as a dependent variable, examining the processes that lead to the outbreak or evolution of rivalry.

Rivalry as a Case Selection Mechanism

One way that the notion of rivalry has improved the study of conflict involves the use of rivalry to identify populations of cases for use in testing propositions about interstate conflict. Wayman (1989), for example, suggests that rivalries represent a dangerous situation, characterized by strong issue disagreements, mutual suspicion, and repeated militarized conflict. Huth and Russett (1993) further suggest that the frequent confrontations involved in rivalries leave one or both rivals dissatisfied with the prevailing status quo, and leave each rival viewing the other as a primary security threat. This mutual suspicion, threat perception, and history of conflict produce a situation in which each rival is aware of the other's actions and reactions, and in which one or both sides might conceivably initiate militarized conflict in response to threatening moves by the other (see also Goertz and Diehl, 1993).

For the reasons described above, rivalries have been used to test propositions about interstate conflict involving arms races (Diehl, 1985b; Diehl and Kingston, 1987), power transitions (Wayman, 1989; Geller, 1993), and general deterrence (Huth and Russett, 1993; Lieberman, 1994). Propositions on arms races, power transitions, and general deterrence suggest that there is an adversarial component to each of these concepts. Arms races or general deterrence can not take place between states that do not regard each other as adversaries, and power transitions are said to be unlikely to lead to war unless they take place between two states that see each other as threatening. In each case, rivalries would seem to offer an ideal ground for empirical analysis, because rivalries represent the type of adversarial relationships where these relationships are expected to apply.

In this sense, rivalry as a case selection mechanism resembles the notion of 'relevant dyads,' or countries that have potentially serious interests under contention and that possess the force-projection capability to fight over these interests (e.g. Maoz and Russett, 1993; Lemke, 1995). Much like 'relevant dyads,' rivalries in this sense are treated as countries with both disputed issues and the frequently demonstrated capability to confront each other. Furthermore, dyads lacking the history of disputed issues and military confrontations that characterize rivalry are treated as unlikely to engage in conflict in any situation – whether or not an arms race or power transition occurs, and whether or not one state pursues general deterrence policies.

As Huth and Russett (1993) point out, studying general deterrence (or arms races, power transitions, or similar factors) in enduring rivalries may not be able to tell us much about the frequency of deterrence successes, arms races, or power transitions in the entire interstate system, because rivalries make up only a small fraction of the number of dyads in the system. Nonetheless, the characteristics of rivalries discussed above can increase our confidence in our conclusions about these phenomena. If arms races or power transitions do not lead to war in dyads that are marked by a history of conflict and by high levels of mutual suspicion, or if a variable does not affect the likelihood of successful deterrence in such a situation, then we can be reasonably certain that these effects will be even weaker in situations lacking such a background of hostility and suspicion.

Another advantage of using enduring rivalry as a case selection mechanism is that it allows us to examine dynamic questions or longitudinal relationships over the course of a rivalry. Lieberman (1994) demonstrates this by examining the longitudinal record of deterrence in the Israeli–Egyptian rivalry from 1948 to 1979, which includes a number of deterrence breakdowns as well as a number of periods of relative deterrence success and stability. By studying a lengthy period of the same rivalry, Lieberman is able to analyze the effects of changes over time in his independent variables. Beyond studying the static impact of factors such as the balance of forces or the balance of interests between two states, a rivalry-based study allows the study of changes in these factors over time. A rivalry-based study also allows the study of factors or strategies that take effect over time, such as learning or attempts to develop a bargaining reputation. In each of these ways, the use of rivalry to select cases for analysis helps to increase the potential contributions that can result from research.

The results of the above studies have helped to increase our understanding of the conditions under which conflict occurs between rivals, as well as our understanding of the effects of arms races, power transition, and general deterrence. Because of the history of hostility and conflict between enduring rival adversaries, rivalries form an ideal population for testing propositions that previously had been difficult to test empirically. As suggested above, these characteristics of rivalries as a population of cases for analysis can increase our confidence that the scholars' research findings are meaningful and do not result from the inclusion of inappropriate cases. For example, Diehl and Kingston (1987) find that enduring rival adversaries are no more likely to initiate militarized conflict while undergoing either a dyadic arms race or a unilateral military build-up by either side than in the absence of such conditions. If arms races and military build-ups do not seem to lead to the outbreak of conflict between enduring rivals, then it seems even less likely that these factors will lead to conflict between states that do not have the same suspicion or hostility between them as enduring rivals.

Additionally, these analyses offer some implicit lessons about the factors that influence the timing of conflict within ongoing rivalries. Research by Wayman and by Geller, for example, has suggested the importance of power transitions (or 'rapid approaches') for conflict between rivals, similar to Diehl's research on arms races and Huth and Russett's work with general deterrence. Even if such studies are originally intended primarily to test propositions about power transitions, arms races, or deterrence theory – rather than propositions about the timing of conflict within rivalries – their results nonetheless add to our understanding of when rivals are most likely to engage in conflict or war.

Rivalry as an Independent Variable

When used as a case selection mechanism, the concept of rivalry has helped to improve the study of numerous other propositions of interest. Yet we can learn little about the effects or consequences of rivalry when the rivalry concept is only used to identify a set of cases to be studied or to define a particular phenomenon of interest (e.g. by defining arms races as requiring a history of conflict and suspicion between two adversaries). A second application of rivalry in international relations research treats rivalry as a phenomenon of interest in its own right. Research using this latter approach has used rivalry as an independent variable, in order to study the effects of rivalry on such dependent variables as the frequency or escalation levels of conflict.

Research treating rivalry as an independent variable argues that an understanding of the processes of interstate conflict depends on studying the impact of rivalry, beyond the effects of other potential explanatory factors such as arms races or power transitions. For example, Brecher (1984, 1993) argues that prolonged hostility between two adversaries creates deeply rooted mistrust and the mutual anticipation of violent behavior, which is expected to make the crisis behavior of rivals more escalatory than the behavior of non-rival adversaries. Similarly, Bercovitch and Regan (1994) suggest that peaceful conflict management should be more difficult in enduring rivalries, because of the frequency and duration of hostile interactions characterizing rivalry. On the other hand, Brecher (1984) and Brecher and James (1988) suggest that external intervention should be more likely in crises involving protracted conflict than in other crises, because such crises are more likely to be seen as potentially destabilizing to the regional or world system. Similarly, the latter authors expect outside involvement to be more effective in protracted conflict crises than in other crises, partly for the same reasons. When a crisis breaks out between two long-term adversaries, outside actors are expected to take stronger actions to preserve regional or global stability than they would be willing to do for crises in less prominently conflictual or unstable settings. Treating rivalry as an independent variable also allows us to understand the effects of rivalry as a context affecting interstate conflict, by studying whether or not the results of arms races, power transitions, or crisis management differ between rivalry and other types of international contexts.

Goertz and Diehl (1992b) offer one example of research treating rivalry as a phenomenon or an independent variable. The authors examine the frequency of different forms of conflict behavior between enduring rivals, proto-rivals, and isolated conflict adversaries. They find that proto-rivals and enduring rivals account for the vast majority of all modern interstate conflict, with 'isolated conflict' accounting for less than one-fourth of all interstate wars, militarized disputes, and violent territorial changes. Also, the probability of war at some point between two adversaries increases greatly for adversaries in more advanced forms of rivalry, increasing from 6.9 per cent for isolated conflict dyads to 17.6 per cent for proto-rivals, 28.3 per cent for enduring rivals with under ten militarized disputes, and 55.6 per cent for the most advanced enduring rivals.

Beyond the frequency of conflict in different types of rivalry relationships, several scholars have studied the impact of rivalry on crisis behavior and escalation patterns. Brecher (1984, 1993) and Brecher and James (1988) find that crises in protracted conflicts are much more likely than other crises to be triggered by direct violence or non-violent military acts, instead of internal or political triggers. Crises in protracted conflicts are much more likely than other crises to involve threats to greater stakes, such as threats of grave damage or threats to an actor's existence. Protracted conflict crises are much more likely to involve military crisis management techniques and to involve severe levels of violence than crises in other contexts. Crises occurring in protracted conflicts are also more likely than other crises to end in ambiguous outcomes or stalemates, and the actors in protracted conflict crises are much less likely to be satisfied with the crisis outcome than protagonists in other settings.

Several studies have also examined the impact of protracted conflict or rivalry on mediation or intervention by outside actors. Bercovitch and Regan (1994) and Bercovitch and Diehl (1995) find that conflict management attempts are common both in enduring rivalries and in other contexts. Bercovitch and Diehl (1995), for example, find that over half of all enduring rivalries are the subject of conflict management efforts, drawing over forty per cent of all management attempts with an average of more than ten attempts per rivalry. Examining specific actors, Brecher (1984) and Brecher and James (1988) found the United States, the Soviet Union, and the United Nations to be more likely to reach high levels of involvement in protracted conflict crises than in other crises, and roughly half as likely to avoid involvement in such crises altogether.

Despite the frequency of conflict management attempts in rivalries, though, Bercovitch and Diehl find that the world community seems to be ineffective at anticipating serious conflicts or taking early action. Few conflict management attempts take place before the start of militarized competitions in eventual rivalries; conflict management attempts in proto-rivalries and enduring rivalries are generally spread across the entire period of rivalry. Bercovitch and Diehl (1995) also find little difference in the form of conflict management or the identity of actors attempting conflict management between the different types of rivalry. Bercovitch and Regan (1994) find some slight differences, with enduring rivals being somewhat less likely than other adversaries to submit disputes to arbitration and somewhat more likely to engage in direct negotiations and to submit their grievances to international organizations.

Conflict management attempts within enduring rivalries are also less likely to be successful than attempts involving other adversaries, particularly when the adversaries possess roughly equal national capabilities (Bercovitch and Regan, 1994). Somewhat differently, Brecher (1984) and Brecher and James (1988) found the United States, the Soviet Union, and the United Nations to be somewhat more effective contributors to crisis abatement in protracted conflict crises than in other crises. The United States and the United Nations are also somewhat more likely to contribute negatively to conflict resolution, though, in that their involvement is more likely to lead to crisis escalation in protracted conflict crises than in other crises. Bercovitch and Diehl (1995) also find that conflict management attempts within rivalries do not substantially reduce or prevent subsequent conflict between the same adversaries. Although conflict management in enduring rivalries significantly increases the time until the recurrence of militarized conflict between the rivals, future conflict is only postponed by around one year and the likelihood of future conflict remains unchanged.

There is also reason to believe that rivalries or protracted conflicts throughout the world show similar patterns of conflict behavior, but that rivalries and non-rivalry relationships show very different patterns. For example, Brecher and James (1988:452–3) conclude that protracted conflict crises from different regions of the world exhibit nearly identical conflict behavior, while protracted conflict crises differ noticeably from non-protracted conflict crises in either the same region or other regions. Similarly, Wayman (1989) finds that the occurrence of relative power shifts slightly increases the risk of war for non-rivals, but these results are generally weak. Power shifts have a much stronger effect on rival adversaries, though, more than doubling the likelihood of war. The conflictual effects of power shifts thus seem to differ greatly between rivalries and non-rivalry relationships.

The use of rivalry as an independent variable in the studies reviewed above has demonstrated the importance of rivalry and protracted conflict. Rivalry has been found to account for a majority of all interstate conflict behaviour. Militarized disputes and crises in enduring rivalries tend to be more violent and more escalatory than confrontations between non-rival adversaries, from their initial crisis trigger to their eventual termination. Crises occurring within enduring rivalries may be more likely to attract external conflict management efforts, but such efforts are less likely to succeed in a rivalry context than in other types of interstate relationships. As Wayman finds, the impact of additional sources of interstate conflict also seems to be stronger (and more likely to lead to the outbreak of militarized conflict) within enduring rivalries.

On the basis of results such as these, Goertz and Diehl (1992b:161) argue that scholars can not reasonably assume that conflicts are independent of one another. They conclude that interstate conflict behavior is context-dependent, with conflict being more frequent and more severe within enduring rivalries than in isolation or in proto-rivalries. They then suggest (Goertz and Diehl, 1992b:162) that the concept of rivalry is important for the study of interstate conflict, with the rivalry framework being better able than other approaches 'to reflect actual conflict patterns and to allow scholars to understand irregular, but interconnected, conflict over long periods of time.' Similarly, Brecher (1984:292) concludes that crises within protracted conflicts differ along a number of dimensions from crises outside of such an 'environment of cumulative hostility,' and Brecher and James (1988) – as noted above – conclude that there are great differences between the conflict behavior of rivals and non-rival adversaries.

As a result of these studies that employed rivalry as an independent variable, we now have a great deal of evidence that conflict behavior within the context of enduring rivalry differs from conflict behavior in other contexts. Yet we still have little understanding of the reasons for these observed differences. That is, these studies tell us little about the factors that make relationships between enduring rivals more conflict-prone or more escalatory than relations between other types of adversaries. Even if enduring rivalries or protracted conflicts differ from non-protracted conflicts, the studies discussed so far can tell us little about the factors that give rise to these protracted relationships. The next section of this review examines studies that move rivalry from the role of independent variable – or influence on conflict behavior – to that of dependent variable, in order to account for the origins of rivalry and for the observed effects of rivalry.

The Evolutionary Approach: Rivalry as a Dependent Variable

The final approach to rivalry is what Hensel (1994b, 1996a) and Maoz and Mor (1996a, 1996b, 1996c) call the 'evolutionary approach.' Rather than using rivalry as a case selection mechanism or an independent variable, studies from an evolutionary approach examine the origins of rivalry itself. Such studies treat rivalry as a dependent variable, or as a changing phenomenon that we must attempt to explain. Evolutionary studies have focused attention on the interactions or dynamics that can lead to rivalry, as well as the way that relations between two adversaries can change as the result of past events in the rivalry. These studies typically emphasize the changing context of relations across earlier and later phases of the same rivalry, and attempt to account for the movement of certain adversaries to full enduring rivalry while other adversaries resolve their differences much earlier.

Evolution and Conflict Behaviour
Several studies have contributed to an understanding of evolutionary processes by examining the relationships between episodes of interstate conflict, even though these studies did not focus on rivalry explicitly. One such study is Leng's (1983) examination of experiential learning processes in recurrent crises between the same adversaries. Leng (1983) argues that statesmen tend to learn lessons from crisis

outcomes, and that these lessons are especially important if their state becomes involved in a subsequent crisis against the same adversary. Leng's empirical analyses of recurrent crises generally support his hypotheses. In particular, states that obtained unsuccessful outcomes in previous crises tend to shift to more coercive bargaining behavior in later crises with the same adversaries, and five of the six dyads in his study had escalated a crisis to full-scale war at least once by the end of their third crisis.

Similarly, in a study of arms races and escalation that uses enduring rivalry as a case selection mechanism, Diehl (1985b) finds that arms races alone do not substantially increase the escalation of militarized disputes to war between major power enduring rivals. Further analysis reveals, though, that arms races do increase the risk of escalation to war when – among other factors – the adversaries have a history of recent militarized conflict. That is, 19 of the 22 rivalries in Diehl's study engaged in war (in either the presence or absence of an arms race) only after engaging in a number of sub-war militarized disputes. These studies by Leng and by Diehl offer some important evidence of evolution in conflict behavior between adversaries, with previous confrontations appearing to influence subsequent relations between the same adversaries.

Studies of deterrence crises offer further support for an evolutionary conception of interstate rivalry. Huth (1988a), for example, argues that the potential attacker in a deterrence situation can use the defender's behavior in previous crises as a measure of the defender's likely actions in a later crisis. If the defender had backed down in the previous crisis, Huth suggests, its subsequent deterrent threats are likely to be less successful because the defender's behavior in the previous crisis should weaken its credibility. Similarly, if the defender had been intransigent and forced the attacker to back down in the previous crisis, then its subsequent deterrent threats might also be less successful because the potential attacker can not afford to risk further weakening of its own credibility and bargaining reputation. These hypotheses are supported by Huth's empirical analyses: a record of either conciliation or intransigence by the defender decreases the probability of deterrence success in the next deterrence crisis between the same adversaries. Past behavior by the defender in crises against other adversaries does not have a systematic impact on subsequent deterrence crises, though, leading Huth (1988a:81) to conclude that past behavior and reputations are primarily important 'in continuing rivalries between adversaries who have a history of prior confrontations.'

Fearon (1994) offers a broader alternative to Huth's conception of the impact of previous conflict behavior. Rather than focusing on details such as the outcome or escalation level of the previous crisis, Fearon (1994:264) argues that what matters most is simply that the previous crisis occurred. The occurrence of the crisis can be seen as a 'costly signal,' indicating the defender's willingness to resist the challenger – even if the defender ultimately backed down before the previous crisis ended. In subsequent general deterrence situations, when the challenger must decide whether or not to initiate a new crisis, such a signal of the defender's willingness to resist is expected to make general deterrence more successful than if the two adversaries had not been involved in any previous crises. To Fearon, only a highly motivated challenger is likely to initiate a crisis under the expectation that the defender will resist – which he then suggests makes crisis escalation (immediate deterrence failure) more likely. Alternatively, when the challenger expects the defender to prefer concessions to war, then general deterrence is less likely to succeed, but if a crisis begins and the defender makes an (unexpected) immediate deterrent threat then immediate deterrence should be more likely to succeed.

Fearon (1994) finds support for his hypotheses. Much as Huth had suggested, the effect of past crises is strongest when the defender had previously used a bullying or conciliatory strategy. Yet Fearon also finds a weak but negative effect after a crisis in which the defender had used a firm-but-flexible strategy, indicating that all three types of previous defender strategies tend to decrease the likelihood of subsequent deterrence success. Fearon then finds a strong negative result for a combined indicator of any previous deterrence crisis between the adversaries (regardless of the outcome or strategy used in the past crisis). While Fearon's evidence does not rule out a reputational effect based on past crisis behaviour or outcomes, it does support his model. That is, any previous deterrence crisis between the same adversaries seems to increase the likelihood of general deterrence success, while decreasing the likelihood of immediate deterrence success if general deterrence should break down.

Fearon's formal model seems to fit the observed patterns of escalation in recurrent crises, and is compatible with Leng's finding of increasingly coercive crisis behavior in recurrent crises. A number of scholars suggest alternative views of the effect of past conflict on subsequent crisis initiation, though, arguing that past episodes of conflict often make the outbreak of recurrent conflict more likely in their aftermath. For example, Anderson and McKeown (1987) suggest that when a state's decision-makers decide to become involved in interstate conflict, they are not equally likely to choose each country in the interstate system as their target. Instead, Anderson and McKeown (1987:5) argue, governmental attention is focused by prior interaction, with leaders being more likely to target a state with which they had interacted previously – such as a past adversary[1] – than some other, randomly selected state: '*casus belli* do not exist for governments that have not had prior substantial interaction.' They also suggest that states should be especially likely to target a state that is currently the source of conflict and friction, such as a current rival.

Similarly, Maoz (1984) and Hensel (1994a) study the likelihood and timing of recurrent conflict between states that had already been involved in at least one confrontation. Maoz (1984) suggests that conflict can be seen as a turning-point in relations between states, and that the outcome of a confrontation helps to shape the adversaries' subsequent attitudes toward the status quo and their subsequent decisions related to the recurrence of militarized conflict. Hensel (1994a) also suggests that a confrontation can influence subsequent relations between the protagonists both by creating or augmenting tension, hostility and suspicion, and by producing potential changes to the status quo ante.

Both Maoz (1984) and Hensel (1994a) see dispute outcomes as important sources of recurrent conflict. Hensel, for example, suggests that recurrent conflict should be more likely after stalemated outcomes than after decisive outcomes (where one side emerges victorious) or compromises (where the two sides reach a negotiated settlement). In such cases, Hensel (1994a:283) suggests, 'neither side was able to produce the desired changes in the status quo, neither was defeated and rendered unable or unwilling to mount another serious challenge, and no mutually satisfactory settlement was reached to resolve the two sides' differences.' Hensel also examines contentious issues as a potential source of recurrent conflict, arguing that issues that are seen as unimportant are unlikely to produce recurrent conflict regardless of the outcome of a previous crisis, while highly salient issues might be likely to produce recurrent conflict after any outcome because of the importance of the issues.

Empirical analyses have supported many of the above hypotheses on the relationship between past conflict and subsequent relations between the adversaries. Anderson and McKeown (1987), for example, find that militarized conflict behavior is influenced greatly by the history of interaction between states: states with a history of recent militarized conflict are much more likely than other states to become involved in militarized conflict in a given year. Maoz (1984) and Hensel (1994a) also find that former adversaries are likely to become involved in recurrent conflict overall, regardless of the outcome of their past confrontation.

Important differences are found in the likelihood and timing of conflict recurrence, though, particularly with regard to dispute outcomes and issues. Maoz (1984) finds that decisive outcomes and imposed settlements tend to produce longer periods of post-dispute stability without the recurrence of conflict than do tied disputes or formal, mutually agreed settlements. Similarly, Hensel (1994a) finds that both decisive outcomes and negotiated compromises tend to produce greater stability in their aftermath than do stalemated outcomes, particularly when territorial issues are at stake between the former adversaries. Hensel (1994a) also finds that the effects of dispute outcomes and contentious issues on recurrent conflict are strongest when considering recurrent conflict over the same contentious issue(s) as in the previous dispute. That is, decisive and compromise outcomes are much more likely to end conflict over a specific contentious issue than they are to end conflict overall.

Accounting for Evolution
The studies discussed so far have examined processes involved in the recurrence and escalation of conflict, although they have not focused explicitly on interstate rivalry. Several recent studies have begun to study the evolution of recurrence and escalation processes from a more explicit rivalry framework, putting these processes in more of a long-term context. Wayman and Jones (1991) call for an evolutionary approach to the study of rivalry, involving questions such as how rivalries start, how rivalries end, and how we can account for fluctuations in conflict severity during ongoing rivalries. Hensel (1994b, 1995, 1996a) and Maoz and Mor (1996a, 1996b, 1996c) each present an explicit evolutionary framework, treating interstate rivalry as a dynamic relationship that comes into being over time as the result of interactions between two states. Under this evolutionary approach, two states do not begin their relationship with the knowledge that they are long-term enemies. Instead, the relationship between those states changes over time as the result of past actions and future expectations, perhaps evolving towards rivalry if they should continue to engage in confrontations, and perhaps stopping short of rivalry if they can reach a mutually acceptable settlement of their differences. Continued involvement

in crises or wars is seen as likely to build up suspicion, distrust, and hostility, along with grievances and desires for revenge if their confrontations should lead to the loss of life or changes in the status quo ante. If these elements of suspicion, hostility, and grievances accumulate enough over time, then the adversaries' relationship might reach full-fledged rivalry (see especially Hensel, 1996a).

Under such an evolutionary conception of rivalry, two states that eventually reach the level of enduring rivalry must pass through several less severe phases. All interstate adversaries begin their conflictual relationships in the early phase of rivalry, in which the adversaries have turned to militarized means of pursuing their goals at least once. Adversaries in the early phase are distinguished from most other dyads by their demonstrated willingness to threaten or use military force, but they have not yet engaged in a prolonged series of conflicts and – while they are very likely suspicious of each other's motives – have not yet accumulated substantial grievances against each other. If the same adversaries engage in several more confrontations, they can be considered to have reached the intermediate phase of a rivalry relationship. At this point, it is becoming clear to them that their differences are serious, and that neither side is likely to let matters drop peacefully. The continued confrontations between these states also typically exacerbate the tension and suspicion between them, and are likely to have produced serious grievances if any territory has changed hands, lives have been lost, or similar changes have occurred. If the confrontations continue beyond this point, the adversaries eventually reach what is considered the advanced phase of rivalry, which is analogous to the notion of full-fledged enduring rivalry. Once two adversaries reach the advanced phase of rivalry, there is little doubt on either side that they are involved in a protracted, conflictual relationship, and both sides expect the conflict to continue for some time into the future.

Hensel (1995, 1996a) and Maoz and Mor (1996a, 1996b, 1996c) attempt to account for the movement of dyads along this evolutionary path from the early phase through the intermediate and advanced phases to enduring rivalry. As with much of the research discussed above, these scholars argue that previous interactions set the stage for subsequent relations between two states. In particular, past conflicts often set the stage for recurrent conflict. Hensel's (1994b, 1996) evolutionary approach to rivalry differs from the previous studies on temporal linkages between conflicts by incorporating the effects of more than one previous confrontation. That is, the evolutionary approach explicitly studies how relations between two adversaries change (or evolve) over the course of a conflictual relationship. Beyond the effects of past dispute outcomes or escalation levels, then, the evolutionary approach suggests that relations between adversaries will tend to become more conflict-prone and more escalatory later in a rivalry relationship, regardless of the outcome or severity level reached in their single most recent dispute.

Similarly, Maoz and Mor's (1996a, 1996b, 1996c) game theoretic model of the evolution of rivalry allows for learning and preference changes by one or both sides during an ongoing relationship. Two potential rivals can learn from earlier interactions with each other in their model, with each side revising its expectations or beliefs if the opponent's behavior departs from expectations. Preferences can also change due to the outcomes of previous plays of the game: a previously satisfied state can become dissatisfied if it loses in a dispute, and a previously dissatisfied state can become satisfied if it wins.

Goertz and Diehl (1995b) offer an alternative conception of the evolution of rivalry, where rivalry relationships are essentially centered around some 'basic rivalry level' of conflict severity for the dyad. Goertz and Diehl suggest that rival states become 'locked in' to this basic rivalry level at an early point in their relationship, with no secular trend towards more conflictual or more peaceful relations. Except perhaps for short periods at the beginning and ending of rivalries, or perhaps during periods of dramatic political shocks, they argue that relations between rivals fluctuate around this basic level. This conception differs from the evolutionary approach that has been proposed by Wayman and Jones, Hensel, and Maoz and Mor (and that draws from earlier work by Leng, Huth, and others), which suggests that one event or set of events in a relationship directly affects subsequent relations between the adversaries.

With regard to empirical results, Wayman and Jones (1991) find that the likelihood of dispute escalation to war does not change much during ongoing periods of rivalry. They identify 18 wars between rivals in the period of their study, and note that these wars are evenly distributed over time. That is, five of these wars occurred in the first five years of rivalry, followed by either three or four wars for each subsequent five-year period.

Goertz and Diehl (1995b) also fail to identify a single evolutionary pattern of ever-increasing conflict severity in the early development of rivalries. Looking only at dyads that eventually reach full enduring rivalry, they search for patterns in the severity levels of the first three and last three militarized disputes within each rivalry. They find that 26.6 per cent of their rivalries – a 'significant subset of our cases,' although 'far from universally valid' (Goertz and Diehl, 1995b:11) – fit some version of the 'volcano model' (an evolutionary model featuring increasing severity) in terms of dispute severity, and 20 per cent of their rivalries fit this model for dispute duration. A similar number of rivalries exhibit 'wavy' patterns, showing variation but not following a secular trend, and very few rivalries show trends of decreasing severity or duration. Over half of their rivalries, then, show largely flat patterns of dispute severity and duration, offering little evidence of any systematic trends and offering support for a basic rivalry level approach.

Similarly, Hensel (1996a) finds that relations between rivals do not consistently fit a pattern of ever-increasing conflict severity in every dimension studied. For example, there is little systematic difference over time in the tendency for rival states to reach decisive, compromise, or stalemated outcomes in their militarized disputes. Hensel (1996a) also finds little systematic tendency for disputes between rival states to become consistently more escalatory in later rivalry phases. Disputes between proto-rivals become significantly more escalatory between the early and intermediate rivalry phases, but there is little systematic difference in escalation levels for eventual enduring rivals.

On the basis of the above results, it seems clear that not all rivalries show evolution in the sense of ever-increasing conflict severity, at least with the indicators that have been studied so far. More likely, there are probably several different patterns of evolution, each involving different dynamics and having different effects on conflict severity. It may be, for example, that major power rivalries involve different dynamics than do minor power rivalries. It may also be that rivalries involving certain types of issues (perhaps those involving territorial issues) are especially likely to show rapid escalation in their early years and throughout the period of rivalry, while rivalries over less inflammatory stakes may take longer to reach high levels of escalation (if they reach these levels at all).

It may also be that evolution in conflict behavior only takes place under certain circumstances. Leng (1983), for example, suggests that states should be most likely to adopt more coercive strategies after a previous crisis that ended in an unsuccessful outcome. Huth (1988a) suggests that the outcomes and bargaining strategies of previous deterrence crises affect escalation in future crises. Gochman and Leng (1983) and Hensel (1996b) also show that the issues at stake in a given confrontation can exert a great influence on escalation levels. Such studies suggest that a more meaningful analysis of possible evolution in crisis escalation levels must consider the effects of additional factors beyond simply the rivalry phase in which conflict occurs. Even if the current research finds little evidence of evolution in crisis escalation, evolutionary trends may be identified in the aftermath of certain types of dispute outcomes. Also, otherwise strong evolutionary trends may be repressed when highly salient issues like territory are at stake – in which case the rivals may begin at high escalation levels, leaving little room for subsequent change.

We must also consider that evolution may not occur in every dimension of international relations. It is very possible that certain types of behavior may show evidence of evolution, while other types of behavior may show little such evidence or may even show opposite trends. Several studies of dynamics within rivalries support this suggestion. That is, although the evidence presented above suggests that rivals do not show a systematic tendency toward ever-increasing conflict severity, several studies offer evidence that evolution does occur within ongoing rivalries.

Focusing on relations below the threshold of militarized conflict, Hensel (1997) finds that non-militarized interaction between rivals shows evolution in several ways. First, a disaggregated analysis of the conflictual and cooperative dimensions of interstate relations reveals that relations between rivals become both more intensely cooperative and more intensely conflictual in later phases of rivalry. Also, consistent with much of the existing work cited earlier, overall relations between rivals become much more conflictual in later phases of rivalry, from the non-militarized phase and the early phase to the intermediate and advanced rivalry phases. Overall, the increase in conflictual relations thus seems to outweigh the increase in cooperative relations.

Hensel (1996a) also finds evidence of evolution in militarized interaction along the path to rivalry. In particular, two adversaries are more likely to become involved in recurrent conflict after the conclusion of one militarized dispute when they have a longer history of past conflict. Recurrent conflict occurs after around half of all disputes in the early phase of rivalry (54.1 per cent), as compared to 71.1 per cent of all disputes in the intermediate phase of rivalry and 89.0 per cent of all disputes in the advanced phase. The likelihood of experiencing a tenth dispute after the conclusion of the ninth dispute between the same two adversaries is thus much greater than the likelihood of a fourth dispute after the conclusion of a third, which in turn is greater than the likelihood of a second dispute between two adversaries that have just concluded their first confrontation. A longer legacy of conflict thus contributes greatly to the renewal of conflict, making it more difficult over time to resolve the contentious issues, tension, and hostility that separate two adversaries.

Hensel (1996a; Hensel 1997) attempts to account for the evolution of adversaries toward full-fledged enduring rivalry. Several factors identified by previous studies (Maoz, 1984; Hensel, 1994a) are found to affect evolution towards rivalry. As with these previous studies, the recurrence of conflict is much more likely after a dispute that ended in a stalemated outcome than after a dispute that ended in a compromise or decisive outcome. Conflict recurrence is also much more likely after a dispute that involved territorial issues than after a dispute over non-territorial issues. Hensel (1996a) also finds several control variables to be important influences on the recurrence of conflict and thus the evolution of rivalry. Recurrence is much more likely between two adversaries characterized by military parity, for example, and much less likely between two adversaries that are both classified as political democracies.

Supporting the earlier bivariate analyses of rivalry phase and dispute recurrence, Hensel's (1996a) multivariate analyses of dispute recurrence also find rivalry phase to be an especially important influence on the likelihood of recurrence. Thus, even after controlling for the impact of dispute outcomes, contentious issues, military capabilities, and political regime type, dispute recurrence is much more likely in the intermediate and – especially – advanced phases of rivalry than in the early phase. This finding greatly increases our confidence in the earlier bivariate results, which did not take such factors into account. Similarly, the analyses of Hensel (1997) find the same impact of evolutionary rivalry phases on dispute recurrence while considering the effect of non-militarized events, which further adds to our understanding of conflict recurrence. The more conflictual the non-militarized relationship between two states, the more likely those states are to become involved in renewed militarized conflict. Conversely, the more cooperative the basic relationship between two states, the less likely they are to resort to renewed militarized force in pursuit of their goals.

Focusing more on the evolution of perceptions and preferences than on the recurrence of militarized conflict, Maoz and Mor (1996a, 1996b, 1996c) test several propositions derived from their game-theoretic model of the evolution of rivalry. Maoz and Mor (1996a, 1996b) apply their model to the early portions of four rivalries, attempting to identify the rivals' preferences at key points in the rivalry and seeking to trace changes in these preferences over time. They find that conflictual games dominate the early years of the four rivalries being studied. They also find that one or both states' perceptions of the game changed at most of the points where their model had predicted that learning should occur, although half of these changes were not in the expected direction and many changes occurred where their model would not predict any learning (Maoz and Mor, 1996a).[2]

Maoz and Mor's findings offer some suggestions about the early paths taken by states that eventually reach rivalry. The prevalence of conflictual games, especially Deadlock (where both players prefer a conflictual DD outcome to a cooperative CC outcome), suggests that a peaceful resolution of differences is difficult for eventual rivals to reach. Even games with a cooperative CC equilibrium outcome tend to be followed by (or tend to lead to) highly conflictual games. To Maoz and Mor (1996a:156), this indicates that 'in the early stages of rivalries there is a constant motivation to renew the conflict (and with a vengeance), even during periods of relative calm.' Maoz and Mor (1996c) also find statistical support for the implications of their model, with militarized conflict being much more likely when the adversaries' preferences place them in a conflictual game.

In short, there is evidence that conflict behavior does evolve on certain dimensions within ongoing rivalries or potential rivalry relationships. The existing studies in this area, though, are best regarded as preliminary, offering an early overview of a new topic but not resolving their research questions definitively. Goertz and Diehl (1995b), for example, argue that the conflict level between two rivals at any given point in time can be divided into two parts: one determined by the adversaries' basic rivalry level, and one determined by characteristics of the individual disputes or the individual adversaries. Studies such as that of Goertz and Diehl (1995b) focus on the former part, while studies such as those of Hensel (1996a; Hensel 1997) and Maoz and Mor (1996a, 1996b, 1996c) focus on the latter. Future research might profitably try to integrate both parts, and might even attempt to identify the factors that produce the basic rivalry level itself. Goertz and Diehl (1995b), for example, suggest that the disputed issues between two states or the structure of the international system might contribute heavily to this basic rivalry level, although they do not study this issue explicitly.

A final topic related to the evolution of rivalry is the termination of rivalry, which has been addressed by several recent studies. Goertz and Diehl (1995a) see rivalries as continuous, essentially stable interstate relationships, which become deeply ingrained in domestic and international political life. A political shock, or 'a dramatic change in the international system or its subsystems that fundamentally alters the processes, relationships, and expectations that drive nation-state interactions' (Goertz and Diehl, 1995a:31), is seen as virtually necessary to interrupt this stability and end a period of rivalry. Goertz and Diehl identify five types of political shocks at the levels of the interstate system and the nation-state: world wars, periods of widespread global territorial change, periods of rapid change in the global power distribution, newfound state independence, and civil war.

Bennett (1993, 1995) also studies the termination of ongoing rivalries, focusing on political, economic, and security conditions within the rivalry. Bennett (1993) suggests that domestic economic factors, such as a weak domestic economy and a high military burden on the economy, should increase the likelihood of rivalry termination because these factors tend to be difficult to overcome without ending a rivalry. Bennett (1993) also suggests that military threats to one or both of the rivals, such as a threat to one or both from actors outside of the rivalry itself, should increase the likelihood of rivalry termination, because of the incentive to improve a state's military security by resolving at least one of its serious threats. Bennett (1995) focuses on domestic politics within the rivalry, applying the democratic peace proposition to the termination of rivalry. He expects that domestic political change within the rivalry should increase the likelihood of rivalry termination, particularly if the change pushes one or both states toward greater democracy or if it creates a situation where both rivals are political democracies.

Goertz and Diehl (1995a) find that political shocks do seem to be closely related to the process of rivalry termination. Over 90 per cent of the enduring rivalries that had ended within their period of study did so shortly after a political shock. World wars in the interstate system and civil war in one of the rival states seem to have the strongest impact on rivalry termination. Major power rivalries tend to be more sensitive to system-level shocks, while minor power rivalries tend to be more sensitive to shocks at the nation-state level. Furthermore, full enduring rivalries are entrenched more deeply, with proto-rivalries being more vulnerable to disruption by political shocks.

Bennett (1993, 1995) also finds support for several hypotheses on the termination of rivalry. A worsening security situation in one or both rivals is closely associated with the end of rivalries, as is the magnitude of mutual threats facing both rivals (Bennett, 1993). Each rival's domestic economic situation has a weak and inconsistent effect on the likelihood of rivalry termination, as does the salience of issues at stake in the rivalry; high military burdens and high expected war costs seem to have little systematic impact (Bennett, 1993). Polity change in one of the rivals and the level of democracy in the two rivals also seem closely associated with rivalry termination, despite somewhat inconsistent results (Bennett, 1995).

In conclusion, recent research on the recurrence of conflict and the evolution of rivalry has extended our understanding of the sources and consequences of rivalry. Just as the research on rivalry discussed above indicates that the conflict behavior of rivals differs from that of other adversaries, evolutionary studies have shown that conflict behavior is not necessarily constant over time within the same dyad types. Relations between the same adversaries tend to become more conflict-prone over time.

Research using an evolutionary approach has also helped to account for the origins and early development of rivalry. As two adversaries accumulate a history of past conflict, they become increasingly likely to become involved in even more conflict in the future. Evolutionary research has identified some of the factors that contribute to this recurrence of conflict, including the outcomes of past confrontations and the issues at stake. Such research thus helps to account for certain dyads' movement toward rivalry, which offers the possibility of identifying likely enduring rivals and perhaps offering policy prescriptions that can help such adversaries resolve their differences before reaching the most dangerous levels of full-fledged rivalry.

THE IMPORTANCE OF RIVALRY: EMPIRICAL ANALYSES

The remainder of this chapter presents a series of original analyses on the importance of rivalry. These analyses begin with the prominence of rivalry as a context for the occurrence of interstate conflict, in terms of militarized interstate disputes, interstate wars, territorial changes, and international crises. The analyses of the aftermath of conflict then examine the impact of past conflict on the likelihood of future conflict between the former adversaries. The analyses of conflict aftermath involve the evolutionary approach to rivalry, examining how the impact of one confrontation on subsequent relations changes as a rivalry relationship evolves.

As noted earlier, the present study uses a recently updated version of the COW militarized dispute data that covers a longer time period and includes roughly twice as many cases as previous versions of the data set. This study thus allows us to reexamine some of the most important findings from the current published research on rivalry. Similarly, much of the research on protracted conflicts was based on older versions of the International Crisis Behavior (ICB) Project's crisis data. Brecher's (1984) study covered the time through 1975, while Brecher and James (1988) went up to 1979. The present chapter employs a recently updated version of the ICB crisis data that runs through 1988.

Research using the ICB crisis data has also employed the ICB Project's designation of certain cases as protracted conflicts (Brecher, 1993), which does not overlap completely with the COW-based measures of interstate rivalry used by Goertz and Diehl, Maoz and Mor, Hensel, and others. The present chapter merges the ICB crisis data with the COW-based list of interstate rivalries, in order to maximize the consistency of the empirical analyses. Thus, both ICB crises and COW disputes, wars, and territorial changes are studied with the same measure of rivalry, rather than using a COW rivalry measure for some analyses and the ICB protracted conflict indicator for others.

Spatial-Temporal Domain

The analyses presented in this chapter examine the conflict behavior of members of the modern interstate system (Small and Singer, 1982) over the past two centuries. The analyses based on militarized interstate disputes and interstate wars cover the years 1816–1992, using the latest version of the COW militarized dispute data set. Analyses based on the COW territorial change data cover 1816–1980, which is the current temporal limit of that data set. Analyses based on the ICB crisis data set cover 1946–88, which is the domain covered by the dyadic crisis data employed in this chapter (see Diehl, et al., 1996).

Operationalization of Variables

Rivalry
The present study operationalizes rivalry through the occurrence of militarized conflict between two states. A focus on militarized conflict allows us to capture the major theoretical dimensions of rivalry identified in the scholarly literature (Hensel, 1996a; Goertz and Diehl, 1993): regular interaction, competitive relations, threat perception, and a temporal dimension. The occurrence of militarized conflict between two states demonstrates an important degree of both interaction and competition

between them; the adversaries took the risks of a militarized confrontation because they disagreed over something that at least one considered important. Militarized confrontations reflect the existence of hostility and the perception of threat between the adversaries, especially if the same adversaries become involved in multiple disputes over a relatively short period of time.[3] Furthermore, we can see the entrance of the temporal dimension of relations between adversaries as more confrontations occur over time – or the absence of this dimension if no later confrontations follow the first.[4]

Periods of interstate rivalry and evolutionary phases within ongoing rivalries are identified by the occurrence of a sufficient number of COW militarized interstate disputes.[5] Following Goertz and Diehl (1995a), an 'isolated conflict' relationship involves one or two militarized disputes, a proto-rivalry involves three to five disputes, and an enduring rivalry involves six or more disputes. Given these thresholds, though, a temporal cutoff is needed to determine when a period of rivalry ends. After a sufficiently long time elapses after the end of one dispute without the recurrence of militarized conflict, the lack of a subsequent dispute can be taken as evidence that the militarized portion of that particular period of rivalry has ended (even if relations between the former rivals are not necessarily cooperative or friendly). Each rivalry (and each evolutionary rivalry phase) is thus considered to have ended after a 15-year gap with no further disputes (Hensel, 1996a). After such a gap, the dyad returns to the status of 'non-militarized interaction' and any subsequent disputes would mark the beginning of a new period of rivalry. This definition identifies 885 periods of isolated conflict, 195 periods of proto-rivalry, and 103 periods of enduring rivalry between 1816–1992 (ranging from six to 53 disputes per enduring rivalry). Further details on this data set are provided in discussing this study's analyses, and the rivalry data set is discussed in greater length by Hensel (1996a).

In the evolutionary sense, all potential interstate rivalries start in the early rivalry phase, which begins with the outbreak of the first militarized dispute between two adversaries. Once the early phase of rivalry has begun, further militarized disputes between the same adversaries extend the period of rivalry as they occur, and may advance the dyad to the next phase of rivalry.[6] For the purposes of the present study, movement between the different rivalry phases is based on the frequency of militarized conflict. If the dyad eventually engages in three or more militarized disputes, then the dyadic rivalry relationship enters the 'intermediate phase' with the outbreak of the third dispute.

Interstate Rivalry and the Study of Militarized Conflict 187

Finally, if the dyad eventually engages in six or more disputes, then the 'advanced phase' of rivalry begins with the outbreak of the sixth dispute.

As Hensel (1996a) points out, this study's evolutionary conception of early, intermediate, and advanced phases of rivalry is roughly analogous to Goertz and Diehl's (1992b, 1993) contexts of isolated conflict, proto-rivalry, and enduring rivalry, except that the evolutionary approach focuses on changes of context within a given rivalry as the adversaries' relationship evolves over time. A relationship that Goertz and Diehl would classify as 'isolated conflict' never advances past the early stage of rivalry in this evolutionary classification, but more severe forms of rivalry pass through several phases. What Goertz and Diehl classify as a 'proto-rivalry' begins in the early stage of a rivalry relationship, and the remainder of their relationship after the third dispute is classified as occurring in the intermediate rivalry phase. Similarly, a Goertz and Diehl 'enduring rivalry' must spend time in both the early and intermediate phases of the rivalry relationship before the adversaries engage in a sixth dispute and their subsequent relations are classified as the advanced phase.

Interstate Conflict
This study examines the frequency of four different forms of interstate conflict. The first is militarized interstate disputes, as described earlier. The second form of conflict is interstate wars, as identified by the COW Project. Interstate wars are militarized disputes that involve extended combat between the regular armed forces of two or more states, resulting in at least 1000 battle deaths among the participants (Small and Singer, 1982).

The third form of conflict is international crises, as defined and collected by the ICB Project. ICB crises are defined as involving (1) a 'distortion in the type and an increase in the intensity of disruptive interactions between two or more adversaries, with an accompanying high probability of military hostilities, or, during a war an adverse change in military balance, and (2) a challenge to the existing structure of an international system ... posed by the higher than normal conflict interactions' (Wilkenfeld, Brecher, and Moser, 1988:3). In order to study crises in the context of dyadic rivalries (and for consistency with the existing research on rivalry), the ICB crisis data set was broken up into crisis dyads, producing a set of 262 dyadic crisis adversaries in the period 1946–88.[7] I also examine a subset of these cases, violent international crises, which are ICB crises that are classified as involving 'serious clashes' or 'full-scale war' instead of 'no violence' or 'minor clashes.'

The final form of conflict involved in the present study involves territorial changes, as identified by the Correlates of War Project. Territorial changes are defined as the formal transfer of territorial sovereignty between two members of the interstate system. I also examine a sub-class of these exchanges, violent territorial changes, which are territorial changes that involve armed conflict between organized forces of the two participants within one year prior to the transfer (Goertz and Diehl, 1992a). I limit the population of territorial changes in this study to those exchanges involving the transfer of homeland territory between two members of the interstate system, in order to avoid distorting the results by including transfers of colonial territory that may not have the same salience to states as transfers of their own homeland territory.

Conflict Aftermath

This study's analysis of the aftermath of militarized conflict focuses on the recurrence of militarized conflict after a given confrontation. Conflict recurrence refers to whether or not another militarized dispute occurs between the same adversaries in the aftermath of a given dispute. Because it might be misleading to consider two confrontations to be connected, it is necessary to set a temporal limit for the later confrontation to be considered an example of 'recurrent' conflict.[8] Drawing from previous work (Hensel, 1996a) and consistent with the measure of rivalry developed earlier, this limit is set at 15 years, after which any further confrontations are considered to be sufficiently unrelated that they do not represent recurrent conflict.[9]

Previous research (Maoz, 1984; Hensel, 1994a) has shown that the likelihood of recurrent conflict is affected by characteristics of the initial confrontation, particularly the outcome of the confrontation and the issues at stake between the disputants. In order to examine the effects of the evolution of rivalry, this study goes beyond the likelihood of recurrence to see whether evolution also affects patterns of recurrence, in terms of the effects of dispute outcomes or contentious issues on dispute recurrence.

Dispute outcomes are included in the updated version of the Correlates of War militarized dispute data set, and are described briefly by Hensel (1996a). This chapter's analyses compare the effects of three general types of outcomes: decisive outcomes, compromises, and stalemates. A decisive outcome is one in which the dispute had a clear

Table 7.1 Frequency of militarized interstate disputes and wars

Rivalry type	Number of disputes		Number of wars	
Isolated conflict	1078	(35.4%)	186	(54.4%)
Proto-rivalry	709	(23.3%)	73	(21.4%)
Enduring rivalry	1259	(41.3%)	83	(24.3%)
Total	3046		342	

winner and loser, either through a battlefield victory or by the loser backing down or granting concessions without the large-scale use of military force.[10] Compromise outcomes involve mutually acceptable agreements between the adversaries. Stalemated outcomes reflect the absence of either of these forms of settlement – i.e., the dispute ended without either a clear victor or a negotiated compromise.

Contentious issues refer to the stakes over which two or more parties are contending, which can range from territory to specific governmental policies like immigration policy or support for terrorists. It should be noted that any given dispute is not necessarily limited to one type of issue. Thus, the same dispute could involve elements of contention over both territory and one or more governmental policies, as long as each element is under explicit contention in the dispute. Following previous research in this area (Hensel, 1994a, 1996a), the issues at stake in a dispute are coded dichotomously, indicating the presence or absence of explicit contention over some territorial issue(s) in the dispute.

The Frequency of Militarized Conflict

Rivalry and Conflict Frequency
Tables 7.1 to 7.3 summarize the frequency of a number of forms of interstate conflict, broken down by the rivalry status that the adversaries eventually reached (enduring rivalry, proto-rivalry, or only isolated conflict). As Table 7.1 shows, only around one-third of all militarized disputes occur between adversaries involved in isolated conflict. The remaining two-thirds occur between adversaries that would qualify as proto-rivals (23.3 per cent) or enduring rivals (41.3 per cent). Around half of all interstate wars occur between adversaries in isolated conflict, with the remaining half occurring between proto-rivals (21.4 per cent) or enduring rivals (24.3 per cent).

Using a very different data set, Table 7.2 reveals similar patterns in the distribution of international crises, as reported by the ICB Project. About half of all ICB crises (50.4 per cent) occur between eventual

Table 7.2 Frequency of international crises

Rivalry type	Number of crises		Number of violent crises	
Isolated conflict	92	(35.1%)	64	(37.0%)
Proto-rivalry	38	(14.5%)	25	(14.5%)
Enduring rivalry	132	(50.4%)	84	(48.6%)
Total	262		173	

enduring rivals, with barely one-third (35.1 per cent) taking place between isolated conflict adversaries. About half of all violent ICB crises (48.6 per cent) also take place between enduring rivals, with another 14.5 per cent occurring between proto-rivals.

Territorial changes have been less concentrated in the realm of rivalry than either militarized disputes or interstate wars. Table 7.3 shows that 70 per cent of all territorial changes since 1816 have occurred between states involved in isolated conflict (or those that were not involved in any militarized conflict), with only 5.1 per cent occurring between proto-rivals and 25 per cent occurring between enduring rivals. Territorial changes, though, are not necessarily conflictual in nature: many of the changes in the data set involve small transfers of territory as minor border adjustments between friendly states. As a result, it should not be very surprising that the fraction of all territorial changes accounted for by rival adversaries should be so low. Violent territorial changes are much more conflictual by nature, and – not too surprisingly – the fraction occurring between rivals is much higher. Around half of all violent territorial changes have taken place in isolated conflict or conflict-free dyads, with another 8.1 per cent occurring between proto-rivals and 38.7 per cent between enduring rivals.

In examining the frequency of conflict in Tables 7.1 to 7.3 we should remember that rival adversaries represent a very small fraction of all dyads in the interstate system or of all dyads that have been involved in militarized conflict. In the data used for this study, a total of 1183 dyads became involved in at least one militarized dispute between 1816 and 1992, and there were many thousands of possible dyads in the interstate system in the same time frame that could have engaged in conflict. Of these dyads, though, only 195 qualify as proto-rivalries and 103 more reach enduring rivalry status. Rivalry, then, accounts for a disproportionate fraction of all militarized interstate disputes, interstate wars, and violent territorial changes, considering the small number of dyads that qualify as rivals.

Table 7.3 Frequency of homeland territorial changes

Rivalry type	Number of changes		Number of violent changes	
Isolated conflict	305	(70.0%)	59	(53.2%)
Proto-rivalry	22	(5.1%)	9	(8.1%)
Enduring rivalry	109	(25.0%)	43	(38.7%)
Total	436		43	

These results complement the findings of previous research on rivalry. Using an older version of the COW militarized dispute data and a somewhat different definition of rivalry, for example, Goertz and Diehl (1992b) find that rivals account for the majority of all militarized disputes, wars, and violent territorial changes. Between revisions to the previously existing data and the addition of a further 16 years of temporal coverage, the updated militarized dispute data set employed in the present study contains nearly twice as many dyadic disputes as the older data set used by Goertz and Diehl. Despite the large number of changes to the data set, though, this study's results closely follow those of Goertz and Diehl, which helps to increase our confidence in the results of both studies.

This confidence level is increased even further by the finding that ICB crises and COW territorial changes produce results that are very similar to COW militarized disputes and wars. It may seem unsurprising that a large fraction of all militarized disputes occur between enduring rivals, because the frequency of disputes is a central component in most empirical definitions of rivalry. Yet only 103 dyadic relationships qualify as enduring rivals under the present study's definition, out of tens of thousands of dyads in the history of the interstate system. Considering that only 103 dyads out of tens of thousands account for such a large proportion of interstate conflict over the past two centuries, these results do appear to make a meaningful statement about the importance of rivalry. Furthermore, ICB crises and COW territorial changes represent very different forms of interstate interaction that were collected for very different purposes than the militarized dispute data, and that are not represented in this study's measure of rivalry. The similarity in patterns of militarized dispute, war, crisis, and territorial change involvement suggests that the importance of rivalry goes well beyond the possibility of tautology due to a dispute-based definition.

Evolution and Conflict Frequency

Tables 7.4 to 7.6 reexamine the frequency of conflict through evolutionary lenses. In order to give a meaningful depiction of how conflict behavior in the same set of dyads changes over time, these tables are limited to the 103 dyads that eventually reached the status of enduring rivalry. These tables thus show the conflict behavior of these 103 enduring rival dyads in all three evolutionary phases, allowing us to compare how their conflict behavior changed as they evolved through the different phases of rivalry.[11]

For all six forms of conflict, the majority of events occurred in the advanced phase of rivalry. That is, enduring rivals engaged in 59.1 per cent of all of their militarized disputes, 57.8 per cent of their wars, 53.0 per cent of their international crises, 48.8 per cent of their violent international crises, 50.5 per cent of their territorial changes, and 51.2 per cent of their violent territorial changes in the advanced phase of their rivalries. The remaining events were generally split evenly between the early and intermediate phases. Just as many cases of interstate conflict in general occur between eventual rival adversaries, most cases of conflict between these eventual rival adversaries occur after they have already reached the advanced phase of rivalry and qualified as enduring rivals. As before, this finding is especially meaningful because five of the six types of conflict were not used in identifying the time frame for each rivalry phase.

The results presented in Tables 7.4 to 7.6 suggest that the evolution of rivalry is an important topic to study. The definition of rivalry used in the present chapter does not include any requirement about the frequency of conflict between two adversaries once they reach the advanced phase and qualify as full-fledged enduring rivals; an enduring rivalry could end after the sixth dispute or could go on through dozens of additional confrontations. Yet once the enduring rivals studied in Tables 7.4 to 7.6 reached the advanced phase, they typically continued to engage in frequent episodes of conflict, with more disputes, wars, and territorial changes occurring in the advanced phase itself than in the early and intermediate phases combined. In fact, only 25 of the enduring rivalries in the present study stopped after six disputes, with 39 going on to become involved in at least twenty militarized disputes each (up to a maximum of 53 disputes).

Particularly in light of earlier research on escalation patterns in recurrent crises, this frequency of conflict in the advanced phase of rivalry seems especially dangerous and worthy of further study. As noted earlier, Leng (1983) found a tendency for bargaining strategies to be-

Table 7.4 Frequency of militarized interstate disputes and wars in enduring rivalries

Rivalry phase	Number of disputes		Number of wars	
Early phase	206	(16.4%)	19	(22.9%)
Intermediate phase	309	(24.5%)	16	(19.3%)
Advanced phase	744	(59.1%)	48	(57.8%)
Total	1259		83	

Table 7.5 Frequency of international crises in enduring rivalries

Rivalry phase	Number of crises		Number of violent crises	
Early phase	30	(22.7%)	26	(31.0%)
Intermediate phase	32	(24.2%)	17	(20.2%)
Advanced phase	70	(53.0%)	41	(48.8%)
Total	132		84	

Table 7.6 Frequency of homeland territorial changes in enduring rivalries

Rivalry type	Number of changes		Number of violent changes	
Early phase	29	(26.6%)	11	(25.6%)
Intermediate phase	25	(22.9%)	10	(23.3%)
Advanced phase	55	(50.5%)	22	(51.2%)
Total	109		43	

come increasingly coercive and war-prone in recurrent crises between the same adversaries, and Diehl (1985b) found that arms races were only likely to lead to war between previous adversaries with histories of recent conflict. By the advanced phase of rivalry, a given pair of adversaries has engaged in a number of previous confrontations, and the observed tendency toward more coercive or escalatory crisis-bargaining in recurrent crises suggests that it is even more important for policy-makers and academics to prevent the occurrence of further, potentially dangerous confrontations in the future. The next section of this chapter examines this likelihood of renewed confrontation, in order to explore whether or not the evolutionary phase of rivalry affects relations between two adversaries in the aftermath of a militarized confrontation.

Table 7.7 Militarized dispute recurrence

Rivalry type	Followed by recurrent dispute		Last dispute in rivalry	Total
Early phase	789	(47.1%)	885	1674
Intermediate phase	433	(68.9%)	195	628
Advanced phase	641	(86.2%)	103	744
Total	1863	(61.2%)	1183	3046

$X^2 = 350.40$ (2 d.f., $p < .001$)

The Aftermath of Militarized Conflict

Evolution and Militarized Conflict Recurrence
The remaining analyses examine the recurrence of militarized conflict in the aftermath of a given confrontation. Table 7.7 examines the impact of a given dyad's evolutionary rivalry status on the likelihood of dispute recurrence between the same adversaries within 15 years. As noted earlier, this table (and the subsequent tables on conflict recurrence) includes all conflictual dyads in the present study, rather than simply those that would eventually qualify as enduring rivalries. The results presented in Table 7.7 indicate that the likelihood of conflict recurrence increases greatly across the three rivalry phases. Of the 1674 militarized disputes that occurred in the early phase of rivalry, 789 (47.1 per cent) were soon followed by another dispute between the same adversaries. This figure increased to 433 of 628 (68.9 per cent) for disputes in the intermediate phase of rivalry, and to 641 of 744 (86.2 per cent) for disputes in the advanced phase.[12] Beyond the substantive or theoretical significance of this trend, the results presented in Table 7.7 are also highly statistically significant ($X^2 = 350.40$, 2 d.f., $p < .001$).[13]

Tables 7.8 and 7.9 examine the impact of evolution on the bivariate relationships between dispute outcomes or contentious issues and conflict recurrence. Earlier research (Hensel, 1994a) has found both outcomes and issues to have a substantial impact on the likelihood of conflict recurrence, although that earlier work did not consider the impact of the rivalry context between two adversaries at the time of their previous dispute. The results presented in these two tables indicate that the effects of both outcomes and issues change substantially from one rivalry phase to the next. Although important differences remain between different types of dispute outcomes or different types of contentious issues, the overall likelihood of recurrent conflict increases as

Table 7.8 Dispute outcomes and militarized dispute recurrence

A. Decisive Outcomes

Rivalry type	Followed by recurrent dispute		Last dispute in rivalry	Total
Early phase	121	(28.9%)	298	419
Intermediate phase	62	(54.4%)	52	114
Advanced phase	89	(85.6%)	15	104
Total	272	(42.7%)	365	637

$X^2 = 117.22$ (2 d.f., $p < .001$)

B. Compromise Outcomes

Rivalry type	Followed by recurrent dispute		Last dispute in rivalry	Total
Early phase	56	(49.6%)	57	113
Intermediate phase	35	(77.8%)	10	45
Advanced phase	22	(75.9%)	7	29
Total	113	(60.4%)	74	187

$X^2 = 14.14$ (2 d.f., $p < .001$)

C. Stalemate Outcomes

Rivalry type	Followed by recurrent dispute		Last dispute in rivalry	Total
Early phase	465	(58.3%)	333	798
Intermediate phase	276	(73.0%)	102	378
Advanced phase	435	(86.3%)	69	504
Total	1176	(70.0%)	504	1680

$X^2 = 117.76$ (2 d.f., $p < .001$)

rivalry evolves, regardless of the issues at stake in the dispute or the type of outcome that was reached.

Recurrent conflict becomes much more likely to occur in later rivalry phases, regardless of the type of dispute outcome or contentious issues that were involved in the previous confrontation. As Table 7.8 reveals, the likelihood of recurrent conflict increases by about 30 to 40 per cent for each outcome type between the early and advanced rivalry phases. Even compromise outcomes – the least likely to be followed by recurrent conflict – are followed by another dispute 75.9 per cent of the time in the advanced phase. Similarly, Table 7.9 reveals corresponding increases in the likelihood of recurrent conflict in later rivalry phases, regardless of the types of issues at stake in an earlier confrontation. Each of these increases is highly statistically

Table 7.9 Contentious issues and militarized dispute recurrence

A. Territorial Issues

Rivalry type	Followed by recurrent dispute		Last dispute in rivalry	Total
Early phase	208	(55.8%)	165	373
Intermediate phase	121	(77.6%)	35	156
Advanced phase	240	(89.9%)	27	267
Total	569	(71.5%)	227	796

$X^2 = 92.41$ (2 d.f., $p < .001$)

B. Non-Territorial Issues

Rivalry type	Followed by recurrent dispute		Last dispute in rivalry	Total
Early phase	581	(44.7%)	720	1301
Intermediate phase	312	(66.1%)	160	472
Advanced phase	401	(84.1%)	76	477
Total	1294	(57.5%)	956	2250

$X^2 = 239.87$ (2 d.f., $p < .001$)

significant at the .001 level, indicating that the differences revealed in these tables are much greater than we would expect by chance alone if there were no relationship between rivalry phase and dispute recurrence. In fact, both Tables 7.8 and 7.9 show that the least conflict-prone outcome or issue type in one rivalry phase is more likely to be followed by recurrent conflict than the most conflict-prone outcome or issue type in the previous phase. For example, 58.3 per cent of stalemates in the early phase of rivalry were followed by recurrent conflict, but by the advanced phase all three outcome types were more likely to lead to further conflict (ranging from 68.9 per cent for decisive outcomes to 77.8 per cent for compromises).

Together, Tables 7.7 to 7.9 show a clear impact of rivalry phase on dispute recurrence, which offers strong evidence in favour of evolution in rivalry and conflict behaviour. As two adversaries accumulate a longer history of confrontation, they become much more likely to engage in renewed conflict in the immediate future. In other words, conflict begets conflict, and adversaries that are not careful to resolve their differences early face a great risk of becoming trapped in a protracted string of conflict.

Table 7.10 Logistic regression analysis of militarized dispute recurrence

Variable	Est.	(S.E.)	X^2	(p)	Odds ratio
Intercept	0.13	(0.07)	3.78	(.05)	–
Intermediate phase	0.82	(0.11)	54.13	(.001)	2.276
Advanced phase	1.69	(0.13)	171.91	(.001)	5.422
Decisive outcome	−1.10	(0.10)	110.60	(.001)	0.334
Compromise outcome	−0.34	(0.17)	4.13	(.04)	0.711
Territorial issues	0.64	(0.11)	36.49	(.001)	1.906

N: 2504
Log likelihood (null model): 3317.17
Log likelihood (full model): 2890.94
Improvement: 426.23
Significance: $p < .001$ (5 d.f.)

Logistic Regression Analysis of Militarized Conflict Recurrence
Table 7.10 presents the results of a logistic regression analysis of militarized dispute recurrence, incorporating the effects of dispute outcomes and contentious issues in a multivariate model along with the evolutionary rivalry phase indicators.[14] The model as a whole fits the data very well, producing a highly significant improvement over a baseline model ($X^2 = 426.23$, 5 d.f., $p < .001$). With regard to the individual covariates being studied, the model produces positive and highly significant coefficients for both the intermediate ($X^2 = 54.13$, $p < .001$) and advanced phases of rivalry ($X^2 = 171.91$, $p < .001$). Recurrence is thus much more likely in each of these phases than in the early phase of rivalry. The control variables in the model also produce the expected effects. Dispute recurrence is significant less likely after disputes that ended in a decisive outcome ($X^2 = 110.60$, $p < .001$) or a compromise ($X^2 = 4.13$, $p < .04$), and significant more likely when territorial issues are at stake ($X^2 = 36.49$, $p < .001$).

Beyond statistical significance, the odds ratio column in Table 7.10 allows us to evaluate the practical or substantive significance of each element of the model.[15] The odds ratio (OR) values in Table 7.10 reveal that the different variables included in this model all carry great substantive significance. The odds of militarized dispute recurrence are over twice as great (OR = 2.276) after a dispute in the intermediate phase and over five times as great (OR = 5.422) after a dispute in the advanced phase of rivalry, even when controlling for the impact of dispute outcomes and territorial issues. The odds of dispute recurrence are nearly twice as great (OR = 1.906) when territorial issues were involved in the dispute. Furthermore, the odds are one-third as great (OR = 0.334) after a dispute that ended in a decisive outcome and are somewhat lower (OR = 0.711) after a compromise outcome.

Another way to evaluate the impact of variables or combinations of variables is to examine their marginal impact on the expected probability of the dependent variable, while holding all other variables in the model to their mean values or to some theoretically meaningful values. If all other variables are held to their means, then a dispute in the intermediate phase of rivalry increases the expected probability of dispute recurrence from 0.60 to 0.78, and a dispute in the advanced phase increases the expected probability from 0.55 to 0.87. Both of these changes are substantial, and help to demonstrate the impact of rivalry phase on two states' conflict behavior. The overall expected probability of dispute recurrence in this model is 0.65, but this probability varies widely with rivalry phase and the control variables included in the model. Thus, a dispute in the early phase of rivalry that involved non-territorial issues and ended in a decisive outcome is much less likely to be followed by another dispute, with a probability of 0.28 that recurrent conflict will erupt. After a dispute in the advanced phase of rivalry over territorial issues that ended in stalemate, though, this probability rises to 0.92 – a virtual certainty that future conflict will arise.

Taken together, the results presented in Table 7.10 offer strong evidence of the importance of rivalry in processes of conflict recurrence. Dispute outcomes and territorial issues continue to have a strong impact on recurrent conflict, as in previous studies. Even after controlling for their effects, though, the evidence presented in this table reveals that the rivalry context in which a confrontation occurs has a large effect on subsequent relations between the adversaries. Recurrence is much more likely between two adversaries who have reached the intermediate phase of rivalry, and even more likely between adversaries in the advanced phase.

CONCLUSIONS

This chapter's empirical results, along with the earlier discussion of the contributions of existing research in this area, offer a number of implications for future research. Many current studies of rivalry, particularly those on the evolution of rivalry, have suggested promising new paths of research to follow up on their findings. This chapter concludes by summarizing the previous research on rivalry and the empirical analyses presented herein, and by suggesting some new directions for research related to rivalry.

The first half of this chapter reviewed current research on interstate rivalry, organized by three different uses of the rivalry concept. Research using rivalry as a case selection mechanism has shown the value of the rivalry concept in testing other propositions about interstate conflict. Research employing rivalry as an independent variable has shown that conflict behavior differs along a number of dimensions between rivals and non-rival adversaries. Research using rivalry as a dependent variable has shown that conflict behavior changes over time along many dimensions as rivalry evolves, particularly with respect to the aftermath of conflict and the likelihood or timing of future conflict between the same adversaries.

The empirical analyses presented in the second half of the chapter support and extend many of these previous research findings discussed above. Rival adversaries are found to account for a highly disproportionate fraction of all interstate conflict, given the small number of rivalries in the modern interstate system and the large number of confrontations between them. This finding holds across six different measures of interstate conflict, including both peaceful and violent exchanges of territory, militarized disputes, both low-level and violent international crises, and full-fledged interstate wars. This finding remains equally impressive when rivalry is considered from an evolutionary perspective. The majority of each of the six forms of conflict occurs after two adversaries have reached the advanced phase of interstate rivalry, although only one of these six measures is actually used to define the different phases of rivalry.

Analysis of conflict aftermath shows even stronger results for the importance of an evolutionary approach to rivalry. The likelihood of conflict recurrence increases dramatically in each subsequent rivalry phase, both overall and after each individual type of outcome or contentious issue examined. A logistic regression analysis also showed similar results while controlling for both past dispute outcomes and contentious issues, with the statistical odds of recurrence in a given year more than doubling in the intermediate phase and being over five times greater in the advanced phase of rivalry. Clearly, then, the aftermath of conflict behavior between two adversaries shows important signs of evolution over time as their rivalry continues.

The review and analyses presented in this chapter suggest a number of new directions for future research. The use of rivalry as a case selection mechanism has aided in the analysis of a number of concepts such as arms races, power transitions, and general deterrence. Future research on each of these topics could benefit from an extension of the domain of cases studied, in order to determine the extent to which the results depend on the use of rivalry to identify cases for analysis. Wayman (1989), for example, found that the effects of capability shifts or rapid approaches were only statistically significant for rivalries, with much weaker results when the same tests were run on a population of non-rival adversaries. Our understanding of these topics, and our confidence in the empirical results, should be much greater upon determining the extent to which each proposition holds for non-rival adversaries as well as for rivalries.

Studies using rivalry as a case selection mechanism could also be improved by considering the evolution of rivalry. If arms races, power transitions, and similar concepts are argued to have their strongest effects on conflict behavior between enduring rivals, then their effects might be expected to change over time as rivalry evolves. According to the evolutionary approach to rivalry proposed by Hensel and by Maoz and Mor, enduring rivals do not recognize each other as long-term rivals until a number of crises have occurred between them, and after they have accumulated substantial levels of suspicion, tension, or grievances because of this history of conflict. Empirical relationships depending on a history of rivalry might thus be expected to begin with weak results in the early phase of rivalry, becoming stronger in later phases of the relationship. Research using rivalry as a case selection mechanism would do well to consider this possibility.

Studies using rivalry as an independent variable have shown that rivalries differ from non-rivalry relationships along many dimensions of conflict behavior. Studies using rivalry as a dependent variable have also shown that conflict behavior changes over time within ongoing rivalries as the relationships between rivals evolve. Empirical studies of both types have generally been preliminary, though, and have typically been more concerned with identifying differences between different types of dyads or different phases of rivalry than with accounting for these differences.

Studies using rivalry as either a dependent variable or an independent variable could benefit from a more sophisticated analysis to help account for the observed differences. Empirical analyses of conflict recurrence and rivalry evolution have attempted to account for the recurrence of militarized conflict with dispute outcomes, contentious issues, relative capabilities, political regime types, and other variables as well as the evolutionary rivalry phase (e.g. Hensel, 1996a). Yet analyses of conflict escalation have focused primarily on the type of rivalry relationship or the evolutionary rivalry phase, without much consideration of other factors affecting escalation behavior. Future research should examine such factors as well as rivalry type or rivalry phase, in order to see whether the largely bivariate relationships observed so far change in more sophisticated analyses.

Additional factors should also be examined in future research on rivalry. Nincic (1989) and Vasquez (1993), among others, discuss at great length the importance of domestic political factors in establishing and maintaining interstate rivalries. With the exception of political regime type, though, domestic factors have been overlooked in most current research on rivalry. Hensel (1996a), for example, did not examine any domestic factors besides regime type in his statistical analyses of rivalry, but after examining several case studies of rivalry Hensel (1996a) concludes that domestic factors seem to have helped to prolong or exacerbate the rivalries being studied. Several potentially important domestic factors that might profitably be examined in future research on rivalry includes public opinion, domestic economic conditions, or societal militarization (e.g. Holsti, 1992; Russett, 1990; Bremer, 1992).

Similarly, research on topics such as external conflict management, political shocks, and the growth of external threats to one or both rivals has typically been conducted separately, in isolation from the evolutionary analyses discussed above. Future research on rivalry – and particularly future research attempting to account for the evolution of rivalry – could benefit from an effort to integrate these previously separate strands of research. If dispute outcomes, contentious issues, conflict management attempts, political shocks, and external military threats are all important individually, then we could presumably learn even more about rivalry from studying them in combination.

In conclusion, this chapter has reviewed the existing literature on interstate rivalry, and has supplemented this review with original analyses on rivalry. Rivalry has been found to make many contributions to the study of interstate conflict, from improving research designs (when used as a case selection mechanism) to improving our understanding of the connections between recurrent confrontations (when used as an independent variable). Nonetheless, the study of rivalry is still a relatively new topic, and much remains to be done. Throughout the text, and particularly in the concluding remarks, I have suggested a number of ways that future research can make continued improvements.

NOTES

1. Anderson and McKeown also investigated the possibility that subsequent conflict would be more likely between states that had prior interaction of either a cooperative or conflictual nature. For the purposes of this chapter, I focus on conflictual interactions, because of the similarity of this approach to the notions of rivalry and of evolution.
2. Many of the unexpected or unpredicted changes occur in the presence of exogenous changes in one or both rivals, particularly changes in capabilities resulting from wars, foreign military aid, or domestic politics.
3. A single militarized confrontation is obviously an insufficient basis for a full-fledged enduring rivalry relationship. In the continuous view of rivalry employed in this study, though, the outbreak of militarized conflict between two states represents an important break from non-militarized relations between states (as mentioned earlier), and can be seen as moving the adversaries along the rivalry continuum toward the extreme of enduring rivalry.
4. Some scholars (e.g. Thompson, 1995) have called for a more detailed measure of rivalry, possibly incorporating some explicit identification of each side's perceptions of the other as a primary security threat or a 'principal rival.' Nonetheless, such a measure would make the study of more than a few rivalries an unmanageable task, and an operational measure based on dispute involvement – such as has been used in the existing systematic research on rivalry – is sufficient for the purposes of the present study.
5. A militarized interstate dispute is defined as a set of overt, explicit, non-accidental, and government-sanctioned incidents involving the threat, display, or use of military force between two or more states (Gochman and Maoz, 1984).
6. The present study treats all militarized disputes as equivalent for identifying rivalries or phases of rivalry. This is consistent with much of the published research on rivalry (Gochman and Maoz, 1984; Goertz and Diehl, 1992b, 1993, 1995a). It could be argued, though, that some disputes have a greater impact than others. A full-scale interstate war, for example, might be expected to produce a greater long-term impact on relations between the protagonists than might a minor border incident. To maximize consistency with the previous published research relevant to this study's analyses (Goertz and Diehl, 1992b; Maoz, 1984; Hensel, 1994a), the present study continues treating each dispute as equivalent for the purposes of identifying rivalries. Future research, though, could certainly benefit from a closer examination and reconsideration of this approach, perhaps weighting the impact of each dispute by some severity criterion or requiring disputes to reach a certain severity threshold before counting toward a dyad's rivalry status.
7. For more details see Diehl, et al. (1996).
8. It might be argued that recurrent conflict can only meaningfully be studied in terms of contentious issues. Hensel (1994a), for example, examined both recurrent conflict overall and recurrent conflict over the same contentious issues that were involved in a previous dispute. Viewed from a rivalry perspective, though, issue consistency does not seem to be a vital

condition for two disputes to be considered 'connected' to each other. Goertz and Diehl (1993) note that a given rivalry can involve numerous contentious issues, and that the specific issues at stake in a given rivalry can change over time. Even if the Cuban Missile Crisis and the various Berlin crises during the Cold War technically involved separate issues and separate geographic locations, it would be difficult to argue that these crises were not related to each other. Future researchers, of course, can always attempt to identify the specific issues involved in each dispute for the purpose of studying issue consistency. For the purposes of the present study, though, issue consistency is left to future research and is not considered theoretically vital to the study of recurrent conflict in evolving rivalries.
9. Fifteen years is a common threshold in empirical definitions of rivalry. If a gap of more than 15 years elapses without the recurrence of militarized conflict, many definitions of rivalry would consider the rivalry in question to have ended (Goertz and Diehl, 1992b, 1993). Yet because this figure of 15 years may appear somewhat arbitrary, further analyses were run with 20- and 25-year thresholds for the ending of rivalry, as well as with no threshold (leaving an unlimited temporal horizon). These alternative thresholds did not produce any substantially different results.
10. This 'decisive' category is produced by combining four separate outcome types from the dispute data set: victory by side A, victory by side B, yield by A, and yield by B. These categories are combined because I have no good theoretical reason to distinguish between these different forms of decisive outcomes. Furthermore, keeping them separate would leave many of the analyses with an insufficient number of cases to allow meaningful interpretation of the results.
11. Hensel (1996a) presented similar evolutionary analyses for all of the dyads in the dispute data set, rather than just those that eventually qualified as enduring rivals; the results did not change substantially.
12. Some readers might question the treatment of all dyads as equivalent in Tables 7.7 through 7.10, regardless of their eventual rivalry status. That is, if a given dyad's period of conflict ended after one or two disputes, it could be argued that the dyad should not be considered to have been in the early phase of rivalry (since there were no later rivalry phases in that dyadic relationship). When viewed in an evolutionary sense, though, this decision appears reasonable. Under an evolutionary approach to rivalry, two states do not know with certainty what their eventual rivalry status will be. Thus, in the first two disputes in a given dyad (i.e., the early phase of rivalry), the potential rivals do not know whether their conflictual relationship will end or whether it will continue on to the intermediate or advanced phase. As a result, it appears reasonable to study all dyads that have engaged in one dispute to see whether they become involved in a second, or to study all dyads that have engaged in four disputes to see whether they become involved in a fifth.
13. The chi-square (χ^2) statistic indicates the statistical significance of the relationship between rivalry phase and recurrence, or the likelihood that the distribution of cases in the table could have arisen by chance if the variables are statistically independent (Reynolds, 1984; Phillips, 1992).

14. Logistic regression (or logit analysis) is appropriate for studying discrete dependent variables, such as the outbreak or avoidance of recurrent conflict, which cause problems for traditional methods such as OLS regression (Aldrich and Nelson, 1984; Liao, 1994).
15. The odds ratio presents the ratio of the statistical odds of a certain dependent variable, given a certain value of the independent variable. An odds ratio of 1.0 would tell us that the odds of recurrence after a dispute in the advanced phase, for example, are identical to the odds of dispute recurrence after a dispute in either of the earlier rivalry phases. Odds ratios above 1.0 indicate how much greater are the odds of dispute recurrence when the independent variable is present, while odds ratios below 1.0 indicate how much lower are the odds of dispute recurrence in the presence of the independent variable (Liao, 1994).

Part Three
War and Peace

8 The Steps to War in Europe, 1933–41
John A. Vasquez

The scientific study of peace and war has generated a number of important empirical findings over the past thirty years about the onset and expansion of war. With the exception of the First World War (see for example Holsti, North and Brody, 1968; Zinnes, Zinnes and McClure, 1972; and Choucri and North, 1975), not much attention has been devoted to individual wars. The main reason for this is that a search for general patterns cannot be conducted except by a comparison of a large number of cases. As findings have accumulated, however, and attempts have been made to move from the identification of the correlates of war to the weaving of theoretical explanations, a new challenge has arisen for the scientific approach: can its theory and research tell us anything new and interesting about well-known wars? In particular, can its theory and research be utilized to develop a scientific explanation of specific wars? One of the new directions that scientific peace research has begun to take is to confront its findings and hypotheses with what we know about individual wars. This new theoretical conversation between history and peace research has a potential to enrich and stimulate both disciplines.

In order for such a conversation to live up to its potential, more thought has to be given within international relations to whether and how we can explain well-known wars scientifically, and precisely what that would mean and entail. In the physical sciences, particular events are explained all the time. Hempel (1966:51) argues that scientific explanation of individual events involves applying a 'covering law.' While Hempel has been challenged on various grounds (e.g. Ringer, 1989), his notion that scientific explanation involves applying a general theory of the class of events to a specific event in history is the obvious place to start.

One of the functions of good theory is that it should be able to account for the fundamental and often underlying causes of specific cases, such as individual wars.[1] Since causal inferences can logically only be made by comparing across cases, a general theory of war that has been tested and corroborated provides the most assurance that the explanation is actually distinguishing fundamental causes from idiosyncratic factors that may be coincidental. It is the promise of creating just such a general explanation that separates social science from history. To explain a war scientifically entails: (1) seeing if the war fits a pattern (i.e. a postulated causal sequence or path) known to bring about war, and (2) tracing out how that pattern brought about the war. Such an explanation, if properly conducted in light of the historical record, should offer a plausible account of both why and how the war came about. At the same time, it should be able to show how this war is typical of the wars of its class or in what ways it deviates significantly.

This analysis will attempt to offer a new scientific explanation of the Second World War.[2] Explaining this war scientifically will be done by first seeing whether the Second World War follows the common theoretical pattern that a war of this type would be expected to evince. The scientific study of peace and war has produced a critical mass of findings so that it is now in a position to begin at least to tackle this goal. Attempts to see whether individual wars follow theoretically predicted patterns should tell us something about the adequacy of our theory and research, as well as perhaps provide new insights about what of the welter of events associated with a particular war are really of theoretical significance.

The second way to explain a war scientifically is to show how the various correlates that make up a general pattern bring about the war in terms of a causal sequence. This entails showing not only how each step toward war increased the probability of war, but also tracing out within the case how the step caused (or brought) the parties to come closer to war. Explaining war along these lines is much more challenging for the field given the current state of empirical knowledge, so only a preliminary attempt will be made to explain the Second World War in this manner. Nevertheless, efforts along these lines are useful because they highlight those areas where we may need to learn more about how the general factors interact with each other. In addition, trying to think about how a factor that increases the probability of war actually produces a sequence of action that causes (or results in) war in a specific historical instance aids the theory-building process.

The above discussion should make it clear that the purpose of this chapter is explanation and not testing. Likewise, it is not a case study in the classic sense, in that its purpose is not to examine the Second World War, inductively, in the hopes of identifying causes, but to explain the war in light of what are thought to be 'theoretically known' (or at least specified) general causes of war. While the purpose is primarily explanation, such an exercise must perforce say something about the explanatory power of the theory being applied and thus about its adequacy. A theory that cannot explain the well-known events of an important social phenomenon would seem to be deficient. A theory that provides no new understanding or insight would appear to be redundant of existing understandings.

This analysis also seeks to demonstrate that the scientific approach can provide two basic contributions to the larger endeavour of seeking the causes of war. First, it can identify general patterns, corroborate these with replicable evidence, and weave them into explanations that are falsifiable. Second, these patterns may provide us with new information about the dynamics of the war, and how it came to be a world war. The explanation in this chapter is new in the sense that not only does it differ from most existing political science explanations (see Midlarsky, 1989; Levy, 1989c), but also in that it provides new insights and a new way of describing the facts associated with the onset of world war.

Part I of the analysis will outline the theory; Part II will apply it to the specific events to explain the onset of the Second World War, and Part III will apply it to explain the expansion of the war.

I. EXPLAINING WORLD WAR

Over the past thirty years, a number of peace researchers have tested numerous hypotheses about the onset of war. In *The War Puzzle* (Vasquez, 1993), I have attempted to integrate these findings into a coherent explanation of the onset and expansion of war. One of the first things that becomes clear in any sustained analysis about war is that there are different paths to war and different types of war, each with their own set of causes. Some of this complexity is made manageable, however, by the fact that it appears that the strongest states in the system get involved in wars by following a typical path – one associated with power politics and its foreign policy practices.

To explain the Second World War, it is necessary to first discern what type of war it was. The Second World War consisted of an interstate war among the strongest states in the system that spread to encompass a very large number of states. In many ways, the Second World War was a number of ongoing wars that became linked together. Technically a world war is defined as 'a large-scale severe war among major states that involves the leading states at some point in the war and most other major states in a struggle to resolve the most fundamental issues on the global political agenda' (Vasquez, 1993:63). While such wars are rare in the international system, they are not unique. In fact Levy (1985b:364-65), who refers to such world wars as general wars, identifies ten of them. One of the failures of previous analyses is that they do not distinguish between the factors that bring about the initial interstate war and the factors that make the war spread to encompass most of the world. This requires two explanations – one of the onset of interstate war and one of the conditions making for the expansion of war.

Table 8.1 summarizes the typical path by which major states become embroiled in world war. The path is conceptualized as a series of steps that leads to interstate war and then a set of conditions that makes the interstate war expand.

Existing peace research has found that most interstate wars are fought between neighbours and involve territorial issues (see Vasquez, 1993:130–4; see also Holsti, 1991:307–13). This is a basic finding not only for wars between equals, like France and Germany, but also for wars between unequals, like Germany and Poland. Consequently, when crises occur over territorial issues or on a site contiguous to the territory of a state, the probability of escalating to war goes up (see Brecher, 1993, and Diehl, 1985b, respectively).

For all these reasons, territorial disputes are seen as an underlying cause of all interstate wars. While they are not sufficient to bring about war, their presence as a contentious issue makes war more *probable*. Preliminary empirical analyses of militarized interstate dispute data consistently show this to be the case (see Hensel, 1996b; Senese, forthcoming; see also Huth, forthcoming). These studies show that militarized disputes that seek to revise the existing territorial distribution are much more likely to escalate to war than disputes over other issues (e.g. those that seek to revise a state's policy or form of government).

One of the reasons territorial issues serve as an underlying cause of war is that their salience, both in terms of their intrinsic importance and public awareness of them, tends to make disputes recur (see Roy, 1994). The repetition of disputes is one of the main factors most associated with war among equals (see Wayman, 1996; Goertz and Diehl, 1992b). Presumably this recurrence engenders increasing hostility and a sense of rivalry with all that this entails (see Vasquez, 1993:75–83). Whether this potential for war is actualized depends very much on how the issue is handled. It is hypothesized that the use of power

Table 8.1 Typical path associated with world war
(Application to Second World War in Europe)

Steps to interstate war

Rise of territorial disputes
  (underlying cause)
handled in a power politics fashion
  (proximate causes):
Military build-ups
Alliance making
Repeated crises
one crisis escalates to war when
—— Physical threat to vital issue
—— Ongoing arms race
—— Escalatory bargaining across crises
—— Hostile spiral
—— Hard-liners on at least one side

Factors promoting expansion of war

Allied non-belligerents brought in
Bordering states brought in
Rivals brought in
Bandwagon effects present
Breakdown of political order
States brought in because of economic dependence

Systemic factors necessary for world war

—— Multipolar distribution of capability
—— (reduced by) Polarization into two hostile blocs
—— Neither bloc preponderant

---

politics to handle territorial issues increases the probability of war.

This analysis assumes that war is a social invention learned in history that tells actors when it is appropriate to handle a certain situation through the use of deadly force (see Mead, 1940:402–3; Vasquez, 1993:30–2, 40–2). In the modern global system, realist folklore has provided an intellectual culture for the strongest states that guides the foreign policy actions of states. This realist social construction, which is based on deriving lessons from war and inventing practices and policies to deal with the prospect of war, in effect tells leaders how to handle various situations they might face in their relations with other states. For example, if threatened they should build up their capability. Power, according to realist wisdom, can be increased either by making alliances or building up one's armaments. A variety of other prescriptions, some ambiguous and others contradictory, are part of the realist construction of reality (see Morgenthau, 1960).

Among the great ironies of this folklore is that between equals the practices of power politics, instead of increasing security, produce a security dilemma, and instead of producing peace, increase the probability of war. Thus, while the use of power politics between unequals to settle territorial disputes may lead to success for the strong without war, among equal states the opposite occurs. If equals try to resolve territorial issues through the use of power politics, the probability of war will increase. When coercion is threatened or applied between equals, political actors will resort to a series of realist practices.

The adoption of realist practices can be seen as taking a series of steps toward war. The idea of steps to war is meant to convey that each step in and of itself increases the probability of war. The steps to war, however, need not occur in a particular order, nor is it necessary that each step be taken for war to break out. As a probabilistic explanation, it is assumed that the more steps to war that are taken, the higher the probability of war. Together these steps can be viewed as proximate causes of war among equals. While none of the steps make war inevitable, the taking of one step increases the probability of taking the next, making the avoidance of war increasingly difficult for decision-makers. The precise impact of each step on the probability of war cannot be determined *a priori*, but interaction effects are likely.[3]

As a situation emerges that portends the use of force, realist folklore recommends the making of alliances and/or the building up of one's military. Both of these, however, usually increase the probability of war because they threaten one's opponent and produce a counter-response.

The empirical evidence shows that alliances, particularly among major states, are generally followed by war not peace. Levy (1981:597–8) finds that from 1495 on (with the exception of the nineteenth century) 56 per cent to 100 per cent of alliances are followed by war.[4] Since there is often an interval between the making of an alliance and the onset of war, alliances probably do not cause wars immediately, but can be seen as aggravating a situation, thereby making war more likely.[5] Clearly, one of the ways in which this occurs is that the making of alliances increases the threat to the other side and leads to a counter-alliance. The end result, in relative terms, is that there has been no increase in power, but in absolute terms both sides now face a greater threat and a greater bloc of capability that must be overcome. Overall, insecurity has increased.

The most fundamental way in which alliances cause war, then, is that they increase threat-perception, hostility, and general tension. Threat perception gets parties to start thinking about war and defining who their enemies are. In doing so it generates more hostility. Hostility intensifies rivalry and makes parties define their issue positions (interests) more in terms of who is opposing them rather than the specific stakes at issue (see Vasquez, 1993:76–82). General tension promotes war scares and an atmosphere conducive to hard-liners in each side. While the initial formation of an alliance and the formation of a counter-alliance are the events that produce these effects, the renewing or tightening of older alliances or the formation of alignments within crises could produce similar effects.[6]

The second way in which alliances can cause war is that they mesh the interests of several different actors, thereby increasing the number of situations and *casus belli* that can give rise to war. On the whole, multi-party disputes are more apt to escalate to war than dyadic disputes (see Cusack and Eberwein, 1982; Gochman and Maoz, 1984:601–602; James and Wilkenfeld, 1984). To the extent that alliances bring third parties into a crisis, they make it more difficult for the crisis to be managed and more likely that things might get out of control.[7]

An increase in hostility also results from attempts to build up one's military. Unlike the making of an alliance, this step is both more costly in terms of resources and more time consuming. The building up of one's military frequently leads to an arms race, although such a race may not always take the technical form outlined by Richardson (1960a)(see Ward, 1984).

The empirical evidence on the relationship between military build-ups and the onset of war is not as clear as the evidence on alliances and war. Suffice it to say here that (at most) military build-ups of some kind seem to increase the probability that militarized disputes will escalate to war. Whether these military build-ups need to be mutual ongoing arms races and whether this relationship holds only for arms races of a certain type is still a matter of debate (see Wallace, 1979; 1982; 1990; and Diehl, 1983; 1985a; cf. Morrow, 1989).[8] Nevertheless, there seems to be at least a statistically significant relationship between the presence of arms races and the escalation of crises to war. Sample (1996), in particular, shows that most of the cases Diehl's index identifies as not escalating to war in the presence of a mutual military build-up are in fact followed, in a few years, by disputes that do escalate to war. Furthermore, it is clear from the empirical evidence that hardly any crises escalate to war in the *absence* of arms races (see Wallace, 1982, 1990). In terms of the analysis here, it is also important to note that the relationship between arms racing and war is strongest before world wars (Weede, 1980; Diehl, 1983). Overall, the effects of arms racing are not unlike those of alliance making; namely they tend to increase threat perception, hostility, and general tension. The precise effects of arms racing must await further in-depth case studies, but theoretically it appears that arms racing can be a very important element in generating a rivalry, as was the case in the Anglo-German rivalry, which was brought about in no small part by the German decision to build up a navy (see Kennedy, 1982:251-2, 467). More typically, military build-ups may put decision-makers (and/ or certain bureaucratic actors) under time pressure to act now before the enemy reaps the benefit of a build-up. Such pressures generated by the building of railroads in Russia, for example, seemed to be an element in hard-line arguments in Japan favoring war against Russia in 1904 (see Richardson, 1994:119-20) and in Germany favoring war against Russia in 1914. Arms races also help identify the enemy and are often related to war scares. The latter are not only an indicator of the high level of tension, but help generate self-amplifying feedback that serves to buttress the arguments of hard-liners in each side and weaken the influence of accommodationists. In this manner, arms races promote a domestic political atmosphere for hard-line bargaining, increasing the probability of crises escalating, while at the same time making it difficult for accommodationist actions to be taken at crucial junctures within a crisis.

From the above analysis, it can be concluded that alliances and military build-ups constitute two steps toward war among equals. The making of alliances and building up of militaries do not occur in isolation. They are usually punctuated by crises because, in an intense rivalry, realism preaches that states test their rivals and demonstrate resolve by relying on threats and coercive tactics (Rummel, 1979:186; Maoz, 1983). In a crisis, equal states tend to employ realpolitik tactics (Leng, 1983). As these crises repeat, the probability of war goes way up, especially if all the other steps to war have already been taken (Wallensteen 1981:74-5, 84; Leng, 1983; Brecher and Wilkenfeld, 1989; Brecher, 1993).

The repetition of crises are the real engines of war for they make it highly likely that eventually a crisis will emerge that escalates to war. This is another way of saying that as crises repeat, actors tend to intensify their bargaining tactics, getting closer and closer to war. This escalation in turn is a function of the increased influence of hard-liners within each side. A crisis is most likely to escalate to war if: (1) it is triggered by a physical threat to a territorial issue (Gochman and Leng, 1983; Brecher and James, 1988), (2) it is the third crisis in a series of crises with the same rival (usually resulting in realpolitik tactics becoming more coercive and hostile) (Leng, 1983; see also Leng, 1993), (3) a hostile interaction spiral emerges in the crisis (Holsti, North and Brody, 1968), and (4) hard-liners dominate the leadership of at least one side.

Through successive crises, the making of alliances and the building up of their respective militaries, states have engaged in interactions that have taught them that force and war are the best or only way of handling the situation at hand. The previous steps that have been taken constitute a set of external constraints under which decision-makers must act. In the meantime, the interactions have also had important domestic effects on each collectivity, creating a domestic political context that also constrains the choices of decision-makers. In short, each step to war and the threatening reaction it generates in the other side help to create a constituency for hard-liners within a state and reduce the number and influence of those who wish to seek accommodation and avoid war (see Vasquez, 1987b). The balance between hard-liners and accommodationists tips more and more in favor of the former as hostile actions persist and grow.

How long it will take for hard-liners to predominate within a polity depends not only on the external interaction, but also on the initial balance between them and the accommodationists. It is hypothesized that the initial balance between the two is a function of the outcome of the last major war. Victory in war that is seen as worth the costs generates hard-liners; whereas defeat that is seen as not worth the costs generates accommodationists. Victory that is seen as not worth the costs and defeat that is seen as worth the costs produce unstable situations because of cognitive dissonance, with the former favoring accommodationists and the latter hard-liners.[9] States that were initially dominated by accommodationists will have a longer fuse than those dominated by hard-liners, but neither will be able to resist the prevailing tendency of interactions (i.e. over the long run hostile actions increase the influence of hard-liners and cooperative actions the influence of accommodationists). The combined effect of hostile external relations and the rise of hard-liners domestically produces a number of psychological effects that help mobilize the society for war and make it difficult to turn the tide to avoid war at the last minute (see Barringer, 1972:102–15; White, 1966:4–5).

On the basis of the above cursory review, it would be expected that the typical dyadic interstate war between equal states in the modern global system would be between neighbors over a territorial dispute. Rivals engaged in a territorial dispute and who make alliances against each other and build up their militaries would be expected to be simultaneously involved in repeated crises. Successive crises would result in each side's increasing its escalatory actions, with war becoming increasingly probable.

Territorial issues, however, do not need to be handled by power politics, and if they are not, the probability for war will decrease. Whether power politics will be employed depends very much on the extent to which there are clear norms for transferring territory and whether the demands of revisionist states for territorial changes can easily be handled by those norms. Territorial demands that are seen as legitimate are obviously going to require less coercion than those that are not. Nevertheless, the more extensive and complicated the territorial demands, the greater the likelihood the existing norms of the system will be unable to handle them. Thus, the norms of the Concert of Europe could handle minor adjustments to the territorial distribution, but could not have been expected to accommodate the ambitions of nineteenth-century German and Italian nationalists seeking to create respective states for their respective 'nations.'

Often war will occur because norms and the global institutional order have been put under too much stress or have simply decayed and no longer exist. In either case, revisionist states act unilaterally to bring about territorial changes, thereby initiating a steps-to-war process. If, however, there is an agreement on norms and a rich global institutional context for handling political issues and bringing about peaceful change, then there is a lower probability that revisionist states will: (1) resort to unilateral practices like power politics, or (2) go to war.[10] The nature of the existing global institutional context and, in particular, its norms for the transfer of territory are important factors for explaining the onset of war.

The above outlines one path to war taken by major states that are involved in a rivalry, but it does not explain why most wars remain dyadic in the international system and only a few expand to include more than two parties (Richardson, 1960b:257, 275). For example, in the Correlates of War data, only 8 of 50 interstate wars from 1815–1965 expand (see Yamamoto and Bremer, 1980). To fully explain world war, it is necessary to develop a model of how and why wars expand.

Six factors are posited as increasing the probability that war will spread to include third parties. These are: the presence of alliances, territorial contiguity, ongoing rivalry, bandwagon effects associated with the weakening of norms prohibiting violence, the breakdown of political order, and economic dependence. The first three are the basic factors bringing about initial intervention, and once this has occurred the last three serve to expand the war even further.

Alliances are the most important factor in increasing the probability that a war will spread; in fact the most pernicious and unanticipated effect of alliances is to increase the likelihood that once war breaks out in the system it will spread. Siverson and King (1979) find that states that have an alliance with a belligerent are much more apt to be drawn into an ongoing war than other states (see also Siverson and Starr, 1991). Alliances, particularly those involving major and minor states (see Siverson and King, 1980), act as a contagion mechanism to spread war. While alliances increase the probability that war will spread, it must be kept in mind that they are far from a sufficient condition of war expansion, since most wars (42 of 50) do not spread, even if alliances are present.

Nevertheless, it is equally true that prior to the world wars in the twentieth century, alliances built up (statistically) in the system (Midlarsky, 1983; McGowan and Rood, 1975). Alliances seem to spread wars in two ways: first by drawing in an ally because its interests are affected and/or it has become so intertwined with the belligerent that it feels it must fight. Second, because the growth of alliances in a system of multiple rivalries has poisoned the atmosphere and increased hostility to such an extent that the system is like a powder keg waiting for a spark.

Territorial contiguity is the second factor that increases the probability that war will spread. Most and Starr (1980) found that states in the post-1945 period that share a border with a belligerent are much more apt to become involved in a war than states that do not share such a border (see also Starr and Most, 1976, 1978). Siverson and Starr (1990, 1991) extend this study back to 1816. They also find that sharing a border with a belligerent increases the probability of becoming involved in a war (keeping in mind, once again, that the overall probability of war spreading is low and that most bordering states do not become involved in most wars or experience subsequent wars). Much of this is due to considerations of military strategy, which is a major channel for war diffusion. Evidence marshalled by Houweling and Siccama (1988b: chap. 7) showing that wars are clustered in space is consistent with this conclusion. Part of this diffusion is also due to learning that violence can be successful for attaining goals (see bandwagon effects below).

While geography serves as an important focus for understanding war (see Starr, 1991), its effects on spreading war are not necessarily stronger than alliances. Siverson and Starr (1990:57–60; 1991:58–61) find that alliance is a more potent variable. Interestingly, alliances and borders have a cumulative effect, so having both an alliance and a shared border makes a state more prone to contagion than having just one of these effects (see Siverson and Starr, 1990:55–7, 60–1).

A third factor posited as spreading war once it breaks out is the presence of an ongoing rivalry. *Ceteris paribus*, wars breaking out in the absence of a rivalry are much less likely to spread than wars that break out in the presence of an outside ongoing rivalry.[11] The presence of multiple rivalries, especially if these become intertwined through alliances, can be assumed to make the probability of war's spreading even higher. While these are plausible expectations, existing research has not yet tested this claim.

Rivalry is a factor that is likely to interact with the other factors, as well as the steps to war themselves. Many rivalries occur between neighbors that have territorial disputes (see Vasquez, 1993:134, Table 4.2c). Rivalry is also associated with the search for allies. This has the effect of bringing together major and minor states, which may make serious disputes accumulate in a unstable fashion, a condition Midlarsky (1984, 1988) finds associated with the onset of world war.[12] It is not an accident then that Sabrosky (1985:151, 181) finds that wars that begin with major states on each side are less likely to expand than wars that begin with a major state on one side and a minor state on the other. This suggests that rivalry plays a role in enlarging certain wars by encouraging a non-belligerent ally to intervene on behalf of a minor state when it has been attacked by a rival (Sabrosky, 1985; see also Midlarsky, 1988).

Once a major state intervenes in an ongoing war, then it becomes more likely that other major states will intervene (Yamamoto and Bremer, 1980). This bandwagon effect reflects the fact that violence begets violence, which is probably a function of the breakdown of norms against violence (see Gurr, 1970:170). This finding is also consistent with other studies that show that the use of force in serious disputes is contagious, i.e. clustered (Bremer, 1992:42–6, 53–4; Maoz, 1989:225).

As fighting spreads, a momentum builds that makes fighting spread even more, which leads naturally to a breakdown of the global or regional political order. The main effect of this is that now minor states and other actors (e.g. revolutionary movements or ethnic groups) use the breakdown of the political order to fight their own wars. Ongoing war provides an opportunity for those who have wanted to use force to attain their ends, but have been prevented by the political order from doing so. World wars are particularly prone to this phenomenon. In addition, major states may bargain for the intervention of minor states or drag in their client states.

Lastly, the economic needs of belligerents draw in states that can meet those needs. On the one hand, this can occur through trade which then makes the neutral state a potential target of the side hurt by the trade in order to deny the enemy access. On the other hand, a state that can provide raw material might be attacked by the side that needs it.

These six factors increase the probability that war will spread. They do not, however, ensure that the war will spread so far as to become a world war encompassing most of the major states in the system. World wars are so rare that they probably occur only under certain systemic conditions, which can be seen as necessary conditions. Based on an analysis of statistical conditions associated with the biggest wars in the post-1816 period, three systemic processes are posited as being associated with the onset of world war: (1) there is a multipolar distribution of capability in the system;[13] (2) through the making of alliances this multipolarity is reduced to a polarized system of two hostile blocs;[14] and (3) the two blocs are generated in such a way that neither has a preponderance of capability over the other.[15]

Alliance-making, because it affects each of these conditions, has the peculiar consequence of bringing these factors together in their most explosive combination. What is equally tragic is that each of these effects is an unanticipated consequence of the making of alliances. In addition to making war spread, alliances make each side better prepared for war so that when war comes, it is much costlier and more severe than it would have been in the absence of alliances (Bueno de Mesquita, 1978:262-3; Kennedy, 1984). On the positive side, because these conditions act as necessary conditions, their absence will help prevent a war from expanding to a full-fledged world war even in the presence of factors that promote expansion. Let us now turn to see how the factors listed in Table 8.1 can be used to identify the causes of the Second World War in Europe.

II. THE ONSET OF THE SECOND WORLD WAR[16]

The general explanation of world war offered here would lead one to expect that the underlying causes of the Second World War lie in territorial disputes. This seems to be amply borne out by the immediate start of the war, the series of militarized disputes that preceded the war, and the attack on the Soviet Union in 1941. The war was initiated because of specific territorial demands made by Germany on Poland. These demands reflected a string of claims coming out of the Versailles settlement that sought to bring all 'Germans' under the sovereignty of the Third Reich. These included the militarization of the Rhineland, the *Anschluss*, and the absorption of the Sudetenland. Each of these involved sovereign control or transfer of territory. The prevailing norms of nationalism helped ease the transfer of territory prior to September 1939 (Kaiser, 1990:375). The Poles, however, were not to be bullied and saw the territory in question as legally theirs and vitally important to their survival.

According to the theoretical explanation offered here, such an issue (i.e. one involving territory) is best handled by force when faced with the threat of force. The war, then, was initiated with a major state attacking a minor state over an intractable territorial dispute. According to this explanation, such a war might be expected to expand since there were ongoing rivalries and alliances. In fact, the war expanded along a path that is often typical of world war, namely, a rival of the major state came to the aid of a minor state ally (Vasquez, 1993:230–1; see also Sabrosky, 1985; Midlarsky, 1988). In this case two rivals of Germany – France and Britain – came to the aid of Poland, whose territorial integrity they had both guaranteed. Territory can be seen, in part, as a guiding force bringing about German initiation and Polish resistance.

In a more fundamental sense, territory can be seen as an underlying cause of the Second World War in that it was the key goal guiding Hitler's overall foreign policy and diplomacy. The call for *Lebensraum* going back to *Mein Kampf*, repeated several times once he was Chancellor (particularly in the Hossbach conference in 1937), and more or less relentlessly pursued in Austria, Czechoslovakia, Poland and in the attack on the USSR, was a major element in Hitler's motivation for war (see Bell, 1986:85, 152, 155, 194, 257, 272, 284; Watt, 1989:24, 35, 40, 167, 321; Kaiser, 1990:370–4, 377–84). To the extent that Hitler's foreign policy brought about war, the goal that persistently raised the question of war and produced it in 1939 (Poland) and in 1941 (USSR) was the idea of replacing people and colonizing the territory to the East (Bullock, 1952:651, cited in Bell, 1986:285). The racial element and eventual exterminations went hand in hand with this extreme framing of the territorial issue (Weinberg, 1994:2)[17] In this sense, the 1939 war and the 1941 attack can be seen as intimately connected and part of a larger long-term strategy, even if not a reflection of a blueprint.[18]

A host of other territorial claims by other states – some long-ongoing disputes, others the product of new demands – were present prior to the outbreak of the war that added potential fuel to the conflagration and worked to disrupt the earlier norm against the use of violence to transfer territory or revise the Versailles settlement. These included, among others: Polish claims against Teschen (in Czechoslovakia); Hungarian claims for the Magyar area of Slovakia, for Ruthenia, and for Transylvania (in Romania); Italian desires for Albania and Corfu and demands on France for 'Corsica, Nice, and Tunisia'; Russian desires in Finland, the Baltic states and Romania; German desires for Memel; as well as a host of nationalist sentiments, as that of the Ukrainian nationalists, for a shifting of territory.[19] Some of these disputes, like the Italian attack on Albania, would lead directly to war on their own; most others would occur under the cover of other significant military action and can be seen as a product of contagion due to the breakdown of political order. The latter would include the Polish occupation of Teschen and Russian attacks taken in light of the Hitler-Stalin Non-Aggression Pact.

While territorial demands explain what brought about the initiation of the attacks in 1939 and 1941, they do not explain, directly, British and French intervention. Here one must look at the steps to war, for while territory is an underlying cause of war, the proximate causes of wars between rivals lie in how the territorial issues are treated and handled (see Vasquez, 1993: chap. 9). British and French intervention is generally thought of as resulting from a series of repeated crises in which they learned that the only way to deal with Hitler was to fight. The reason war was necessary from their perspective was that the territorial demands became relentless and began to spill over to non-German areas, such as Bohemia and Moravia (Watt, 1989:167; Rosecrance and Steiner, 1993:140) violating the prevailing norm of nationalist self-determination. It was the move on non-Germans that convinced Chamberlain that Hitler could not be satisfied (Watt, 1989:168). The commitment to Poland by Britain was made in this context after the occupation of Prague.[20]

The repeated crises themselves reflected a deeper set of processes that increased hostility and the perception of threat within the context of an enduring rivalry. The Anglo-German and Franco-German rivalries went back to before the First World War. It was these two rivalries and the festering that resulted on the German side that made Germany raise demand after demand. Hitler's aim of *Lebensraum*, which went way beyond revising the Versailles settlement, made appeasement unworkable, and that realization propelled Britain and France to defend Poland, as much as they did not want war. This ongoing rivalry, which had a power politics cast to it in the fear of German domination, brought about British and French intervention.[21]

While the repeated crises were a product of the territorial goals of Hitler's foreign policy, the crises had their own effects and fueled rivalry (and the hostility and fear underlying it) by making each side take steps to build up their military and make alliances, each of which are posited as proximate causes of the war (Vasquez, 1993:155ff). The building up of armaments was a drawn-out process that eventually resulted in multiple arms races. The process can be seen as beginning with German rearmament, begun in secret under Weimar and intensified by Hitler. The collapse of the Geneva Disarmament Conference in 1934, the public announcement of German rearmament on 10 March 1935, and the existence of the *Luftwaffe* followed by the reintroduction of conscription six days later, were initial steps down the road to war. They were not irreversible steps, however, as indicated by the separate Anglo-German Naval Accord, in which Hitler tried to avoid the mistake he saw the Kaiser making of unnecessarily alienating Britain by threatening her naval dominance (Bell, 1986:82, 83). German rearmament led to the Rhineland crisis in which Hitler, in violation of the Versailles Treaty and the Treaty of Locarno, militarized the Rhineland, undercutting French strategy that would make the next war one fought on German soil (Bell, 1986:211).

After the March 1936 Rhineland crisis, France and eventually Britain began to consider their own military build-ups, although both were constrained by domestic considerations (see Bell, 1989: chap. 11). Thus, in September 1936 even the anti-militarist Popular Front government of France passed a major rearmament program (Bell, 1986:167; Kaiser, 1990:387). Up to 1939, Germany and to a considerably lesser extent, Italy, can be seen as engaged in a military build-up, with Britain and France reluctantly responding, although technological developments in airplanes would have resulted in some kind of arms race in the absence of any agreement on managing this new form of warfare. Each new dispute or crisis made for another spurt in their activity; thus, Britain removed all restraints on the purchase of aircraft in April 1938 and ended other financial restraints on the navy and army after the Munich crisis (Bell, 1986:176; Watt, 1989:82–3).

Unlike Britain and France, Hitler had long-term plans, most clearly evinced in his program for self-sufficiency, such as the production of synthetics for oil and rubber (Bell, 1986:153). The German rearmament program was so ambitious that it failed to meet its goals in 1937 and 1938 (Bell, 1986:154) because of lack of raw materials. The rearmament program placed such a strain on the German economy that it provided a separate impetus for conquering new territory that would have some of the raw materials. Out of this, as well as concerns about access raised by the Great Depression, came the notion that in order to continue to rearm, Germany would have to expand (see Bell, 1986: 151–2; see also Rosecrance and Steiner, 1993:141–3).[22]

By early 1939, all sides were rushing to build up their militaries. Britain, in response to the war scare of January and February, took major steps to build up its air force and even to make a commitment to an expeditionary force (Watt, 1989: chap. 6) and for the first time introduced conscription during peacetime, although in the end they were able to deploy at the beginning of armed hostilities only four divisions, compared to 84 for the French and 103 for the Germans (Bell, 1986:175). By 1939 France had made impressive gains (Kaiser, 1990:387). These historical impressions are confirmed by Wallace (1982: Appendix) whose arms race index for Germany–UK and for Germany–France increase dramatically in 1939 over their 1938 levels.

On the whole, the military build-ups of each side moved each closer to war, thus providing support for the general steps to war explanation. Moreover they did this in a manner consistent with the rationale of the explanation. Namely, the inability to reach any agreement on disarmament in the 1932–4 conference and to control new technological developments led to a race in air capability. Each crisis led to new concerns on the British and French side about their capability, with the Rhineland crisis, Munich, and the war scare of early 1939 providing the greatest impetus. Throughout, the build-ups reflected bureaucratic and leadership concerns that they be ready to go to war, even though they might not be planning war immediately. When the war did come in September 1939, no one felt fully prepared – France, Britain, Italy, not even Hitler, whose rearmament program was not yet due for completion.

The military build-ups seemed to have had three effects: initially, when coupled with the Rhineland crisis, rearmament produced a sense of threat on the British and French sides. This was particularly the case since Britain and France expected Germany to begin by opening negotiations rather than just moving in with troops (Bell, 1986:208). Next, each crisis increased British and French hostility and raised concerns of insecurity and thereby led to an increase in military expenditures and preparations. Meanwhile, Hitler and Mussolini pursued their military build-ups spurred on by their success to prepare for bigger battles. Finally, as war seemed to loom on the horizon, each side rushed to arm so that the war would be timed to give it the most advantage it could get given the circumstances.

Did the military build-ups produce the war? Such inferences are very difficult to make, but military build-ups did seem to have an impact on each side. To the extent that Hitler wanted to avoid a war on the Western front and aimed at *Lebensraum* in the East, his military build-up and the way he flaunted it was a primary factor in bringing about British and French intervention. If he had handled his territorial ambitions more diplomatically and more shrewdly, war with Poland and even the USSR need not have provoked intervention by Britain and France. Instead, his military build-up provoked theirs, and increased hostility on both sides, including Hitler's own, which in 1939 seemed out of control in terms of his rage toward Britain (Watt, 1989:100–1, 106).

Of equal importance to note is that the military build-ups did not prevent war. Hitler's build-up failed to keep France and Britain out of the war. They were intimidated, but could be pushed only so far. Instead, they responded with their own military build-up. As late as March 1939, Chamberlain apparently thought that British rearmament would prevent Hitler from going to war against Britain (Watt, 1989:164–6). Peace through strength was also one of Chamberlain's illusions.

In the end, the military build-ups can be seen as a step to war because the fear and hostility they generated interacted with the repeated crises in a manner that increased the probability of war. For Britain and France it led to the conclusion among important domestic foreign policy elites that force was the only way to deal with Hitler. They had to prepare as best they could.

The military build-ups coupled with the crises in the late 1930s helped produce war in another way – they created a sense of threat sufficient to increase hard-liners and produce a domestic context able to overcome French and British aversion to war and anything connected with militarism. According to the steps-to-war model, the balance between hard-liners and accommodationists in any society is determined by whether the last major war was won or lost and by whether the war was seen as 'worth the costs' (see Vasquez, 1993: chap. 6). Losing a war and more importantly regarding the effort as 'not worth the costs' tends to produce accommodationists; whereas winning a war and seeing it as worth the costs produces hard-liners, all other factors being equal. In mixed situations, dissonance is present, but the psychological variable of 'worth the cost' is specified as more potent. Since Britain and France won the last war, but did not see it as worth the costs, it would be expected that accommodationists would prevail and this, of course, was very much the case (Mueller, 1989; Bell, 1986: chap. 7). In Germany, the situation was just the opposite – the war was lost, but seen as worth the costs, so hard-liners would be expected to prevail. This, in fact, occurred with hard-liners accusing accommodationists with having stabbed Germany in the back in 1918.

Hard-liners can be seen as coming to power with Hitler in 1933. The success of their rearmament program and more importantly their use of threats and force increased the number of hard-liners, eventually converting the reluctant military and silencing the accommodationists and risk-averse, and generally providing wide public support for Hitler's foreign policy (Kaiser, 1990:381–2).[23] In Britain and France, accommodationists tended to prevail, even within the complicated ideological situation of France. The continuing German build-up in armaments alarmed the British and French military establishments, moving them toward a hard-line direction early on. France, being much closer to the threat, moved more quickly than Britain. Here, the anti-fascist coalition of the Popular Front took away a natural accommodationist constituency. In Britain, Lord Halifax, the Foreign Secretary, became an important spokesman for taking a hard line, but this was only after Munich (Watt, 1989: chap. 6). It took Munich, and for others the fall of Prague, to make them hard-liners.[24] By September 1939 there were not only hard-liners on one side, as required by the steps to war model, but on both sides. This had the anticipated hard-line effect on bargaining and produced escalation to war in 1939.

A second process in the steps to war is the making of alliances. Immediately after Versailles, France's rivalry with Germany spurred her on to make a number of alliances as a way of fencing in Germany (Belgium 1920, Poland 1921, Czechoslovakia 1925, Romania 1926, Yugoslavia 1927). The French military was convinced that it would have to fight another war with Germany and that, without allies, it was no match for Germany (Bell, 1986:167). For this France needed major states, and the obvious ones were Britain, the Soviet Union, and Italy. With the rise of Hitler, the concern over allies took on more urgency, and in 1935 France was able to sign an alliance with the Soviet Union and much to its elation reach a military agreement with Italy (Watt, 1989:21). The Italian invasion of Abyssinia forced France to choose between Italy and Britain so that the military agreement with Italy proved abortive.

France was not the only one that felt the need for allies; a number of minor states did so as well. Czechoslovakia, Romania, and Yugoslavia – all of whom benefitted from the Versailles settlement at the expense of Hungary – came together early on to form the 'Little Entente.' France signed bilateral alliances with each of these (Chambers, 1962:173–4) enmeshing her with their territorial concerns. The remaining Balkan states came together periodically in the 1930s to meet their mutual security needs, eventually producing the Balkan Entente composed of Greece, Turkey, Yugoslavia, Romania, and Bulgaria (Chambers, 1962:395–7). This alliance added to the complicated diplomacy of the area without ultimately providing a collective defense of any of the states (see Watt, 1989: chaps 16 and 17).

While Britain eschewed alliances, it was not above making economic agreements, such as that with Romania in 1938 (Bell, 1986:156–7, 256), to undercut German influence. Towards the end, public guarantees to support France in case of war and to protect the territorial integrity of Romania and Greece were substituted for formal alliances. The latter two guarantees were issued jointly with France on 13 April 1939 and aimed at both Germany and Italy, the latter having invaded Albania on 7 April 1939. After the German occupation of Prague, Britain made an alliance with Poland, and France reconfirmed her alliance with Poland.

These public guarantees spurred the Pact of Steel between Germany and Italy signed on 22 May 1939. Mussolini had long felt that, given his ambitions in the Mediterranean, he would ultimately be opposed by France and Britain and that the only major state on whom he could rely for support was Germany (Bell, 1986:67). The ideological link, the early personal affinity between Mussolini and Hitler, and the cooperation during the Spanish Civil War made this a natural alliance. Still, Italy could wander and could be courted by France and Britain, as she was on more than one occasion, including at Munich. Furthermore, Italy and Germany had had early differences on Austria; on Poland, Mussolini and Ciano could not believe Hitler would fight over Danzig (see Watt, 1989:526–7, 536).

Since 1938, Hitler had been trying to develop a tripartite pact with Italy and Japan as a way of menacing Britain on three fronts. Now, given the guarantee to Greece, and Italian territorial demands on France, Italy had come on board, although Ciano wanted to avoid a major war until 1943 (Bell, 1986:257; Watt, 1989:240–1). Japan could not be brought in until 1940, because she wanted the alliance to be directed toward the Soviet Union, which obviously went against Hitler's immediate plans (Bell, 1986:257). Nevertheless, Japan had been aligned with Germany in 1936 in the Anti-Comintern Pact, which Italy had joined in 1937, and this was to be the real herald of the eventual war coalition.

In the meantime, the rush for alliances continued. All efforts focused now on the Soviet Union. Stalin had long taken an anti-fascist stance, supporting popular front coalitions throughout Europe and providing material support to the Republic in the Spanish Civil War. He and his Foreign Minister, Litvinov, had sought in vain some sort of united anti-German alliance with Britain and France. This would also provide a way of combating the Anti-Comintern Pact which faced the USSR with the prospect of a two-front war (Watt, 1989:112). After Munich, Stalin grew increasingly suspicious that Britain wanted Germany to turn toward the East (Watt, 1989: chap. 7). The Anglo-German agreement that called for solving all problems through consultation, the subsequent German–French Declaration along the same lines, the Anglo-Italian agreement on the Mediterranean following Munich, and Chamberlain's visit to Rome in early 1939 fueled these suspicions to almost a frenzy. So when the chance came for a reversal of relations with Germany and the opportunity to gain territory that might be useful in a future war and that restored areas lost after the First World War, Stalin seized it and signed the Non-Aggression Pact with Germany in August 1939. Overtures were made by Britain and France after Prague, between April and August, but now it was too late; furthermore, Germany offered Russia opportunities for territorial expansion.

The failure of Britain and France to join with the Soviet Union is a major anomaly for the balance-of-power hypothesis that maintains that states will coalesce to meet a hegemonic challenge. If there ever was a hegemonic challenge in Europe, then Hitler posed it. Yet Britain and France did not respond to Stalin's overtures, primarily for ideological reasons. To call this 'passing the buck,' as Christensen and Snyder (1990) do, simply hides the discrepant evidence with a catchy phrase (see Vasquez, forthcoming). According to this version of balance-of-power theory, balancing against a hegemonic threat must outweigh all other considerations because survival is at stake.

Interestingly, the same failure occurred with Napoleon's hegemonic bid (see Schroeder, 1994). With Napoleon, a balancing coalition emerged not because of a rational calculation on the part of other major states, but because the challenger eventually attacked each state (Schroeder, 1994; Rosecrance, 1992). The same thing occurred in 1941 when Hitler attacked the Soviet Union and Japan attacked the US. If, as realists argue, world wars are always wars over power, then the failure of Britain and France to join the Soviet Union, as well as the failure of the US to join this coalition in order to balance Hitler, is an anomaly for realism. To claim that if the allies could have put together a preponderant coalition, war could have been avoided, and that this somehow supports realist analysis, is irrelevant, since the allies failed to put together such a coalition. In the end, it was ideology rather than concerns about balancing power that were uppermost in their minds.

Generally, the statistical findings (see Singer and Small, 1966; Levy, 1981) indicate that alliances, especially among major states, do not prevent war but are followed by war within five years. This was certainly the case with the Second World War. Alliances provoked counteralliances and, as will be seen in the next section, dragged in states once war broke out. They did not seem to cause war directly, since they were symptomatic of a deeper underlying jockeying for position. They may, however, have been indirect causes of war in that they increased insecurity, uncertainty, and hostility.

Two things are clear from this case that make alliances much more complex than realists think. First, alliances are not simply attempts to balance power or prevent war. Alliances reflect a variety of purposes and are sometimes entered into for contradictory purposes. Mussolini and Ciano entered the Pact of Steel hoping that it would add leverage in their negotiation with France, and explicitly did not see this as a green light for Germany to go into Poland, a crisis they genuinely attempted to mediate (Watt, 1989:526–7). Often states use alliances as a way of proposing or even making a settlement of outstanding differences. The Hitler-Stalin Non-Aggression Pact illustrates that function, as does the 1935 Franco-Italian military agreement. Frequently, alliances are made to isolate states and limit war – Hitler attempted to do this in 1939 and was in part successful.

Second, the rather extensive alliance activity, which reflected much more flexibility than before the First World War (especially with regard to Italy and the Soviet Union), did not prevent war. Mostly, this is because what is usually needed to prevent war is not a balance of power but a preponderance of power.

When all is said and done, however, the flexible alliances and various agreements signaling political and economic alignments at some point shifted from their initial stated purpose to a preparation for war. In 1939 the various public guarantees and attempts to prevent war by marshalling a winning coalition simply did not work. Instead they led to increased preparation on the other side, as predicted by the steps to war model and denied by mainstream realist analysis.[25]

Military build-ups and alliance-making are important variables that move states indirectly toward war through their increase in hostility and insecurity. In this process they fuel rivalry. Repeated crises, however, move the states more directly toward war (Bell, 1986:26). The turning-point in the Second World War occurred with the Munich crisis and the failure of the British and French agreements with Hitler to reach an overall mutually acceptable settlement. This in turn was a strict function of Hitler's grandiose territorial ambitions, which he knew could only be attained by war. In hindsight, it can be seen that one attempt to use force would just lead to another because the underlying territorial issues at stake were inherently war prone. It was these specific territorial demands, not the vague musings about conquering the world, that brought about each crisis and made an overall settlement difficult to obtain.

The presence of territorial issues, military build-ups, alliances and repeated crises in this case raise the question of whether one is of greater causal significance than another. Another way of addressing this question is to ask if any were absent would this be sufficient to have avoided war. Theoretically, territorial issues are posited as the underlying cause of war and repeated crises as the engine that drives political actors toward rivalry and war. The more extensive the territorial issues, of course, the greater the probability that they would lead to war and be unable to be handled by existing norms. Alliance-making and military build-ups are ways of dealing with this insecurity by trying to increase capability. Such efforts would not be apt to lead to war in the absence of serious territorial issues, but their presence does increase tension and hostility and thereby fuels rivalry. Nevertheless, if there were no serious territorial disputes such practices would probably be insufficient to bring about war.[26] Thus, while each step increases the probability of war, they do not have a uniform impact – territorial disputes that challenge existing norms and repeated crises are the most weighty.

The Second World War provides some evidence for this theoretical specification. It is important to make clear that one of the reasons Hitler was able to succeed earlier on was that all his territorial claims were made on the basis of existing norms for transferring territory.

Hitler based his claims to Austria and the Sudetenland on the principles of nationalism and self-determination that all Germans should have the right to be part of Germany. The treaty of Versailles was seen as unjust because it denied these principles to Germans, whereas it granted them to others. Likewise, the remilitarization of the Rhineland was justified on the basis of the principle that the German government should have sovereignty over all its territory. So long as Hitler was able to couch his territorial demands on the basis of legitimate norms, then war and power politics were avoided. Once he sought territory that was not German, as in Bohemia and Moravia, then France and Britain were prepared to resist.

Likewise, the plans for *Lebensraum* in Poland and in the Ukraine were in violation of existing norms and made unilateral actions on Germany's part inevitable. In this sense, Germany's alliances and military build-ups were a function of his larger territorial ambitions, but these ambitions were not known by Chamberlain and Daladier. To them, Germany's alliances and military build-ups were regarded as threatening and led to a questioning of appeasement by hard-liners within each country. Nevertheless, it was only with the occupation of Prague that Chamberlain abandoned appeasement and prepared for war. If Hitler would have confined himself to including only Germans within the Reich, then war might well have been avoided, even over Danzig. Instead, there was a series of recurrent crises that resulted in war.

The general statistical findings show that repeated crises greatly increase the probability of war, and this is supported for the major states in the pre-Second World War period. Leng (1983: table 2) identifies three crises between Britain and Germany – Rhineland, Munich, Polish-Danzig – with the third escalating to war. Not too much emphasis should be placed on the exact number, since there are many crises and incidents that fuel hostility. Brecher, Wilkenfeld and Moser (1988:25–7), for example, find that Germany is a source of threat in at least eleven crises, albeit not all directly involve the UK and France. Likewise, Midlarsky (1988) finds a destabilizing build-up of militarized disputes prior to each of the twentieth-century world wars. What is critical is that the escalatory actions of the next crisis increase over the previous one (Leng, 1983). This is consistent with Brecher's (1993) finding that crises in a protracted conflict are more likely to escalate to violence. States 'learn' that the only way to deal with each other is to increase their use or threat of force, and this certainly fits the pattern of behavior exhibited prior to the Second World War. These lessons become even more evident as one examines the perceptions and discussions of the principles that follow each crisis (see Watt, 1989).

When the 1939 Polish crisis did come, it was not a surprise that it escalated to war. The Poles were not going to capitulate, and after Prague the British and French were going to fight. This was all a function of the lessons derived from the previous crises. As such, the crisis has most of the characteristics predicted by the steps-to-war model. It began as a physical threat to a vital territorial issue. It came at the end of a series of escalating crises. There was an ongoing arms race, and hard-liners were now in charge on all sides, including Poland (see Watt, 1989:158–61, 500, 512–13; Rosecrance and Steiner, 1993).[27]

The steps to war constitute the proximate causes of war. They also set up the factors that helped bring about the expansion of the war and the initial major state intervention by Britain and France. It is to a more detailed discussion of this process that we must now turn.

III. THE EXPANSION OF WAR

The general explanation of the expansion of war maintains that the presence of an ongoing rivalry and an alliance with a belligerent increases the probability that a war that breaks out will expand. Both of these factors clearly account for British and French intervention. As noted above, the ongoing rivalry led Britain and France to form an alliance with Poland and give public guarantees to Romania and Greece. When the attack came on Poland, they declared war.

The model also points to possible Soviet intervention. Here traditional Russo-German rivalry coupled with resentment over the Treaty of Brest-Litovsk, as well as territorial contiguity (once Poland was occupied) would be factors promoting contagion. Hitler anticipated this and neutralized the factors by the Non-Aggression Pact which provided a mutually acceptable territorial settlement and reversed essential parts of Brest-Litovsk. Thus, rivalry was successfully managed and territorial contiguity neutralized, demonstrating that the variables making for war form a structure that humans can manipulate and change by their policies. The Non-Aggression Pact, however, was just a respite; in the long run, Hitler's territorial ambitions made contiguity operate as a base from which to diffuse war.

Territorial contiguity also played an important role in facilitating the diffusion of war to several minor states. The German attacks on Norway and Denmark, which ended the phony war, were done for strategic reasons. Denmark was occupied primarily to get to Norway (Weinberg, 1994:115). Norway was attacked, in part, to serve as a potential base against the British (Weinberg, 1994:113-14), but also to protect the Swedish supply of iron ore (see below). Neither of these advantages were lost on the British, who actually made the first belligerent move by announcing that they would mine Norwegian waters and by taking naval action (Hughes, 1961:309; Bell, 1986:272-3). The Germans then moved quickly.

Territorial contiguity, in terms of questions of military strategy, obviously was a key consideration in the German attack on the Netherlands, Belgium, and Luxembourg (Weinberg, 1994:115). It also was a motive in the Soviet attack on Finland in that the area annexed was important for defending Leningrad (Hughes, 1961:309). In Eastern Europe, territorial contiguity, coupled with territorial ambitions, played an important role in bringing in Hungary, Romania, and Bulgaria on the side of the Axis. Hitler needed them for strategic reasons, and they were willing to be bought in order to secure new territory and/or protect what they had (Hughes, 1961:318; Weinberg, 1994:219).

Siverson and Starr (1991) find that, generally, the presence of a warring state on one's border and an alliance with a belligerent increases the probability of war. This path of expansion operated in a highly explosive fashion in the Second World War. Interestingly, most of the minor states that entered the war also made alliances with the belligerents (e.g. Hungary, Romania, Slovakia and Bulgaria entered the Tripartite Pact) between November 1940 and March 1941 (i.e. before the attack on the USSR) and Germany and Finland signed a treaty of friendship, as well as having staff talks in December 1940 (Bell, 1986:289).

In these ways, rivalry, alliances, and territorial contiguity all served to expand the war. Of these three factors that bring about the initial expansion of the war, rivalry is the most fundamental in that it is the rivalry and sense of threat it embodied that led to the formation of alliances in the first place. The presence of alliances, once Germany invaded Poland, acted as a very potent contagion mechanism, locking third parties into a decision for war. By locking in parties, alliances can make actors intervene in a war even when they are hesitant to actually go to war, as the phony war demonstrated. The formation of alliances also interacted with rivalry to help increase hostility, which made intervention more probable. They also better prepared each side for war once it came. Lastly, territorial contiguity served as a plane to diffuse the war, because of questions of military strategy and geopolitical considerations.

The onset of the war in September and quick German victory also had a major bandwagon effect on Italy. Italy used the opportunity to fight its own wars in France, Greece, and Yugoslavia. The declaration of war on France should not be seen simply as a craven attempt to get in on the spoils, but as something deeper. Mussolini, despite the cautiousness of Ciano, felt that he could not 'stand by with folded arms while others make history' (Bell, 1986:279). He did not want to get in just on the spoils, but into the battle. Hitler's actions and success were highly contagious for Mussolini.

Two other factors operated to expand the war – the breakdown of the political order, which promoted additional interventions, particularly by states that used the opportunity to fight their own wars, and economic dependence. The German–Soviet Non-Aggression Pact broke down the existing political order in Eastern Europe and led Stalin to pursue a number of his own ambitions in Poland, Finland, Romania, and the Baltic states. Later, the Soviet war against Hitler provided Stalin with the opportunity to extend Soviet borders and impose a sphere of influence, even if this involved expanding the war, as in the declarations of war against Bulgaria in 1944 and on Japan in 1945.

Economic dependence played a role in the attack on Norway. In addition to its strategic position near Britain, Norway was brought in because she was a vital point in the supply line of Swedish iron ore to Germany, on which Germany was economically dependent.[28] German economic dependence on Romanian oil was an element in Hitler's thinking throughout the war. Early on, Hitler in his pre-war diplomacy toward Romania, Yugoslavia, Bulgaria, Turkey, Sweden, and Hungary aimed at securing from them needed economic resources in the event of war (Bell, 1986:257). Once war broke out, Britain and France contemplated taking military action against some of these sources of supply, specifically the Romanian oil fields, the Baku oil fields in the Soviet Union, and at one point, the Swedish iron ore mines (Bell, 1986:269–70).

The economic needs of Britain and of France also spurred FDR into action as early as 1938 (after Munich), when he made a secret offer to build planes for them in Canada (Watt, 1989:129–30). The offer greatly heartened Chamberlain. Later, Roosevelt may have used his undeclared war in the Atlantic to taunt Hitler into attacking the US Navy, but Hitler would have none of that (see Divine, 1969). Ultimately, the US was brought in by Japan, which attacked it because its economic dependence on US oil led it to conquer an alternative source in the Dutch East Indies.

Lastly, the attack on the Soviet Union was brought about by Hitler's feeling that his economic dependence on Soviet raw materials and foodstuffs was untenable. Given the fact that Stalin was more than compliant, this rationale must be seen as reflecting the more fundamental goal of *Lebensraum*. Despite this last point, economic dependence turns out to be much more of a major factor in spreading the war than had been believed to be the case.

The various interventions led to a complete breakdown of the political order in Europe and led to all kinds of groups fighting their own wars and battles, since prohibitions against violence were completely dissipated. Italy is a classic example of a weaker major state that could now pursue its own agenda. Minor states, however, were more likely to be brought in through this path. War provided an opportunity to achieve long-held objectives. Bulgaria and the Yugoslav regime of Prince Paul (regent of the boy king) providing bases for a German attack in exchange for a promise of Greek territory is a major example. Additional examples could be drawn from Romania, Hungary and even Finland, which joined Germany in 1941 for revenge.

The breakdown in political order also provided an opportunity for domestic wars to be fought. The civil war in Yugoslavia is a prime example of this kind of contagion. But the actions of the resistance in France and in Italy are not that different. Likewise, it is not an accident that the so-called *Mafia* in Sicily should provide aid to the US against Mussolini, one of its most dangerous enemies. Indeed, Hitler's domestic war on communists and on Jews and then on Jews throughout Europe is the most extreme example of this phenomenon. To this one would add other massacres, such as that of gypsies and the Croatian killing of Serbs within its borders. All of these were opportunities (to fight wars and battles of one's choosing) brought about by the larger ongoing war.

The six factors promoting war expansion were clearly all at work in the Second World War, with a certain amount of interaction among them. In many instances, but not all, the expansion of war was overdetermined. Each of the factors made it difficult to contain and limit the war, even though there were many opportunities to do so, given certain lulls in battles. As each factor brought more and more actors into the war, it became harder for others not to be dragged in. Nevertheless, some important strategically located countries, like Sweden, Switzerland, Turkey and Spain, did avoid the war, but they had to work against the *tide*. What distinguishes a social science explanation of the Second World War from an historical one, is that the scientific explanation seeks to identify the variables that compose the *tidal forces* at work. The above analysis explains how the Second World War expanded by describing how each of the six factors brought in various belligerents.

The general explanation of world war, however, suggests that in addition to these six factors that generate expansion, there are deeper systemic factors that will restrain the six factors so that, of the wars that expand, only a rare few become world wars. The Second World War became a world war because three necessary conditions were in place. In fact, one could argue that until they were in place, the German war with Britain and France did not become a world war.

According to the general explanation, the preconditions of a world war reflect a dynamic interaction of three factors: a multipolar distribution of capability is polarized into two hostile blocs in which one is not preponderant over the other. The major states in 1939 are Britain, France, Germany, Italy, the USSR, the US, and Japan – clearly a multipolar structure. The process by which this multipolar structure becomes polarized into two hostile blocs in which one bloc is not preponderant is critical, because it accounts for (a) how the war expands to become global, involving all major non-belligerent states, and (b) how the war in Europe becomes intimately linked to the war in the Pacific.

The major culprits were alliances and the foreign policy decisions of Hitler and Japan, who as allies took independent actions that brought about a realignment in the system, placing the two remaining major non-belligerents – the US and the USSR – in an unwitting alliance with each other and with Britain. The process began with the signing of the Tripartite Pact in September 1940. The Pact helped Hitler provide a threat to Britain and the US, putting before them the prospect of a two-front war. It did the same thing to the Soviet Union, even though Article 5 specifically named the Soviet Union as unaffected by the Pact (Bell, 1986:289). Both of these conditions were, for different reasons, important to Japan. The treaty also constituted a settlement among the three in that it recognized clear spheres of influence (see Bell:277–8).

The attacks on the Soviet Union and then on Pearl Harbor were fatal decisions for the Axis. They destroyed Hitler's previous attempt to win through salami tactics and by divide and rule. Pearl Harbor worked against Hitler because it allowed Roosevelt to now enter the war legitimately and with full domestic support. The Pact did not really weaken the US effort in Europe, because Roosevelt was willing and could afford to put the Pacific on the back burner. The Axis decisions of 1941 would probably not have been taken by a unitary rational actor, and reflect the contradictions of a coalition and its inability to anticipate negative consequences from drastic decisions. Operation Barbarossa and Pearl Harbor in the context of the Tripartite Pact polarized the world and spread war from Europe to Eurasia, from Asia to the Pacific, and from the Pacific to the Western Hemisphere, and back to Europe. Prior to 1941 the Second World War was not really a world war either in terms of its geography or its magnitude and severity. The meeting of the three conditions made the war a truly *world* war.

Alliances not only helped bring about these three conditions, but also helped each side be better prepared for the war, making it quite severe once it broke out. Additional interventions, particularly that of the US, extended the duration of the war, thereby further increasing its severity. Eventually, pressure by the US would even bring the Soviet Union into the Pacific war in 1945.

IV. CONCLUSION

Table 8.2 summarizes the findings of the analysis. It shows that the Second World War does indeed fit the hypothesized typical pattern that world wars are said to follow.

The Second World War occurred because salient territorial issues were handled in such a way that they gave rise to rivalries among major states. These states took a number of steps such as building up their militaries, making alliances, and engaging in repeated crises that brought them closer and closer to war. The steps they took made them learn that the only way of dealing with each other was through force. Simultaneously, each step taken increased the number and influence of hard-liners within each state. Eventually, a crisis with certain specified characteristics emerged that escalated to war.

Given certain systemic factors and the presence of alliances, territorial contiguity, and rivalry, it was highly likely that the initial dyadic war between Germany and Poland would expand. Once it did, other states were brought in because of bandwagon effects, territorial contiguity, the breakdown of political order, and economic dependence. The conversion in 1941 of the multipolar distribution of capability into a polarized system of two blocs made the war truly global and produced a war of the highest magnitude and severity that has been seen in history.

Table 8.2 Factors related to onset and expansion of war: the Second World War in Europe

Expected	Observed
Onset	
Territorial disputes, military build-ups, Alliance making, repeated crises	Yes
one crisis escalates to war when:	
——— Physical threat to territorial issue	Yes
——— Ongoing arms race	Yes
——— Escalatory bargaining across crises	Yes
——— Hostile spiral	?
——— Hard-liners on at least one side	Yes
Expansion	
Six factors promoting contagion	Yes
Three systemic factors	Yes

The path states took to the dyadic war and the path that led that war to expand to a world war were not unique to 1939–41, but fit a pattern that is thought to be typical of how world wars begin. This chapter has shown that a scientific analysis can clearly identify the underlying factors guiding states along the paths to war. Knowledge of these factors does not eliminate the need for historical explanation, but helps direct the writing of historical narratives toward the events that have the most impact on bringing about war and its expansion.

NOTES

* My thanks to Michael Brecher, Mats Hammarstrom, Marie T. Henehan, Frank Harvey, Patrick James, and Jack Levy for valuable comments. None, however, are responsible for this final version.
1. A justification of the use of causal language is provided in Vasquez (1993: 8–9). For those who object for philosophical reasons to this language, the use of 'causes' can be interpreted as 'the factors that have been found to be associated with war after the effects of other variables have been controlled.'

2. This book chapter is an expansion of Vasquez (1996).
3. Likewise, whether the factors should be seen as additive or multiplicative must await further empirical research.
4. Gibler and Vasquez (1995) are able to improve on Levy's predictions by developing a typology of alliances that distinguishes those that are more war prone from those that are not. Basically, alliances that are pacts to resolve territorial issues are rarely followed by war within five years of their formation. Alliances consisting of major states that were successful in their last war are most war prone; whereas alliances consisting exclusively of minor states that were not successful in their last war are least war prone. Additional evidence on the war-proneness of alliances and the absence of a relationship between alliances and peace may be found in Singer and Small (1966). For a detailed discussion of their findings and Levy's, see Vasquez (1993:162–9).
5. Ostrom and Hoole (1978) find in an analysis of alliances after 1815 that war is most apt to occur within three years after they are made; thereafter alliances are negatively related to war until an alliance is in its twelfth year. After twelve years the relationship between alliances and war is random.
6. The renewing and/or tightening of older alliances (as was done in the Dual Alliance and the 1904 Anglo-French Entente before 1914) can also produce these effects. In addition, alignments can be as important as formal alliances in bringing about war, as Richardson (1994:221) notes. Of course, one must make sure in studying the effect of alignments not to select on the dependent variable; i.e. not to study effects of alignment just by studying crises that are already highly war prone.
7. For example, the crisis leading up to the Crimean war was initiated by Napoleon III of France, and in the early stages he was responsible for taking escalatory actions. Britain became involved as an ally of France and was pushed along this escalatory path by Napoleon III. However, as the crisis unfolded, Napoleon III was prepared to settle without war, but Britain, whose press and certain members of its cabinet were taking a very hard line, was not. Rather than betray Britain, France went along with the actions that led to the war (see Richardson, 1994:85). Here we have an example of where, if there had been no alignment, Britain would not have become involved, and France would have settled.
8. For a detailed discussion of the evidence on arms races that concludes that there is some relationship between building up one's military and the escalation of crises to war, see Vasquez (1993:177–84), Vasquez and Henehan (1992:88–90, 103–8), and Sample (1996).
9. It is hypothesized that perceptions of whether the war was worth the costs are more powerful than the actual outcome, so that when a war is not seen as worth the costs, accommodationists predominate (see Vasquez, 1987b and Vasquez, 1993: chap. 6).
10. On the role norms and rules of the game play in reducing the likelihood of war between major states (see Wallensteen, 1984; Kegley and Raymond, 1990; Vasquez, 1993: chap. 8).
11. See Vasquez (1993:240–2) for caveats about how this factor might be muted by the proper management of the rivalry.

12. Since this occurs simultaneously with an accumulation of alliances (Midlarsky, 1983), the reason disputes accumulate may be that major states have made the disputes of minor states their own and vice versa. Rivalry has the tendency to link issues together into one grand overarching issue. This in turn makes it harder to resolve the issue because to resolve one issue would require an overall settlement. These considerations help explain why repeated confrontations occur and eventually give rise to a crisis that escalates to war.
13. Both Wayman (1984) and Levy (1985a), using different data-bases, find large wars occurring in periods of multipolarity and smaller wars occurring in periods of bipolarity. Levy and Morgan (1984) find that in periods when wars are frequent, they tend not to be severe, and in periods when wars are infrequent they tend to be severe.
14. Bueno de Mesquita (1978) finds that when alliances are polarizing a system into two blocs, this is associated with large wars. Almost 80 per cent of the wars (1815–1965) involving more than one participant occur in periods of rising tightness of alliances, and none of the big wars occur after a decline in systemic tightness (Bueno de Mesquita, 1978:259–60). Wayman (1984), using different measures of alliance polarization, also finds it associated with high magnitude wars (see Vasquez, 1993:253–4).
15. Evidence that world wars are associated with relative parity rather than preponderance can be derived from Singer, Bremer, and Stuckey (1972), who find that in the twentieth century, relative parity in the system is associated with high nation-months of war.
16. Because of the voluminous literature on the Second World War coupled with limitations on space in a book chapter, I will confine my documentation primarily to historical accounts published since 1980.
17. On the connection between the goals of living space and racial policy, see Weinberg (1994:2). It should be noted that many of these ideas did not need the racial element and were discussed in connection with German foreign policy in the First World War (Bell, 1986:85). Nevertheless, what is more important is that the idea that Germany needed *Lebensraum* because it could not rely on trade to meet its needs was a misguided economic theory (Kaiser, 1990:371; see also Bell, 1986:155). At times, and especially with the attack on the Soviet Union, the goal of *Lebensraum* jeopardized the existing access Germany had to the foodstuffs and raw materials being provided by Stalin (see Bell, 1986:290).
18. On the question of whether Hitler had a blueprint or reacted to opportunities and events, see Bell (1986:85 and especially 273).
19. For documentation of these territorial claims, on Teschen see Bell (1986:236), Watt (1989:59); on Ruthenia see Bell (1986:250), Watt (1989:63, 67); on Transylvania see Bell (1986:288); on Italian ambitions see Bell (1986:248), Watt (1989:74); on Russian ambitions see Bell (1986:260, 288); on Memel see Bell (1986:250), Watt (1989:156–57); on Ukrainian nationalists see Watt (1989:59, 61, 64); Bell (1986:286). For a summary of the crises these generated, see Brecher and Wilkenfeld (forthcoming).
20. Bell (1986:252–3) makes this point strongly. See Watt's (1989:108) qualification on this point, saying that Halifax and others were alarmed by

Hitler before the occupation of Prague, but also note his discussion of Chamberlain on pp. 162–72.
21. Rivalry between neighbors usually has a territorial dimension to it, as does the Franco-German rivalry. Rivalries that do not, such as the Anglo-German rivalry, are posited as going to war by having one rival come to the aid of another state, usually a minor state, over a territorial issue. This of course was the case with Britain in both 1914 (Belgium) and 1939 (Poland).
22. Initially, war did have a short-term positive impact on their armament program, especially their labor shortage (Kaiser, 1990:378–80).
23. See Steinert (1977), whom Kaiser cites to support his contention that success made for public and bureaucratic support for Hitler. Nevertheless, there probably remained within the German populace, as well as the Italian, an aversion to war indicated by the outpouring of affection that Chamberlain received from the public on his visits to Munich and to Rome after the Munich agreement, a response that miffed both Hitler and Mussolini (Watt, 1989:30, 96).
24. Rosecrance and Steiner (1993) argue convincingly that it was domestic political pressures that brought about the British decision for war even though the military and economic capability of Britain (from a realist perspective) would not have warranted that decision. They see the domestic pressures as arising from the series of crises and provocations initiated by Hitler that now required 'that Britain should not give way again, war or no war' (Rosecrance and Steiner, 1993:148, 126).
25. In this regard, the realist practice of attempting to balance power no more prevented war than did the idealist policy of appeasement.
26. It may be noted for example, that almost all the steps to war were present between the US and USSR during the Cold War, but no war occurred. The major reason for this is that the conflict was mainly ideological and lacked serious territorial disputes between the two parties. When even relatively minor territorial issues were raised at the periphery in Berlin and Cuba, nuclear deterrence came close to failing and throwing the world into the abyss of nuclear war (see Vasquez, 1991).
27. The only possible characteristic not present is a hostile spiral in the technical sense of the Holsti, North, and Brody (1968) action–reaction model. Whether this is the case will have to await the creation of the appropriate data to measure the dynamics of interaction process in the 1939 Polish crisis.
28. Bell (1986:272–3) places emphasis on the role of economic dependence, whereas Weinberg (1994:113–14) sees economics as less significant.

9 Threat Perception and Surprise: In Search of the Intervening Variable
Abraham Ben-Zvi

I. SURPRISE ATTACK AS A RESEARCH FIELD

During the years following the Second World War, intensive research was undertaken on the subject of surprise attacks and their origins. Confronted with the recurrent inability of nations to respond adequately to warnings of an impending onslaught, many scholars concentrated on such events as the Pearl Harbor attack, the Barbarossa Operation, the outbreak of the Korean War and the Yom Kippur surprise, and produced a voluminous body of literature.

In addition to the multitude of works which sought explanations solely in terms of the specific and ideographic conditions operating at the time of the event scrutinized, other inquiries attempted to incorporate the case under scrutiny into a broader theoretical framework in the hope of better elucidating the inherent patterns by which nations cope with threatening situations. And while explanations which were patterned on the logic and premises of the analytic-revisionist category of research gained initial salience and occasionally even dominance in the immediate aftermath of the event analyzed, it was the category of cognitive-perceptual works which eventually became the major focus of the endeavor to explain the prevalent patterns of response to warning.[1]

In general, studies which rely largely on cognitive premises as their basic analytical tool for the explanation of the prevalent patterns of response to warning are largely skeptical about the prospects for fully overcoming the screens of confusion, ambiguity and deception. Seeking an explanation in terms of the perceptual mechanisms and predispositions which obscured the relevant warning signals gathered by the 'victim state,' these studies maintain that 'the possibility of surprise at any time lies in the conditions of human perception and stems from uncertainties so basic that they are not likely to be eliminated, though they might be reduced.' As a result of this innate propensity to see ambiguous information as confirming pre-existing images and beliefs 'about how the world works and what patterns it is likely to present us with,'[2] policy-makers are bound, according to this category, to distort or dismiss as unreliable and unfounded information which is incompatible with initial beliefs, particularly those which comprise the core of their belief systems (Jervis, 1976:187–90; Kam, 1988:89; Holsti and Fagen, 1967:15, 19).

In view of the welter of obstacles in the way of accurate and timely threat perception 'that are both profound and numerous, and therefore also practically insurmountable,' strategic surprises are depicted by representatives of the cognitive orientation not as the exception but rather the rule – 'practically every strategic surprise attempt is said to succeed' (Vertzberger, 1987:18; Jervis, 1979:306).

Although various cognitive interpretations diverge in terms of emphasis, focus and nuance, they all share Wohlstetter's pessimism regarding the inherent difficulties surrounding the effort to *a priori* distinguish between credible warning signals and the accompanying barriers of obfuscating, misleading noise. Indeed, George's and Smoke's analysis of the reward-cost implications of correct and timely signal detection, which originate in a specific policy background; Jervis' review of an entire cluster of motivated (rather than purely cognitive) biases affecting threat perception, and Lebow's findings regarding the domestic sources of brinkmanship – these are but a few efforts to integrate cognitive premises into a differentiated explanation of the roots of human behavior on the eve of and during acute international crises, which are predicated – explicitly or implicitly – upon Wohlstetter's work and pioneering conceptualization (George and Smoke, 1974:574; Jervis, 1985:24–7; Lebow, 1981:57–97).

In assessing the cognitive-perceptual explanations of the recurrent failure of national entities to adequately cope with the challenge of an imminent attack, it appears that at least some of them underestimate the human capacity to deviate from pre-existing cognitive constraints, and thus to adopt policies which are incompatible with preconceived images and beliefs. In other words, preoccupied with the cognitive, political and strategic sources of misperception of the opponent's intentions, this research category has remained, at least partially, oblivious of the ability of decision-making units to predicate their crisis behavior upon the dynamics of the unfolding situation rather than on the premises of certain fixed belief systems. In the process, it did not assign adequate weight to the cluster of constraints and difficulties (including cognitive and doctrinal biases and barriers), which may arise *after* the adversary's basic intentions had been accurately perceived and diagnosed by the 'victim state' and after the initial barriers to receptivity had been completely overcome.[3] Notwithstanding the insightful efforts of representatives of the cognitive-perceptual orientation to incorporate concepts and analytical tools from attribution theory, prospect theory and schema theory, insufficient attention has been paid to the multitude of cognitive, political, strategic and bureaucratic factors and constraints which may intervene between threat perception and response, and which may doom the prospects of effectively responding to the threat of the approaching attack (George, 1979b:109). The existence of this intervening phase between threat perception and response therefore implies that threat perception may remain decoupled from any concrete and timely action when decision-makers are convinced that it is unnecessary to resort to certain emergency measures to counter the imminent danger. It further entails the possibility that even when policy-makers do perceive a threat and believe some response to be feasible, desirable and necessary, unpreparedness may still be the final outcome (Levite, 1987:151, 158).

As a step toward further differentiation, not only between divergent sources of misperception, but also between the distinct phases of threat perception and response, the following analysis will juxtapose between the Japanese attack on Pearl Harbor on 7 December 1941, and the outbreak on 6 October 1973, of the Yom Kippur War. It is hoped that the sequential review of the factors and variables which intervene between threat perception and response will help explain at least some of the remaining anomalies and paradoxes associated with the outbreak of the war and will provide the impetus for more comprehensive and comparative research on the types of linkage between perception and action.

In conclusion, the main purpose of the following comparison between the Pearl Harbor and the Yom Kippur case studies is to proceed beyond the parameters and bounds of the existing cognitive explanations by focusing on two neglected dimensions: the role of processes which took place after the recognition of war as imminent had permeated the thinking of the leadership of the defending state, and the role of capability assessment as a variable which contributed most decisively to the initial success of the challenger.

II. PERCEPTIONS OF INTENTIONS AND CAPABILITIES

In order to reconstruct systematically the perceptual and behavioral patterns by which the victim states attempted to cope with the welter of tactical indicators, which increasingly warned of an impending attack, the two major determinants of expectations about future adversarial behavior, which pertain to the opponents' intentions and capabilities, should be carefully scrutinized. Although it is widely assumed that intention assessment, which is believed to be intrinsically fraught with ambiguities and ambivalence, is considerably more difficult than capability assessment, which is at least partially based on hard evidence (which is relatively easy to obtain) (Shlaim, 1976:362),[4] one should not overlook the broad complex of intangible capability components and dimensions which are particularly susceptible to misperception (Levy, 1983b:82). These include the enemy's motivation and morale; the quality of military intelligence, control systems and communications; the nature of the prevailing military doctrine and the ability to absorb and effectively employ new and sophisticated weapon systems (Levy, 1983b:82–3). And indeed, as the following analysis will seek to demonstrate, in the context of both the Pearl Harbor and the Yom Kippur case studies, policy-makers in the defending states found it more difficult to diagnose changes in their opponents' capabilities than in their intentions. And while the recognition that the opponents' intentions underwent a significant change did not entail that all the elements that are associated with this determinant of behavior have been fully explored and exposed, still it provided the defender with a crucial index which could have been used as a precipitant for tracing and identifying additional clusters of components of the adversary's overall strategic design.

Intention assessment may be divided into two sub-categories: (1) perceptions of the adversary's basic intentions, and (2) perceptions of the adversary's immediate intentions,[5] which also incorporate assessments of the behavior of the adversary's allies and assessments of the specific manner in which these immediate intentions will be translated into action.

Perceptions of the adversary's basic intentions are perceptions of the opponent's general behavioral style, approach to calculating political action, motivational calculus and ideology (George and Smoke, 1974:582–3). Altogether, these components comprise a coherent set of beliefs and expectations concerning the opponent's operational code, frame of reference, and overall cultural and conceptual frameworks (George and Smoke, 1974). Perceptions of the adversary's immediate

Threat Perception and Surprise: Intervening Variables 245

intentions are perceptions of the opponent's anticipated short-term behavior. Whereas perceptions of the adversary's basic intentions represent the potential and the desired, perceptions of the adversary's immediate intentions represent the tangible and the operational, with the initiator prepared to act forthwith in order to promote his basic objectives and thus to convert the hypothetical into the actual and observable (Kam, 1988:66).[6] Notwithstanding the importance of deciphering the changes in the opponent's immediate intentions, the defender's recognition that war was imminent should be viewed as but the tip of the iceberg rather than as an ironclad, definitive proof that all facets associated with the challenger's decision to strike have been comprehensively diagnosed and adequately addressed. Thus the conviction that a Japanese attack was imminent did not eliminate from the scene pertinent questions such as the exact timing and specific location of the onslaught. Similarly, Israel's policy-makers, while expecting an immediate Arab attack, failed in their assessments of the exact timing of the strike as well as in their estimates of the behavior of such Arab powers and allies as Saudi Arabia.

While most of the works, which seek to elucidate the origins of surprise, focus on the opponent's intentions (both basic and immediate) as the central independent variable and as the main determinant which precipitated complacency and lack of preparedness in the face of the approaching attack, it appears that, at least within the delimited parameters of the two cases under scrutiny, intention assessment (in terms of the basic decision to attack, albeit not in terms of all behavioral tenets which comprise this category) did not comprise the main source of misperception and miscalculation. Instead, it was the continued inability of the political and military leaders of the victim states to update their assessments of the adversary's military capabilities during the period preceding the onslaught which proved to be the main factor responsible for the inadequate response in the face of the clearly perceived threat of war.

Thus, while perceptions of the enemy's immediate intentions were revised and updated in view of the accumulating tactical indicators of the approaching war, no such change took place in the perceptions of the adversary's capabilities, which remained largely outdated and depreciatory.

Although confined largely to the specific context within which these episodes unfolded, this examination of the manner in which the American and Israeli leaders perceived and responded to the mounting indicators of the approaching attack is conceived as an illustration of 'some larger phenomenon' or a class to which it belongs. Treated as an instance of a wider type of undertaking that occurs repeatedly throughout history, the present inquiry can also provide – together with other case studies – the necessary empirical building blocks for the cumulative development of a typological explanatory theory of threat perception and action. In other words, patterned on the method of the 'structured, focused comparison,' it seeks to explain the origins of surprise in 1941 and 1973 in terms of certain theoretically relevant and general variables (George, 1979a:44–5). These surpass the ideographic idiosyncrasies of the cases under scrutiny and thus comprise an integral part of the search to refine and further develop 'generalizations and general laws of at least a probabilistic character covering all ... the cases of each type of phenomena' (George, 1979a:45).[7]

III. CASE STUDIES

A juxtaposition of the patterns by which American and Israeli military and political leaders assessed their opponents' intentions on the eve of war indicates that in both cases the screen of obfuscating, misleading and distracting noise and outdated policy background did not overshadow the relevant warning signals that were gathered. Specifically, the pre-existing belief that Japan, Egypt and Syria would be deterred from action as long as an asymmetry in the balance of military capabilities favoring 'the observing states' continued to exist, was ultimately abandoned on the eve of war, when the accumulating stream of tactical indicators which portrayed a picture of an impending onslaught ultimately overshadowed and outweighed all discrepant interpretations of the unfolding crises.

In the Pearl Harbor case, the widespread belief, shared by most members of the Roosevelt Administration, that war in the Pacific was unlikely to break out so long as the U.S. pursued a 'pure' coercive posture *vis-à-vis* Japan, progressively receded into the background during the period which immediately preceded the Japanese attack as the result of the accumulating tactical data which indicated that war was imminent. Thus, during November 1941 it became increasingly evident to Secretary of War Henry Stimson and Secretary of the Treasury Henry Morgenthau Jr., that their advocated policy of imposing upon Japan a series of comprehensive economic sanctions as a means of deterring and restraining Japanese expansionist moves completely failed, and that – confronted with an irreconcilable coercive drive – the Japanese government was bound to resort ultimately to a defiant, recalcitrant course of militarily challenging the status quo in the Pacific (George and Simons, 1994:283; Levite, 1987:39–41; Jervis, 1979:306–7; Utley, 1985:173–5; Jervis, 1988:679; Ben-Zvi, 1987: *passim*).

Whereas, prior to November 1941, Stimson, Morgenthau and their allies in the State Department remained convinced that the Japanese would not attack American territory 'even if the U.S. put an embargo on raw materials for arms' and that 'all the evidence indicates that they are more afraid of war with the U.S. than anything else,'[8] this expectation that Tokyo's immediate intentions would invariably be derived from Japanese military and economic capabilities (which were perceived as inferior to American capabilities) was abandoned on the eve of war. Instead, the assessment of the American Ambassador in Tokyo, Joseph Grew, according to which Japan's capacity 'to rush headlong into a suicidal conflict with the U.S.' (*President's Secretary's File*, Box 30) should not be underestimated, gained credence in Washington with his cryptic warning that 'a progressively firm policy' entailed 'the risks of sudden uncalculated strokes' ultimately becoming the basis of the revised and updated American posture (*President's Secretary's File*, Box 59).

Similarly, during the period immediately preceding the outbreak of the Yom Kippur War, the assumption – previously adhered to by most Israeli decision-makers and high-ranking military officers – that Egypt (or Syria) would not resort to war unless it could secure control of the skies, or at least have enough air power to support military operations (Kam, 1988:59), gradually evaporated in the face of the accumulating welter of tactical indicators which unequivocally warned of an impending attack. Thus, although Israel continuously estimated – until the outbreak of war – that it could maintain its perceived air superiority into the mid-1970s, this assessment was decoupled from the growing recognition that Egypt and Syria made a strategic decision to go to war despite the vast risks involved. Having acquired ironclad and fully credible warning signals regarding the adversary's determination to take military action (which, as such, were less vulnerable to cognitive and political distortions than other forms of intelligence), members of Israel's political and military elite therefore opted *de facto* to abandon their belief that 'Egypt would not attack Israel unless it achieved the capability to strike Israel's centers of population by air and neutralize Israel's air force' (Ben-Zvi, 1976:386).

Notwithstanding this growing propensity of the American and Israeli policy elites to set aside their pre-existing strategic assumptions which ruled out the outbreak of war as a short-term eventuality, there remained the problem of estimating their adversaries' military capabilities (Kam, 1988:59, 62) (as well as of coping with a multitude of questions, which were inextricably linked to the assessment of their opponents' intentions, such as the assessment of the intentions of their allies or the exact timing of the attack). Although in both cases, estimates of the opponents' intentions were ultimately revised as the expectation of war increasingly permeated the thinking of most (albeit not all) of American and Israeli leaders, the concurrent estimates of the Japanese, Egyptian and Syrian capabilities remained largely intact (Handel, 1984:239). Indeed, while the opponents' intentions to strike were correctly diagnosed, their military capabilities were – in all three cases – significantly underestimated.

In other words, the fact that the decision-makers of the two victim states perceived the war as imminent by no means guaranteed an effective and appropriate response (Ben-Zvi, 1990:23). Although the adversaries' intentions were accurately diagnosed on both occasions, perceptions of the military balance remained static and biased, thus precipitating a military response which did not match the severity of the threat. Comprising a cluster of intervening or 'filtering' variables between the phases of intention assessment and response, capability assessments therefore considerably outweighed and neutralized the accurate assessments of the opponents' immediate intentions. Thus, whereas most studies of threat perception explain strategic surprise in terms of an inadequate intention assessment (which is further reinforced by an equally erroneous capability assessment), it is argued here that surprise should be defined in relative rather than in absolute terms: namely, in terms of the relative weight assigned to each category of assessment when juxtaposed with its counterpart.

Furthermore, although it is widely believed that 'it is far simpler to obtain information about capabilities than about intentions' (Levite, 1987:64), a juxtaposition of the two cases under consideration indicates that what happened in them was in fact the reverse. Thus, on the eve of the 1941 and 1973 wars, it was the category of capability assessments which proved the major impediment to an early and effective response to the impending challenge (or to the formulation of a more realistic political posture, which could have prevented war). In other words, although in both cases the attributes of 'behavioral surprise' were absent, the nature and timing of the response to the perceived threat was still highly inappropriate as a result of the relative dominance of the cluster of intervening considerations related to or derived from capability assessment over those pertaining to intention evaluation (Knorr, 1976:98–9; Ben-Zvi, 1990:23–4) (as well as a result of purely technical factors and failures, such as the erroneous way in which Israel's armoured units in the Sinai peninsula were deployed, or the fact that the alert orders were not always fully implemented). It is to a more detailed analysis of these two clusters of factors in the contexts of the two case studies under scrutiny, that we now turn.

IV. THE PEARL HARBOR ATTACK

The Perception of Intentions

Although the warning signals which pointed directly and specifically to Pearl Harbor as the likely target of the approaching Japanese attack were inconclusive, the deciphered Japanese diplomatic communication (*Magic*), particularly in its most confidential form (*Purple*), consistently provided the United States 'with much useful information on Japan ... by revealing many of the most intimate and confidential thoughts, meetings, and other actions of the Japanese diplomats around the world and their immediate superiors in Tokyo' (Levite, 1987:27). Thus, while the information which was obtained through Magic, which could have suggested that Tokyo was contemplating an air strike against Pearl Harbor as the spectacular opening move in a Japanese–American war, was fragmentary and partial, it still portrayed a general picture of a highly strained and rapidly deteriorating dyad, with the Japanese expecting their conflict with the United States to escalate to the point of open hostilities in the Pacific (Levite, 1987:70).[9]

And indeed, during the month preceding the Pearl Harbor attack it became abundantly clear to American negotiators and primarily to Secretary of State Cordell Hull, that Japan had set a deadline (28 November) for reaching an agreement with the United States on a variety of issues including its relations with the Axis powers, American oil embargo and Japan's continued occupation of China. Concurrently, American decision-makers were fully aware that the messages originating in Tokyo were permeated with a sense of despair and deep concern that the United States would refuse to accept the latest and final Japanese proposals for a *modus vivendi*. No less than nine messages of this type were intercepted before 7 December. One of them, dated 4 November, informed the Japanese Ambassador to the United States, Kichisaburo Nomura, that the proposal he was instructed to submit was Japan's last effort 'to prevent something from happening.' A recurrent theme in all intercepted messages was that 'time was becoming exceedingly short and the situation very critical...' and that an 'extreme danger of war between Japan and the Anglo-Saxon nations, which might break out with an abrupt suddenness,' existed (Wohlstetter, 1962:193).[10]

Against this backdrop, the Japanese decision to reject Secretary Hull's final proposals, namely his uncompromising Ten-Point Plan of 26 November (which amounted to an ultimatum which demanded the immediate and drastic transformation in the direction and course of Japan's foreign policy) clearly signaled that the era of negotiations had effectively reached its end and was not to be resumed (Ben-Zvi, 1976:386).

And indeed, the bulk of the messages originating in Tokyo after 26 November indisputably indicated that Japan did not intend to return to the negotiating table, but that it wished to deceive the United States into believing that it still desired the diplomatic dialogue to continue: 'The situation continues to be increasingly critical,' the Japanese government informed its representatives in the United States in a typical message. 'However, to prevent the U.S. from becoming unduly suspicious, we have been advising the press and others that although there are some wide differences between Japan and the U.S., the negotiations are continuing' (Wohlstetter, 1962:200).[11] Whereas the intercepted messages sent before the rejection of Japan's final proposals contained a faint hope that war would be averted, the later messages made it clear that Japan had finally abandoned the political option. Combined with a plethora of signal intelligence (*Sigint*) which, in late 1941, portrayed an increasingly ominous picture of the Japanese navy completing preparations for massive operations in the Far East, this spate of diplomatic and military signals provided the impetus for Washington's decision-makers to modify drastically their perceptions and expectations regarding the immediate intentions of the Japanese. Against the backdrop of the alarming signal intelligence, which in late November 1941 revealed intensive Japanese naval activity in the vicinity of the Marshall Islands, the massive movements of troops, equipment, and warships from Chinese and Japanese ports into the South China Sea and Indochina, and the intensification of intelligence collection in the Pacific, all residual hopes that Japan could still be deterred from launching a large-scale military campaign in Southeast Asia completely evaporated (Levite, 1987:66).

And indeed, notwithstanding the initial expectation of Secretaries

Stimson and Morgenthau that, confronted with 'clear language and bold actions ... in the Pacific, Japan will yield to that policy even though it conflicts with her own Asiatic policy and conceived interests' (Morgenthau, 2-3 October 1940: Book 318),[12] and notwithstanding the long-standing American belief that the Japanese would refrain from directly challenging the American deterrence (and later coercive) posture in the Pacific, it became clear, in early November 1941, that these images had receded into the background, having been replaced by a cluster of immediate images which were predicated upon the newly formed conviction that an American–Japanese war was imminent (Utley, 1985:162-75).[13]

Whereas, prior to November 1941, Ambassador Grew's repeated warnings of the dangers inherent in the indiscriminate and inflexible pursuit of coercive diplomacy *vis-à-vis* Japan were not heeded by most members of Washington's high policy elite, his assessments – of early November – that the Japanese were likely to undertake 'an all-out, do-or-die attempt, actually risking national hara-kiri, to make Japan impervious to economic embargoes abroad rather than to yield to foreign pressure,' and that 'to believe that Japan would back down rather than go to war with the United States' was 'an uncertain and dangerous hypothesis upon which to base considered United States policy and measures' (Utley, 1985:162),[14] quickly became the basis upon which the new American perceptions of the immediate Japanese intentions were now shaped and delineated.

The diary entries of Secretary Stimson for the entire month of November provide ample evidence for this cognitive transformation of Washington's leading decision-makers from an unbounded, uncritical reliance on the premises of coercive diplomacy as the most effective means for averting a Pacific War, to an equally unmitigated conviction that Japan was about to instigate a military confrontation with the United States (or with its British ally) in the Pacific. Apparently, the prolonged impasse in the Hull–Nomura negotiations, and the accelerated pace of the Japanese military preparations precipitated a frame change in the thinking of Secretaries Hull, Stimson and Morgenthau, and ultimately of President Roosevelt himself.[15] With the expectation that the posture of economic and political pressure would compel Japan to acquiesce in the American demands rapidly diminishing, the Administration was now prepared to view the Japanese intention to challenge the status quo as a short-term and highly probable contingency rather than as a long-term, amorphous dream, which was devoid of any concrete ramifications. Thus, in a cabinet meeting which was held on

7 November 1941, the subject of discussion was not whether war would break out, but whether public opinion would rally around the president during the impending Pacific war. As Secretary Stimson confided in his diary: 'He [President Roosevelt] went around the table – first Hull and then myself, and then around through the whole number and it was unanimous in feeling the country would support us' (Stimson, 1973:3). Similarly, on 25 November, in the course of a meeting which Stimson held with Secretary Hull and Secretary of the Navy Frank Knox, when presented – by the secretary of state – with the draft of the far-reaching, uncompromising Ten-Point Plan which he intended to submit to the Japanese negotiators on the following day, the secretary of war stated: 'It [the Ten-Point Plan] adequately safeguarded all our interests ... but I don't think there is any chance of the Japanese accepting it, because it was so drastic' (Stimson, 1973:1).[16] A few hours later, at a meeting with the president and Chief-of-Staff General George C. Marshall, President Roosevelt – who for many months supported an accommodative posture towards Japan – was unequivocal and quite explicit in addressing the prospects of war. His remarks clearly indicate that while the question of the specific location of the Japanese strike remained permeated with confusion and fraught with uncertainty, he was not distracted or misled by any screens of noise regarding the Japanese immediate intentions to initiate war with the United States. According to Stimson's diary:

> He [President Roosevelt] brought up the event that we were likely to be attacked perhaps next Monday, for the Japanese are notorious for making an attack without warning, and the question was what we should do. *The question was how we should maneuver them into the position of firing the first shot without allowing too much danger to ourselves* (Stimson, 1973:1–2, emphasis added).

Against this background, it is clear that all remaining residues of hope that Japan could still be effectively deterred as a result of a coercive, punitive American posture – completely evaporated in late November. Convinced that war was imminent, the American leadership (which remained in the dark regarding the specific location of the initial combat zone) focused on the question of how to respond most effectively (militarily as well as in terms of domestic support) to the challenge it clearly perceived.

And indeed, even Secretary Hull himself, who for many months invested much of his time and energy in trying to promote an American–Japanese accord, no longer entertained any hopes of a diplomatic breakthrough when he opted to submit to the Japanese negotiators, on 26 November, his most comprehensive and irreconcilable Ten-Point Plan. Believing that this statement would not be an impetus for progress but a direct trigger for escalation and war (Hull was fully aware, from the Magic intercepts, of the Japanese deadline), he remained disillusioned and thoroughly pessimistic even before his scheduled meeting with Ambassador Nomura took place. As Stimson's diary reveals: 'Hull told me over the telephone this morning [26 November] that he had about made up his mind ... to kick the whole thing over – to tell [the Japanese] that he has no other proposition at all' (Stimson, 1973:1). The following day, in the wake of his stormy meeting with Ambassador Nomura, which *de facto* sealed the fate of the diplomatic process, he acknowledged to Secretary Stimson that he indeed 'had broken the whole matter off ... and it is in the hands of ... the Army and the Navy' (Stimson, 1973:1). Combined with President Roosevelt's growing conviction that the Japanese did not conduct the entire negotiations in good faith and were about to attack Indochina (Stimson, 1973:1), there can be little doubt that, during the fortnight which preceded Pearl Harbor, all members of Washington's high policy elite looked upon a Pacific conflagration as a virtual certainty. That they failed to identify the first target in the war they all anticipated is, of course, quite a different matter.

The Perception of Capabilities

The fact that, on the eve of the Pacific War, the immediate Japanese intentions were correctly diagnosed by the American leadership, could by no means guarantee that their initial response to the challenge would be adequate. Thus, although the barrier of noise generated by political misperceptions did not confuse or mislead the president and his civilian and military advisers in late November and early December, a variety of bureaucratic, organizational, technical, cultural, communications, political and perceptual factors intervened between threat perception and response, and ultimately obfuscated or reduced, in the minds of American policy-makers, the magnitude and scope of the military encounter they clearly expected to shortly break out in the Pacific.[17] Central among the multitude of these variables, which prevented the administration from taking full advantage of its success in deciphering Japanese strategic (albeit not tactical) intentions pertains to the level of capability assessment. Thus, while the opponent's intentions (which were at least partially shaped and delineated by an intransigent and belligerent American posture) were accurately perceived even by those members of the administration who, for many months, continuously believed that Tokyo would not dare to confront directly the United States in the Pacific, perceptions of the Japanese capabilities remained static and outdated up to the Pearl Harbor attack. It was indeed in the sphere of capability assessment that a major miscalculation was to abort the American effort to cope with the rapidly escalating crisis in the Pacific. On the eve of war, certain deeply held and pervasive attitudes of condescension toward the Japanese, which had permeated American military thinking since the 1930s and which vitiated any serious effort to analyze Japanese military skills, merged with and were further reinforced by vastly inflated visions of American air power. Specifically, convinced that in air power, the United States 'possessed an almost magical solvent' which could not only deter a Japanese attack on Luzon, but 'defeat one if made' (Weigley, 1973:182-3, 186), American military planners had no doubt that the newly produced B-17 Flying Fortress could easily defend the Philippines by 'destroying the convoys and landing ships of a Japanese attack.' It was further widely believed that even a moderate number of B-17s 'could carry destruction to Japanese expeditions against other friendly territories ... and perhaps to Japan itself' (Weigley, 1973:183). Thus, in October 1941, Major-General Leonard T. Gerow, chief of the War Plans Division, announced that the ongoing reinforcement in air strength of the Philippines had changed 'the entire picture in the Asiatic area.' Gerow further indicated that a Japanese movement toward Malaya and the Indies west of the Philippines would now expose itself to American air attack from the islands and that, consequently, 'American air strength provided new abilities to counter Japanese movements in any other direction as well' (Weigley, 1973:183).[18] Clearly, in the fall of 1941, 'it began to seem possible to establish in the Philippines a force not only sufficient to hold the Islands but also ... strong enough to make it foolhardy for the Japanese to carry their expansion southward through the China Sea' (Stimson and Bundy, 1947:388).

And indeed, on 21 October 1941, these assessments and expectations were comprehensively manifested in a memorandum which was sent by Secretary Stimson to President Roosevelt. In the memorandum, the secretary of war – who repeatedly maintained that 'a showdown [with Japan] could not be long delayed,' enthusiastically asserted:

> A strategic opportunity of the utmost importance has suddenly arisen in the southwestern Pacific. Our whole strategic possibilities in the last twenty years have been revolutionized ... From being impotent

Threat Perception and Surprise: Intervening Variables

to influence events in the area, we suddenly find ourselves vested with the possibility of great effective power. (Sagen, 1994:79)[19]

Against this background of unbounded optimism regarding the air (and naval) capacity 'to destroy Japanese expeditionary forces' and to assault 'the very bases and installations from which the Japanese might mount attacks' (Weigley, 1973:183), there was hardly any reason for concern when the military leadership became convinced that war with Japan was imminent. And indeed, on 15 November 1941, believing that a Pacific war could not be averted, General Marshall expressed confidence that the army's air power was capable of defeating Japan singlehandedly, without much need for the navy. He further observed that the United States was not only prepared 'to defend the Philippine islands' but could use them 'as bases for an air offensive against ... Japan itself.' Marshall concluded:

Already the build-up, begun in the early fall, had placed thirty-five B-17s in the Philippines. This was the largest concentration of heavy bomber strength in the world ... If Japan chose war, the B-17s would bomb Japanese bases and destroy the 'paper' cities of the Japanese home islands. (Weigley, 1973:184)[20]

Combined with the pervasive belief that the Japanese fleet could not carry out a massive air attack against Pearl Harbor due to the insufficient range of its carrier-based planes, it is clear why the perception of war as a short-term eventuality did not result in an acute sense of alarm and vulnerability which called for extraordinary precautionary measures among Washington's military and political leaders. And while successive alert messages were sent to the military commanders in the Pacific by both the army and navy during the last week of November in the wake of the collapse of the Hull–Nomura negotiations, they were couched in broad and general terms and, as a result, were not translated into military alert in either Hawaii or the Philippines (Levite, 1987:88–9). Approaching the war with equanimity and complacency, the architects of American diplomacy and strategy remained oblivious to certain technological capabilities of the Japanese navy (such as the range, speed and maneuverability of the Zero fighter) (Ben-Zvi, 1976–1977:86). And while such members of the administration as Secretary Knox expressed concern about the danger of a Japanese attack with aerial torpedoes on Hawaii despite the fact that the harbor was shallow, this concern was not translated into precautionary action (Weigley, 1973:187). With complacency permeating the thinking of most decision-makers and high-ranking army officers (including General Marshall and General Douglas MacArthur) the possibility that the Japanese could develop torpedoes that would function even in the minimal depth of Pearl Harbor was downgraded despite the 'Taranto precedent,' in which the British demonstrated, in attacking the Italian fleet at Taranto, that torpedoes could be used in shallow water (Betts, 1982:112; Wohlstetter, 1962:358–61).

In Weigley's words:

> As for the Japanese army as a possible adversary, the U.S. army in part affected a condescension toward the Japanese as toward all Orientals. However, impressive as the Japanese army might have been in fighting the Japanese, most American soldiers seem to have thought it not up to Western standards in tactics or military technology. In this view lay the implication that the Japanese army would be an adversary not quite worthy of American mettle, so that a contest with it would be an unfortunate distraction from greater military concerns ... A persistence of prejudices, assumptions and mistaken judgments ... helps to account for the army's spasms of optimism ... in particular for the readiness of otherwise reasonable officers as General Marshall to profess the belief that a handful of B-17s could turn back the military might of Japan without much help from the navy. (Weigley, 1973:167–168)

Indeed, viewing Japan as 'not a particularly significant military power,' American leaders considered the Japanese aircraft second rate, 'when in fact many were of superb quality.' Similarly, American estimates of Japanese aircraft production 'were too low by about half,' and Japanese pilots were viewed as poor in quality, although they were to turn out to be exceedingly well trained (Morgan, 1984:55). Clinging tenaciously to certain stereotyped and widely distorted images of Japan which underscored Japanese 'lack of creative ability,' they were to witness, on 7 December, the total bankruptcy of their own culturally bound, deeply held cluster of capability assessments.

V. THE OUTBREAK OF THE YOM KIPPUR WAR

The Perception of Intentions

In analyzing Israeli perceptions of their opponent's intentions, it is clear that during the period immediately preceding the Yom Kippur

War, the basic strategic preconception – previously adhered to by most Israeli decision-makers and high-ranking military officers – that Syria (or Egypt) would not resort to war unless it could secure control of the skies, gradually and incrementally receded into the background (particularly with regard to the northern front) in the face of the accumulating complex of tactical indicators which increasingly warned of an impending attack.

During the years and months which preceded the war, Israeli leaders were predisposed to perceive basic Arab intentions as divorced from their immediate intentions. For example, while Defense Minister Dayan repeatedly reiterated his belief that Arab frustration with the status quo might ultimately lead Egypt and Syria to embark on a confrontational course *vis-à-vis* Israel, this assessment remained – at least until late September 1973 – general, amorphous and long-term, and as such did not entail any immediate and operational ramifications for Israel.[21]

For all its salience and durability, this perception of the Arab threat as middle-range or long-term (which was predicated upon the premise that Egypt and Syria would not attack Israel unless they achieved the capability to strike Israel's centers of population), was progressively abandoned by several (albeit not all) members of Israel's political and military elite on the eve of war. Thus, although the Israeli leadership continued to estimate – until the outbreak of hostilities – that it could maintain its perceived air superiority into the mid-1970s, this assessment became decoupled from the growing recognition that Egypt and Syria made a strategic decision to go to war despite the high risks involved. Notwithstanding the innate human propensity to remain fully committed to preconceived beliefs and images of the world in the face of discrepant information, such policy makers as Defense Minister Dayan became increasingly predisposed to set aside their long-standing strategic assumptions and expectations during the period immediately preceding the war as a result of their direct encounter with a broad cluster of tactical indicators which – particularly in the Syrian zone – portrayed a picture of imminent war.

Alongside this growing propensity to differentiate between the strategic and the tactical, a new symbiosis between two hitherto distinctive perceptions clearly emerged on the eve of war. With the basic and long-term transformed and converted into the immediate and concrete, the gap between the potential and the actual finally disappeared.

And while such military leaders as Major General Zeira, the director of the Israeli Military Intelligence (AMAN), continuously believed that the opponent's recognition of its own inadequate military capabilities would ultimately outweigh and mitigate the desire to challenge the status quo and thus dictate a restrained Arab posture, Defense Minister Dayan became increasingly convinced that an Arab decision to initiate war could well be reached even in a perceived asymmetric military context, and that the perception of insufficient capabilities by no means comprised an unbridgeable barrier to the Arab margin of maneuverability and latitude of choice in seeking to dramatically alter the strategic regional environment.

Believing that Arab frustration with the continued status quo and diplomatic deadlock might dictate a recalcitrant, defiant posture despite an overall military inferiority, Dayan – like Hull, Stimson and Grew in 1941 – ultimately assigned priority in his strategic assessment of the unfolding crisis, to considerations and factors related to Arab intentions over those pertaining to their capabilities.

An analysis of the process by which the threat of an imminent Egyptian and Syrian attack came to permeate the thinking of Israel's decisionmakers, thus overshadowing the pre-existing perception of the Arab threat as a long-term and diffuse contingency, reveals an asymmetry between the northern and southern fronts. Whereas, in the Golan Heights, the screens of deception and ambiguity completely evaporated as early as late September 1973, in Sinai the change was slower, with residues of the initial perception of war as a long-term eventuality continuously preoccupying and distracting the architects of Israel's foreign and defense policy up to the very eve of war.

The initial precipitant or 'trigger event,' which provided the impetus for changing Defense Minister Dayan's assessment of the prospects of war with Syria was the briefing, which was given by Major General Hoffi, Commander of the Northern Command, to members of the Israel Defense Forces general staff and the defense minister on 24 September. Emphasizing the fact that, unlike the situation on the Egyptian front, Israel lacked strategic depth or any natural barrier in the Golan area, Hoffi reported that Syrian armored forces were massing on the border at an unprecedented rate. Equally unprecedented, he further pointed out, were the surface-to-air missile (SAM) batteries, which were deployed along the border (Handel, 1976:32; Brecher, 1980:64; Keller, 1992:16). Reacting to Hoffi's report, Dayan – who expressed concern in view of the threat to the Golan Heights settlements posed by the Syrian deployment – instructed the general staff to assess the possibility of a limited Syrian offensive in the Golan. This was the first occasion in which Israel's defense minister portrayed a very concrete and

Threat Perception and Surprise: Intervening Variables 259

highly menacing scenario of a strategically vulnerable region becoming the target of a Syrian surprise attack designed to achieve limited territorial gains (including the seizure of a few Israeli civilian settlements) despite Damascus' perceived overall strategic inferiority (*Agranat*:18–21).[22] This perception of a local war in the Golan as an immediate rather than long-range contingency was to become increasingly dominant and salient in Dayan's thinking in the aftermath of his visit, which took place on 26 September, to the Golan front. Whereas, prior to this visit, Dayan alluded to the 'war scenario' as one among several contingencies that he considered in view of the mounting tension along Israel's northern border, it is clear that his first-hand impressions of Israel's tactical vulnerabilities in the Golan, which were reinforced by additional data indicating that the Syrian build-up was indeed unprecedented, led him to reframe the entire regional situation.

In this context, the element which affected Dayan's definition of the situation most profoundly, and which played a dominant role in the frame change he underwent in the course of the crisis, was his recognition (which surfaced for the first time on 26 September, upon concluding his visit of the area) that the Syrians had concentrated their SAM batteries at the front rather than around Damascus. Convinced that this missile deployment unequivocally indicated an offensive design and could not be explained in any non-threatening fashion, Dayan repeatedly asserted his belief that Syria sought to place the entire Golan Heights under a dense missile umbrella so as to provide its advancing ground and artillery units with greater freedom of action and maneuverability. Thus, viewing the new Syrian missile formation (which consisted of 31 batteries covering the Golan Heights as compared with only one battery which was deployed near the Israeli border in January 1973) as a definitive clue or index of Syria's war intentions, the minister became highly sensitive to the dangers to Israel, which were inherent in the approaching northern confrontation. With the war perceived now as a virtual certainty, Dayan – who was further alarmed by King Hussein's warning of an impending Arab attack on both fronts, which was issued in the course of his secret visit to Israel on 25 September – became increasingly affected by its anticipated short-term outcome. In particular, he began to demonstrate – during the last week of September – an ever increasing concern for the safety of the Israeli settlements in the Golan Heights.

And indeed during the two weeks that preceded the outbreak of war Dayan – as well as Major-General Hoffi and the Chief of Staff Lieutenant-General Elazar – were not in the least distracted or misled by any barrier of noise, ambiguity or deception in their assessment of

Syrian intentions. While all of them remained convinced that Israel would ultimately take advantage of its perceived overall military superiority to prevail in the war, their attention shifted, during the fortnight which preceded the outbreak of hostilities, from overall strategic calculations and assessments to specific islands of vulnerability and weakness. As a result of this perceptual shift in the pattern by which the Golan crisis was defined and framed, several precautionary measures were taken in the immediate aftermath of Dayan's visit to the Syrian border to strengthen the Israeli forces in the Golan area. Specifically, elements of the Seventh Armored Brigade (including 25 tank crews) and some heavy artillery units were dispatched to the north. Concurrently, as a measure of precaution, anti-tank positions, ditches and mines were added and strengthened, and a higher level of alert was introduced. On 3 October, after the Syrians had moved 850 tanks into jump-off positions, Dayan decided to reinforce the Seventh Armored Brigade. Instead of the 70 tanks in place two weeks earlier, the total reached 188 by 5 October. On the same day, Major-General Hoffi was authorized to strengthen fortifications with an increase of manpower, bringing them up to an average of 20 men per fortification (*Agranat*:18–20).

Turning to the southern front, it is clear that the perceptual shift from the remote and abstract to the immediate and concrete was sequential and phased, with the pre-existing strategic perception which ruled out the outbreak of general war with Egypt as a short-term eventuality only slowly and unobtrusively receding into the background. Unlike the situation in the Golan Heights, where war was broadly perceived as imminent as early as on 26 September, the significance of at least some of the tactical data gathered by Israeli military intelligence along the southern front did not fully penetrate the screens of strategic preconceptions and deception until the very eve of war.

It is true that during the week preceding the war, Israeli military intelligence (AMAN) accumulated a broad complex of credible indicators concerning Egyptian activity along the Suez Canal, which pointed to several deviations from certain established patterns of behavior in apparently similar circumstances. However, this recognition that Egypt infringed upon the tacit rules of the game with Israel and crossed the demarcation line between the permissible and the forbidden did not trigger an early and comprehensive Israeli response. Not until the evening of 4 October was this gap between the two fronts, in terms of the respective assessments of the opponents' immediate intentions, fully closed. The precipitant for this frame change in Dayan's perceptions of the Egyptian intentions (as well as in the perceptions of most members of Israel's military and political leadership) was inherent in the accumulating reports which indicated that Antonov-22 aircraft had arrived in Cairo (and Damascus) to evacuate the families of Soviet advisors (Stein, 1985b:74).[23]

Coming in the wake of a plethora of indicators, such as aerial photographs from a special reconnaissance mission of the canal zone (which was carried out on 4 October), which revealed an unprecedented build-up of Egyptian forces (with 1100 artillery pieces poised on the canal's west bank and five forward-deployed infantry divisions), as well as reports of an unusual and massive earth-removal operation, which was carried out by the Egyptians along the northern sector of the Suez Canal, the news of the Soviet airlift constituted for Dayan the last straw or catalyst, leading him to abandon – at long last – his belief that war would be confined to the northern front. This perception of war, on both fronts, as imminent was further reinforced early in the morning of 5 October, when Zvi Zamir, the director of the Mossad, obtained a piece of information which he considered to be most reliable and conclusive, which confirmed that war would break out on both fronts at sunset on 6 October. This information was delivered to the prime minister and the defense minister on the same day (Braun, 1992:1987). And indeed, in a meeting which took place at the Defense Ministry on the morning of 5 October, Defense Minister Dayan expressed his belief that the ongoing military exercise in Egypt was merely a cover and a prelude for an impending attack (*Agranat*:21).

In conclusion, by the morning of 5 October, Israeli decision-makers and military leaders (with the notable exception of the director of military intelligence) had already completely abandoned the preconception which categorically precluded the possibility of a full-scale war in 1973. Their decisions on the very eve of war were therefore not in the least affected by any obfuscating noise regarding their opponents' intentions to strike instantly. Faced with mounting indicators which were depicted as inextricably related to Egypt's and Syria's war aims and which, as such, could not be reconciled with any other interpretation, they moved to reframe the crisis as a matter of direct and immediate concern which called for an immediate response. Furthermore, shortly after these definitive indices had reached Prime Minister Meir, she approved Dayan's suggestion for a partial (100 000) defensive reserve mobilization. However, Lieutenant-General Elazar's request for full mobilization of combat reserves and for a preemptive air strike against Syrian airfields and missile emplacements was rejected by Defense Minister Dayan and subsequently by the prime minister.

That these expectations, which were based on the assumption that 'the regular army, supported by the airforce... could withstand a combined attack on two fronts... thus allowing ample time to mobilize the reserves...' (Vertzberger, 1990:66), failed to materialize is, of course, quite a different matter and cannot be attributed to any misperception of the opponent's intentions. And while it is true that this mobilization process started only 10 hours before the actual outbreak of war, thus depriving the army of a sufficient warning time, it is doubtful whether – in view of the erroneous way in which the armored units were deployed in the Sinai peninsula along the bank of the Suez canal and the state of negligence which prevailed in some of the army's positions – the immediate outcome would have been significantly different had Israel been provided with additional time.

The Perception of Capabilities

Whereas several key indicators of Egypt's and Syria's immediate intentions underwent a rapid and far-reaching transformation during the week preceding 6 October 1973, the changes in the indicators of their military capability were considerably slower and, as such, could not erode the preconceived Israeli conviction that an asymmetry in military capabilities favoring Israel still existed on the eve of war. Furthermore, whereas intention assessment was closely patterned on the distinction between the routine and the deviant, no self-evident, clearcut demarcation lines and boundaries between divergent categories and components of the opponents' capabilities emerged in Israel's strategic thinking during the period preceding the war.

In assessing the Arabs' capabilities, the Israeli political and military leadership was particularly impressed with evidence of the Egyptian perception of its own military and political weakness. Perceived as an ironclad and single index of future behavior, which was inextricably related to basic dimensions and characteristics which could not be controlled or manipulated by Egypt,[24] this evidence of the Egyptian evaluation of its own inferior capability *vis-à-vis* Israel (which was accumulated between 1971 and 1972) became a central and immutable component in Israel's strategic planning. Relying heavily on the early assessments of the Egyptian general staff (which argued, before 1973, that even a limited ground operation without adequate defensive capability in the air could be turned into a disastrous defeat, and which expressed skepticism regarding Egypt's capacity to absorb and integrate modern Soviet weaponry into its armed forces), the conservative

Israeli general staff remained oblivious to the overall significance of subsequent incremental indications of change in this category. Irreversibly committed to a static and immutable vision of Egypt's capabilities (and highly skeptical regarding its ability to effectively operate sophisticated weapon systems), it failed to recognize the fact that by the spring of 1973, this pessimistic Egyptian evaluation of the military balance largely receded into the background, giving way to a considerably more optimistic cluster of predictions regarding the likely outcome of war (Stein, 1985b:79–80).

Indeed, during the months immediately preceding the war, the evaluation of the Egyptian general staff of the military balance had changed significantly as a result of accelerated arms deliveries from the Soviet Union (which had resumed in early 1973) as well as the reorientation of Egypt's military strategy (Stein, 1985a:46). The receipt in late August 1973 of SCUD missiles which could strike at Israel's population centers, as well as of the highly effective and mobile anti-aircraft missiles (the SAM-6, and the infantry-fired SAM-7) and the anti-tank missiles (the SAGGER and SWATTER) constituted for President Sadat the last precipitant which convinced him that Egypt, though still inferior to Israel, had nevertheless reached the zenith of its military capability and should therefore exploit this window of opportunity in order to accomplish a set of limited military objectives as a springboard for promoting a considerably broader cluster of political and strategic goals (Stein, 1985a:47; Handel, 1983:138).[25]

Although AMAN closely monitored and fully reported the acquisition by Egypt of these improved military capabilities, these reports could not effectively permeate the barriers of staunchly held preconceptions and beliefs (based on Egypt's *early* assessments of the military balance of power), which envisaged Egypt as being incapable of effectively absorbing advanced weapon systems, and hence of launching a successful general attack across the canal before 1975. And while the situation in the north was perceived as somewhat different, with Syria depicted as capable of occupying Israeli civilian settlements and of securing temporary tactical gains in the Golan, the overall Israeli picture of the military balance on both fronts remained one of total asymmetry up to the very eve of war. Indeed, fully and irrevocably committed to such notions as the belief that Israel's aerial superiority was of such magnitude that its air force could not only comprehensively defend Israel's entire air space in case of war, but concurrently provide an umbrella of effective support for ground operations during the early phases of any large-scale conflagration, Israel's military leadership remained unaware of the possibility that the deployment to the front, by Egypt and Syria, of the advanced SAM-6 and SAM-7 anti-aircraft missiles could well engage the Israeli airforce to such a degree that it would not be capable of significantly contributing to the containment effort during the early stages of the war (Vertzberger, 1990:61).[26] Thus, while believing that Egypt and Syria did intend to attack Israel in the immediate future, Israel's political and military leaders remained confident that the perceived balance of power guaranteed a comprehensive victory for the IDF and thus approached the confrontation with relative equanimity. Oblivious to the fact that their opponents had acquired the necessary capabilities for launching an effective limited offensive, they clung on tenaciously to their initial, obsolete perceptions of the balance of military power, and were therefore largely preoccupied, on the very eve of war, with questions pertaining to the global political context rather than to the more immediate strategic setting along Israel's borders with Egypt and Syria (Handel, 1983:139).

In other words, incapable of recognizing the fact that both categories of intention and capability constituted highly dynamic determinants of behavior which could significantly change, Israeli leaders downgraded the significance of Egypt's recent acquisition of sophisticated weapon systems and thus failed to perceive the possibility that this change in the military balance could provide President Sadat with the option of a limited war.

VI. SYNTHESIS AND CONCLUSIONS

In Search of an Explanation

The two cases juxtaposed above cannot be thought of as identical historical episodes. Not only do they differ from one another in terms of the regional and global setting, the 'operational code' of each initiating party and its specific mode of calculating utility and assessing risks (with the Japanese prepared to take higher risks than their Egyptian and Syrian counterparts), but they diverge in the quality of the intelligence collected by the 'observing states' on the eve of war as well as in the intrinsic structure of each episode. Confronted with a continued irreconcilable posture, a desperate Japanese government ultimately chose the high-risk, low-confidence strategy of war with the United States.[27] By comparison, while Egypt and Syria respectively regarded the continued territorial status quo in the Sinai peninsula and the Golan Heights as unacceptable, the risks involved in their decision to challenge Israel, on 6 October 1973, were considerably lower than those taken by Japan in December 1941.

By virtue of resorting to the strategy of limited war which – particularly on the Sinai front – sought to accomplish minimal territorial gains as a springboard for establishing a new political and strategic environment in the region, and by virtue of forging a broad inter-Arab coalition which – through the imposition of an oil embargo on the West – exerted pressure on major actors on the global international scene, Egypt (and to a lesser extent Syria) initially succeeded, unlike Japan three decades earlier, in controlling the risks of escalation by pursuing a constrained and delimited military strategy which – at least during the first phase of the war – managed to maximize its tactical assets and advantages against an overall stronger Israeli opponent. Thus, whereas the Japanese expectation that the Pacific War would remain limited and short was unrealistic and myopic (Jervis, 1982-3:30), the vastly different international configuration of forces in 1973, combined with his specific war strategy, enabled Egypt's President Sadat to achieve at least some of his strategic-political aims despite the military setbacks which were inflicted upon him during the last phase of the conflagration.

Similarly, although – in the Pearl Harbor case – Washington's high policy elite became convinced, during late November, that war between the United States and Japan was imminent but remained in doubt regarding the specific location of the Japanese attack, no such ambiguity existed among the Israeli political and military leadership in early October 1973. Convinced that war along Israel's southern and northern borders was imminent, the question which preoccupied Prime Minister Meir, Defense Minister Dayan and Chief-of-Staff Elazar on the morning of 5 October, was whether to launch a preemptive air strike against Syria and whether to authorize a large-scale mobilization of reserves. Ultimately, believing that, by virtue of its superior military capabilities and secure borders (particularly in the south), Israel could absorb and contain the Arab attack while avoiding international condemnation which a preemptive strike was bound to precipitate, the Israeli leadership – seeking to eliminate any residue of doubt regarding Arab responsibility for the war – was fully prepared to pay a perceived marginal military price for securing a highly desired set of political goals (*Agranat*:39).[28]

Notwithstanding these differences, as well as the difference in the scope and quality of the intelligence which was gathered in the two cases during the period immediately preceding the outbreak of war (with the quality of the data compiled by Israeli military intelligence far outweighing the level of the intelligence gathered by the U.S. in 1941), it is clear that in both episodes it was the category of capability assessment which came to intervene between the phases of intention-recognition and response, thus dictating a behavioral pattern which proved inadequate and insufficient.

Notwithstanding the contextual and structural differences between these two cases, the basic similarities between Pearl Harbor and Yom Kippur should not be overlooked. Central among them was the decision of both initiating states to resort to force after reaching the conclusion that there was no hope any longer of diplomatic progress.[29] In 1941, it was the uncompromising Ten-Point Plan which indicated to the Japanese that it had no viable diplomatic option for securing at least some of its objectives in the Pacific. In 1973, it was Sadat's growing conviction that there was no hope of reaching an interim agreement on a partial Israeli withdrawal from the Suez Canal which led him to challenge deterrence and embark on a recalcitrant, belligerent course of action. Thus believing, as the Japanese leadership did three decades earlier, that his margin of diplomatic maneuverability had been drastically reduced in the wake of the failure to conclude even a partial disengagement agreement with Israel in Sinai, he resorted to the same posture of defiance which characterized the Japanese behavioral pattern when it became clear that the prolonged diplomatic effort to reach even a partial *modus vivendi* agreement in the Pacific ended in a complete deadlock.

Turning to the 'victim states' it is clear that in both the cases juxtaposed, the main impediment to an effective and timely response to the looming military challenge originated in static and outdated perceptions of the opponents' capabilities rather than in misperception of their immediate intentions. Whereas most of the cognitive literature has remained preoccupied with the effort to identify and underscore the patterns and types of misperception which repeatedly prevented the victim from recognizing their adversary's belligerent intentions, much less emphasis has been placed on subsequent cognitive (and bureaucratic) reactions which help shape the actual response to the clearly perceived threat of attack. Accurate intention assessment, then, should be viewed as the tip of the iceberg and as nothing more than the initial phase in a long and multifaceted cognitive process. Deciphering the opponent's immediate intentions and immediate goals by no means guarantees, therefore, that one's response will be appropriate or satisfactory. Nor does it indicate that all facets of the adversary's decision to strike have been accurately perceived. Hence, attention should be paid to a variety of constraints and factors which may surface *after* the initial barriers to accurate intention assessment have been overcome, and which may ultimately reduce the chances of effectively coping with the anticipated assault. As the preceding review of the Pearl Harbor and Yom Kippur cases sought to demonstrate, perceptions of the opponent's military capability (which were inextricably related to a wide complex of cultural factors and images) proved to be the major obstacle to effective and timely response by downgrading and minimizing the threatening ramifications of the approaching confrontation. In other words, whereas American and Israeli decision-makers initially believed that their opponents would predicate their behavior upon their perceptions of the balance of capabilities and would consequently refrain from initiating war, the change which ultimately took place in their beliefs about the Japanese, Egyptian, and Syrian immediate intentions did not lead them to reassess their preliminary assumptions concerning their opponents' capabilities. Thus while the defenders in both instances surmised that the adversaries would delineate their intentions in accordance with their perceived capabilities, this view of an inextricable link between the adversary's capabilities (the independent variable) and intentions (the dependent variable) did not spill over to its logical conclusion. Specifically, it did not entail the recognition that the diagnosed change in the challengers' intentions could reflect changes in their perceived capabilities. Instead, these changes of the opponent's immediate intentions were perceived in isolation, decoupled from any effort to examine to what extent they originated in the adversary's revised capability assessments. Clearly, the growing expectation of war did not induce the defender, in both cases, to focus on the opponent's capabilities in an effort to determine if, indeed, these modified intentions reflected a revised assessment, on the part of the challenger, of the balance of capabilities.

In trying to account for the discrepancy and asymmetry between these two determinants (which was also manifested in other cases such as the outbreak of the Border War between China and India in October 1962), it appears that by virtue of their highly dynamic nature and the fact that they underwent drastic modifications in their structure, formation and configuration during the period immediately preceding the war, indicators of the opponents' short-term intentions were susceptible to early detection and accurate interpretation. So drastic was the deviation from certain long-standing, well-established patterns of behavior (both military and political), that the infringement of the rules of the game (which routinely regulate permissible behavior between allies and adversaries) was quickly recognized and diagnosed by both American and Israeli decision-makers as a statement of intent, and thus as the prelude to the violent repudiation and disruption of the entire pre-existing system of non-verbal communications (in the 1973 case) or direct verbal and explicit communication (in the 1941 case).[30]

By comparison, the fact that capability assessments (particularly on the strategic level) inevitably dealt with prolonged processes which changed only gradually and incrementally, led the American and Israeli leaderships to fit new and discrepant capability indicators into their preconceived theories and images. To paraphrase Jervis, the contradiction between the incoming pieces of discrepant data (concerning the opponents' capabilities) and the prevailing view was small enough to go unnoticed or to be dismissed as unimportant (Jervis, 1968:465–6).[31] Whereas the change in some of the indicators of the opponents' immediate intentions was quite overwhelming and unequivocal and thus precipitated a major cognitive reorganization among most members of high policy elites of the victim states, no clear-cut and conclusive criteria for updating and revising the opponents' capabilities emerged on the eve of war. Furthermore, the fact that capability assessments were inextricably related to an entire cluster of deeply ingrained political, cultural and philosophical beliefs, made discrepant information particularly susceptible to the dangers of misperception, rejection and erroneous interpretation. Thus, in the absence of ironclad and definitive evidence (of the sort that was obtained with respect to the opponents' intentions) that a dramatic change in the capabilities of the Japanese, Egyptian, and Syrian armies had indeed taken place, Israel's policymakers were predisposed to adhere tenaciously to their preexisting images of the opponent's overall military capabilities in defiance of all fragments of contradictory information (*Agranat*:85),[32] and in defiance of their own initial belief that their adversary was a rational actor who was sensitive to cost and would therefore refrain from resorting to exceedingly high-risk courses of action.

Thus, in view of this powerful durable screen of culturally bound capability assessments, the disjointed trickling of discrepant data was insufficient to counterbalance the cumulative impact of deeply held national images and stereotypes, which were reflected in the pervasive belief that neither Japan nor Egypt and Syria were capable of absorbing modern technology and making full use of sophisticated weapons systems.

And while it is virtually impossible to separate completely the assessment of the opponent's intentions from the appraisal of its capabilities (any assessment of the opponent's immediate intentions is at least partially based on the analysis of the specific configuration, deployment and location of its military forces), more attention should be given to the tactical and tangible indicators of the adversary's war-related actual behavior than to its basic strategic preconceptions, aspirations, predilections and overall capabilities. In other words, rather than focusing on the general components of the military balance, the leadership of the status quo power should assign priority, in its effort to assess the likelihood of war, to the cluster of ingredients which pertain to an imminent planned action (local, partial or general), by the challenger, which may be carried out even when the perceived overall balance of military capabilities favors the status quo or defending state. Indeed, whether flawed or accurate, assessments of the *overall* military balance should not be viewed as the dominant or exclusive index for evaluating the prospects of a limited or even general military action. Such a challenge may be derived from a broad cluster of political, ideological, economic, psychological and domestic factors and is, therefore, only seldom predicated entirely upon purely military considerations.

Although the foregoing reconstruction of the divergent patterns of perception and misperception was confined to two specific case studies, the Pearl Harbor and Yom Kippur episodes should by no means be approached in purely ideographic terms. Instead, these cases provide part of the infrastructure for the development of a differentiated and sequential theory of threat perception and action. Additional cases in which apparently similar forms of misperception were evident – such as the Sino-Indian Border War of October 1962, and the Indo-Pakistani War of 1965, as well as a large number of asymmetric low-intensity conflicts – should be scrupulously reconstructed in the hope of establishing the necessary empirical building blocks for the cumulative development of a typological theory of cognition and action in the shadow of war.[33] Knowing what the enemy's proclivities are (to paraphrase Ernest May) cannot be thought of, therefore, as the panacea for successfully coping with the threat (May, 1984:505–41). Instead, it is but a prerequisite or a necessary condition, which must be augmented and accompanied by compatible and accurate capability assessments so as to guarantee that the counter-measures adopted indeed correspond to the nature and magnitude of the threat.

As this juxtaposition clearly indicates, then, the study of the cognitive, political and strategic roots of surprise should be approached sequentially. Such a sequential research agenda, and an emphasis on the various types of threat indicators as they unfold over time, should sensitize us to the possibility that the recognition of an impending threat in terms of the opponent's immediate intentions may be decoupled and completely divorced from subsequent processes which shape the actual response to the perceived threat of attack.

And while a surprise attack by definition is one that is truly understood only in retrospect, it is hoped that this dissection of the problem and the identification of certain interacting variables pertaining to the divergent patterns of perception and response may help to prevent situations which make such postmortems necessary.

NOTES

1. Some of the author's earlier works on the subject of surprise are used as the point of departure and basis for the present comparative analysis. For a review of the analytic-revisionist category of research, see Ben-Zvi (1995:5–29). Another recent article which addresses the revisionist category is Bar-Joseph (1995:584–609). The article focuses on the role of the director of Israeli Military Intelligence, Major-General Zeira, on the shaping of Israeli strategy on the eve of war rather than on capability and intention assessments, which comprise the major focus of the present analysis. Similarly, Lebow and Stein in their comprehensive book analyze various facets of the Yom Kippur War, but primarily from the vantage point of the superpowers. See also Wohlstetter (1962:127–41) and Cohen and Gooch (1990:40).
2. See also Vertzberger (1990:57).
3. For exceptions, see Betts (1982; 1989:330–4) and Ben-Zvi (1990:21–2). While underscoring the importance of capability assessments, Ben-Zvi's article did not address the issue of frame-change and its ramifications, nor could it make use of the multitude of recently published documents and memoirs of some of the Israeli participants in the decision-making process on the eve of the Yom Kippur War. It should also be added that the 1990 article juxtaposed the 1973 war with the 1962 border war between India and China.
4. See also, in this connection, Levy (1983b:82, 92).
5. See Jervis' definition of 'basic intentions' in Jervis (1976:50).
6. See also, in this connection, Knorr (1976:78, 84).
7. See also Eckstein (1975:99) and George and Smoke (1989:171).
8. Quoted from a letter which was sent by Stimson to the *New York Times*, dated 11 January 1940.

9. See also Weigley (1973:185).
10. See also Sagen (1994:81); Utley (1985:173-4) and Levite (1987:64-5).
11. The quoted despatch was intercepted on 1 December 1941.
12. Quoted from a 'Historical Memorandum as to Japan's relations with the United States,' which was sent on 2 October 1940 by Secretary Stimson to Secretary Morgenthau. See Morgenthau (Hyde Park, New York: Franklin D. Roosevelt Library: Book 318: 2-3 October 1940).
13. For an analysis of the distinction between 'background images' and 'immediate images' see Snyder and Diesing (1977:291-310).
14. See also Ben-Zvi (1987:87-91).
15. For an analysis of the process of frame change in the context of the Munich Crisis, see Farnham (1992:205-35).
16. Among other things, the Ten-Point Plan demanded the immediate evacuation of *all* Japanese troops from China.
17. For a review of these factors see Ben-Zvi (1976:85-6). See also Wohlstetter (1962:310, 312-19, 322-3).
18. See also Sagen (1994: 79) and Utley (1985:162-3).
19. See also, on Stimson's conviction that war was imminent, Stimson and Bundy (1947:389).
20. See also Stimson and Bundy (1947:388-9).
21. For illustrations see Defense Minister Dayan's statement of 22 May 1973, in *Agranat* (page 173).
22. Dayan's statement of 24 September is quoted by *Agranat* (pages 18-21). See also Braun (1992).
23. On the theoretical aspects of frame change, see Farnham (1992:205-7).
24. This definition of indices is based on Jervis (1970:18, 44). See also Vertzberger (1990:66).
25. Earlier, in April 1973, 18 Libyan Mirage-5 fighters were deployed to Egypt (Braun, 1992:23).
26. See also Morgan (1984:200-1).
27. See, in this connection, Grew's message of 30 November 1941, in *President's Secretary's File* (Box 30).
28. See *Agranat* (page 39). See also Braun (1992:72-3).
29. See, with regard to the Yom Kippur case, Stein (1985a:58).
30. See, in this connection, Schelling (1966:126-89).
31. See also Heuer (1982:39).
32. See also, in this connection, Kam (1988:94-5) and Nisbett and Ross (1980:370).
33. For a preliminary effort to juxtapose the cases of the Yom Kippur War and the Sino-Indian Border War of October 1962, see Ben-Zvi (1990: *passim*). See also, on the Sino-Indian Border War, Vertzberger (1984:124; 1982:370-89) and Mullik (1971). For similar findings see Cohen and Gooch (1990:176-8) and Lebow (1981:150). For a similar analysis of the Indo-Pakistani War of 1965 see Ganguly (1990:76-80).

10 Democratic Change and Defense Allocation in East Asia
Steve Chan

In this chapter, I undertake a preliminary analysis to clarify the effects, if any, of the 'democratic opening' in three East Asian countries on their military expenditures. In the context of a two-level game (Evans et al., 1993; Putnam, 1988), democratization can simultaneously influence these expenditures by promoting a more relaxed international environment and by altering domestic priorities for resource allocation. Because the central concern of the democratic peace proposition has been war occurrence rather than defence spending, this analysis shares an interest of several other recent attempts that probe this proposition's 'cosilience' (Olson, 1982) by extending its logic beyond the original domain to additional empirical phenomena such as foreign intervention, dispute mediation, and civil strife (Kegley and Hermann, 1995; Kozhemiakin, 1994; Raymond, 1994; Zerbinos, 1994). In line with this volume's theme of new directions in international relations research, this chapter pursues a potentially important 'missing link' – namely, defense expenditures – through which domestic regime change can affect international peace.

This chapter is organized as follows: (1) explaining the research rationale for studying East Asian defense expenditures, (2) presenting the logic of inquiry, (3) specifying the methodology of interrupted time series, and (4) interpreting the analysis results by making comparisons between most similar systems.

I. RESEARCH RATIONALE

The democratic peace proposition has received much analytic attention in the past decade (for two major works on this topic, see Ray, 1995, and Russett, 1993). Although some scholars continue to question the empirical validity or coverage of this proposition, others consider the practical absence of war *among* democracies as representing 'as close as anything we have to an empirical law in international relations' (Levy, 1989c:270), and as constituting 'one of the strongest nontrivial or nontautological generalizations that can be made about international relations' (Russett, 1990:123).

Instead of focusing on the historical association between the democratic attributes of states and their frequency of war involvement, I address in this analysis the question of *'democratic armament.'* Two rationales underlie this choice of focus. First, it seems appropriate to shift from an interest with comparative statics to a concern with dynamic process. Rather than treating democracy as a set outcome, it is useful to examine democratization as an ongoing evolution. In particular, this analysis seeks to understand how the *initiation* of a democratic opening is likely to affect policy choices (in this case, defence expenditures). The inquiry is therefore extended to the newly democratizing polities. Instead of focusing on the possible differences in the war involvement record of established democracies and non-democracies, one is led to ask whether *major regime changes* in the direction of greater democracy matters for public policy.

Second, it seems important to penetrate the 'black box' that most analysts have so far employed in studying the democratic peace proposition. That is, the general tendency has been to ascertain some historical association (or the lack thereof) between the presence (or level) of democracy for states and their war records. The *policy medium* through which democratic politics is likely to affect a country's propensity to be involved in belligerence is usually left unspecified and unexplored. In this analysis, I investigate one such possible policy medium, namely, a country's decision to spend on the military. Dating at least from Richardson's (1960a) classic work, there has been a long tradition of scholarship on the determinants of arms expenditures and on the effects that such expenditures can have for the outbreak of war. Wallace (1982, 1979) presented especially persuasive evidence that arms races, as indicated by reciprocal escalation of defense expenditures, have promoted war. Thus, budgetary decisions about military spending offer an important conduit through which changes at the domestic level (e.g. democratization) can produce consequences at the international level (e.g. detente).

In short, this analysis asks whether democratic changes matter for policy choices. It shares with those past studies (e.g. Ames, 1987, 1977; Bunce, 1986, 1981, 1980; Huang, 1992; Dixon and Moon, 1986; Roeder, 1986, 1985) an interest in inquiring about the effects, if any, of regime transition or leadership succession on the government's decisions on resource allocations. East Asia offers an especially appealing area for pursuing this inquiry because, unlike some other regions, it features simultaneously rapid and sustained economic expansion, substantial armament in the midst of seemingly intractable enduring rivalries, and significant democratic opening in the recent past.

As will be explained in greater detail below, four East Asian countries – Malaysia, the Philippines, South Korea, and Taiwan – are selected for analysis. Malaysia serves as the 'control case,' where there was not a sharp break in regime continuity. In the other three cases, such a shift occurred in the form of a major democratic opening.

The nature of democratic transition should have an effect on defense allocations. More specifically, this expectation can be stated as the following hypotheses:

H1: Compared to countries with regime continuity, those having undergone a democratic opening tend to experience changes in their defense allocations. The greater the regime change, the sharper and more immediate tend to be the alterations in the latter allocations.

H2: If the democratic transformation is initiated and controlled by an incumbent elite, military expenditures tend to show milder discontinuities, or smaller departures from the period preceding the regime change. In such 'top down' political transitions, we expect greater continuity in the personalities of the ruling coalition and also in its policy orientations. Accordingly, major or abrupt shifts in fiscal allocations are less likely to occur. One would instead expect considerable persistence in the prior pattern of defense allocation. Changes in such allocation, if any, tend to be marginal and incremental.

Conversely, if a democratic change is forced from below as a result of mass revolt, we expect sharper changes in fiscal decisions. In this case, there is more likely to be a new ruling coalition interested in pursuing a different policy agenda. However, the direction for changes in defense expenditures is uncertain in this scenario. These expenditures can increase or decrease, depending in part on the strength or fragility of the new regime.

H3: If a new regime is politically precarious, it tends to resort to using foreign threat as a way of providing the military with an external mission, and to increasing the defense budget as a way of securing the support of the armed forces (Huntington, 1991). We would therefore expect military allocation to rise, when there are intense intra-elite competition and opposition from the supporters of the *ancien régime*. In contrast, a more secure democratic leadership does not have to rely on the armed forces to quell its opposition or to neutralize challenges from the military establishment itself. Of course, appeasement of the latter is not mutually exclusive with other attempts by the regime to secure support from alternative interest groups.

H4: Regimes with strong institutional ties with the military tend not to raise the defense budget significantly after the democratic opening. These regimes have less to fear about being overthrown by the armed forces. Conversely and paradoxically, regimes without strong institutional ties with the military are more likely to appease the armed forces by raising their budget. The need for this appeasement, as hypothesized earlier, is greatest when a newly democratizing regime is most vulnerable to conservative challenges.

The above expectations about defense allocations hinge not only on the presence or absence of democratic opening, but also on the *interaction* effect between the source of political change, the strength of the new regime's political control, and the depth and extent of its institutional ties with the armed forces. They echo Russett's (1993:33) emphasis that the operation of democratic peace can be quite context dependent. They also point to the need for multivariate analysis. This said, it is important to acknowledge that with only four cases being studied here, one cannot possibly resolve conclusively the permutations sketched above. This chapter should therefore be seen as exploratory rather than definitive.

II. LOGIC OF INQUIRY

How do we propose to determine any non-random change in defense expenditures in response to democratization? This analysis combines the logic of quasi-experimental design with the logic for comparing most similar systems in order to infer cause–effect relationships and to reduce the danger of spurious interpretation (Campbell and Stanley, 1963; Przeworski and Teune, 1970). It studies the historical time series of defense expenditures for the four East Asian countries already mentioned: the Philippines, Malaysia, South Korea, and Taiwan (recent surveys of these countries' political economies can be found in Borthwick, 1992; Friedman, 1994; Simone and Feraru, 1995).

The ouster of Ferdinand Marcos by Corazon Aquino in 1986 represents the 'test intervention' in the quasi-experimental design. Because the Aquino administration had a tenuous grip on political power and was constantly challenged by various entrenched oligarchs and rightwing military leaders, the rationale presented earlier led me to expect a sharp increase in defense budget in the post-test period as a sign of the regime's attempt to secure the military's support. There is, of course, always the possibility that the observed post-test change in the Philippine time-series can be an artefact of some other event that just happened to coincide with the popular uprising against Marcos and the subsequent installation of the Aquino presidency. To check against the danger of irrelevance (that is, different experimental treatments producing the same results), Malaysia – which has not experienced a comparable regime change – is introduced as a control case. Thus, causal inference is attempted not only on the basis of pre- and post-test observations for the same country, but also on the basis of comparing this country's time series with its most similar counterpart that has not been subjected to the quasi-experimental stimulus.

If the Philippines presents us with a case of democratic transition due to popular uprising from below, Taiwan offers an example of political liberalization initiated from above. Although this liberalization is an ongoing process, the critical turning point was mid-1987 when the then president, Chiang Ching-kuo, lifted martial law and abolished the Emergency Decree on the basis of which the Kuomintang had ruled the island since 1949. This action subsequently led to the legalization of opposition parties and the introduction of popular elections at the national level. In contrast to the Philippines case, democratic transition in Taiwan – if the reasoning given earlier is valid – should not be accompanied by any major or abrupt changes in defense allocations.

South Korea, however, presents a more appropriate counterpart for making pairwise comparison with Taiwan than the Philippines. It so happens that this country also underwent a democratic transition in late 1987. In that year mass demonstrations and student riots finally forced the regime to accept the popular election of the president. Roh Tae Woo, with 35.9 per cent of the popular votes, won this election over a badly split opposition (Kim Young Sam with 27.5 per cent of the votes and Kim Dae Jung with 26.5 per cent). While the election was forced by pressure from below, Roh appeared to enjoy greater political authority and control than Aquino. Moreover, Roh was a former general with extensive military ties. He should presumably be more able to count on the support of the armed forces, and thus had less need to placate them. Therefore, the prospects for major reallocations of military resources should be less in South Korea than in the Philippines and, more speculatively, perhaps less than in Taiwan as well. Moreover, according to the logic laid out earlier, should these changes occur, they are more likely to signal a fall than a rise in Seoul's defense budget (or perhaps a slower increase than previously).

III. QUASI-EXPERIMENTAL DESIGN

Box and Tiao (1975) offer one popular approach to studying interrupted time series (for other examples, see Campbell, 1969; Campbell and Ross, 1968; Caporaso and Pelowski, 1971). This approach requires the analyst to identify and estimate a noise model for the pre-test period so that it can be used as a basis for determining the effect, if any, of the test intervention. Because, however, of the small number of pretest observations (12 for the Philippines and Malaysia, and 14 for South Korea and Taiwan) in this study, it would be inappropriate to apply this approach.

Instead, I follow Lewis-Beck's (1986, 1979; see also, Lewis-Beck and Alford, 1980) suggestions which seek to take advantage of the information contained in the entire data series. This alternative approach was most recently exemplified by Huang (1992). It treats the analysis of interrupted time series as a variation of the classic multiple regression model. In this approach, various independent variables – intended to capture the effects of trends, events, and intervening factors – are introduced in the regression to explain the overtime variation in the dependent variable. The test event is represented by (1) a dichotomous dummy variable designed to indicate any intercept change, and (2) a post-test time counter intended to reflect any slope change. Any significant change in intercept could be interpreted to indicate the test event's immediate and short-term effect in affecting the level of the dependent variable, while that in slope suggests a longer-term effect in altering the dependent variable's pre-test trend.

The two pairs of countries studied here are quite similar in some respects, but they are hardly identical. Thus, for instance, trade and cultural factors are not represented in the regression model, because the countries selected for the pairwise comparisons are relatively alike in these respects. There are, however, important differences as well. Because there have been rather sharp distinctions in the rate of economic growth among these countries (with the poor performance of the

Philippines being the obvious deviant case), this variable is explicitly introduced in the regression model. Economic growth, of course, can provide the wherewithal to finance defense spending (as has been suggested often in conventional explanations of East Asia's rising military expenditures). However, economic growth could also promote post-material concerns that augur a shift away from such spending (Inglehart and Abramson, 1994). Moreover, it could be linked to stronger trade and investment ties with other states, thus presenting another factor in neoliberal accounts of international peace.

The rate of change in US military spending is also entered in the regression model as a control variable. This variable is used as a proxy to indicate declining international tension after the Cold War, and to reflect diminished opportunity for the East Asians to count on Washington to provide for their collective defense (Olson and Zeckhauser, 1966). It provides an explicit basis for assessing the influence of a changing external environment on defense appropriations, thus enabling us to compare its potency with that of other factors of a domestic origin. Finally, in the cases of Taiwan and South Korea, I also incorporate in the regression equations the defense allocations of their rivals, China and North Korea respectively, in order to capture the dynamics of their enduring contests. In the interest of preserving the maximum number of data points, the regression model tests only the contemporaneous effects of the control variables.

The regression model is specified with the following terms:

$$Y_t = b_0 + b_1 T_t + b_2 D_t + b_3 C_t + b_4 Growth_t + b_4 USDef_t + b_5 RivalDef_t + e_t$$

where

Y_t = rate of change in defense spending;
b_0 = regression intercept;
T_t = trend variable, a time counter that assigns 1, 2, 3 ... from the first to the last year in the entire series;
D_t = dichotomous dummy variable indicating the test event, scoring 0 for the pre-test years and 1 for the post-test years;
C_t = post-test time counter, scoring 0 for the pre-test years and 1, 2, 3 ... for the post-test years;
$Growth_t$ = rate of change in gross national product;
$USDef_t$ = rate of change in US defense spending;
$RivalDef_t$ = rate of change of China's or North Korea's defense spending, applied only to Taiwan and South Korea respectively;
e_t = error term.

All data, covering the years 1974–93, are stated in constant US dollars, and are based on the United States Arms Control and Disarmament Agency (various years). Ordinary least-squares regression was used by Lewis-Beck (1986) to demonstrate its general usefulness in pursuing this approach to analyzing interrupted time series. The OLS method assumes that the regression errors are not auto-correlated. I account explicitly for first-order auto-regressive process in the following analysis and, as can be seen from the Durbin-Watson statistics, auto-correlation is not a problem.

IV. PATTERN INTERPRETATION

Before interpreting the analysis results, three caveats should be noted. First, the data series for military expenditures show considerable volatility. There are frequent surges or declines in annual changes exceeding 20 per cent and even 30 per cent. Second, the post-test period is quite short (with only 8 observations for the Philippines and Malaysia, 6 for Taiwan, and 5 for South Korea). Given this limited data basis (not just for the post-test period, but also for the entire series for which $N = 20$), the stability of the results reported here is subject to further examination. Moreover, the relative imbalance in the number of pre-test and post-test observations raises concern about the danger of multicollinearity between b_2 and b_3 (both of which have a large number of zero values for the pre-test observations; see Lewis-Beck, 1986:228).

Third, determining the exact timing of the test intervention is not unproblematic. It is sometimes difficult to establish definite cut-points in marking this intervention, and this decision can in turn affect the analysis results (Lewis-Beck, 1986:228–9). I apply the following rationale to the specification of the test interventions' timing. The Philippine election and the subsequent People's Revolution deposing Ferdinand Marcos took place in February 1986, that is, close to the beginning of 1986. Thus, for this case as well as for the Malaysian case that serves as its control, I treat 1986 as the first post-test year. The Emergency Decree was lifted in Taiwan in July 1987; and the South Korean presidential election, preceded by mass protests, took place in December 1987. In these two cases, 1988 is taken to be the first post-test year.

The regression results are reported in Table 10.1. We begin by noting what we failed to find. Except for South Korea, percentage changes in defense allocations were not significantly related to economic performance – perhaps because this performance has cross-cutting effects (such as those mentioned earlier) that tend to neutralize one another. In the case of South Korea, a rising GNP tended to boost military expenditures. Asian defense allocations were also not related in a systematic fashion to changes in US military expenditures, used here as an approximate index of international tension and the opportunity to engage in defense free-riding. And, in the cases of Taiwan and South Korea, we found little evidence suggesting that their defense spending was linked to changes in the military expenditures of their respective civil-war adversaries (China and North Korea). With the partial exception of South Korea just noted, these results suggest that, for the cases and periods studied here, defense spending did not appear to have responded to or been motivated by changes in the domestic economy or in the external security environment. This spending had risen – and fallen – sharply during periods of both major GNP contraction and expansion, and during periods of both heightened and declining international tension.

Turning to the main concern of this analysis, there appears to be strong support for the expectation that a fragile democracy installed by mass uprising is likely to resort to major increases in military spending as a means to improve its power grip. The dummy variable for the Philippine case indicates a statistically significant (at the 0.03 level) hike in this spending in the wake of Marcos's ouster, a hike that reversed the ongoing trend of declining military allocations (note the trend coefficient is negative and significant at the 0.05 level). This increase in base level, however, was only temporary because, as shown by the insignificant coefficient for the post-test counter, it did not initiate a new trend in the subsequent years. The latter finding is in itself interesting, suggesting that the Aquino administration did not engage in a systematic pattern of escalating funding for the military as a way of securing its support. In other words, the slope for defense allocation did not rise in the 1986–93 post-test period. Thus, the democratic opening did not have a lasting impact on this allocation.

Is it likely that the short-term post-test jump in the level of Philippine military expenditures just noted was due to some test intervention other than the People's Revolution but happening coincidentally with that uprising? To guard against this possibility of spurious interpretation, let us examine the evidence from Malaysia which serves as a control case. The Malaysian data were investigated by the identical method used for the Philippines. If some unidentified 'third variable'

Table 10.1 Democratic change and defense allocation

	Philippines	Malaysia	Taiwan	Korea
Constant	50.56**	25.61	9.40	13.44**
	(22.96)	(20.73)	(9.30)	(4.49)
Trend	−6.82**	−3.25	−1.48	−1.87**
	(3.15)	(2.18)	(0.88)	(0.68)
Dummy	72.63**	7.87	30.21*	13.67
	(28.27)	(21.26)	(14.37)	(10.20)
Counter	1.50	8.27*	−1.60	1.01
	(4.03)	(4.51)	(2.80)	(2.27)
Growth	−1.62	−0.33	0.45	1.03**
	(1.69)	(1.91)	(0.95)	(0.23)
US defense	0.55	1.57	1.04	0.21
	(1.31)	(1.32)	(0.72)	(0.47)
Rival defense			−0.70	0.14
			(0.76)	(0.21)
N	20	20	20	19
R^2	0.51	0.24	0.33	0.77
Durbin-Watson	2.17	2.02	1.95	2.17

Note: figures without parentheses are the regression coefficients, and those in parentheses are the standard errors.

* significant at the 0.10 level
** significant at the 0.05 level

other than the People's Revolution was responsible for the observed level change in the Philippine data, one would expect it to have similarly affected the Malaysian data. If, however, the Malaysian data failed to behave like the Philippine data in the 1987–93 period, one could be more confident that the intercept change in the latter's military spending was indeed a response to its democratic transition.

The pertinent coefficient for determining the presence of any post-test intercept change (that of the dichotomous dummy variable) indicates that the Malaysian time series did not experience any perturbation. That is, as expected, the Malaysian data did not 'respond' in the absence of receiving a 'stimulus' comparable to that of the People's Revolution in the Philippines. This null finding for Malaysia, in turn, enhances confidence in the interpretation given earlier to the Philippines post-test 'response.'

Interestingly, the post-test time counter for Malaysia is positive and significant at the 0.09 level. Although not statistically significant at conventional levels, the pre-test pattern for this country's military allocation pointed to a declining trend as in the Philippines. Thus, the

Malaysian time series suggests that defense spending was generally falling during 1973–85, but it started to climb subsequently. Following the same logic of comparing the Philippines (the experimental case) and Malaysia (the control case) applied in the last paragraph, an intriguing hypothesis emerges.

Specifically, being 'most similar (though hardly identical) systems,' one would expect the Philippines and Malaysia to follow generally the same trajectories in military allocation, had it not been for the People's Revolution in the former country. Indeed, judging from the coefficients for the trend variable, both countries were experiencing declining defense spending prior to 1986. However, as just noted, this trend was reversed in Malaysia and it undertook an accelerated program of military expansion since 1986. Such a pattern was absent in the Philippines, for which the slope for defense spending during the post-test period was relatively flat. Using the Malaysian evidence for this period as a benchmark for posing a counter-factual for the Philippines, one comes to the hypothesis that, in the longer term, the People's Revolution could have had the effect of slowing down the pace of military expansion in the Philippines by flattening what would have otherwise been a rising slope as in Malaysia. Seen in this light, the lack of statistical significance for the counter-variable in the Philippine case – when juxtaposed against its statistical significance (at the 0.09 level) in the Malaysian case – gains a substantive significance analogous to the 'dog that did not bark.' Given the data limitations already noted, however, these comments are necessarily quite speculative.

Turning to our other pair of cases, Taiwan and South Korea, we see from Table 10.1 that both were undergoing a process of military downsizing during the pre-test period. The coefficients for the trend variable are negative and highly significant (at the 0.02 level) for South Korea, and somewhat less significant (at the 0.12 level) for Taiwan. This convergence offers some *prima facie* evidence that these two cases constitute 'most similar systems.' It was implied earlier that, in the case of Taiwan, a top-down and more gradual approach to political liberalization is less likely to influence military spending. In contrast, the more violent and bottom-up push for electoral reform in South Korea is more likely to produce major fiscal reallocations (although not quite as likely as in the Philippines). However, because of Roh Tae Woo's stronger military connections, he might also have less need to appease the armed forces than Chiang Ching-kuo. This latter inference would in turn imply a greater prospect for the defense budget to rise in Taiwan than in South Korea.

The regression results show that Taiwan's experience was more similar to that of the Philippines than that of South Korea. That is, Taiwan's armed forces received a major budgetary increase following that island's initial democratic opening in 1987. Though smaller in its magnitude than in the Philippines, this boost was statistically significant (at the 0.06 level). And, as in the Philippines, it was only a short-term change in level that did not have a lasting impact in affecting the posttest trend. The general similarities in the data patterns of these two countries contradict my earlier expectation regarding the budgetary consequences of democratic changes initiated by an incumbent elite versus those forced by mass uprising. Differences in the sources of democratic changes in these two cases did not produce different budgetary outcomes as originally hypothesized. The similarities in these outcomes suggest that whether the democratic changes were brought about by top-down or bottom-up reforms are irrelevant for explaining defense allocations. As mentioned already, concern for irrelevance is heightened when different experimental stimuli produce apparently similar responses.

Comparing the analysis results for Taiwan and South Korea, we are moreover alerted to the danger of idiosyncrasy – namely, similar experimental stimuli have produced different responses. In this regard, the greater political control and elite continuity characterizing these two countries were not sufficient for producing similar short-term outcomes in defense allocations. Whereas, as already discussed, Taiwan's military expenditures temporarily went up after 1987, South Korea's defense budget did not experience a comparable boost. As can be seen in Table 10.1, the dummy variable was not significant for the latter country.

By inductive elimination, we are therefore led to infer that, among all the independent variables mentioned earlier, the extent to which a democratizing regime can exercise effective control over and resist potential challenges from the armed forces appears to be most effective in discriminating the patterns shown by the three cases undergoing democratic transition. Institutional rapport with the military was strongest for the South Korean regime, less strong in Taiwan, and the weakest in the Philippines. This rapport in turn appeared to be inversely related to a democratizing regime's felt need to appease the armed forces in the short run by raising their budget.

Significantly, the results in Table 10.1 consistently fail to support an expectation of falling military allocations (compared to the preexisting historical pattern), either in the short term or in the long term, following the initiation of the democratization process. There is little support for the view that a more democratic regime will trim military expenditures or slow their overtime rise, thereby perhaps creating more resources for public welfare programs. Similarly, the results do not enhance confidence in the belief that a more democratic regime will cut the defense budget, thereby helping to relax external tension and promote international peace. However, the popular election of Roh's presidency may not be an ideal candidate for locating the turning point in South Korea's democratic transition. Pending the availability of more post-test observations, the December 1992 presidential election of Kim Young Sam offers another test event for making this assessment. Similarly, the March 1996 popular election of president in Taiwan offers another such test event.

V. CONCLUSION

Although motivated by recent interests in democratic peace, this paper moves beyond the phenomenon of war occurrence. It has sought to examine the effects, if any, that democratic changes can have on defense allocations. To the extent that military expenditures, especially those involving disputants caught in an arms race (e.g. Wallace, 1982, 1979), play an important role in conflict escalation, the study of the relationship between democratization and armament presents a potentially rewarding topic for clarifying further the dynamics of democratic peace. Moreover, it invites scholars to attend more systematically to the domestic redistributive consequences, if any, of democratization. Does political liberalization, regime change, or leadership succession make any difference in the fiscal choices between guns and butter?

Given the limited length of the data series, especially for the post-test period, the results reported in this paper must be treated tentatively. Nevertheless, it is quite striking that, at least for the four countries studied here, defense spending has not responded significantly to changes in either the international environment or, with the exception of South Korea, the domestic economy. The end of the Cold War and the changes in economic performance have not had a significant impact on these countries' defense allocations. Thus, neither the realist perspective (which tends to stress defense spending as a result of foreign tension) nor the Keynesian perspective (which tends to see government spending, including that for defense, as a counter-cyclical tool for managing domestic economy) receives support from this analysis.

There is some evidence that when measured in annual rates of change, defense allocation in our four cases has been characterized by some inertia pointing to a generally downward trend over the entire period being analyzed (albeit in a context of considerable volatility as noted earlier). This declining pattern was especially noticeable for South Korea and the Philippines, and their respective democratic transition did not initiate a significantly different new trend. Only in Malaysia was there a recent (i.e., post-1985) resurgence in military expenditures as reflected by a statistically significant change in the slope of this spending.

Returning to our differential expectations regarding the effects of democratic change in the defense allocations of the four countries, only the Philippine case offered strong and unambiguous support. In that country, leadership succession that replaced a long-standing authoritarian regime, accompanied by political disorder and conservative (including important military factions) challenges to the new regime, did bring about an acceleration in defense allocation as expected. This appeared, however, to be only a one-time hike (in intercept), and did not bring about a more permanent shift (in slope) in fiscal decisions. Parenthetically, one would expect policy making in general to become more incremental as a democracy matures; the diverse competing interests in such a polity would tend to work against drastic policy swings.

The results are less clear-cut and more confusing when we try to juxtapose the Philippine experience with those of Taiwan and South Korea. Contrary to our original expectation, Taiwan's democratic transition was, as in the Philippine experience, accompanied by a short-term positive shift in the level of that island's defense spending, even though this transition was initiated by an incumbent elite enjoying a comparatively strong position over its political opposition. At the same time, even though South Korea's democratic transition received an important impetus from mass movements (making its experience in this respect more similar to the Philippines than Taiwan), Seoul's military expenditures were not affected by this political change. We are therefore led to infer that the closer institutional ties between Roh's regime and the armed forces made any budgetary appeasement of the latter less necessary. Conversely, the reliability of the military was much more in doubt and its support was much more imperative for the survival of the fragile Aquino regime. Hence, we have rather strong evidence of this regime boosting military expenditures in the short run, apparently as a means of securing support from the armed forces. The

Taiwan case lies somewhere between the Philippines and South Korea although, rather surprisingly according to our initial expectations, its experience turned out to be more similar to that of the Philippines than to that of South Korea. If the reasoning just presented contains some validity, it implies paradoxically that reformist governments with few military ties will be under greater pressure to appease the armed forces during the initial stages of the democratization process, whereas those with stronger military ties will be in a better position to control and discipline them.

Future research ought to take into explicit account concerns such as leadership continuity, regime security, and especially existing institutional rapport with the armed forces. It should also examine more explicitly the presence and nature of any budgetary tradeoffs between defense and welfare as a result of democratization. Because we do not have authoritarian regime changes as a comparison group, it could be argued that the observed fluctuations in military spending may be a result of regime changes in general rather than democratic regime changes *per se*. Yet, as already reported, the nature of these defense fluctuations is quite diverse even among the three cases experiencing democratic regime change – so that these fluctuations can hardly be assigned to a generic explanation of regime change, or even to democratic regime change. We need to develop more context-sensitive categories to capture the variety of regime changes, and to discriminate their effects on budgetary decisions. Future research should attend to this concern as well as the issue of whether democratic opening in a country can produce declining military spending by its neighbors, thus contributing to more congenial dyadic relations that are the core of the democratic peace proposition.

Increasing the number of observation points since the initiation of democratic opening should help to rule out spurious explanations and enhance our confidence in the validity of the analysis results. A longer time series would enable one to separate the effects of decision structures (stressed in institutional explanations of democratic peace) from the effects of mass attitudes (stressed in normative explanations). Democratic reforms altering governing structures presumably present discrete interventions; they introduce clear breaks from past institutional arrangements and should therefore promise sharper discontinuities from historical patterns if they have the predicted effects in changing resource allocations. Conversely, the evolution of mass attitudes takes more time and its effects on policy conduct should likewise become discernible more gradually over a longer period. The approach used in this analysis is suitable for examining simultaneously these rationales, as appropriate data become more available. It can incorporate in one regression model both the discrete interventions of structural change and the continuous transformation of popular norms in order to assess their relative impact on public policies bearing on democratic peace.

11 A Prospect-Based Analysis of War Termination*
Alex Mintz and Nehemia Geva

Throughout history, countless wars have been initiated without the benefit of foresight as to how these conflicts would, and should be terminated. Yet this ought to be a fundamental concern to those who initiate conflict as well as to those who study it. What are some of the factors that lead to the termination of war? How is the decision to terminate a war arrived at? These questions are addressed in this chapter.

In a series of articles, Jack Levy (1992a, 1992b, this volume), introduced Kahneman and Tversky's prospect theory to the realm of international relations (see also Farnham, 1994). According to Levy (1992a:171): (1) individuals evaluate outcomes with respect to deviations from a reference point rather than with respect to net asset levels; (2) their identification of this reference point is a critical variable in influencing their choice; (3) they assign more weight to losses than to comparable gains; and (4) they are generally risk-averse with respect to gains and risk-acceptant with respect to losses. In a subsequent article Levy (1992b) notes that these four tenets of prospect theory have critical implications for the study of international relations.

In this chapter we apply prospect-theory to the study of war termination. Most studies of war termination model the decision to terminate war as a choice between the 'continue the war' option and the 'stop the war' option. Here we suggest that:

- the domain in which a leader operates (gain vs. loss) also affects the decision to terminate war;
- the loss–gain domain is defined by political leaders in political terms;
- decisions made by political leaders often correspond to a non-compensatory principle of decision-making;
- whereas in previous applications of prospect theory to international relations, the gain or loss domains were defined by the same dimension that underlined the risky choice, i.e. international politics (see Boettcher, 1995), this chapter goes one step further by exploring risky decisions in one arena (foreign policy) while proposing that the calculations (utilities) of war termination are performed in an-

other arena (domestic politics). Rather than using monetary currency to account for the decision as is common in 'prospect' studies, risk-aversion in the domain of gain and risk-seeking in the domain of loss are explained using a political 'currency' (i.e. levels of public approval). The chapter contributes to the *new directions* theme of this book by introducing a prospect-based theory of war termination and testing it utilizing an experimental methodology.

PROSPECT THEORY

Prospect theory is a formal model of individual decision-making which assumes that decisions are made under conditions of risk. Kahneman and Tversky (1979) formulated the theory based on the notion that decision-makers do not necessarily operate according to subjective expected-utility theory, with its accompanying normative implications based on final asset positions (see von Neumann and Morgenstern, 1947); instead individuals evaluate decision outcomes as gains and losses as a function of their departure from some 'reference point' (Quattrone and Tversky, 1988:722; Garland and Newport, 1991:57).

Decision-makers exhibit risk-aversion in the domain of gains and risk-seeking in the domain of losses. This is referred to as the 'reflection effect' (see Kahneman and Tversky, 1979; 1981; 1984; see also Tversky and Kahneman, 1986; and Quattrone and Tversky, 1988:719).

Prospect theory also implies that losses loom larger than corresponding gains. The theory replaces the traditional concave utility function for wealth by an S-shaped function for changes of wealth. Thus, the utility function for gains is proposed to be concave, while that for losses is proposed to be convex and steeper than that for gains (Garland and Newport, 1991:57; Levy, this volume). Quattrone and Tversky (1988:724) observed that the displeasure associated with losing a sum of money is generally greater than the pleasure associated with winning the same amount. In the political context, Anderson (1983:201) found that leaders are more concerned with avoiding failure than with achieving success in their decisions, and that they do not necessarily seek an optimal or 'satisfactory' solution to a problem but a course of action that does not have a high probability of making matters worse (Anderson, 1983:203). Whether the action will solve the problem, is 'a secondary concern' according to Anderson (1983:203).

Decision-makers are also known to be influenced by a 'certainty effect' (see Quattrone and Tversky, 1988:732; Garland and Newport,

1991:57) which implies that probable outcomes are underweighted in comparison to certain outcomes. Quattrone and Tversky (1988:732) observed that 'reducing the probability of an outcome by a constant factor has a greater impact when the outcome was initially certain than when it was merely possible.'

Prospect Theory, Sunk Costs and the Framing of Policy Alternatives

Garland and Newport (1991:55) pointed out that when decision-makers are faced with decisions involving the continuance or discontinuance of a previously initiated course of action, sunk costs are taken into account. A sunk cost involves 'any prior investment of money, effort, or time' (Garland and Newport, 1991:124; see also Arkes and Blumer, 1985).

Garland and Newport (1991:63) found a strong sunk cost effect on decisions to continue with an *unprofitable* course of action. This may explain President Johnson's decision to continue the war in Vietnam and Israeli Prime Minister Shamir's decision to continue the war in Lebanon. Prospect theory also implies that shifts in the reference point induced by the framing of the problem might have predictable effects on people's risk preferences (Quattrone and Tversky, 1988:721; Frisch, 1993). Thus, the situation can be framed as a choice between risky prospects or as a choice between gains (Garland and Newport, 1991). In the context of war termination, a loss situation can be framed as a choice between a sure loss of sunk costs, versus continued fighting, with some chance of recovery and a higher chance of additional loss.

Framing has important implications for the study of foreign policy decision-making. Holsti (1992) reminds us that war is a foreign policy act that requires public support. The public's perception of a problem can be reversed by framing a given choice problem differently, without distorting or suppressing information, and 'without anyone being aware of the impact of the frame on the ultimate decision' but merely by the framing of outcomes. The formulation of the issue may affect the attitude of the target audience. If it is presented 'as a choice between gains, one will typically choose the less risky option. However, if it is presented as a choice between losses, then one will opt for the riskier option' (Maoz, 1990c:88). Furthermore, public sentiment can also be swayed by framing differently the certainties or probabilities associated with the different options of stopping versus continuing the fighting.

War termination can be framed in different ways. These frames are naturally related to the frames that were used during the initiation of the war. Usually, frames used prior to initiation of war focus on garnering national support for the war, while framing of war termination attempts to color the result of the war as a success. The war's objectives can be presented as an attempt to force a rival leader from power, or can be framed as defending the sovereignty of independent states. President George Bush, for example, framed Operation Desert Storm in terms of defending the sovereignty and independence of Kuwait from Iraqi aggression. Termination of the military operation could have then been framed as an overwhelming success. However, the same operation is perceived as less successful had the initial frame emphasized overthrowing Saddam Hussein. This interpretation is consistent with the common observation regarding the political significance of how issues are labeled (Quattrone and Tversky, 1988:727).

Prospect Theory, Framing, and the Non-compensatory Rule

Political leaders virtually always take into account (explicitly or implicitly) political factors and consequences while making policy decisions. Mintz (1993, 1995) has recently introduced the non-compensatory theory of the use of force. The non-compensatory principle suggests that in a choice situation, if a certain alternative is unacceptable politically, then a high score on another dimension (e.g. military) cannot compensate/counteract for this low score, and hence, the alternative is eliminated. Politicians will not shoot themselves in the foot, so to speak, by selecting alternatives that may hurt them politically. The non-compensatory principle in foreign policy decisions suggests, then, that leaders will eliminate an option that is below a 'cutoff' level on the political dimension, or will adopt a policy that fares highest on the political dimension. The first rule corresponds to Tversky and Kahneman's (1974) Elimination by Aspect (EBA), whereas the second rule is compatible with the lexicographic principle of choice. Elsewhere (Mintz and Geva, 1996) we propose that the EBA rule is more likely to be applied when the political leader is operating in the domain of gain, while the lexicographic rule is more applicable when the decision maker is operating in the domain of loss.[1] A necessary (though obviously not sufficient) condition for most choices by political leaders is that the decision will not damage them politically.[2] This usually translates to factoring domestic considerations into foreign policy decisions.

Domestic politics is 'the essence of decision,' and public support is the 'currency' of political leaders. The predominant importance of domestic politics in foreign policy-making by democratic leaders is well documented in the literature (see Russett, 1990; Russett and Barzilai, 1992; Mintz and Russett, 1992). Taking this one step further it also implies that when information-processing heuristic models of decision-making ('elimination by aspects,' 'lexicographic,' 'preference reversal,' etc.) are applied to political situations, gains or losses and risks or rewards should be viewed in political (and not in monetary) terms.[3]

Indeed, previous studies showed that leaders use force in the international arena when their approval rating is in the critical 40–60 per cent range, i.e. when a boost is most needed (see Ostrom and Job, 1986; Russett, 1990; Mintz and Russett, 1992) and even more often when their popularity decreases among their supporters (Morgan and Bickers, 1992). A rough estimate of James and Oneal's data (1991) shows that 22 out of 69 cases of the use of force by American presidents in the post-World War II era (i.e. 32 per cent) occurred when public support for the president had declined. Only ten out of 69 cases (14 per cent) occurred one quarter after a sharp (more than 20 per cent) increase in presidential popularity. In contrast, 32 out of 73 crises did not result in the use of force (44 per cent) following a sharp rise in public support for the president, versus 12 incidents out of 73 that did not result in the use of force following a decline in support. Very similar results are obtained when the use of force lags two quarters behind change in public support for the president (see James and Oneal's data set, 1991).

The influence of the domain in which decision-makers operate (gain vs. loss) on the risk propensity of national leaders in the context of decisions concerning the termination of wars will be explored below using an experimental methodology.

The application of prospect theory to foreign policy decision-making has raised a number of concerns that centre on how representative of foreign policy decisions are the laboratory experiments on which prospect theory is based. Jervis (1992) and Levy (1992) point out that prospect theory was developed in a context of highly structured experimental designs where the risks and utilities that are associated with the decision option are specific and clear. However, decision situations in the international arena are rather vague. Moreover, Levy (1992:293) states that while the focus of prospect theory is on the extent of risk that underlies various options, foreign policy decisions are better characterized by levels of uncertainty. Boettcher (1995) adds that many foreign policy decisions are made by groups, while prospect theory attempts to model an individual decision-maker. Wittman (1979) criticizes the relatively trivial issues analyzed by prospect theory in experimental settings, and suggests that in cases of politically relevant topics, framing effects will be minimal due to feedback and learning. The experimental methodology allows, however, for testing hypotheses about war termination that otherwise cannot be tested. As will be shown below, we take these concerns into account in the analysis of the relevance of political (gain–loss) calculations in decisions on war termination.

WAR TERMINATION

The termination of hostilities is treated in the conflict theory literature as a phase in a larger process (see Stein, 1975:7).[4] Actual participation in a conflict allows the leader to perceive lucidly 'what the war is actually costing him in its social, economic, military and political dimensions' (Staudenmaier, 1987:27). Because war conveys information about the consequences of using force, war itself may be a potent cause of peace (Wagner, 1993:258). The decision to terminate hostilities may therefore differ considerably from the one made to enter the conflict, when costs and utilities are more uncertain.

The 'conventional wisdom' on war termination is represented by Wittman's (1979) rational choice approach. A commitment to a current course of action (war) is a function of the comparison between the perceived utility of continuing the action and the perceived utility of terminating hostilities. Leaders will terminate hostilities if such a settlement exceeds the expected costs of continuing the war. Bueno de Mesquita (1981) employs a similar logic in his book *The War Trap*. Massoud (1993) also utilizes this line of reasoning in a comparative case study of termination of the Korean, Arab–Israeli, and Falklands Wars.

Based on premises of strategic calculation, theorists argue that in order to terminate war at least one of the participants 'must revise his estimate of the relative advantages and disadvantages of continuing hostilities' (Stein, 1975:6). A change in the calculus of costs and benefits is therefore the essential prerequisite to the termination of war.

Stein (1975) notes, however, that the attempt to predict the likelihood of termination from exclusively military indicators misses the point. Stein (1975:5) has noted that the termination of hostilities, like other phases of interstate conflict, is the product of multiple factors. She observes on the basis of a detailed analysis of the termination of the October War of 1973 (Stein, 1982) that wars do not necessarily end when one of the participants is recognized as a victor. Similarly, Kaplan's (1980) analysis of the termination of World War I points to the difficulties the Allies had in coming to terms on termination policy. He suggests that in many other cases of war termination, the military victory does not translate into a political victory (Kaplan, 1980:73).

The termination of war is a process in which political and military power merge so that a solution tolerable to all sides can be reached (Fabyanic, 1987). According to Stein (1975:20), the decision to terminate a war also depends on political constraints. Stein (1975:22) writes that 'often opinion has been aroused during the phase of hostilities and is resistant to a process of accommodation ... Policy-makers are constrained not only by the actions of their opponent, but also by the limits imposed by domestic audiences. The use of threat by the opponent reinforces those domestic groups who are most resistant to change and weakens those who are prepared to risk an innovative policy.' Negative mass public opinion can thus serve as a major impediment to the process of conflict reduction.

Escalation, and de-escalation, or termination of conflict, obviously entail political benefits and/or costs. For example, a leader may be seen as either too weak or too aggressive during peace negotiations and lose domestic support and subsequently power (Ikle, 1971: chap. 4). Public opinion may dictate that the leader terminate hostilities when war casualties are excessive or when the conflict has run on for too long – e.g. French public opinion regarding the conflict in Indochina in the 1950s (Randle, 1973:432–3), and American public opinion concerning further involvement in the Vietnam War. When the public perceives the war to be immoral or illegal, the public mood may shift to one of cooperation – e.g. Italy in 1943 (Randle, 1973:432–3). Finally, if the citizens of a nation sense that their country could eventually become the target of an invasion, the public mood is likely to swing to one of non-hostility (Randle, 1973:432–3).

The importance of domestic factors in war termination is also addressed by Ikle (1971) and Shillony (1982). Ikle observed that peace between Japan and the US was only barely accomplished in 1945 because those favoring peace in Japan had great difficulty in pleading their case in Tokyo. Shillony, who has also analyzed the negotiations surrounding the termination of hostilities in World War II, notes that Japan's surrender was made easier by the fact that it did not have to contend with public opinion and seek an 'honorable peace' because of the autocratic nature of the regime (1982:101).

While much of the literature emphasizes the expected utility of each side continuing or terminating hostilities, little has been done to formulate and test alternative explanations of war termination, such as prospect theory. Prospect theory highlights the importance of the domain in which decision-makers operate on their propensity to choose risky options. The process of making compromises and reaching agreement on the termination of hostilities may be hindered by loss-aversion because each side may view its own concessions as losses that appear to loom larger than the gains achieved by the concessions of the adversary. The very willingness of one party to make a particular concession (e.g. to propose a ceasefire) immediately reduces the perceived value of the concession. Political loss aversion also constrains national decision-makers through the manifestation of public opinion. We feel that a prospect-based analysis may provide important insight into understanding the underlying reasons for the termination of war.

A Prospect-Based Analysis of War Termination: An Experimental Demonstration

To illustrate the relevance of prospect theory to the study of war termination, and in lieu of the methodological concerns mentioned earlier in this paper, we presented a simulated international crisis that involved the United States and an 'aggressive' non-democratic regime to a group of 184 students. We then replicated the experiment using a group of 120 non-student adults. The crisis 'required' a choice between two options: (1) to 'continue the war' and capture the aggressor's leader with all the uncertainties and risks that are associated with such an action, or (2) to 'stop the war' and accomplish the mission, but without overthrowing the aggressor's regime.[5]

The construction of the simulated international crisis borrowed from Pillar's extensive analysis on war termination (Pillar, 1983). Accordingly, an end of a war is not necessarily a negotiated settlement. War can be terminated by a unilateral decision of one party. The study was set to analyze the influence of domestic consideration on imposing a reference point and defining the domain (gain or loss) in which leaders operate. Thus, the experiment may shed light on potential effects of domestic factors that trigger leaders' interest in negotiated options rather than continuing the war.

To test the prospect explanation, the experiment varied the domains in which the decision-maker operated. Gains and losses were defined in clear terms as an increase or decrease in public support. Moreover, since the decision question was embedded in a multi-dimensional space where framing of gain or loss was on one dimension (political) while the decision had to be made on another dimension (international), we introduced into the experiment a control factor that varied the salience of the political costs and benefits.

The experimental procedure was also designed to avoid a situation where risky choices can be interpreted as having higher subjective expected utilities rather than reflecting risk propensity that is triggered by the domain in which the decision-maker operates. Hence, we did not change the probabilities of success of either option (stop the war versus continue the fighting), nor did we change the cost and benefits of these options. The same two options were presented across all the four experimental conditions. Our focus was on the impact of changes of values in the political domain on the choice of a military option.[6]

The central hypothesis of the experiment was that there is an association between the domain in which the decision-maker operates and his or her choice, and that this association is contingent on the salience of the political dimension.

STUDY I

Method

Subjects. One hundred and eighty-four students participated in the study. Subjects were randomly assigned to one of four different experimental conditions.

Design. The study employed a 2 × 2 between groups factorial design. The factors were: (a) framing (loss vs. gain); and (b) political sensitization (exposure vs. no exposure to political tips). The main dependent measure was the choice subjects made between two options: 'continue the war' or 'stop the war.' Several additional indices were assessed in order to ascertain the internal validity of the study.[7]

Research Instrument.[8] The decision task placed the subjects in the role of a president facing an international crisis. In the scenario a war erupted between two small Pacific Ocean nations over control of one of the world's largest concentrations of uranium. According to the scenario, US forces intervened militarily against the aggressor nation in order to stop their invasion of the neighboring country. The description indicated that the US military was successful in this mission; however, the ruler of the aggressive nation remained in power. The advice of the military establishment was that a continuation of the war for a few more days, while risky, might oust the aggressor nation's leader and prevent future problems in the area.

The two independent variables were manipulated as follows. First, the domain of the decision was introduced at the beginning of the international scenario. In the domain of gain condition, subjects read that the 'public rating of the president increased by 20 per cent.' In the domain of loss, the description stated that the 'public rating of the president decreased by 20 per cent.'

The 'sensitization' of the subjects to the political dimension was performed prior to the introduction of the international scenario. In the instructions preceding the decision task, half of the subjects were told that 'in order to help you perform the decision, we have provided you with some critical political tips on presidential decision-making which are based on recent research.' These tips included (a) leaders are concerned about their popularity and about their chances for reelection; (b) leaders know that the use of force brings about a 'rally round the flag' effect; and (c) leaders know that defeat on the battlefield is likely to reduce their popularity. The other half of the subjects were not exposed to these tips.

Procedure. The instructions and scenario were presented in a small booklet format, and the experiment took about 8–10 minutes. Upon completing the experiment subjects were fully debriefed about the study.

Results

As observed in Table 11.1, the tendency to choose to terminate the war conformed to the prospect conceptualization discussed above. When decision-makers were sensitized to the political dimension (i.e. exposed to political tips), being in a political domain of gain (e.g. increased public rating) led them to select a more risk-averse policy as compared to being in a political domain of loss.[9] Specifically, among the four conditions in the experiment, the highest 'resistance' to continuation of the war was in the political tips condition when operating in the domain of gain (26.1 per cent). On the other hand, the least concern with stopping the war (i.e. risk-prone) was expressed by decision-makers who were equipped with political tips, but operated in the domain of loss (8.70 per cent). It is interesting to note, however, that

Table 11.1 Proportion of students choosing the 'Stop the War' alternative*

	Domain of decision	
	Gain	Loss
Political tips	.261	.087
No tips	.152	.196

* N in each cell = 46

without sensitization to the political 'rules of the game' this effect dissipated. The statistical interaction between the two independent variables was tested utilizing a Z test for proportion data (see Langer and Abelson, 1972) and yielded a significant result of $z = 2.08$ $p < .05$.

Additional data collected in this experiment help to shed some light on other, related questions. For example, subjects who chose to 'stop the war' were less confident in their choice (M = 6.06) than those who chose the 'continue the war' alternative (M = 7.57) $t(1,182) = 4.74$ $p < .0001$. Moreover, these subjects perceived the force option as more of a policy failure (M = 5.16) than those who selected the 'Continue the War' option (M = 2.67) $t(1,182) = -5.64$ $p < .0001$.

STUDY II

Method

Subjects. One hundred and twenty non-student adults participated in the study. The median age of this group was 44.0 (ranging from 22 to 86 years). Their educational background was quite heterogeneous, ranging from some high school to a PhD degree, with the median being 'some college.' Subjects were recruited at several local churches. They were randomly assigned to one of the four different experimental conditions.

Design and Procedure. The experiment replicated the same 2 × 2 between groups factorial design of the previous experiment (i.e. loss vs. gain framing and political sensitization). The main dependent measure was the choice subjects made between two options: 'continue the war' or 'stop the war.' The material and procedures used in this experiment were similar to those reported in Study I.

Table 11.2 Proportion of adult subjects choosing the 'stop the war' alternative*

	Domain of decision	
	Gain	Loss
Political tips	.53	.27
No tips	.33	.33

* N in each cell = 30

Results

The experiment shows that the 'prospect' results are robust. As depicted in Table 11.2, being in the domain of gain increased the preference for the safer option of stopping the war as compared with making the same decision while operating in the domain of loss. However, when subjects were not sensitized to the political dimension the preference for a policy option was not affected by being in the domain of gain or loss. The statistical interaction between the two independent variables was tested, as in the previous experiment, using a Z test for proportion data (Langer and Abelson, 1972). The analysis yielded a $z = 1.45$ $p < .07$ (one tailed), which corroborates the findings obtained with the student sample.

Similar to the previous experiment, subjects who chose to 'stop the war' were less confident in their choice ($M = 6.89$) than those who chose the 'continue the war' alternative ($M = 8.05$) $t(1,118) = 3.03$ $p < .005$. In addition, as in the first experiment, subjects perceived the 'stop the war' option as more of a policy failure ($M = 4.73$) than those who selected the 'continue the war' option ($M = 3.08$) $t(1,118) = -3.18$ $p < .005$.

Several points warrant further elaboration. First, we found that the majority of subjects in both experiments (77.2 per cent in the first experiment and 63.5 per cent in the second experiment) opted for the continuation of the war, rather than terminating it. This finding, however, should not come as a surprise to students of the use of force in lieu of the extensive body of literature on the 'rally round the flag' effect (Mueller, 1973; Russett, 1990). When military intervention is under way, the public rallies in support of its leaders. Public support is especially strong when the consequences of the intervention are viewed as favorable and the costs (in casualties) are low. The scenario used in our experiments is compatible with these defining conditions.[10] Furthermore, applying the 'sunk-cost' notion to this case would also imply a strong push toward continuing the fighting. Since resources have already been invested in the fighting, the natural inclination would be to invest 'a little more' in the hope of reaping the gains associated with the overall endeavor. In light of the 'rally round the flag' and the 'sunk-cost' effects that loaded our experimental design against our hypothesis, it is almost surprising that the gain–loss manipulation had such a strong effect on the choices in our study. Hence, the findings we obtained in a conservative test yield credence to our proposition.

When faced with several alternatives, leaders are likely to evaluate policies based on probabilities of success and failure and not necessarily based on the payoffs alone. The public on the other hand may aspire to the 'best' solution while focusing on the expected payoffs. This phenomenon (preference reversal) and the results of our simulated experiment may also explain why, for example, President Bush and the public viewed the results of the 1991 war in the Gulf so differently. To illustrate, a public opinion poll conducted shortly after the war indicated that less than one-fourth of those surveyed agreed with President Bush's decision to stop the war short of overthrowing Saddam Hussein. Even many of those surveyed within the President's own party thought that Saddam should have been ousted.

This difference of opinion between the President and the public can also be explained in terms of self-interest or hedonic relevance, i.e. the direct bearings and consequences of an action on a given individual's life. It is natural to expect the President to stop the war because of the direct bearing of the consequences on his political future – the potential decline in public approval from a continuing protracted conflict that may result in a foreign quagmire. Conversely, the subjects in the experiment felt no such 'hedonic relevance' because of the fact that such an experiment had no bearing on their daily lives. These results coincide with earlier studies (see Geva and Andrade, 1993; Geva, Astorino-Courtois, and Mintz, 1994) that suggest that hedonic relevance sensitizes public opinion by minute variations in the way foreign policies are framed.

In calculating the payoffs, the public focused on the sunk costs already invested in the war. The public assessment of the outcome searched for an acceptable level of equity (Austine et al., 1976). The sub-par results of the campaign to oust Saddam Hussein, considered together with the sunk costs, led to the public's belief that an additional investment was worthwhile as means to obtain a better payoff. Tversky and

Kahneman (1986) pointed out that alternative framing of the same situation (for example, in terms of gains vs. losses) produce inconsistent preferences. Here, however, we found that leaders and the public may perceive the same situation in different ways.

CONCLUSIONS

This study attempted to contribute to our understanding of how and why hostilities are terminated. The chapter showed that decision-makers who operate in the domain of gains (when their popularity is on the rise) are less likely to use force (assumed to be the risky option in this study) than when they operate in the domain of loss (when their popularity decreases). Losses loom larger than gains, and avoiding failures, mistakes and risks is typically more important to political leaders than trying to optimize success. The theory differs considerably from theories of war termination that have been previously introduced in the literature, e.g. game-theoretical models (see Brams, 1985; Zagare, 1983) or expected-utility models (see Wittman, 1979) as it emphasizes information-processing heuristics such as the gain–loss position *vis-à-vis* a reference point, that are embedded in rational calculations, and integrates political factors into a cognitive model of decision-making.

During the Gulf crisis of 1990–91, US President Bush was faced with the decision of when to stop the war. With his popularity skyrocketing as a result of the swift and effective air and ground campaigns, and with General Powell warning General Schwarzkopf that 'the mood was shifting to an early end to the fighting' (*Newsweek*, 1991:24), the President selected the risk-averse alternative of stopping the war and rejected the risk-seeking alternative of ousting Saddam from power. The political and military risks involved in continuing the war could not have been 'compensated' for by increasing the gap in the military balance between the Allied forces and Saddam Hussein's forces. President Bush decided that the potential costs involved in continuing the military operation were excessive and therefore chose to terminate hostilities. The success of the military operation placed the president in the domain of gain both politically and militarily, and led to the rejection of the 'continue the march to Baghdad' alternative.

In addition, it is clear that decisions on the termination of war are not always based on a comprehensive and comparative evaluation of all alternatives along all dimensions, but often rely on cognitive shortcuts and heuristics (see Mintz and Geva, 1995). This by itself does not violate expected utility theory. However, the experiments presented in this chapter contained a 'control condition' to the gain situation – a situation where the termination of war is placed in the context of the domain of loss. Prospect theory is sensitive to the domain in which the decision-maker operates and always predicts (except for cases with small probabilities) risk-averse behavior in the domain of gains and risk-seeking behavior in the domain of loss. The experiments reported in this chapter provide support for the notion that 'where you stand in the polls determines where you stand on the issues.'

NOTES

* An earlier version of this paper was presented at the annual meeting of the American Political Science Association, Washington, D.C., 2–5 September 1993. The authors thank Steven B. Redd, Karl R. DeRouen and Sarah Lynch for research assistance and Ben Mor and Frank P. Harvey for their insightful comments.
1. The above arguments do not imply that the political leader is always risk averse and predominantly apprehensive of the consequences his or her decisions in terms of public support. We posit, along the notion of diversionary theory of war, that leaders may initiate use of force when their popularity is dropping, assuming that such a decisive policy may increase their public support. Moreover, when the political currency is extremely salient (e.g. at eve of election), the national leader will seek the first policy option to alleviate this problem (i.e. using a lexicographic approach). Such an interpretation coincides with McDermott's (1992) analysis of the Teheran hostage crisis. Yet, when the extent of public support is rising (due to the 'rally round the flag' effect), the reference point changes. The new situation (pending the results of the use of force) can be defined politically as being in the domain of gain. In this situation the decision to terminate the war (especially when still short of accomplishing all the war's goals) is an indication of political risk-aversion. Moreover, our present analysis proposes that when the political consequences of an ongoing war become sour (e.g. a result of high number of casualties), the leader situated in a domain of loss is likely to be risk prone and continue the war. This proposition coincides also with the sunk-cost argument stated above. Hence, the defining characteristics of the domain of gain and of loss during an ongoing war are a function of two *interrelated* factors: the accomplishment of the military objectives and the political support the leader has.
2. Obviously, every decision that a leader makes will antagonize some part of the constituency. Yet, the leader will try to avoid an overall decrease in the level of his or her critical support groups. In a non-democratic

regime leaders may be sensitive to the elite group that enables them to rule (e.g. the military). In a democratic regime the leader may attend to the overall polls or partisan support indices (Morgan and Bickers, 1992). This argument follows Merritt and Zinnes' (1991) analysis and review of the democratic peace phenomenon. They suggest that leaders are accountable to followers, though the definition of relevant followers changes with regime type.
3. Levy (this volume) entertains this idea when he addresses the plausibility of employing forceful or aggressive international policies to divert attention from deteriorating domestic political positions. The latter would lead leaders to perceive themselves in the domain of loss.
4. Barringer (1972), for example, establishes six phases in a conflict, of which termination is only one.
5. The reader should be aware that such phrasing of the alternatives colors the 'war continuation' option as riskier than the war termination. The continuation of a war is usually riskier than a negotiated settlement (the outcome of a war typically being more uncertain than the results of a particular settlement, see Stein, 1975).
6. Recently, Boettcher's (1995) experimental study on the application of prospect theory in international relations shows that the conversion of the international environment to numeric probabilistic terms is a rather complex issue.
7. We assessed subjects' perception of the domestic conditions (which served as the manipulation of the decision-making domain), and the confidence subjects had in their decision.
8. Appendix A contains the research material we used in this study.
9. As depicted in Appendix A, the manipulations of the gain and loss domains did not imply that the increase or decrease of public ratings of the President was related to the crisis or the actions taken by the President.
10. One could also argue that the political tips were phrased towards a stronger support of the continuation of the use of force, but then one would expect that in the 'political tips' conditions the propensity of the risky (war prone) choice would have been greater than in the 'no tips' conditions. While such a trend is suggested in Table 11.2, it does not exist in Table 11.1.

APPENDIX 11.A

The experimental material is described below. Please note that the 'political salience' manipulation is introduced on Page One and is accompanied by the 'Political Tips' page. The latter is omitted when the political salience is not introduced in the first page.

The scenario page included the manipulation of the 'gain' or 'loss' manipulation. The text in the square brackets identifies the text that was employed for each of the two domains. The italicized texts appeared in the domain of loss while the regular font text appeared in the gain manipulation.

The final page includes the questions to which the subjects responded.

INSTRUCTIONS
Page 1

Political Decision Making

In this study we are interested to learn about *decision making* in various international events. Specifically, we are interested in your ability to comprehend national level decision making. This comprehension will be expressed by the quality of a decision you make in the context of a simulated international crisis.

In the next pages you'll be confronted with a hypothetical international crisis. The case will contain information that a president is exposed to by his various advisors. Read the information carefully, and then respond to the situation, *assuming the role of the president.*

POLITICAL SENSITIZATION →

⌐ — — — — — — — — — — — — — — — — — — — ¬
| In order to help you perform the role, we have provided you with some critical political tips on presidential decision making which are based on current research in political science. |
| Read the Political Tips *and then move on to read about the international crisis for which you'll make the policy decisions.* |
└ — — — — — — — — — — — — — — — — — — — ┘

Following the case is a questionnaire in which you'll record your decision and responses to the situation. Please respond to all the questions.

Thank you for your cooperation
The Research Team

⌐ — — — — — — — — — — — — — — — — — — — ¬
Page 2 (*only where applicable*)

Political Tips

1. Leaders are concerned about their popularity and about their chances of being reelected.
2. Leaders know that the use of force (low cost incidents as Grenada, Panama) bring about a 'rally around the flag' effect (i.e. emotional support of national leaders) and thus increase their popularity.
3. Leaders know that a defeat in the battlefield is likely to reduce their popularity.
└ — — — — — — — — — — — — — — — — — — — ┘

Page 3

The Degania-Raggol Crisis

During the past few weeks the media has focused almost exclusively on the military crisis in Degania-Raggol. News reports indicate that U.S. forces who fought Degania's forces in the Pacific Ocean faced strong military opposition.

Loss/Gain Manip. → [Public rating of the president decreased by 20 per cent.]/ [Public rating of the president increased by 20 per cent.]

The President was advised by the Chairman of the Chiefs of Staff that the limited mission of kicking out Degania from the Raggol Islands, was accomplished but that Degania's leader is still in power. Continuing the war for a few more days is much riskier but may outset Degania's leader and prevent future problems in the area.

The Raggol Island region has an enormous importance to the world since it was discovered that near the shores of the Raggol Island is one the world's largest concentrations of Uranium (the basis for nuclear power).

The president has to make a decision whether to 'continue the war' (and overthrow the agressor's regime) or to 'stop the war'. Please, turn the page and evaluate the president's alternatives.

Page 4

The choice that I think the U.S. should make is: (mark one)

'Continue the War': _____
'Stop the War': _____

How confident are you that this choice will be successful: (circle a number on the scale)

Low confidence 0 1 2 3 4 5 6 7 8 9 10 High confidence

12 Camp David: Was the Agreement Fair?
Steven J. Brams and Jeffrey M. Togman

I. INTRODUCTION

Two approaches to the study of dispute resolution in international relations can be distinguished. The first explores how *actual* disputes were – or, for that matter, were not – resolved by the participants. This approach, which might be called inductive, seeks to provide generalizations from historically specific examples of which strategies of conflict resolution proved successful or not, and to offer explanations of why this was the case.

The second approach, which might be called deductive, has received less attention in international relations. It involves the construction of theoretical models, usually based in game theory, whose consequences are applicable to the study of dispute resolution. This work, which goes under the rubric of 'negotiation analysis' (Young, 1991), has only rarely been applied to cases of real-world disputes in international relations, like that between Egypt and Israel at Camp David in 1978 (see Brams, 1990, for an analysis of this case using game-theoretic models of bargaining).

We seek to illustrate the relevance of the deductive approach in this article by showing how a newly developed procedure for dividing up goods in a dispute, or resolving issues in a conflict, can be applied to a real-world territorial dispute that involved sovereignty and security issues as well. The procedure is called Adjusted Winner (AW), which heretofore has been applied to only one other international dispute – that between Panama and the United States over the Panama Canal, which, after prolonged negotiations (Raiffa, 1982; Brams and Taylor, 1996), culminated in a treaty signed and ratified by the two countries in 1979.

In this article we will apply AW to the Camp David Accords of 1978, comparing the resolution that AW hypothetically would have given with the agreement that was actually reached. This comparison will enable us to draw conclusions about the potential use of AW in aiding negotiators to resolve disputes fairly and expeditiously. While AW is applicable to numerous types of disputes, the Camp David case allows us to illustrate how conflicts with a significant territorial component can be resolved using this procedure, and how deductive analysis can serve normative as well as explanatory ends.

II. PROPORTIONALITY AND ENVY-FREENESS

There are several important criteria by which to judge fairness. One criterion is that all parties to a dispute are entitled to a 'fair share' of a heterogeneous good, like a cake, which each party may value different parts of differently (e.g. one party might like the cherry in the middle, another the nuts on the side). The simplest notion of a fair share is a proportional share; that is, each of the n parties in a dispute is entitled to at least $1/n$ of the cake, as he or she views it. Fair-division procedures that guarantee a proportional share are said to satisfy the property of *proportionality*.

Another criterion of fairness, and one that is more difficult to obtain, is *'envy-freeness.'* An *envy-free* division is one in which each party believes he or she has received the most valuable portion of that division. One way of conceptualizing such a division is to imagine an allocation in which no party believes he or she could do better by trading his or her portion for someone else's.

To illustrate how fair-division procedures can ensure proportionality and envy-freeness, consider the well-known procedure, applicable to two people, of 'one divides, the other chooses.' Suppose that Bob and Carol wish to divide a heterogeneous cake between themselves. If Bob cuts the cake into two pieces, and Carol gets to choose whichever piece she prefers, each can ensure both proportionality and envy-freeness by adhering to the following strategies:

1. By cutting the cake into two pieces that he considers to be of equal value, Bob can guarantee himself what he believes to be half the cake, regardless of which piece Carol chooses. Similarly, by choosing first, Carol can guarantee herself what she believes to be at least half the cake. Thus, this procedure, in conjunction with these strategies, guarantees proportionality.
2. Given that these strategies are followed, this procedure guarantees that neither Bob nor Carol will believe that the other person

received a larger portion of the cake than what he or she received. Thus, this procedure produces an allocation that is envy-free.

Envy-freeness and proportionality are equivalent when there are only two players – that is, the existence of one property implies the existence of the other. However, there is no such equivalence when there are three or more players. For example, if each of three players thinks he or she received at least one-third of the cake, it may still be the case that one player thinks another received a larger piece (say, half), so proportionality does not imply envy-freeness. Envy-freeness, on the other hand, does imply proportionality, for if none of the players envies another, each must believe that he or she received at least a third of the cake. Thus, envy-freeness is the stronger notion of fairness.

III. ADJUSTED WINNER (AW)

While the simplicity of 'one divides, the other chooses' is appealing, some bundles of goods are not quite analogous to a cake. The Adjusted Winner (AW) procedure is designed for disputes in which there are two parties and a number of discrete goods (or issues), each of which is divisible. Under AW, each of the two players is given 100 points to distribute across the goods. The goods are then allocated to the two players on the basis of their point distributions. We illustrate the procedure for making an allocation with a simple example.

Suppose that Bob and Carol must divide three goods, G_1, G_2, and G_3, between themselves. Based on the importance they attribute to obtaining each good, assume they distribute their points in the following manner:

	G_1	G_2	G_3	Total
Bob's point distribution	6	**67**	27	100
Carol's point distribution	5	34	**61**	100

Initially, Bob and Carol get all the goods they have assigned more points to than the other player has (the greater point assignment is in bold type in the example). Thus, G_1 and G_2 are awarded to Bob, giving him 6 + 67 = 73 of his points, and G_3 is awarded to Carol, giving her 61 of her points. If Bob's total points were equal to Carol's at this juncture, the procedure would end. However, this is not the case: Bob gets more of his points than Carol gets of her points.

Since the initial allocation is unequal, the next step is to transfer from Bob to Carol as much of a certain good or goods as is needed to give both the same point totals. This is called an *equitability adjustment*. The first good to be transferred is that with the lowest ratio of Bob's points to Carol's. In this example, G_1 has a lower ratio (6/5 = 1.20) than G_2 (67/34 ≃ 1.97).

Even transferring all of G_1 to Carol leaves Bob with a slight advantage (67 of his points to 5 + 61 = 66 of hers). Hence, we turn to the good with the second-lowest ratio, G_2, transferring only that fraction of G_2 necessary to give Bob and Carol the same number of points.

Let x denote the fraction of G_2 which Bob will retain, with the rest transferred from him to Carol. We choose x so that the resulting point totals are equal for Bob and Carol. The equation for the equitability adjustment is as follows:

$$67x = 5 + 61 + 34(1 - x)$$

This equation yields $x = 100/101 \simeq 0.99$. Consequently, Bob ends up with 99 per cent of G_2, for a total of 66.3 of his points, whereas Carol ends up with all of G_1, all of G_3, and 1 per cent of G_2, for the same total of 66.3 of her points.

This outcome can be shown to satisfy several important properties (Brams and Taylor, 1996). First, AW guarantees proportionality, because both players are assured of getting at least 50 per cent of their points. Second, because it is a two-person procedure, AW also ensures an envy-free allocation: neither player would trade his or her portion for that of the other. Third, the resulting allocation is *efficient* in that there is no other allocation that would give one player more of his or her points without giving the other player less. Finally, the resulting division is *equitable*: Bob's valuation of his portion is exactly the same as Carol's valuation of her portion.

By comparison, 'one divides, the other chooses' ensures neither efficiency (there may be an allocation better for both players) nor equitability (the chooser may do better than the divider). These and other criteria of fairness, equity, and justice are discussed in, among other places, Young (1994), Zajac (1995), Kolm (1996), and Brams and Taylor (1996).

In order for AW to satisfy the properties we have just described, two important conditions must be met: linearity and additivity. *Linearity* means that the added value, or marginal utility, of obtaining more of a good is constant (instead of diminishing, as is usually assumed), so, for example, $2x$ per cent of G_1 is twice as good as x per cent for each player.

Additivity means that the value of two or more goods is equal to the sum of their points. Put another way, obtaining one good does not affect the value of obtaining another, or winning on one issue is separable from winning on another. Thus, goods or issues can be treated independently of each other, with packages of goods no more nor less than the sum of their individual parts. We will return to the additivity of issues when we discuss Camp David later.

We have illustrated how AW works to solve a hypothetical dispute and indicated the properties it satisfies. But how useful would it be in resolving actual conflicts?

Short of having parties to real-world disputes utilize the procedure, perhaps the best way to evaluate its potential usefulness is to look at what, hypothetically, would have occurred if the parties to an actual conflict had applied AW. It is with this putative application in mind that we now turn to Camp David.

IV. CAMP DAVID AND ADJUSTED WINNER (AW)

On 17 September 1978, after 18 months of negotiation and after a 13-day summit meeting, President Anwar Sadat of Egypt and Prime Minister Menachem Begin of Israel signed the Camp David Accords. Six months later, these accords provided the framework for the peace treaty that the two nations signed on 26 March 1979. This epochal agreement shattered the view of many observers that the 30-year-old Arab–Israeli conflict was probably irreconcilable.

There are a number of factors which make the Camp David negotiations an excellent case for examining the potential usefulness of AW. First, there were several issues over which the Egyptians and Israelis disagreed. These issues can be considered as goods to be divided fairly in the sense of either one or the other side's winning on each, which is analogous to obtaining a good.

Second, most of the issues were to some degree divisible, rendering the equitability-adjustment mechanism of AW applicable in the case of an issue that must be divided. Third, there is now considerable documentation of the positions of the two sides on the issues, including detailed accounts of the negotiations by several of the participants at Camp David. These allow us to make reasonable point assignments to each issue based on the expressed concerns of each side.

The Camp David Accords, of course, need to be seen in the context of the seemingly intractable conflict that existed between Arab nations and Israel from the time of the latter's creation in 1948. The Arab states, including Egypt, did not recognize Israel's right to exist and continually sought to annihilate it. However, Israel was victorious in the 1948–9 war, the 1956 Sinai conflict, and the Six Day War of 1967. As a result of the 1967 war, Israel conquered and laid claim to substantial portions of territory of its Arab neighbors, including the Sinai Peninsula, the West Bank, the Gaza Strip, and the Golan Heights.

In 1973, Egypt and Syria attempted to recapture the Sinai Peninsula and the Golan Heights, respectively, in the Yom Kippur War. Henry Kissinger's shuttle diplomacy in 1973–4 helped bring about two disengagement agreements between the warring sides but no permanent resolution of their conflict.

When Jimmy Carter took office in January 1977, he deemed the amelioration, if not the resolution, of the Middle East conflict one of his top priorities. This conflict had contributed to major increases in the world price of oil; the fallout of these increases had been inflation and slowed economic growth.

From Carter's perspective, stable oil prices required an end to the turmoil in the Middle East (Quandt, 1986:32). Furthermore, Carter believed that the current disengagement was unstable, and that some sort of settlement was necessary to prevent still another Arab–Israeli war and the potential involvement of the United States (Quandt, 1986:36). Thus, after assuming the presidency, Carter began almost immediately to use his office to press for peace in the Middle East.

The original US plan was to involve all the major parties, including the Palestinian Liberation Organization (PLO), in the negotiations. Yet as talks proceeded, it became clear that the most practicable resolution that might be reached would be one between Egypt and Israel. Indeed, Sadat at one point sent the US president a letter urging that 'nothing be done to prevent Israel and Egypt from negotiating directly' (Carter, 1982:294). By the summer of 1978, it seemed to Carter that a summit meeting was necessary to bridge the gap between Egypt and Israel. He invited Sadat and Begin to meet with him at Camp David.

When the Egyptian and Israeli leaders convened at Camp David, there were several major issues on which the two sides disagreed. We have grouped these issues into six categories. Much of the dispute centered on conflictual territorial claims regarding the Sinai Peninsula, the West Bank, the Gaza Strip, and Jerusalem. We next present each side's most serious concerns regarding each issue:

1. The Sinai Peninsula. This large tract of land was conquered by Israel during the Six Day War in 1967 and remained under its control after the Yom Kippur War. In many ways it was the most important issue dividing the two sides in the negotiations. For Israel, the Sinai provided a military buffer that offered considerable warning in case of a possible Egyptian attack. Israel had set up military bases in the peninsula, including three modern airbases of which it was very protective.

Israel had also captured oil fields in the Sinai that were of significant economic importance. Moreover, Israel had established civilian settlements in the Sinai that it was loath to give up. At one point at Camp David, Begin told a member of the American negotiating team, 'My right eye will fall out, my right hand will fall off before I ever agree to the dismantling of a single Jewish settlement' (Brzezinski, 1983:263).

For Egypt, the Sinai was of such great importance that no agreement could be achieved that did not include Egyptian control over this territory. Almost all observers of the negotiations agree that, amongst all his goals, Sadat 'gave primacy to a full withdrawal of Israel's forces from the Sinai' (Stein, 1993:81). He let the United States know at the earliest stages of the negotiations that while he would allow some modifications of the pre-1967 borders, the Sinai must be returned *in toto* (Quandt, 1986:50).

Roughly midway through the 18 months of negotiation leading up to Camp David, Sadat began focusing almost exclusively on the Sinai in his discussions with both the Israelis and Americans (Quandt, 1986:177). From a material perspective, military issues and the oil fields made the return of the Sinai imperative for the Egyptians. But perhaps more importantly, the Sinai was highly valued by Egypt for symbolic reasons. For Egypt, 'the return of the whole of Sinai was a matter of honor and prestige, especially since Sinai had been the scene of Egypt's 1967 humiliation' (Kacowicz, 1994:135).

2. Diplomatic Recognition of Israel. Since its creation in 1948, Israel had not been recognized as a legitimate and sovereign nation by its Arab neighbors. In fact, almost all Arab nations remained officially at war with Israel and, at least for propaganda purposes, sought its liquidation. For Israelis, diplomatic recognition by Egypt, its most powerful neighbor, was an overriding goal.

Israel wanted more than just formal recognition. Israeli leaders desired normal peaceful relations with Egypt, including the exchange of ambassadors and open borders (Brzezinski, 1983:281). Such a breakthrough could help liberate Israel from its pariah status in the region. Egypt balked at normalizing relations with Israel, in part because other Arab nations would oppose such measures. Sadat also believed that normal diplomatic relations would take a generation to develop because they would require such profound psychological adjustments (Telhami, 1990:130).

In the actual negotiations, Sadat went so far as to assert that questions of diplomatic relations, such as the exchange of ambassadors and open borders, involved Egyptian sovereignty and therefore could not be discussed (Quandt, 1986:51). Recognition of Israel became so contentious an issue that it presented one of the major obstacles to the signing of both the Camp David Accords in 1978 and the formal peace treaty in 1979.

3. The West Bank and the Gaza Strip. For most Israelis, these two territories were geographically and historically integral to their nation – at least more so than was the Sinai. Indeed, the Israeli negotiating team held retention of these areas to be one of its central goals (Brzezinski, 1983:236).

Begin, in particular, considered these territories to be part of Eretz Israel (i.e. the land of Israel), not occupied foreign land. As one observer put it, 'Begin was as adamant in refusing to relinquish Judea and Samaria as Sadat was in refusing to give up any of Sinai' (Quandt, 1986:66). By contrast, if Begin were to give up the Sinai, he was intent on getting some recognition of Israel's right to the West Bank and the Gaza Strip in return (Kacowicz, 1994:139).

For Egypt, these two territories had little economic or geo-strategic worth; Sadat did not focus much on them as the negotiations proceeded. However, Egypt did face pressure from other Arab nations not to abandon the Palestinian populations in these territories. Sadat told his aides that he would not leave Camp David without some commitment from the Israelis to withdraw from the West Bank and Gaza (Telhami, 1990:129). In fact, once he arrived at Camp David, Sadat informed Carter, 'I will not sign a Sinai agreement before an agreement is also reached on the West Bank' (Carter, 1982:345).

4. Formal Linkage of Accords and Palestinian Autonomy. One of the major issues of the negotiations was the extent to which an Egyptian–Israeli agreement should be tied to formal, substantive progress on the issue of Palestinian autonomy. Begin held that there should be no linkage.

While Egypt and Israel might agree to some framework for the Palestinian question, Begin claimed that this must be a separate matter from a treaty between the two states (Quandt, 1986:178). Sadat seemed to be of two minds on this issue. On the one hand, he pushed for Israeli recognition of the Palestinians' right to self-determination as part of the treaty, holding that a bilateral agreement could not be signed before an agreement on general principles concerning a Palestinian state was reached. On the other hand, he pointed out that a truly substantive agreement on the this issue could not be negotiated by the Egyptians alone. However, he opposed possible deferral on this issue to an Arab delegation, which he knew could sabotage the talks.

5. Israeli Recognition of Palestinian Rights. From the Israeli perspective, recognizing the rights of the Palestinian people was difficult because of competing sovereignty claims between the Israelis and Palestinians. When President Carter declared in Aswan that any solution to the conflict 'must recognize the legitimate rights of the Palestinian people,' the Israelis reacted negatively (Quandt, 1986:161). But because this recognition was not attached to any substantive changes (see issue 4 above), it was not viewed as excessively harmful to Israeli interests. In fact, Israeli foreign minister Moshe Dayan at one point sent a letter to the American negotiating team, indicating that Israel would be willing to grant equal rights to Arabs in the West Bank (Quandt, 1986:106).

From the Egyptian point of view, some form of Israeli recognition of the rights of Palestinians was deemed necessary. Even if the formulation was vague and largely symbolic, Sadat felt strongly that he needed at least a fig leaf with which to cover himself in the eyes of other Arab nations (Brzezinski, 1983:236; Quandt, 1986:188). Rhetorically, such a declaration would allow Egypt to claim that it had forced Israel finally to recognize the rights of the Palestinian population, an accomplishment that no other Arab state had been able to achieve. Furthermore, this formulation was appealing to Sadat, because it would not require the participation of other Arab states.

6. Jerusalem. Control of Jerusalem had been a delicate issue since 1948. The United Nations demanded in 1949 that the city be internationalized because of competing religious and political claims. Until the Israelis captured and unified the city in 1967, it had been split between an eastern and a western section.

For Israelis, Jerusalem was the capital of their nation and could not be relinquished. At Camp David, Dayan told the Americans that it would take more than a UN resolution to take the city away from Israel: 'They would also need to rewrite the Bible, and nullify three thousand years of our faith, our hopes, our yearnings and our prayers' (Dayan, 1981:177).

As was the case with other territorial claims, Egypt faced pressure from other Arab nations to force Israeli concessions on this issue. An Egyptian representative impressed on the Israelis that a constructive plan for Jerusalem would 'lessen Arab anxiety and draw the sting from Arab hostility' (Dayan, 1981:49). However, Egypt did not push strenuously on this issue and, in fact, seemed willing to leave it for the future.

These were the major issues of dispute dividing Egypt and Israel at the outset of the Camp David talks. We next indicate how AW might have been used to resolve these issues in as fair a manner as possible.

We consider these six issues as goods to be distributed between the two sides. Assuming both Egypt and Israel have 100 points to allocate across them, we now offer a hypothetical point allocation (see Table 12.1). This allocation, to be sure, is somewhat speculative: it is impossible to know exactly how Israeli and Egyptian delegates would have distributed their points had they actually used AW. However, it should be noted that while different point allocations could produce different issue resolutions, this would not alter any of the properties that AW guarantees (i.e. envy-freeness, efficiency, and equitability). Thus, it is the *methodology* of reaching a fair settlement that we emphasize rather than our particular allocation, which we believe to be plausible but certainly not the only plausible allocation.

The allocation of points in Table 12.1 is based on our preceding analysis of each side's interests in the six issues. Briefly, it reflects Egypt's overwhelming interest in the Sinai, Sadat's insistence on at least a vague statement of Israeli recognition of Palestinian rights to protect him from other Arab nations, the Israelis' more limited interests in the Sinai, and Begin's strong views on Eretz Israel (i.e. retaining the West Bank/Gaza Strip and control over Jerusalem). Note that each side has a four-tier ranking of the issues: most important (55 points for Egypt, 35 for Israel), second-most important (20 points), third-most important (10 points), and least important (5 points).

Our hypothetical allocation represents what we believe would be a truthful, rather that a strategic, point distribution of each side. Although in theory it is possible to benefit from deliberately misrepresenting one's valuation of issues, in practice this would be difficult and might succeed only in hurting oneself (Brams and Taylor, 1996).

Table 12.1 Hypothetical Israeli and Egyptian point allocation

Issue	Israel	Egypt
1. Sinai	35	**55**
2. Diplomatic recognition	**10**	5
3. West Bank/Gaza Strip	**20**	10
4. Linkage	**10**	5
5. Palestinian rights	5	**20**
6. Jerusalem	**20**	5
Total	100	100

Initially under AW, Egypt and Israel each win on the issues for which they have allocated more points than the other party (bold type in the table). Thus, Egypt would be awarded issues 1 and 5, for a total of 75 of its points. Israel would be awarded issues 2, 3, 4, and 6, for a total of 60 of its points.

Since Egypt has more of its points than Israel has of its points, some issue or issues must be transferred, in whole or in part, from Egypt to Israel in order to achieve equitability. Because the Sinai (issue 1) has a lower ratio (55/35 = 1.57) of Egyptian to Israeli points than the issue of Palestinian Rights (issue 5) does (20/5 = 4.0), the former must be divided, with some of Egypt's points on issue 1 transferred to Israel to create equitability. This transfer on the lowest-ratio issue ensures that AW is efficient – there is no settlement that is better for both sides.

In this instance, the adjustment is determined as follows:

$$20 + 55x = 60 + 35(1 - x),$$

which yields $x = 75/90 = 5/6 \simeq 0.83$. As a result, Egypt 'wins' 83 per cent of issue 1, along with all of issue 5, for a total of 66 of its points. Israel is given 17 per cent of issue 1, plus all of issues 2, 3, 4, and 6, for the same total of 66 of its points. This final distribution is envy-free, equitable, and efficient.

It should be noted that AW, using the hypothetical point allocations of Table 12.1, produces an outcome that mirrors quite closely the actual agreement reached by Egypt and Israel. From Israel's perspective, it essentially won on issue 2, because Egypt granted it diplomatic recognition, including the exchange of ambassadors. Israel also got its way on issue 3, when Egypt 'openly acknowledged Israel's right to claim in the future its sovereign rights over the West Bank and Gaza'

(Kacowicz, 1994:139). Additionally, Israel won on issue 4, because there was no formal linkage between the Camp David Accords – or the peace treaty later – and the question of a Palestinian state or the idea of Palestinian self-determination. And, finally, Jerusalem was not part of the eventual agreement, which can be seen as Israel's prevailing on issue 6.

Egypt prevailed on issue 5: Israel did agree to the Aswan formulation of recognizing the 'legitimate rights' of Palestinians. That leaves issue 1, on which Egypt wins 83 per cent, according to our hypothetical division.

As we previously noted, AW requires that goods of issues be divisible in order for the equitability-adjustment mechanism to work. In fact, the Sinai issue was multifaceted and thus lent itself to division. Besides the possible territorial divisions, there were also questions about Israeli military bases and airfields, as well as Israeli civilian settlements and the positioning of Egyptian military forces.

Egypt won on most of these issues. All the Sinai was turned over, and the Israelis evacuated its airfields, military bases, and civilian settlements. However, Egypt did agree to demilitarize the Sinai, and to the stationing of US forces to monitor the agreement, which represented a concession to Israel's security concerns. Viewing this concession as representing roughly 1/6 (17 per cent) of the total issue seems to us a plausible interpretation of the outcome.

One problem that arises for our hypothetical case is the question of additivity. We noted in section III that AW requires that the issues or goods be additive. But in the case of Camp David, it can be argued, the recognition of Palestinian rights was not independent of territorial issues. For Sadat, in particular, recognition may have been more important *because* of his failure to win Israeli concessions on the West Bank, the Gaza Strip, and Jerusalem.

Although finding tolerably separable issues – whose points can be summed – is never an easy task, skillful negotiators can attenuate this problem. They seem to have done so in reaching a consensus on the different issues that split the two sides in the Panama Canal Treaty negotiations in the 1970s (Raiffa, 1982). An additional lesson to be drawn from the Panama Canal case is that lumping together issues invariably results in each side's receiving fewer of its points (Brams and Taylor, 1996).

At Camp David, we believe, the two sides might have come up with a different division of issues than we proposed, which might have facilitated the application of AW. Nevertheless, we think our list works well, at least to illustrate the potential of AW, with both sides obtaining nearly two-thirds of their points.

V. PRACTICAL CONSIDERATIONS

A potential problem with AW is its manipulability. One side may try to manipulate its point distribution in an attempt to increase its 'winnings.' Assume, for example, that Israel, anticipating that Egypt would put an overwhelming number of points on Sinai – enabling Egypt almost certainly to 'win' on this issue – reduced its points on Sinai from 35 to 20. Also anticipating that Egypt would not put too many points on Palestinian rights, suppose that Israel increased its own points on this issue from 5 to 20 (corresponding to the amount it took from the Sinai issue), hoping, possibly, to win on Palestinian rights.

Under this scenario, Israel initially is awarded issues 2, 3, 4, and 6, for a total of 60 of its points, the same as before. However, Egypt wins only issue 1, for a total of 55 of its points, because now there is a 20–20 tie on Palestinian rights. The equitability adjustment on this issue, which is the lowest-ratio issue because the two sides tie on it, would give Egypt 12.5 points (62.5 per cent) and Israel 7.5 points (37.5 per cent). Thereby each side would end up with a total of 67.5 points, slightly more than the 66 points each side formerly received.

But this improvement for Israel is illusionary, because it is based on Israel's announced rather than true preferences. In fact, this maneuver backfires in two ways. First, insofar as Israel's point allocations in Table 12.1 reflect its true preferences, it actually ends up with fewer points. Instead of obtaining 37.5 per cent of 20 points on Palestinian rights (its manipulative allocation), it actually obtains 37.5 per cent of 5 points (its true allocation), or 1.875 points in addition to its initial 60 points, giving it a total of 61.875 points. This number is less, not more, than the 66 points it obtains by being honest in its announced allocation, whereas Egypt ends up with more (67.5 points).

The second way in which Israel's manipulative strategy backfires in this scenario is perhaps more costly. In the first example in which both parties announced their true preferences, Israel was awarded part of the Sinai issue according to the equitability-adjustment mechanism. However, in the manipulative scenario, because Israel reduced the number of points it put on the Sinai issue, Egypt wins the issue outright and needs to make no concessions to Israel. In such a case, it could be assumed that Egypt would not have to demilitarize the Sinai or allow the stationing of US forces to monitor the agreement.

Although AW is manipulable in theory (Brams and Taylor, 1996: chap. 4), in practice it is not manipulable unless a player has complete information about how the other side will distribute its points. Only then can the manipulator optimally allocate its points to exploit its knowledge. Short of having a spy in the other side's camp, however, a manipulative strategy like that just described is highly risky. As we illustrated, one side may only succeed in hurting itself and helping the other side, the opposite of what it intended to do.

A party to a dispute might also try to manipulate its point distribution in an attempt to deny the other side a good or issue – a strategy we might call *spite*. Imagine, for example, that Egypt wanted to deny Israel diplomatic recognition, even though Egypt itself did not value this issue highly. Egypt could increase the points it allocated to the diplomatic-recognition issue. However, a point-distribution strategy that is designed to deny something to an adversary rather than to ensure an equitable, envy-free, and efficient division, is potentially costly because the additional points allocated to an issue out of spite would have to come from another issue. As in the previous example of a manipulative strategy, the spiteful party would run the risk of losing on other issues. In this case, Egypt might run the risk of losing part or all of, say, the Sinai issue in order to deny diplomatic recognition to Israel.

To convince the two sides that being 'too clever by half' is a dangerous game to play, it would be useful for them to go through the exercise of allocating points to try to capitalize on their imperfect knowledge of what the other side is likely to do. We think that this exercise, in the absence of each side's having complete information about the other side's point distribution, would convince each player that honest allocations are generally the best strategy. Honest allocations always guarantee each player at least 50 of its points – even if one side has advance information on the other's allocation and follows an optimal manipulative strategy – making the outcome envy-free for an honest player.

An alternative point-allocation procedure, called 'proportional allocation' (PA), provides stronger protection against possible manipulation than does AW. However, we do not recommend it for two reasons. First, it is inefficient (Brams and Taylor, 1996: chap. 4). In the case of the Camp David agreement, PA would give each side 63.2 points instead of the 66 points that AW yields. Second, PA requires that every issue be divisible – not just one, as under AW – because under PA, each side wins only partially on each issue, based on the proportion of points it allocates compared to that allocated by the other side.

While honesty usually pays, it may not be a simple matter to come up with point assignments that mirror one's valuations of the different issues. To facilitate this task, we suggest that players begin by ranking the issues, from most to least important, in terms of getting their way on each.

After the issues have been ranked, players face the problem of turning a ranking into point assignments that reflect their *intensities* of preferences for the different issues. Raiffa (1982) discussed this problem in considerable detail, essentially concluding that a player must carefully weigh how much it would be willing to give up on one issue to obtain more on another. Thus for the Israelis in our example, West Bank/Gaza Strip and Jerusalem are worth twice as much (20 points each) as Diplomatic Recognition and Linkage (10 points each), which in turn are each worth twice as much as Palestinian Rights (5 points).

To come up with such point assignments, we recommend that a player begin by comparing the importance of winning its highest-ranked issue relative to its next-highest ranked issue, asking itself how much it values winning on the first to winning on the second. Continuing down the list, comparing the second-highest ranked issue with the third-highest ranked issue, and so on, a player would indicate, in relative terms, its 'importance ratio' between adjacent issues.

For example, if there were three issues, and the importance ratio was 2:1 on the first issue relative to the second, and 3:2 on the second issue relative to the third, this would translate into a 6:3:2 proportion over the three issues. Rounding to the nearest integer, the point assignments would be 55, 27, and 18, respectively, on the three issues.

In the preceding section, we mentioned the problem of making the issues in a dispute as separable as possible in order to render the addition of points on different issues meaningful. If winning on, say, issue 1 affects how much one wins on issue 2, then the points a player receives on issue 2 can not be simply added to the points he or she receives on other issues – it depends on what happens on issue 1. In this sense, West Bank/Gaza Strip was probably best treated as a single issue – even though the West Bank and the Gaza Strip are two geographically separate territories – because it would have been difficult to make decisions on one independently of the other.

By contrast, in some future possible agreement, it is reasonable to suppose that the withdrawal of a few hundred Israeli settlers from Gaza will much more easily be accomplished than the withdrawal of thousands, or even tens of thousands, of Israeli settlers from the West Bank. Although the 1993 Oslo accord between Israel and the PLO intricately linked the withdrawal of Israeli administrative and security personnel from the West Bank and from Gaza, the withdrawal of settlers is an

Camp David: Was the Agreement Fair? 321

entirely different story. In a future agreement, we believe it would probably be better to treat the withdrawal of settlers from Gaza and from the West Bank as separate issues, especially because Gaza has no biblical significance for the Israelis whereas the West Bank (also known as Judea and Samaria) does.

A final practical problem is that of timing. Specifically, when is it most advantageous for disputants to invoke AW? According to Henry Kissinger, 'Stalemate is the most propitious condition for settlement' (*New York Times*, 12 October 1974). Following this view, it might be best to let the disputants try, on their own, to reach an agreement without AW. If, after repeated attempts, they fail, they may well become frustrated and weary enough to consider using AW to break the impasse.

Of course, leaving the final shape of an agreement to AW is somewhat of a gamble. It becomes an acceptable risk to the degree that the disputants see AW as a procedure from which they can benefit equally, which equitability ensures. Moreover, because AW is efficient, the disputants can rest assured that there is no equitable agreement that can benefit both more.

However, if one side thinks that it can frighten the other side into submission by posturing, or that it can wear down the other side through endless haggling, then the equitability and efficiency of AW will not appear so compelling. Indeed, it may take months or even years of impasse, as was the case in the negotiations leading up to Camp David, before the two sides are willing to contemplate certain compromises and then hammer out an agreement. By comparison, AW allows them to reach closure immediately – once they agree as to what winning and losing on each issue means.

To be sure, spelling out what constitutes winning and losing on each issue may require protracted negotiations before AW can be applied. But if the costs of delay are substantial, and the issues are quite narrowly defined, then the two sides should be able to reach agreements on these issues more quickly than they could reach a consensus, without AW, on an entire package of issues.

The two sides will also have to decide, after AW is applied, what winning and losing partially means on the issue on which there is an equitability adjustment. In the case of Camp David, we view the demilitarization of the Sinai and the stationing of US forces to monitor the agreement as Israel's winning one-sixth of the Sinai issue. Negotiations on what partially winning and losing mean can await the application of AW, however, which will stipulate exactly what equitability adjustment is required on what issue.

We think that none of the aforementioned practical considerations presents insuperable barriers to the use of AW. In order for the procedure to work best, the two sides would have to be educated as to the hazards of trying to manipulate AW to their advantage or out of spite, including the likelihood that such manipulative strategies could backfire. They would also have to be advised on how best to define issues to make them as separable as possible, thereby ensuring that the addition of points across different issues, once AW is applied, is sensible.

The determination of what is entailed by winning and losing for each side on the issues would have to be worked out beforehand. As with the definition of the issues, this determination will require good-faith negotiations, perhaps aided by a mediator. Also, some way of monitoring and enforcing the agreements reached on each issue – whoever wins or loses – would have to be built into the agreement once it is implemented.

AW does not so much eliminate negotiations as require that they be structured in a certain way. Once this structuring is accomplished, AW finds the unique settlement that is envy-free, equitable, and efficient.

This method of achieving closure, we think, is likely not only to save the two sides time but also to result in a better agreement than one produced after exhaustive and rancorous negotiations, which often leave both sides with a bitter taste that impedes future negotiations. Not only does AW attenuate this problem, but it also offers a quick way of *re*negotiating agreements should priorities change due to changes in governments or other circumstances.

VI. CONCLUSIONS

Was the Camp David agreement fair? Many Egyptians were disappointed with the results of the Camp David talks. A former foreign minister of Egypt, Ismail Fahmy, wrote, 'The treaty gives all the advantages to Israel while Egypt pays the price. As a result, peace cannot last unless the treaty undergoes radical revision' (Fahmy, 1983:292).

Quandt (1986:255) also takes the view that Israel did better in the negotiations, but our reconstruction of the negotiations using AW suggests that the settlement was probably as fair as it could be. If Fahmy were correct in his belief that an unfair peace could not last, then the last two decades of peaceful relations (albeit a 'cold' peace) between Israel and Egypt is testimony to the contrary.

Reinforcing this view is the fact that the negotiators, while undoubtedly desiring to 'win,' realized that this was not in the cards because they were not in a zero-sum situation. Abetted by Jimmy Carter, they were driven to seek a settlement that, because it benefitted both sides more or less equally, could be considered fair.

While it might be debatable that a fair agreement was reached at Camp David, the biggest surprise, we think, is that *any* agreement was reached. In political disputes in general, and in international disputes in particular, players often spend much time and energy on procedural matters before substantive questions are ever addressed. The Egyptian–Israeli negotiations were no exception: the two sides fought vigorously over procedural issues at several points in the negotiations (Quandt, 1986:108).

Disputants have a strong incentive to do this because procedures can be manipulated to bring about different outcomes (Riker, 1986; Brams, 1990). By guaranteeing a resolution that is fair according to several important criteria, AW, by contrast, affords disputants the opportunity to focus on substantive issues – while largely protecting them from manipulation of the kind we illustrated earlier.

Another problem that plagues international disputes is that one side may worry that it will come out looking worse than the other, inducing it to abandon talks altogether rather than settling for a one-sided resolution – and explaining it back home. At Camp David, Sadat at one point expressed such fear and packed his bags with the intent of returning to Egypt. Only a strong personal appeal from Jimmy Carter, coupled with certain threats, kept Sadat from breaking off the negotiations (Brzezinski, 1983:272).

By guaranteeing an outcome that is envy-free, equitable, and efficient, AW can reduce such fears and help keep negotiations on track. We believe it would have worked well at Camp David, producing a less crisis-driven settlement, even if the outcome would not have differed much from that which actually was achieved.

This is not to say that fair-division procedures such as AW are without shortcomings. For one thing, formal algorithms do not have the flexibility of informal procedures. Furthermore, as we have already mentioned, the synergies that various combinations of issues can create could pose difficulties for the additivity requirement of AW.

Nonetheless, the benefits of a straightforward procedure that guarantees certain properties of fairness are considerable. The failure of negotiations has caused great human misery throughout history. To the extent that it can help resolve some of these conflicts, AW, we believe, offers substantial promise for the future.

Appendix
Survey of War Literature by Category

collections of articles on war: Pruitt and Snyder (1969), Falk and Kim (1980), Vasquez and Henehan (1992).

critical reviews: Zinnes (1980) on quantitative studies of the outbreak of war, Singer (1981) on the 'state of the discipline,' Eberwein (1981) and Levy (1989c) on the causes of war, Luterbacher (1984) on recent contributions, Vasquez (1987a) on the Correlates of War Project, and Midlarsky (1989) on theories and findings until the late 1980s.

causes of war: Blainey (1973), Nelson and Olin (1979), Beer (1981), Howard (1984), Brown (1987), Vasquez (1993).

conflict and war: M. Haas (1974), Rummel (1975–81), Gurr (1980).

crisis and war: O.R. Holsti (1972), Nomikos and North (1976), Brecher and Wilkenfeld (1989, 1997), Brecher, Wilkenfeld and Moser (1988), James (1988), Wilkenfeld, Brecher and Moser (1988), Brecher (1993), Morgan (1994).

deterrence: Morgan (1977), Huth and Russett (1984, 1988, 1990), Lebow and Stein (1987, 1989a,b, 1990), Zagare (1987), Huth (1988a,b), Harvey (1995), 1996a, 1996b, 1997; Harvey and James (1992).

diversionary theory of war: Levy (1989a).

domestic aspects of war: A. Stein (1980), Levy and Morgan (1986), Levy (1989d).

expected utility theory: Bueno de Mesquita (1981, 1985, 1989), Bueno de Mesquita and Lalman (1992); Morrow, 1985, Witol (1995).

game theory: Brams and Kilgour (1987c), Morrow (1994), Bueno de Mesquita and Lalman (1992).

hegemonic war: Gilpin (1981, 1989), Levy (1983a).

hierarchical equilibria theory: Midlarsky (1986, 1988).

historical approach: Stoessinger (1985), Nogee and Spanier (1988), K.J. Holsti (1991), Keegan (1993).

historical sociology approach: Aron (1957, 1959), S. Hoffmann (1965), Luard (1987).

Appendix 325

inadvertent war: George (1991).

lateral pressure theory: Choucri and North (1975, 1989).

levels of analysis and war: Waltz (1959), Singer (1961).

long cycles and war: Modelski and Morgan (1985), Thompson (1986, 1988), Modelski (1987), Goldstein (1988), Modelski and Thompson (1989).

nuclear war: Kahn (1960, 1962, 1965, 1970), Bracken (1983), Harvey and James (1992).

obsolescence of major power war: Mueller (1989), van Creveld (1991).

outcome and consequences of war: A. Stein and Russett (1980).

paradoxes of war: Maoz (1990a).

polarity and war: Morgenthau (1960), M.A. Kaplan (1957), Deutsch and Singer (1964), Waltz (1964, 1967), Rosecrance (1966), M. Haas (1970), Singer, Bremer and Stuckey (1972), Wallace (1973), Bueno de Mesquita (1975, 1978, 1981), Rapkin, Thompson with Christopherson (1979), Wayman (1984), Garnham (1985), Levy (1985), Sabrosky (1985), Thompson (1986, 1988), Domke (1988), Midlarsky (1988), Brecher, James and Wilkenfeld (1990), Mearsheimer (1990), Hopf (1991), Saperstein (1991), Wagner (1993).

political economy of war: Ashley (1980), Gilpin (1987).

power transition theory: Organski and Kugler (1980), Kugler and Organski (1989).

prospect theory: Farnham (1994), Stein and Pauly (1993), Witol (1995).

psychological dimension of war: Glad (1990).

quantitative (aggregate data) research: (Correlates of War project): Singer and Small (1972), Singer et al. (1979), Small and Singer (1982).

regime type (democracy) and war: Kant (1969 [1795]), Small and Singer (1976), Rummel (1983), Doyle (1986), Maoz and Abdolali (1989), Levy (1988), Lake (1992), Dixon (1993, 1994), Maoz and Russett (1993), Ray (1993, 1995), Russett (1993), Hagan (1994), Layne (1994), Owen (1994), Raymond (1994), Spiro (1994), Hermann and Kegley (1995), Fukuyama (1992).

revolution and war: Walt (1992).

search for patterns of war: Barringer (1972).

strategic theory: Earle (1943), Schelling (1960), Kahn (1960, 1965), (Brodie (1973), Paret (1986), Luttwak (1987).

technology and war: McNeill (1982), van Creveld (1989).

territory and war: Vasquez (1993).

war termination: Wright (1942), Kecscemeti (1958), Holsti (1966), Carroll (1969), Fox (1970), Kahn (1970), Stein (1975), Handel (1978), Sigal (1988), Beer and Mayer (1986).

Bibliography

Achen, C.H., and D. Snidal. 1989. 'Rational Deterrence Theory and Comparative Case Studies.' *World Politics* 41:143–69.
Adomeit, H. 1982. *Soviet Risk-Taking and Crisis Behavior: A Theoretical and Empirical Analysis.* London: Allen & Unwin.
Agranat Commission Supplementary Report: The Yom Kippur War, 1 (Givatayim: IDF Archives, declassified in 1955).
Aldrich, J., and F. D. Nelson. 1984. *Linear Probability, Logit, and Probit Models.* Beverly Hills: Sage Publications.
Allais, M. 1953. 'Le Comportement de L'Homme Rationnel Devant le Risque: Critique des Postulats et Axiomes et l'Ecole Americaine.' *Econometrica* 21:503–46.
Allan, P. 1983. *Crisis Bargaining and the Arms Race: A Theoretical Model.* Cambridge: Ballinger.
Allison, G.T. 1971. *The Essence of Decision: Explaining the Cuban Missile Crisis.* Boston: Little, Brown.
Allison, P.D. 1984. *Event History Analysis: Regression for Longitudinal Event Data.* Beverly Hills: Sage Publications.
Altfeld, M.F. 1983. 'Arms Races? And Escalation? A Comment on Wallace.' *International Studies Quarterly* 27:225–31.
Alves, M.H.M. 1989. 'Interclass Alliances in the Opposition to the Military in Brazil: Consequences for the Transition Period.' In S. Eckstein, ed., *Power and Popular Protest Latin American Social Movements.* Berkeley: University of California Press.
Ames, B. 1977. 'The Politics of Public Spending in Latin America.' *American Journal of Political Science* 21:149–76.
———. 1987. *Political Survival: Politicians and Public Policy in Latin America.* Berkeley: University of California Press.
Anderson, P.A. 1983. 'Decision Making by Objection and the Cuban Missile Crisis.' *Administrative Science Quarterly* 28:201–22.
Anderson, P.A., and T. McKeown. 1987. 'Changing Aspirations, Limited Attention, and War.' *World Politics,* 30:1–29.
Andriole, S.J. 1978. 'The Levels-of-Analysis Problems and the Study of Foreign, International, and Global Affairs: A Review Critique and Another Final Solution.' *International Interactions* 5:113–33.
Aron, R. 1957. 'Conflict and War from the Viewpoint of Historical Sociology.' *The Nature of Conflict.* Paris: UNESCO.
———. 1959. *On War.* New York: Doubleday.
Arkes, H.R., and C. Blumer. 1985. 'The Psychology of Sunk Cost.' *Organizational Behavior and Human Decision Processes* 35:124–40.
Arrow, K.J. 1982. 'Risk Perception in Psychology and Economics.' *Economic Inquiry* 20:1–9.
Ashley, R.K. 1976. 'Noticing Pre-Paradigmatic Progress.' In J.N. Rosenau, ed., *In Search of Global Patterns.* New York: Free Press.

———. 1980. *The Political Economy of War and Peace*. London: Frances Pinter.
———. 1986. 'The Poverty of Neorealism.' In R. Keohane, ed., *Neorealism and its Critics*. New York: Columbia University Press.
Ashley, R.K., and R.B.J Walker. 1990. 'Speaking the Language of the Exile: Dissident Thought in International Studies.' *International Studies Quarterly* 34:259-68.
Austine, W., E.W., and M.K. Utne. 1976. 'Equity and the Law.' *Advances in Experimental Social Psychology* 9:163-90.
Axelrod, R. 1984. *The Evolution of Cooperation*. New York: Basic Books.
———. 1986. 'An Evolutionary Approach to Norms.' *American Political Science Review* 80:1095-112.
Azar, E.E. 1972. 'Conflict Escalation and Conflict Reduction in an International Crisis: Suez, 1956.' *Journal of Conflict Resolution*. 16:183-201.
———. 1979. 'Peace Amidst Development: A Conceptual Agenda for Conflict and Peace Research.' *International Interactions* 6:123-43.
———. 1985. 'Protracted International Conflicts: Ten Propositions.' *International Interactions* 12:59-70.
Azar, E.E., and N. Farah. 1981. 'The Structure of Inequalities and Protracted Social Conflict: A Theoretical Framework.' *International Interactions* 7:317-35.
Azar, E.E., P. Jureidini, and R. McLaurin. 1978. 'Protracted Social Conflict: Theory and Practice in the Middle East.' *Journal of Palestine Studies* 8:41-60.
Bar-Joseph, U. 1995. 'Israel's Intelligence Failure of 1973: New Evidence, A New Interpretation and Theoretical Implications.' *Security Studies*, 3: .
Barringer, R.E. 1972. *War: Patterns of Conflict*. Cambridge: MIT Press.
Bazerman, M.H. 1983. 'Negotiator Judgment.' *American Behavioral Scientist* 27:11-28.
Beer, F. 1981. *Peace Against War*. San Francisco: Freeman.
Beer, F., and T.F. Mayer. 1986. 'Why Wars End: Some Hypotheses.' *Review of International Studies* 12:95-106.
Bell, P.M.H. 1986. *The Origins of the Second World War*. London: Longman.
Ben-Zvi, A. 1976. 'Hindsight and Foresight: A Conceptual Framework for the Analysis of Surprise Attacks.' *World Politics* 28:381-95.
———. 1976-7. 'Misperceiving the Role of Perception: A Critique.' *The Jerusalem Journal of International Relations*, 2:
———. 1987. *The Illusion of Deterrence: The Roosevelt Presidency and the Origins of the Pacific War*. Boulder: Westview Press.
———. 1990. 'Intention, Capability and Surprise: A Comparative Analysis.' *Journal of Strategic Studies* 13 no. 4:19-40.
———. 1995. 'Perception, Misperception and Surprise in the Yom Kippur War: A Look at the New Evidence.' *Journal of Conflict Studies* 15:74-93.
Bennett, D.S. 1993. *Security, Economy, and the End of Interstate Rivalry*. PhD dissertation, University of Michigan.
———. 1995. 'Domestic Political Influences on Rivalry Termination.' Paper presented at the Annual Meeting of the American Political Science Association, Chicago, 1995.

Bercovitch, J., and P.F. Diehl. 1995. 'The Conflict Management of Enduring Rivalries: Frequency, Timing, Form, and Short-Term Impact.' Paper presented at the Annual Meeting of the American Political Science Association, Chicago, 1995.

Bercovitch, J., and P. Regan. 1994. 'Managing Enduring International Conflicts: Theoretical Issues and Empirical Evidence.' Paper presented at the Annual Meeting of the American Political Science Association, New York, 1994.

Betts, R.K. 1977. *Soldiers, Statesmen, and Cold War Crises*. Cambridge: Harvard University Press.

———. 1982. *Surprise Attack: Lessons for Defense Planning*. Washington: Brookings Institution.

———. 1989. 'Surprise, Scholasticism, and Strategy: A Review of Ariel Levite's Intelligence and Strategic Surprises.' *International Studies Quarterly* 33:329–43.

Biersteker, T.J. 1989. 'Critical Reflections on Post-Positivism in International Relations.' *International Studies Quarterly* 33:263–67.

Blainey, G. 1973. *The Causes of War*. New York: Free Press.

Bobrow, D.B., S. Chan and J.A. Kringen. 1977. 'Understanding How Others Treat Crises: A Multimethod Approach.' *International Studies Quarterly* 21:199–223.

Boettcher, W. 1995. 'Prospect Theory in International Relations.' *Journal of Conflict Resolution* 39:561–83.

Borthwick, M. 1992. *Pacific Century: The Emergence of Modern Pacific Asia*. Boulder: Westview.

Box, G.E.P., and G.C. Tiao. 1975. 'Intervention Analysis with Applications to Economic and Environmental Problems.' *Journal of the American Statistical Association* 70:70–9.

Bracken, P. 1983. *The Command and Control of Nuclear Forces*. New Haven: Yale University Press.

Brams, S.J. 1985. *Superpower Games: Applying Game Theory to Superpower Conflict*. New Haven: Yale University Press.

———. 1990. *Negotiation Games: Applying Game Theory to Bargaining and Arbitration*. New York: Routledge.

———. 1993. 'Theory of Moves.' *American Scientist* 81:562–70.

———. 1994. *Theory of Moves*. Cambridge: Cambridge University Press.

Brams, S.J., and D.M. Kilgour. 1987a. 'Winding Down if Preemption or Escalation Occurs.' *Journal of Conflict Resolution* 31:547–72.

———. 1987b. 'Threat Escalation and Crisis Stability: A Game-theoretic Analysis.' *American Political Science Review* 81:833–50.

———. 1987c. *Game Theory and National Security*. New York: Blackwell.

Brams, S.J., and W. Mattli. 1993. 'Theory of Moves: Overview and Examples.' *Conflict Management and Peace Science* 12:1–39.

Brams, S.J., and B.D. Mor. 1993. 'When Is It Rational to Be Magnanimous in Victory?' *Rationality and Society* 5:432–54.

Brams, S.J., and A.D. Taylor. 1996. *Fair Division: From Cake-Cutting to Dispute Resolution*. Cambridge: Cambridge University Press.

Bratton, M., and N. van de Walle. 1992. 'Popular Protest and Political Reform in Africa.' *Comparative Politics* 24:419–42.

Braun, A. 1992. *Moshe Dayan and the Yom Kippur War*, (Hebrew). Tel-Aviv: Edanim.
Brecher, M. 1972. *The Foreign Policy System of Israel: Setting, Images, Process.* Oxford: Oxford University Press.
———. 1977. 'Toward a Theory of International Crisis Behavior.' *International Studies Quarterly*, 21:39–74.
———. 1980. *Decisions in Crisis: Israel, 1967 and 1973.* Los Angeles: University of California Press.
———. 1984. 'International Crises, Protracted Conflicts.' *International Interactions* 11:237–98.
———. 1993. *Crises in World Politics: Theory and Reality.* New York: Pergamon Press.
Brecher, M., and H. Ben-Yehuda. 1985. 'System and Crisis in International Politics.' *Review of International Studies* 11:17–36.
Brecher, M., and B. Geist. 1980. *Decisions in Crisis: Israel 1967 and 1973.* Berkeley: University of California Press.
Brecher, M., and P. James. 1988. 'Patterns of Crisis Management.' *Journal of Conflict Resolution* 32:426–56.
Brecher, M., P. James and J. Wilkenfeld. 1990. 'Polarity and Stability: New Concepts, Indicators and Evidence.' *International Interactions* 16:69–100.
Brecher, M., and J. Wilkenfeld. 1989. *Crisis, Conflict and Instability.* Oxford: Pergamon Press.
———. 1991. 'International Crises and Global Instability: The Myth of the Long Peace.' In C. Kegley, ed., *The Long Postwar Peace.* New York: HarperCollins.
———. 1997. *A Study of Crisis.* Ann Arbor: University of Michigan Press.
———. (forthcoming). *Twentieth Century Crises.*
Brecher, M., J. Wilkenfeld, and S. Moser. 1988. *Crises in the Twentieth Century, Volume I: Handbook of International Crises.* Oxford: Pergamon Press.
Bremer, S.A. 1982. 'The Contagiousness of Coercion: The Spread of Serious International Disputes, 1900–1976.' *International Interactions* 9:29–55.
———. 1992. 'Dangerous Dyads: Conditions Affecting the Likelihood of Interstate War, 1816–1965.' *Journal of Conflict Resolution* 36:309–41.
———. 1993. 'Democracy and Militarized Interstate Conflict, 1816–1965.' *International Interactions* 18:231–49.
Brodie, B. 1973. *War and Politics.* New York: Macmillan.
Brookshire, D.S., and D.L. Coursey. 1987. 'Measuring the Value of a Public Good: An Empirical Comparison of Elicitation Procedures.' *American Economic Review* 77:554–66.
Brown, S. 1987. *The Causes and Prevention of War.* New York: St. Martin's Press.
Brussel, G.S. 1989. *Pew Program in Case Teaching and Writing in International Affairs, Case #334: The Cuban Missile Crisis.* Pittsburgh: University of Pittsburgh Press.
Brzezinski, Z. 1983. *Power and Principle: Memoirs of the National Security Adviser, 1977–1981.* New York: Farrar Straus Giroux.
Bueno de Mesquita, B. 1975. 'Measuring Systemic Polarity.' *Journal of Conflict Resolution* 19:187–216.
———. 1978. 'Systemic Polarization and the Occurrence and Duration of War.' *Journal of Conflict Resolution* 22:241–67.

———. 1981. *The War Trap*. New Haven: Yale University Press.
———. 1985. 'The War Trap Revisited: A Revised Expected Utility Model.' *American Political Science Review* 79:156–77.
———. 1989. 'The Contribution of Expected-Utility Theory to the Study of International Conflict.' In R.I. Rotberg and T.K. Rabb, eds, *The Origin and Prevention of Major Wars*. Cambridge: Cambridge University Press.
Bueno de Mesquita, B., and D. Lalman. 1990. 'Domestic Opposition and Foreign War.' *American Political Science Review* 84:747–66.
———. 1992. *War and Reason*. New Haven: Yale University Press.
Bueno de Mesquita, B., and R. Siverson. 1995. 'War and the Survival of Political Leaders.' *American Political Science Review* 89:841–55.
Bueno de Mesquita, B., R. Siverson, and G. Woller. 1992. 'War and the Fate of Regimes.' *American Political Science Review* 86:638–46.
Bullock, A. 1952. *Hitler: A Study in Tyranny*. London: Odhams Press.
Bunce, V. 1980. 'Changing Leaders and Changing Policies: The Impact of Elite Succession on Budgetary Priorities in Democratic Countries.' *American Journal of Political Science* 24:373–95.
———. 1981. *Do Leaders Make a Difference? Executive Succession and Public Policy under Capitalism and Socialism*. Princeton: Princeton University Press.
———. 1986. 'The Effects of Leadership Succession in the Soviet Union.' *American Political Science Review* 80:215–19.
Burke, J.P., and F.I. Greenstein. 1989. *How Presidents Test Reality: Decisions on Vietnam, 1954 and 1965*. New York: Russell Sage Foundation.
Campbell, D.T. 1969. 'Reforms as Experiments.' *American Psychologist* 24:409–29.
Campbell, D.T., and H.L. Ross. 1968. 'The Connecticut Crackdown on Speeding: Time Series Data in Quasi-Experimental Analysis.' *Law and Society Review* 3:33–53.
Campbell, D.T., and J.C. Stanley. 1963. *Experimental and Quasi-Experimental Designs for Research*. Chicago: Rand McNally.
Caporaso, J.A., and A.L. Pelowski. 1971. 'Economic and Political Integration in Europe: A Time Series Quasi-Experimental Analysis.' *American Political Science Review* 65:418–33.
Carroll, B.A. 1969. 'How Wars End: An Analysis of Some Current Hypotheses.' *Journal of Peace Research* 4:295–321.
Carter, J. 1982. *Keeping Faith: Memoirs of a President*. New York: Bantam Books.
Central Intelligence Agency. 1992. *The World Factbook, 1992*. Washington, DC: US Government Printing Office.
Chai, S.-K. 1993. 'An Organizational Economics Theory of Anti-government Violence.' *Comparative Politics* 25:99–110.
Chambers, F.P. 1962. *This Age of Conflict*. New York: Harcourt, Brace & World.
Choucri, N., and R.C. North. 1975. *Nations in Conflict: National Growth and International Violence*. San Francisco: W.H. Freeman.
———. 1989. 'Lateral Pressure in International Relations: Concept and Theory.' In M.I. Midlarsky, ed., *Handbook of War Studies*. Boston: Unwin Hyman.
Christensen, T.J. and J. Snyder. 1990. 'Chain Gangs and Passed Bucks.' *International Organization* 44:137–68.
Cimbala, S.J. 1988. *Nuclear Strategizing: Deterrence and Reality*. New York: Praeger.

Claude, I. Jr. 1962. *Power and International Relations.* New York: Random House.
Clausewitz, K. von 1976 [1832]. *On War.* M. Howard and P. Paret, trans. and ed. Princeton: Princeton University Press.
Cohen, E.A. and J. Gooch. 1990. *Military Misfortunes: The Anatomy of Failure in War.* New York: The Free Press.
Cotton, T. 1986. 'War and American Democracy.' *Journal of Conflict Resolution* 30:616-35.
Coursey, Don L., John L. Hovis, and William D. Schulze. 1987. 'The Disparity between Willingness to Accept and Willingness to Pay Measures of Value.' *Quarterly Journal of Economics* 102:697-90.
Cox, R. 1986. 'Social Forces, States and World Order: Beyond International Relations Theory.' In R. Keohane, ed., *Neorealism and its Critics.* New York: Columbia University Press.
Craig, G.A., and A. George. 1990. *Force and Statecraft: Diplomatic Problems of Our Time.* New York: Oxford University Press.
Crawford, V.P. 1979. 'On Compulsory Arbitration Schemes.' *Journal of Political Economy* 87:131-59.
Cusack, T.R. and W. Eberwein. 1982. 'Prelude to War: Incidence, Escalation and Intervention in International Disputes, 1900-1976.' *International Interactions* 9:9-28.
Dawisha, K. 1984. *The Kremlin and the Prague Spring.* Berkeley and Los Angeles: University of California Press.
Dayan, M. 1981. *Breakthrough: A Personal Account of the Egypt-Israel Peace Negotiations.* New York: Alfred A. Knopf.
DeNardo, J. 1985. *Power in Numbers.* Princeton: Princeton University Press.
Der Derian, J. 1990. 'The (S)pace of International Relations: Simulation, Surveillance, and Speed.' *International Studies Quarterly* 34:295-310.
DeRouen, K. 1995. 'The Indirect Link.' *Journal of Conflict Resolution* 39:671-95.
Deutsch, K.W. 1974. *Politics and Government,* 2nd edn. Boston: Houghton Mifflin.
Deutsch, K.W., and J.D. Singer. 1964. 'Multipolar Power Systems and International Stability.' *World Politics* 16:390-406.
Diehl, P. 1983. 'Arms Races and Escalation: A Closer Look.' *Journal of Peace Research* 20:205-12.
———. 1985a. 'Armaments without War: An Analysis of Some Underlying Effects.' *Journal of Peace Research* 22:249-59.
———. 1985b. 'Arms Races to War: Testing Some Empirical Linkages.' *Sociological Quarterly* 26:331-49.
———. 1985c. 'Contiguity and Military Escalation in Major Power Rivalries, 1816-1980.' *Journal of Politics* 47:1203-11.
Diehl, P.F., and J. Kingston. 1987. 'Messenger or Message? Military Buildups and the Initiation of Conflict.' *Journal of Politics* 49:801-13.
Diehl, P.F., J. Reifschneider, and P.R. Hensel. 1996 (forthcoming). 'United Nations Intervention and Recurring Conflict: A Research Note.' *International Organization.*
Dingman, R. 1988. 'Atomic Diplomacy During the Korean War.' *International Security* 13:50-91.

Divine, R.A. 1969. *Roosevelt and World War II*. Harmondsworth: Penguin.

Dixon, W.J. 1993. 'Democracy and the Management of International Conflict.' *Journal of Conflict Resolution* 37:42–68.

——. 1994. 'Democracy and the Peaceful Settlement of International Conflict.' *American Political Science Review* 88:14–32.

Dixon, W.J., and B.E. Moon. 1986. 'The Military Burden and Basic Human Needs.' *Journal of Conflict Resolution* 30:660–84.

Domke, W.K. 1988. *War and the Changing Global System*. New Haven: Yale University Press.

Dougherty, J.E., and R.L. Pfaltzgraff, Jr. 1990. *Contending Theories of International Relations: A Comprehensive Survey*. New York: Harper & Row.

Dowty, A. 1984. *Middle East Crisis: U.S. Decision-Making in 1958, 1970 and 1973*. Berkeley: University of California Press.

Doyle, M.W. 1986. 'Liberalism and World Politics.' *American Political Science Review* 80:1151–69.

Earle, E.M., ed. 1943. *Makers of Modern Strategy: Military Thought from Machiavelli to Hitler*. Princeton: Princeton University Press.

Eberwein, W.-D. 1981. 'The Quantitative Study of International Conflict: Quantity and Quality?' *Journal of Peace Research* 18:19–38.

Eckstein, H. 1975. 'Case Studies and Theory in Political Science.' In F.I. Greenstein and N.W. Polsby, eds, *Handbook of Political Science, Vol. 7*. Reading: Addison-Wesley.

Eckstein, S. 1989. 'Power and Popular Protest in Latin America.' In S. Eckstein, ed., *Power and Popular Protest Latin American Social Movements*. Berkeley: University of California Press.

Evans, P.B., H.K. Jacobson, and R.D. Putnam, eds. 1993. *Double-Edged Diplomacy: International Bargaining and Domestic Politics*. Berkeley: University of California Press.

Evron, Y. 1987. *War and Intervention in Lebanon*. London: Croom Helm.

Fabyanic, T. 1987. 'Air Power and Conflict Termination.' In S. Cimbala and K. Dunn, eds, *Conflict Termination and Military Strategy*. Boulder: Westview Press.

Fahmy, I. 1983. *Negotiating for Peace in the Middle East*. Baltimore: Johns Hopkins University Press.

Farnham, B. 1992. 'Roosevelt and the Munich Crisis: Insights from Prospect Theory.', *Political Psychology* 13:205–35.

——. ed. 1994. *Avoiding Losses/Taking Risks: Prospect Theory and International Conflict*. Ann Arbor: University of Michigan Press.

Fearon, J. 1994. 'Signaling versus the Balance of Power and Interests: An Empirical Test of a Crisis Bargaining Model.' *Journal of Conflict Resolution* 38:236–69.

Feste, K. 1982. 'International Enemies: A Review.' Paper presented at the Annual Meeting of the International Studies Association, Cincinnati, 1982.

Finlay, D.J., O.R. Holsti, and R.R. Fagen. 1967. *Enemies in Politics*. Chicago: Rand-McNally.

Fishburn, Peter C., and G.A. Kochenberger. 1979. 'Two-Piece Von Neumann-Morgenstern Utility Functions.' *Decision Sciences* 10:503–18.

Fox, W.T.R. 1970. 'The Causes of Peace and Conditions of War.' In W.T.R. Fox, ed., *How Wars End, The Annals* 392:1–13.

Francisco, R. 1993. 'Theories of Protest and the Revolutions of 1989.' *American Journal of Political Science* 27:663–80.
Freedman, L., and E. Karsh. 1993. *The Gulf Conflict 1990–1991*. Princeton: Princeton University Press.
Friedman, E., ed. 1994. *The Politics of Democratization: Generalizing East Asian Experiences*. Boulder: Westview.
Frisch, D. 1993. 'Reasons for Framing Effects.' *Organizational Behavior and Human Decision Processes* 54:399–429.
Fry, M.G. 1989. *Pew Program in Case Teaching and Writing in International Affairs, Case #126: The Suez Crisis, 1956*. Pittsburgh: University of Pittsburgh.
Fukuyama, F. 1992. *The End of History and the Last Man*. New York: Avon Books.
Gamson, W.A. 1975. *The Strategy of Social Protest*. Homewood, IL: Dorsey Press.
Ganguly, S. 1990. 'Deterrence Failure Revisited: The Indo-Pakistani War of 1965.' *The Journal of Strategic Studies* 13:77–93.
Garland, H. and S. Newport. 1991. 'Effects of Absolute and Relative Sunk Costs on the Decision to Persist with a Course of Action.' *Organizational Behavior and Human Decision Processes* 48:55–69.
Garnham, D. 1985. 'The Causes of War: Systemic Findings.' In A.N. Sabrosky, ed., *Polarity and War*. Boulder: Westview Press.
Garreton, M.A.M. 1989. 'Popular Mobilization and the Military Regime in Chile: the Complexities of the Invisible Transition.' In S. Eckstein, ed., *Power and Popular Protest Latin American Social Movements*. Berkeley: University of California Press.
Geddes, B. 1995. 'Games of Intra-Regime Conflict and the Breakdown of Authoritarianism.' Paper presented at the Annual Meeting of the American Political Science Association, Chicago, September 1995.
Geller, D.S. 1987. 'The Impact of Political System Structure on Probability Patterns of Internal Disorder.' *American Journal of Political Science* 31:217–35.
———. 1993. 'Power Differentials and War in Rival Dyads.' *International Studies Quarterly* 37:173–94.
Geller, D.S., and D.S. Jones. 1991. 'The Effect of Dynamic and Static Balances on Conflict Escalation in Rival Dyads.' Paper presented at the Annual Meeting of the American Political Science Association, Washington, DC.
George, A.L. 1979a. 'Case Studies and Theory Development: The Method of Structured, Focused Comparison.' In P.G. Lauren, ed., *Diplomacy: New Approaches in History, Theory and Policy*. New York: The Free Press.
———. 1979b. 'The Causal Nexus Between Cognitive Beliefs and Decision-Making Behavior: The "Operational Code" Belief System.' In L.S. Falkowski, ed., *Psychological Models in International Politics*. Boulder: Westview Press.
———. 1984. 'Crisis Management: The Interplay of Military and Political Considerations.' *Survival* 26:223–34.
———. ed. 1991. *Avoiding War: Problems of Crisis Management*. Boulder: Westview Press.
George, A.L., D.K. Hall and W.E. Simons. 1971. *The Limits of Coercive Diplomacy*. Boston: Little, Brown.

George, A.L. and W.E. Simons, eds. 1994. *The Limits of Coercive Diplomacy*, 2nd edn. Boulder, Westview Press.
George, A.L. and R. Smoke. 1974. *Deterrence in American Foreign Policy: Theory and Practice*. New York: Columbia University Press.
George, J. 1989. 'International Relations and the Search for Thinking Space: Another View of the Third Debate.' *International Studies Quarterly* 33:269–79.
———. 1992. 'Towards a Post-Hegemonic Conceptualization of World Order: Reflection on the Relevancy of Ibn Khaladin.' In J.N. Rosenau and E-O. Czempiel, eds, *Governance Without Government: Order and Change in World Politics*. Cambridge: New York: Cambridge University Press.
George, J., and D. Campbell. 1990. 'Patterns of Dissent and the Celebration of Differences: Critical Social Theory and International Relations.' *International Studies Quarterly* 34:269–93.
Geva, N. and L. Andrade. 1993. 'Foreign and Domestic Policy Decisions: An Experimental Assessment of Public Support.' Paper presented at the annual meeting of the Southern Political Science Association, Savannah, Georgia, November 3–6 1993.
Geva, N., A. Astorino-Courtois and A. Mintz. 1996. 'Marketing the Peace Process in the Middle East: The Effectiveness of Thematic and Evaluative Framing in Jordan and Israel.' In M. Chatterji, J. Fontanel and A. Hattori, eds, *Arms, Security and Development*. New Delhi, India: Aph Publishing Corporation.
Gibler, D. and J. Vasquez. 1995. 'Testing a Typology of Alliances'. Paper presented to the Peace Science Society, International, Ohio State University.
Giddens, A. 1979. *Central Problems in Social Theory*. London: Macmillan.
Gilpin, R. 1981. *War and Change in World Politics*. New York: Cambridge University Press.
———. 1987. *The Political Economy of International Relations*. Princeton: Princeton University Press.
———. 1989. 'The Theory of Hegemonic War.' In R.I. Rotberg and T.K. Rabb, eds, *The Origin and Prevention of Major Wars*. Cambridge: Cambridge University Press.
Glad, B., ed. 1980. *The Psychological Dimension of War*. Newbury Park, CA: Sage.
Glassman, J.D. 1975. *Arms for the Arabs: The Soviet Union and War in the Middle East*. Baltimore: Johns Hopkins University Press.
Gochman, C.S. and R.J. Leng. 1983. 'Realpolitik and the Road to War: An Analysis of Attributes and Behavior.' *International Studies Quarterly* 27:97–120.
Gochman, C.S. and Z. Maoz. 1984. 'Militarized Interstate Disputes, 1816–1976.' *Journal of Conflict Resolution* 28:585–616.
Goertz, G., and P. F. Diehl. 1992a. *Territorial Changes and International Conflict*. London: Routledge.
———. 1992b. 'The Empirical Importance of Enduring Rivalries.' *International Interactions*. 18:151–163.
———. 1993. 'Enduring Rivalries: Theoretical Constructs and Empirical Patterns.' *International Studies Quarterly* 37:147–71.
———. 1995a. 'The Initiation and Termination of Enduring Rivalries: The Impact of Political Shocks.' *American Journal of Political Science* 39:30–52.

———. 1995b. 'The "Volcano Model" and Other Patterns in the Evolution of Enduring Rivalries.' Paper presented at the Annual Meeting of the International Studies Association, Chicago, 1995.

———. 1996. 'Taking "Enduring" out of Enduring Rivalry: The Rivalry Approach to War and Peace.' *International Interactions* 21:291-308.

Golan, G. 1977. *Yom Kippur and After: The Soviet Union and the Middle East Crisis*. Cambridge: Cambridge University Press.

Goldstein, J. 1988. *Long Cycles: Prosperity and War in the Modern Age*. New Haven: Yale University Press.

Goldstein, W.M., and H.J. Einhorn. 1987. 'Expression Theory and the Preference Reversal Phenomena.' *Psychological Review* 94:236-54.

Grether, D.M., and C.R. Plott. 1979. 'Economic Theory of Choice and the Preference Reversal Phenomenon.' *American Economic Review* 69:623-38.

Grieco, J. 1990. *Cooperation among Nations*. Ithaca, NY: Cornell University Press.

Gurr, T.R. 1970. *Why Men Rebel*. Princeton: Princeton University Press.

———. ed. 1980. *Handbook of Political Conflict: Theory and Research*. New York: Free Press.

———. 1988. 'War, Revolution and the Growth of the Coercive State.' *Comparative Political Studies* 21:45-65.

Haas, E.B. 1983. 'Regime Decay: Conflict Management and International Organizations, 1945-1981.' *International Organization*. 37:189-256.

Haas, M. 1970. 'International Subsystems: Stability and Polarity.' *American Political Science Review* 64:98-123.

———. 1974. *International Conflict*. Indianapolis: Bobbs-Merrill.

———. 1986. 'Research on International Crisis: Obsolescence of an Approach?' *International Interactions* 13:23-58.

Haber, E. 1987. *Today War Will Break Out*, (Hebrew). Tel Aviv: Edanim.

Hagan, J.D. 1993. *Political Opposition and Foreign Policy in Comparative Perspective*. Boulder: Lynne Rienner.

———. 1994. 'Domestic Political Systems and War Proneness.' *Mershon International Studies Review* 64:98-123.

Han, S.-J. 1988. 'South Korean Politics and Its Impact on Foreign Relations.' In R.A. Scalapino, S. Sato, J. Wanandi, and S.-J. Han, eds, *Asia and the Major Power: Domestic Politics and Foreign Policy*. Berkeley: University of California Press.

Handel, M.I. 1976. *Perception, Deception and Surprise: The Case of the Yom Kippur War*. Jerusalem: Jerusalem Papers on Peace Problems, The Hebrew University of Jerusalem.

———. 1978. 'The Study of War Termination.' *Journal of Strategic Studies* 1:51-75.

———. 1983. 'Crisis and Surprise in Three Arab-Israeli Wars.' In K. Knorr and P. Morgan, eds, *Strategic Military Surprise*. New Brunswick, NJ: Transaction Books.

———. 1984. 'Intelligence and the Problem of Strategic Surprise.' *Journal of Strategic Studies* 7:229-81.

Hartman, R.S., M.J. Doane, and C.K. Woo. 1991. 'Consumer Rationality and the Status Quo.' *Quarterly Journal of Economics* 106:141-62.

Harvey, F. 1995. 'Rational Deterrence Theory Revisited: A Progress Report.' *Canadian Journal of Political Science* 28:403-36.

——. 1996a. *'Rigor Mortis* or Rigor, More Tests: Deterrence and Compellence in Protracted Crises.' Paper presented at the annual meeting of the International Studies Association, San Diego, California, 1996.

——. 1996b. 'Deterrence and Compellence in Protraced Crises: The Case of Bosnia-Herzegovina, 1993–1995.' *Security Studies* (Winter 1996/1997) 6, no. 3: 181–209.

——. 1997. *The Future's Back: Nuclear Rivalry, Deterrence Theory and Crisis Stability After The Cold War.* Montreal: McGill-Queen's University Press.

Harvey, F., and P. James. 1992. 'Nuclear Deterrence Theory: The Record of Aggregate Testing and an Alternative Research Agenda.' *Conflict Management and Peace Science* 12:17–45.

Hempel, C.G. 1966. *Philosophy of Natural Science.* Englewood Cliffs: Prentice-Hall.

Hensel, P.R. 1994a. 'One Thing Leads to Another: Recurrent Militarized Disputes in Latin America, 1816–1986.' *Journal of Peace Research* 31:281–98.

——. 1994b. 'An Evolutionary Approach to the Study of Interstate Rivalry.' Paper presented at the Annual Meeting of the American Political Science Association, New York, 1994.

——. 1995. 'Political Democracy and Militarized Conflict in Evolving Interstate Rivalries.' Paper presented at the Annual Meeting of the American Political Science Association, Chicago, 1995.

——. 1996a. *The Evolution of Interstate Rivalry.* PhD dissertation, University of Illinois.

——. 1996b. 'Charting a Course to Conflict: Territorial Issues and Interstate Conflict, 1816–1992.' *Conflict Management and Peace Science* 15, no. 1:43–73.

Hensel, P.R., G. Goertz, and P.F. Diehl. 1996. 'The Democratic Peace and Rivalries: A Longitudinal Investigation of Regimes, Regime Change, and Conflict.' Mimeo, Florida State University.

Hensel, P. 1977. 'What Do They Do When They Aren't Fighting: Events Data and the Nonmilitarized Dimensions of Interstate Rivalry.' Unpublished manuscript, Florida State University.

Herek, G.M. 1989. 'Quality of US Decision-Making During the Cuban Missile Crisis: Major Errors in Welch's Reassessment.' *Journal of Conflict Resolution* 33:446–59.

Hermann, C.F. 1969. 'International Crisis as a Situational Variable.' In J.N. Rosenau, ed., *International Politics and Foreign Policy.* New York: Free Press.

Hermann, M.G., and C.W. Kegley, Jr. 1995. 'Rethinking Democracy and International Peace: Perspectives from Political Psychology.' *International Studies Quarterly* 39:511–33.

Hershey, J.C., and P.J.H. Schoemaker. 1980. 'Prospect Theory's Critical Reflection Hypothesis: A Critical Examination.' *Organizational Behavior and Human Performance* 25:395–418.

Herz, J.H. 1950. 'Idealist Internationalism and the Security Dilemma.' *World Politics* 2:157–180.

——. 1951. *Political Realism and Political Idealism.* Chicago: University of Chicago Press.

Heuer, R.J. 1982. 'Cognitive Factors in Deception and Counterdeception.' In

D. Daniel and K.L. Herbig, eds, *Strategic Military Deception*. New York: Pergamon Press.
Hodges, T. 1983. *Western Sahara*. Westport, CT: Lawrence Hill.
Hoffmann, S. 1965. *The State of War*. New York: Praeger.
Holsti, K.J. 1966. 'Resolving International Conflicts: A Taxonomy of Behavior and Some Figures on Procedures.' *Journal of Conflict Resolution* 10:272-96.
———. 1989. 'Mirror, Mirror on the Wall, Which Are the Fairest Theories of All?' *International Studies Quarterly* 33:255-61.
———. 1991. *Peace and War: Armed Conflicts and International Order*. Cambridge: Cambridge University Press.
Holsti, O.R. 1965. 'The 1914 Case.' *American Political Science Review* 59:365-78.
———. 1972. *Crisis Escalation War*. Montreal: McGill-Queen's University Press.
———. 1989. 'Crisis Decision Making.' In P.E. Tetlock, J.L. Husbands, R. Jervis, P.S. Stern, and C. Tilly, eds, *Behavior, Society, and Nuclear War, Vol. 1*. New York: Oxford University Press.
———. 1992. 'Public Opinion and Foreign Policy: Challenges to the Almond-Lippmann Consensus.' *International Studies Quarterly* 36:439-66.
Holsti, O.R. and R.R. Fagen, eds. 1967. *Enemies in Politics*. Chicago: Rand McNally.
Holsti, O.R., and A.L. George. 1975. 'The Effects of Stress on the Performance of Foreign Policy Makers.' *Political Science Annual* 6:255-319.
Holsti, O.R., R. North and R. Brody. 1968. 'Perception and Action in the 1914 Crisis.' In J.D. Singer, ed., *Quantitative International Politics*. New York: Free Press.
Hopf, T. 1991. 'Polarity, the Offense-Defense Balance, and War.' *American Political Science Review* 85:475-93.
Houweling, H.W., and J.G. Siccama. 1988a. 'The Risk of Compulsory Escalation.' *Journal of Peace Research* 25:43-56.
———. 1988b. *Studies of War*. Dordrecht: Martinus Nijhoff.
Howard, M. 1984. *The Causes of War*, 2nd edn. Cambridge: Harvard University Press.
Huang, C. 1992. 'Leadership Change and Government Size in East Asian Authoritarian Regimes.' In C. Clark and S. Chan, eds, *The Evolving Pacific Basin in the Global Political, Economy: Domestic and International Linkages*. Boulder: Lynne Rienner.
Hughes, H.S. 1961. *Contemporary Europe: A History*. Englewood Cliffs: Prentice-Hall.
Huntington, S.P. 1991. *The Third Wave: Democratization in the Late Twentieth Century*. Norman: University of Oklahoma Press.
Huth, P.K. 1988a. *Extended Deterrence and the Prevention of War*. New Haven: Yale University Press.
———. 1988b. 'Deterrence Failure and Crisis Escalation.' *International Studies Quarterly* 32:29-45.
———. 1996. *Standing Your Ground*. Ann Arbor: University of Michigan Press.
———. (forthcoming article in *Conflict Management and Peace Science*).
Huth, P., D.S. Bennett, and C. Gelpi. 1992. 'System Uncertainty, Risk Propensity, and International Conflict Among the Great Powers.' *Journal of Conflict Resolution* 36:478-517.
Huth, P., C. Gelpi, and D.S. Bennett. 1993. 'The Escalation of Great Power

Militarized Disputes.' *American Political Science Review* 87:609-23.
Huth, P., D.S. Jones, and Z. Maoz. 1990. 'An Operational Definition of Enduring International Rivalries.' Unpublished memo.
Huth, P.K., and B.M. Russett. 1984. 'What Makes Deterrence Work? Cases from 1900-1980.' *World Politics* 36:496-526.
———. 1988. 'Deterrence Failure and Crisis Escalation.' *International Studies Quarterly* 32:29-45.
———. 1990. 'Testing Deterrence Theory: Rigour Makes a Difference.' *World Politics* 42:466-501.
———. 1993. 'General Deterrence between Enduring Rivals: Testing Three Competing Models.' *American Political Science Review* 87:61-73.
Ikle, F. 1971. *Every War Must End*. New York: Columbia University Press.
Inglehart, R., and P.R. Abramson. 1984. 'Economic Security and Value Change.' *American Political Science Review* 88:336-54.
Intriligator, M.D., and D.L. Brito. 1984. 'Can Arms Races Lead to the Outbreak of War?' *Journal of Conflict Resolution* 28: no. 1:63-84.
———. 1989. 'Richardsonian Arms Race Models.' In M.I. Midlarsky, ed., *Handbook of War Studies*. Boston: Unwin Hyman.
Isard, W., and C.H. Anderton. 1985. 'Arms Race Models: A Survey and Synthesis.' *Conflict Management and Peace Science* 8:27-98.
Jackson, R.H., and C.G. Rosberg. 1982. 'Why Africa's Weak States Persist.' *World Politics* 35:1-24.
James, P. 1987. 'Conflict and Cohesion: A Review of the Literature and Recommendations for Future Research.' *Cooperation and Conflict: Nordic Journal of International Politics* 22:21-33.
———. 1988. *Crisis and War*. Montreal: McGill-Queen's University Press.
———. 1991. 'Rational Retaliation: Superpower Response to Crisis, 1948-1979.' *Public Choice* 68:117-35.
———. 1993. 'Rational Choice in the Crisis Domain: An Appraisal of Superpower Interactions, 1948-1979.' In W.J. Booth, P. James, and H. Meadwell, eds, *Politics and Rationality*. Cambridge: Cambridge University Press.
James, P., and F. Harvey. 1989. 'Threat Escalation and Crisis Stability: Superpower Cases, 1948-1979.' *Canadian Journal of Political Science* 22:523-45.
———. 1992. 'The Most Dangerous Game: Superpower Rivalry in International Crises, 1948-1985.' *Journal of Politics* 54:25-53.
James, P., and J. Oneal. 1991. 'The Influence of Domestic and International Politics on the President's Use of Force.' *Journal of Conflict Resolution* 35:307-32.
James, P., and J. Wilkenfeld. 1984. 'Structural Factors and International Crisis Behavior.' *Conflict Management and Peace Science* 7:33-53.
Janis, I.L. 1989. *Crucial Decisions: Leadership in Policymaking and Crisis Management*. New York: Free Press/Macmillan.
Janis, I.L., and L. Mann. 1977. *Decision-Making: A Psychological Analysis of Conflict, Choice and Commitment*. New York: Free Press.
Jervis, R. 1968. 'Hypotheses on Misperception.' *World Politics* 20:454-79.
———. 1970. *The Logic of Images in International Relations*. Princeton, Princeton University Press.
———. 1976. *Perception and Misperception in International Politics*. Princeton: Princeton University Press.

———. 1978. 'Cooperation Under the Security Dilemma.' *World Politics* 30:167–214.
———. 1979. 'Deterrence Theory Revisited.' *World Politics* 31:289–324.
———. 1982. 'Deterrence and Perception.' *International Security* 7:3–30.
———. 1986. 'Perceiving and Coping With Threat.' In R. Jervis, R.N. Lebow and J.G. Stein, eds, *Psychology and Deterrence*. Baltimore: Johns Hopkins University Press.
———. 1988. 'War and Misperception.' *Journal of Interdisciplinary History* 18:675–700.
———. 1989. *The Meaning of the Nuclear Revolution*. Ithaca, NY: Cornell University Press.
———. 1991. 'Domino Beliefs and Strategic Behavior.' In Robert Jervis and Jack Snyder, eds, *Dominoes and Bandwagons*. New York: Oxford University Press.
———. 1992. 'Political Implications of Loss Aversion.' *Political Psychology* 13:187–204.
Jervis, R., R.N. Lebow, and J.G. Stein. 1985. *Psychology and Deterrence*. Baltimore: Johns Hopkins University Press.
Kacowicz, A.M. 1994. *Peaceful Territorial Change*. Columbia: University of South Carolina Press.
Kahn, H. 1960. *On Thermonuclear War*. Princeton: Princeton University Press.
———. 1962. *Thinking About the Unthinkable*. New York: Horizon Press.
———. 1965. *On Escalation: Metaphors and Scenarios*. New York: Praeger.
———. 1970. 'Issues of Thermonuclear War Termination.' In W.T.R. Fox, ed., *How Wars End, The Annals*. 392:133–72.
Kahneman, D., J.L. Knetsch, and R.H. Thaler. 1991. 'The Endowment Effect, Loss Aversion, and Status Quo Bias.' *Journal of Economic Perspectives* 5:193–206.
———. 1990. 'Experimental Tests of the Endowment Effect and the Coase Theorem.' *Journal of Political Economy* 98:1325–48.
Kahneman, D. and A. Tversky. 1979. 'Prospect Theory: An Analysis of Decisions Under Risk.' *Econometrica* 47:263–91.
———. 1981. 'The Framing of Decisions and the Psychology of Choice.' *Science* 211:453–8.
———. 1984. 'Choices, Values, and Frames.' *American Psychologist* 39:341–50.
Kaiser, D.E. 1980. *Economic Diplomacy and the Origins of the Second World War*. Princeton: Princeton University Press.
———. 1990. *Politics and War: European Conflict from Philip II to Hitler*. Cambridge: Harvard University Press.
Kam, E. 1988. *Surprise Attack: The Victim's Perspective*. Cambridge: Harvard University Press.
Kant, I. 1974. 'Perpetual Peace.' In P. Gay, ed., *The Enlightenment*. New York: Simon & Shuster.
Kaplan, J. 1980. 'Victor and Vanquished.' In S. Albert and E. Luck, eds, *On the Ending of Wars*. New York: Kennikat Press.
Kaplan, M.A. 1957. *System and Process in International Politics*. New York: John Wiley.
Kecskemeti, P. 1958. *Strategic Surrender*. Stanford: Stanford University Press.
Keegan, J. 1993. *A History of Warfare*. New York: Random House.

Bibliography

Kegley, C.W. Jr., and M.G. Hermann. 1995. 'Military Intervention and the Democratic Peace.' *International Interactions* 21:1–21.

Kegley, C.W., Jr. and G. Raymond. 1994. *A Multipolar Peace?: Great-Power Politics in the Twenty-First Century.* New York: St. Martin's.

Keller, B.A. 1992. *Avoiding Surprise: The Role of Intelligence Collection and Analysis at the Operational Level of War.* Fort Leavenworth: School of Advanced Military Studies.

Kennedy, P. 1982. *The Rise of the Anglo-German Antagonism, 1860–1914.* London: George Allen & Unwin.

———. 1984. 'The First World War and the International Power System.' *International Security* 9:7–40.

Keohane, R.O. 1984. *After Hegemony.* Princeton: Princeton University Press.

Khoury, P.S. 1987. *Syria Under the French Mandate: The Politics of Arab Nationalism: 1920–1945.* Princeton: Princeton University Press.

Kienle, E. 1994. 'The Return of Politics? Scenarios for Syria's Second Infitah.' In E. Kienle, ed., *Contemporary Syria.* London: Academic Press.

Kilgour, D.M., and F. Zagare. 1991. 'Credibility, Uncertainty and Deterrence.' *American Journal of Political Science* 35:305–34.

Knetsch, J.L. 1989. 'The Endowment Effect and Evidence of Nonreversible Indifference Curves.' *American Economic Review* 79:1277–84.

Knetsch, J.L., and J.A. Sinden. 1984. 'Willingness to Pay and Compensation Demanded: Experimental Evidence of an Unexpected Disparity in Measures of Value.' *Quarterly Journal of Economics* 99:507–21.

———. 1987. 'The Persistence of Evaluation Disparities.' *Quarterly Journal of Economics* 102:691–5.

Knez, M., and V.L. Smith. 1987. 'Hypothetical Valuations and Preference Reversals in the Context of Asset Trading.' In A.E. Roth, ed., *Laboratory Experiments in Exonomics: Six Points of View.* Cambridge: Cambridge University Press.

Knorr, K. 1976. 'Threat Perception.' In K. Knorr, ed., *Historical Dimensions of National Security Problems.* Lawrence: University Press of Kansas.

Kolm, S.-C. 1996. *Modern Theories of Justice.* Cambridge: MIT Press.

Kowalewski, D., and D. Hoover. 1995. *Dynamic Models of Conflict and Pacification: Dissenters, Officials and Peacemakers.* Westport, CT: Praeger.

Kowalewski, D., and P. Schumaker. 1981. 'Protest Outcomes in the Soviet Union.' *The Sociological Quarterly* 22:57–68.

Kozhemiakin, A.V. 1994. 'Democratization and International Cooperation: Comparative Analysis of Ukraine's and Kazakhstan's Responses to the Nuclear Non-Proliferation Regime.' Paper presented at the Midwest regional meeting of the International Studies Association, Columbus, Ohio, 30 September – 1 October 1994.

Kugler, J. 1984. 'Terror Without Deterrence.' *Journal of Conflict Resolution* 28:470–506.

Kugler, J., and A.F.K. Organski. 1989. 'The Power Transition: A Retrospective and Prospective Evaluation.' In M.I. Midlarsky, ed., *Handbook of War Studies.* Boston: Unwin Hyman.

Lake, D. 1992. 'Powerful Pacifists: Democratic States and War.' *American Political Science Review* 86:24–37.

Langer, E.J. and R.P. Abelson. 1972. 'The Semantics of Asking a Favor: How to Succeed in Getting Help Without Really Dying.' *Journal of Personality and Social Psychology* 24:26–32.

Lapid, Y. 1989. 'The Third Debate: On the Prospects of International Theory in a Post-Positivist Era.' *International Studies Quarterly* 33:235–54.

Lawson, F. 1984. 'Syria's Intervention in the Lebanese Civil War, 1976.' *International Organization* 38:451–80.

——. 1994. 'Domestic Transformation and Foreign Policy Steadfastness in Contemporary Syria.' *Middle East Journal* 48:47–64.

Layne, C. 1994. 'Kant or Cant: The Myth of the Democratic Peace.' *International Security* 19:5–49.

Lazarus, R.S. 1966. *Psychological Stress and the Coping Process*. New York: McGraw-Hill.

Lebow, R.N. 1981. *Between Peace and War: The Nature of International Crisis*. Baltimore: Johns Hopkins University Press.

——. 1987. *Nuclear Crisis Management: A Dangerous Illusion*. Ithaca: Cornell University Press.

Lebow, R.N., and J.G. Stein. 1987. 'Beyond Deterrence.' *Journal of Social Issues* 43:5–71.

——. 1989a. 'Rational Deterrence Theory: I Think, Therefore I Deter.' *World Politics* 41:208–24.

——. 1989b. 'When Does Deterrence Succeed and How Do We Know?' Paper presented at the Annual Meeting of the International Studies Association.

——. 1990. 'Deterrence: The Elusive Dependent Variable.' *World Politics* 42:336–69.

——. 1995. *We All Lost the Cold War*. Princeton: Princeton University Press.

Lemke, D. 1995. 'The Tyranny of Distance: Redefining Relevant Dyads.' *International Interactions* 21:23–38.

Leng, R.J. 1983. 'When Will They Ever Learn? Coercive Bargaining in Recurrent Crises.' *Journal of Conflict Resolution*. 27:379–419.

——. 1988. 'Crisis Learning Games.' *American Political Science Review* 82:179–194.

——. 1993. *Interstate Crisis Behavior, 1816–1980: Realism versus Reciprocity*. Cambridge: Cambridge University Press.

Leng, R.J., and J.D. Singer. 1988. 'Militarized International Crises: The BCOW Typology and its Applications.' *International Studies Quarterly* 32:155–73.

Lenin, V.I. 1939 [1917]. *Imperialism: The Highest Stage of Capitalism*. New York: International Publishers.

Levite, A. 1987. *Intelligence and Strategic Surprises*. New York: Columbia University Press.

Levy, J.S. 1981. 'Alliance Formation and War Behavior: An Analysis of the Great Powers, 1495–1975.' *Journal of Conflict Resolution* 25:581–613.

——. 1983a. *War in the Modern Great Power System, 1495–1975*. Lexington: University Press of Kentucky.

——. 1983b. 'Misperception and the Causes of War: Theoretical Linkages and Analytical Problems.' *World Politics* 36:76–99.

——. 1985a. 'The Polarity of the System and International Stability: An Empirical Analysis.' In A. Sabrosky, ed., *Polarity and War*. Boulder: Westview.

———. 1985b. 'Theories of General War.' *World Politics* 38:344–74.
———. 1987. 'Declining Power and the Preventive Motivation for War.' *World Politics* 40:82–107.
———. 1988. 'When Do Deterrent Threats Work?' *British Journal of Political Science* 18:485–512.
———. 1989a. 'The Diversionary Theory of War: A Critique.' In Manus I. Midlarsky, ed., *Handbook of War Studies*. Boston: Unwin Hyman.
———. 1989b. 'Quantitative Studies of Deterrence Success and Failure.' In Paul C. Stern, Robert Axelrod, Robert Jervis, and Roy Radner, eds, *Perspectives on Deterrence*. New York: Oxford University Press.
———. 1989c. 'The Causes of War: A Review of Theories and Evidence.' In P.E. Tetlock, J.L. Husbands, R. Jervis, P.S. Stern, and C. Tilly, eds, *Behavior, Society, and Nuclear War, Vol. 1*. New York: Oxford University Press.
———. 1989d. 'Domestic Politics and War.' In R.I. Rotberg and T.K. Rabb, eds, *The Origin and Prevention of Major Wars*. Cambridge: Cambridge University Press.
———. 1992a. 'An Introduction to Prospect Theory.' *Political Psychology* 13:171–86.
———. 1992b. 'Prospect Theory and International Relations: Theoretical Applications and Analytical Problems'. *Political Psychology* 13:283–306.
———. 1994. 'Learning and Foreign Policy: Sweeping a Conceptual Minefield.' *International Organization* 48:279–312.
Levy, J.S. and T. C. Morgan. 1984. 'The Frequency and Seriousness of War: An Inverse Relationship?' *Journal of Conflict Resolution* 28:731–49.
Lewis-Beck, M.S. 1979. 'Some Economic Effects of Revolution: Models, Measurement, and the Cuban Evidence.' *American Journal of Sociology* 84:1127–49.
———. 1986. 'Interrupted Time Series.' In W.D. Berry and M.S. Lewis-Beck, eds, *New Tools for Social Scientists: Advances and Applications in Research Methods*. Beverly Hills: Sage.
Lewis-Beck, M.S., and J.R. Alford. 1980. 'Can Government Regulate Safety? The Coal Mine Example.' *American Political Science Review* 74:745–56.
Lian, B., and J. Oneal. 1993. 'Presidents, the Use of Force, and Public Opinion.' *Journal of Conflict Resolution* 37:277–300.
Liao, T.F. 1994. *Interpreting Probability Models: Logit, Probit, and Other Generalized Linear Models*. Thousand Oaks, CA: Sage.
Lieberman, E. 1994. 'What Makes Deterrence Work? Lessons from the Egyptian–Israeli Enduring Rivalry.' Paper presented at the Annual Meeting of the American Political Science Association, New York, 1994.
Lobmeyer, H.G. 1994. 'The Syrian Opposition at the End of the Asad Era.' In E. Kienle, ed., *Contemporary Syria*. London: Academic Press.
Longrigg, S.H. 1978. *Syria and Lebanon Under the French Mandate*. Beirut: Dar al-Haqiqa.
Luard, E. 1957. *War in International Society*. New Haven: Yale University Press.
Luce, D.R., and H. Raiffa. 1957. *Games and Decisions: Introduction and Critical Survey*. New York: John Wiley.
Lust-Okar, E. 1993. 'The Emergence of Opposition Movements: Syrian Nationalists' Activities in 1941.' MA Thesis, University of Michigan.

Luterbacher, U. 1984. 'Last Words About War?' *Journal of Conflict Resolution* 28:165–82.
Luttwak, E.N. 1987. *Strategy: The Logic of War and Peace.* Cambridge, MA: Belknap Press.
Mansfield, E., and J. Snyder. 1995. 'Democratization and the Danger of War.' *International Security* 20:5–38.
Ma'oz, M. 1995. *Syria and Israel.* Oxford: Clarendon Press.
——. 1982. *Paths to Conflict. International Dispute Initiation 1816–1976.* Boulder: Westview Press.
Maoz, Zeev. 1983. 'Resolve, Capabilities, and the Outcomes of Interstate Disputes, 1816–1976.' *Journal of Conflict Resolution* 27:195–229.
——. 1984. 'Peace By Empire? Conflict Outcomes and International Stability, 1816–1976.' *Journal of Peace Research* 21:227–41.
——. 1989. 'Joining the Club of Nations.' *International Studies Quarterly.* 33:199–231.
——. 1990a. *Paradoxes of War: On the Art of National Self-Entrapment.* Boston: Unwin, Hyman.
——. 1990b. *National Choices and International Processes.* Cambridge: Cambridge University Press.
——. 1990c. 'Framing the National Interest: The Manipulation of Foreign Policy Decisions in Group Settings.' *World Politics* 43:77–110.
——. 1993. 'The Onset and Initiation of Disputes.' *International Interactions* 19:15–33.
——. 1996a. *Domestic Sources of Global Change.* Ann Arbor: University of Michigan Press.
——. 1996b. 'Rearguard Action or Cracks in the Wall? The Debate on the Democratic Peace Proposition.' Mimeo, Tel-Aviv: Jaffee Center for Strategic Studies, Tel Aviv University.
Maoz, Z., and N. Abdolali. 1989. 'Regime Types and International Conflict, 1816–1976.' *Journal of Conflict Resolution* 33:3–35.
Maoz, Z., and B.D. Mor. 1996a. 'Enduring Rivalries: The Early Years.' *International Political Science Review* 17:141–160.
——. 1996b. 'Learning, Preference Change, and the Evolution of Enduring Rivalries.' Paper presented at the Workshop on Enduring Rivalries, Urbana-Champaign, 1996.
——. 1996c. 'Satisfaction, Capabilities, and the Evolution of Enduring Rivalries, 1816–1990: A Statistical Analysis of a Game-Theoretic Model.' Paper presented at the Annual Meeting of the American Political Science Association, Chicago, 1996.
——. 1997. 'Learning, Preference Change, and the Evolution of Enduring Rivalries.' In P.F. Diehl, ed., *The Dynamics of Enduring Rivalries.* Urbana-Champaign: University of Illinois Press.
Maoz, Z., and B.M. Russett. 1993. 'Normative and Structural Causes of Democratic Peace, 1946–1986.' *American Political Science Review* 87:624–38.
Massoud, T.G. 1993. 'The Termination of Wars: A Comparative Case Study of the Korean, 1973 Arab–Israeli, and Falklands Wars.' Paper presented at the 34th annual convention of the International Studies Association, 23–27 March 1993, Acapulco, Mexico.
Maxwell, G., and P. Oliver. 1993. *The Critical Mass in Collective Action: A*

Micro-Social Theory. New York: Cambridge University Press.
May, E.R. 1984. *Knowing One's Enemies: Intelligence Assessment Before the Two World Wars.* Princeton: Princeton University Press.
McClelland, C.A. 1968. 'Access to Berlin: The Quantity and Variety of Events, 1948-1963.' In J.D. Singer, ed., *Quantitative International Politics: Insights and Evidence.* New York: Free Press.
McDermott, R. 1992. 'Prospect Theory in International Relations: The Iranian Hostage Rescue Mission.' *Political Psychology* 13:237-63.
McGowan, P.J. and R.M. Rood. 1975. 'Alliance Behavior in Balance of Power Systems: Applying a Poisson Model to Nineteenth Century Europe.' *American Political Science Review* 69:859-70.
McInerney, A. 1991. 'Prospect Theory and Soviet Policy Towards Syria, 1966-1967.' *Political Psychology* 13:265-82.
McLaurin, R., M. Mughisuddin, and A. Wagner. 1977. *Foreign Policy Making in the Middle East.* New York: Praeger.
McNeil, B.J., S.G. Pauker, H.C. Sox, Jr., and A. Tversky. 1982. 'On the Elicitation of Preferences for Alternative Therapies.' *New England Journal of Medicine* 306:1259-62.
McNeil, W.H. 1982. *The Pursuit of Power: Technology, Armed Force, and Society Since A.D. 1000.* Chicago: University of Chicago Press.
Mead, M. 1940. 'Warfare is only an Invention – Not a Biological Necessity.' *Asia* 40:402-5.
Mearsheimer, J.J. 1990. 'Back to the Future: Instability in Europe after the Cold War.' *International Security* 15:5-56.
Meernik, J. 1994. 'Presidential Decision Making and the Political Use of Military Force.' *International Studies Quarterly* 38:121-38.
Merritt, R.L., and D.A. Zinnes. 1991. 'Democracies and War.' In A. Inkeles, ed., *On Measuring Democracy: Its Consequences and Concomitants.* New Brunswick: Transaction Books.
Midlarsky, M.I. 1983. 'Alliance Behavior and the Approach of World War I: The Use of Bivariate Negative Binomial Distributions.' In D. Zinnes, ed., *Conflict Processes and the Breakdown of International Systems.* University of Denver Monograph Series in World Affairs 20:61-80.
———. 1984. 'Preventing Systemic War.' *Journal of Conflict Resolution* 28:563-84.
———. 1986. 'A Hierarchical Equilibrium Theory of Systemic War.' *International Studies Quarterly* 30:77-105.
———. 1988. *The Onset of World War.* Boston: Allen & Unwin.
———. ed. 1989. *Handbook of War Studies.* Boston: Unwin Hyman.
Migdal, J.S. 1988. *Strong Societies and Weak States: State-Society Relations and State Capabilities in the Third World.* Princeton: Princeton University Press.
Miller, J., and L. Mylroie. 1990. *Saddam Hussein and the Crisis in the Gulf.* New York: Random House.
Mintz, A. 1993. 'The Decision to Attack Iraq: A Noncompensatory Theory of Decision Making.' *Journal of Conflict Resolution* 37:595-618.
———. 1995. 'The Noncompensatory Principle of Coalition Formation.' *Journal of Theoretical Politics* 7:335-49.
Mintz, A., and N. Geva. 1994. 'Framing the Options for Peace in the Middle

East.' Program in Foreign Policy Decision Making, Texas A & M University.
——. 1996. 'The Poliheuristic Theory of Foreign Policy Decision Making.' In N. Geva and A. Mintz, eds, *Decision Making on War and Peace: The Cognitive-Rational Debate*. Boulder: Lynne Rienner Publishers.
——. 1997 (forthcoming). *The Poliheuristic Theory of Decision: A Noncompensatory Approach to Foreign Policy Decision Making*.
Mintz, A., and B.M. Russett. 1992. 'The Dual Economy and Arab–Israeli Use of Force: A Transnational System?' In S. Chan and A. Mintz, eds, *Defense, Welfare, and Growth*. London: Routledge.
Modelski, G. 1987. *Long Cycles in World Politics*. Seattle: University of Washington Press.
Modelski, G., and P.M. Morgan. 1985. 'Understanding Global War.' *Journal of Conflict Resolution* 29:391–417.
Modelski, G., and W.R. Thompson. 1989. 'Long Cycles and Global War.' In M.I. Midlarsky, ed., *Handbook of War Studies*. Boston: Unwin Hyman.
Moll, K.D., and G.M. Luebbert. 1980. 'Arms Race and Military Expenditure Models: A Review.' *Journal of Conflict Resolution* 24:153–85.
Mor, B.D. 1991. 'Nasser's Decision Making in the 1967 Middle East Crisis: A Rational Choice Explanation.' *Journal of Peace Research* 28:359–75.
——. 1993. *Decision and Interaction in Crisis: A Model of International Crisis Behavior*. New York: Praeger.
——. 1995. 'Crisis Initiation and Misperception.' *Journal of Theoretical Politics* 7:351–67.
Mor, B.D., and Z. Maoz. 1997. 'Learning and the Evolution of Enduring Rivalries: A Strategic Approach.' Mimeo, University of Haifa and Jaffee Center for Strategic Studies, Tel Aviv University.
Morgan, P.M. 1977. *Deterrence: A Conceptual Analysis*. Beverly Hills: Sage.
——. 1984. 'Examples of Strategic Surprise in the Far East.' In K. Knorr and P.M. Morgan, eds, *Strategic Military Surprise: Incentives and Opportunities*. New Brunswick: Transaction Books.
Morgan, T.C. 1994. *Untying the Knot of War*. Ann Arbor: University of Michigan Press.
Morgan, T.C. and K.N. Bickers. 1992. 'Domestic Discontent and the External Use of Force.' *Journal of Conflict Resolution* 36:25–52.
Morgan, T.C., and R.K. Wilson. 1989. 'The Spatial Model of Crisis Bargaining: An Experimental Test.' Paper presented at the Annual Meeting of the International Studies Association, London, 1989.
Morgenthau, H.J. 1960. *Politics Among Nations: The Struggle for Power and Peace*, 3rd edn. New York: Knopf.
Morgenthau, H.M., Jr. 1940. *The Morgenthau Diary, 1933–1945*. Book 318, 2–3 October 1940. Hyde Park, New York: Franklin D. Roosevelt Library.
Morrow, J.D. 1985. 'A Continuous-Outcome Expected Utility Theory of War.' *Journal of Conflict Resolution* 29:473–502.
——. 1989. 'Capabilities, Uncertainty, and Resolve: A Limited Information Model of Crisis Bargaining.' *American Journal of Political Science* 33:941–72.
——. 1994. *Game Theory for Political Scientists*. Princeton: Princeton University Press.
Most, B.A. and H. Starr. 1980. 'Diffusion, Reinforcement, Geopolitics, and the Spread of War.' *American Political Science Review* 74:932–46.

Mueller, J.E. 1973. *Wars, Presidents and Public Opinion.* New York: John Wiley.
———. 1988. 'The Essential Irrelevance of Nuclear Weapons: Stability in the Post War World.' *International Security* 13:55–79.
———. 1989. *Retreat from Doomsday: The Obsolescence of Major War.* New York: Basic Books.
Muller, E., and E. Weede. 1990. 'Cross National Variation in Political Violence.' *Journal of Conflict Resolution* 24:524–51.
Mullik, B.N. 1971. *The Chinese Betrayal.* Bombay: Allied Publishers.
Neale, M.A., and M.H. Bazerman. 1985. 'The Effects of Framing and Negotiator Overconfidence on Bargaining Behaviors and Outcomes.' *Academy of Management Journal* 28:34–49.
Nelson, K.L., and S.C. Olin, Jr. 1979. *Why War? Ideology, Theory, and History.* Berkeley and Los Angeles: University of California Press.
Nicholson, M. 1992. *Rationality and the Analysis of International Conflict.* Cambridge: Cambridge University Press.
Nincic, M. 1989. *Anatomy of Hostility: The US–Soviet Rivalry in Perspective.* New York: Harcourt Brace Jovanovich.
Nisbett, R.E. and L. Ross. 1980. *Human Inference: Stategies and Shortcomings of Social Judgment.* Englewood Cliffs: Prentice-Hall.
Nogee, J.L., and J. Spanier. 1988. *Peace Impossible – War Unlikely.* Glenview: Scott, Foresman/Little, Brown.
Nomikos, E.V., and R.C. North. 1976. *International Crisis: The Outbreak of World War I.* Montreal: McGill-Queen's University Press.
O'Keefe, M., and P. Schumaker. 1983. 'Protest Effectiveness in South East Asia.' *American Behavioral Scientist* 26:375–93.
Olson, M. Jr. 1982. *The Rise and Decline of Nations.* New Haven: Yale University Press.
Olson, M. Jr., and R. Zeckhauser. 1966. 'An Economic Theory of Alliances.' *Review of Economics and Statistics* 48:266–79.
Organski, A.F.K. 1958. *World Politics.* New York: Knopf.
Organski, A.F.K., and J. Kugler. 1980. *The War Ledger.* Chicago: University of Chicago Press.
Orme, J. 1987. 'Deterrence Failures: A Second Look.' *International Security* 11:96–124.
Ostrom, C.W. Jr., and F.W. Hoole. 1978. 'Alliances and War Revisited.' *International Studies Quarterly* 22:15–36.
Ostrom, C., and B. Job. 1986. 'The President and the Political Use of Force.' *American Political Science Review* 80:541–66.
Owen, J.M. 1994. 'How Liberalism Produces Democratic Peace.' *International Security* 19:87–125.
Oye, K., ed. 1988. *Cooperation Under Anarchy.* Princeton: Princeton University Press.
Paige, G.D. 1968. *The Korean Decision.* New York: Free Press.
———. 1972. 'Comparative Case Analysis of Crisis Decisions: Korea and Cuba.' In C.F. Hermann, ed., *International Crises: Insights from Behavioral Research.* New York: Free Press.
Paret, P. 1985. *Clausewitz and the State: The Man, His Theories, and His Times.* Princeton: Princeton University Press.

——. ed. 1986. *Makers of Modern Strategy: from Machiavelli to the Nuclear Age.* Princeton: Princeton University Press.

Peterson, S. 1996. *Crisis Bargaining and the State.* Ann Arbor: University of Michigan Press.

Phillips, D.L. 1977. *Wittgenstein and Scientific Knowledge: A Sociological Perspective.* London: Macmillan.

Phillips, J.L., Jr. 1992. *How to Think about Statistics*, rev. edn. New York: W. H. Freeman.

Pillar, P. 1983. *Negotiating Peace.* Princeton: Princeton University Press.

Pipes, D. 1990. *Greater Syria: the History of an Ambition.* New York: Oxford University Press.

Platig, R. 1966. *International Relations Research: Problems of Evaluation and Advancement.* Santa Barbara, CA: Carnegie Endowment for International Peace, Clio Press.

Post, J.M. 1991. 'The Impact of Crisis-Induced Stress on Policy-Makers.' In A.L. George, ed., *Avoiding War: Problems of Crisis Management.* Boulder: Westview Press.

Powell, R. 1987. 'Crisis Bargaining, Escalation and MAD.' *American Political Science Review* 81: no. 3:717–36.

——. 1988. 'Nuclear Brinkmanship with Two-Sided Incomplete Information.' *American Political Science Review* 82: no. 1:155–78.

——. 1990. *Nuclear Deterrence Theory: The Search for Credibility.* New York: Cambridge University Press.

President's Secretary's File; F.D. Roosevelt. 1933–1945 Papers as President. Hyde Park, New York: Franklin D. Roosevelt Library.

Pruitt D.G., and R.C. Snyder. 1969. *Theory and Research on the Causes of War.* Englewood Cliffs: Prentice-Hall.

Przeworski, A., and H. Teune. 1970. *The Logic of Comparative Social Inquiry.* New York: Wiley.

Putnam, R. 1988. 'Diplomacy and Domestic Politics: The Logic of Two-Level Games.' *International Organization* 42:427–60.

Quandt, W.B. 1986. *Camp David: Peacemaking and Politics.* Washington, DC: Brookings Institution.

Quattrone, G.A., and A. Tversky. 1988. 'Contrasting Rational and Psychological Analyses of Political Choice.' *American Political Science Review* 82:719–36.

Raiffa, H. 1982. *The Art and Science of Negotiation.* Cambridge: Harvard University Press.

Randle, R. 1973. *Origins of Peace.* New York: Free Press.

Rapkin, D.P., and W.R. Thompson, with J.A. Christopherson. 1979. 'Bipolarity and Bipolarization in the Cold War Era.' *Journal of Conflict Resolution* 23:261–95.

Rapoport, A. 1960. *Fights, Games and Debates.* Ann Arbor: University of Michigan Press.

——. 1987. 'Conflict Escalation and Conflict Dynamics.' In R. Vavrynen, ed., *The Quest for Peace.* Beverly Hills: Sage.

Ray, J.L. 1993. 'Wars Between Democracies: Rare, or Nonexistent?' *International Interactions* 18:251–76.

——. 1995. *Democracy and International Conflict: An Evaluation of the Democratic Peace Proposition.* Columbia: University of South Carolina Press.

Raymond, G.A. 1994. 'Democracies, Disputes, and Third-Party Intermediaries.' *Journal of Conflict Resolution* 38:24–42.
Reynolds, H.T. 1984. *Analysis of Nominal Data*. 2nd ed. Newbury Park: Sage Publications.
Richardson, J.L. 1994. *Crisis Diplomacy: The Great Powers Since the Mid-Nineteenth Century*. Cambridge: Cambridge University Press.
Richardson, L.F. 1960a. *Arms and Insecurity*. Pacific Grove: Boxwood Press.
———. 1960b. *Statistics of Deadly Quarrels*. Pacific Grove: Boxwood Press.
Richardson, L. 1992. 'Avoiding and Incurring Losses: Decision-Making in the Suez Crisis.' In J.G. Stein and L.W. Pauly, eds, *Choosing to Cooperate: How States Avoid Loss*. Baltimore: Johns Hopkins University Press.
Riker, W.H. 1986. *The Art of Political Manipulation*. New Haven: Yale University Press.
Ringer, F.K. 1989. 'Causal Analysis in Historical Reasoning.' *History and Theory* 28:154–72.
Roeder, P. 1985. 'Do New Soviet Leaders Really Make a Difference? Rethinking the "Succession Connection".' *American Political Science Review* 79:958–76.
———. 1986. 'The Effects of Leadership Succession in the Soviet Union.' *American Political Science Review* 80:219–24.
Rosecrance, R. 1966. 'Bipolarity, Multipolarity, and the Future.' *Journal of Conflict Resolution* 10:314–27.
———. 1992. 'A New Concert of Powers.' *Foreign Affairs* 71:64–82.
Rosecrance, R., and A. Stein, ed. 1993. *The Domestic Bases of Grand Strategy*. Ithaca: Cornell University Press.
Rosecrance, R., and Z. Steiner. 1993. 'British Grand Strategy and the Origins of World War II.' In R. Rosecrance and A. Stein, eds, *The Domestic Bases of Grand Strategy*. Ithaca: Cornell University Press.
Rosenau, J. 1992. 'Governance, Order, and Change in World Politics.' In J. Rosenau and E.-O. Czempiel, eds, *Governance Without Government: Order and Change in World Politics*. Cambridge: Cambridge University Press.
Ross, D. 1984. 'Risk Aversion in Soviet Decisionmaking.' In J. Valenta and W. Potter, eds, *Soviet Decisionmaking for National Security*. London: Allen & Unwin.
Rousseau, D. 1996. 'Domestic Political Institutions and the Evolution of International Conflict.' PhD Thesis, University of Michigan.
Rousseau, D., C. Gelpi, D. Reiter, and P. Huth. 1996. 'Assessing the Dyadic Nature of the Democratic Peace.' *American Political Science Review* 90:512–33.
Roy, A.B. (forthcoming). *Blood and Soil*. Columbia: University of South Carolina Press.
Rummel, R.J. 1963. 'Dimensions of Conflict Behavior Within and Between Nations.' *General Systems* 8:1–50.
———. 1975–81. *Understanding Conflict and War*. Five Volumes. Beverly Hills: Sage.
———. 1979. *War, Power, Peace. Understanding Conflict and War*, Vol. 4. Beverly Hills: Sage.
———. 1983. 'Libertarianism and International Violence.' *Journal of Conflict Resolution* 27:27–71.

———. 1985. 'Libertarian Propositions on Violence Between and Within Nations: A Test Against Published Research Results.' *Journal of Conflict Resolution* 29:419–55.
Russett, B.M. 1990. *Controlling the Sword: The Democratic Governance of National Security*. Cambridge: Harvard University Press.
———. 1993. *Grasping the Democratic Peace: Principles for a Post-Cold War World*. Princeton: Princeton University Press.
Russett, B.M., and G. Barzilai. 1982. 'The Political Economy of Military Actions: The United States and Israel.' In A. Mintz, ed., *The Political Economy of Military Spending in the United States*. London: Routledge.
Sabrosky, A.N. 1985. 'Alliance Aggregation, Capability Distribution, and the Expansion of Interstate War.' In A.N. Sobrosky, ed., *Polarity and War*. Boulder: Westview.
Sagen, S.D. 1994. 'From Deterrence to Coercion to War: The Road to Pearl Harbor.' In A.L. George and W.E. Simons, eds, *The Limits of Coercive Diplomacy*, 2nd edn. Boulder: Westview Press.
Sample, S.G. 1996. *Arms Races to War*. Ph.D. Dissertation, Vanderbilt University.
Samuelson, W., and R. Zechhauser. 1988. 'Status Quo Bias in Decision Making.' *Journal of Risk and Uncertainty* 1:7–59.
Sapperstein, A.M. 1991. 'The "Long Peace Result" of a Bipolar Competitive World?' *Journal of Conflict Resolution* 35:68–79.
Schelling, T.C. 1960. *The Strategy of Conflict*. Cambridge: Harvard University Press.
———. 1966. *Arms and Influence*. New Haven: Yale University Press.
Schroeder, P.W. 1994. 'Historical Reality vs. Neo-Realist Theory.' *International Security* 19:108–48.
Schweller, R.L. 1992. 'Domestic Structure and Preventive War: Are Democracies More Pacific?' *World Politics* 44:235–69.
Segal, U. 1988. 'Does the Preference Reversal Phenomenon Necessarily Contradict the Independence Axiom?' *American Economic Review* 78:233–6.
Selten, R. 1975. 'Reexamination of the Perfectness Concept for Equilibrium Points in Extensive Games.' *International Journal of Game Theory* 4:25–55.
Senese, P. (forthcoming in *Conflict Management and Peace Science*).
Shefrin, H., and M. Statman. 1985. 'The Disposition to Sell Winners too Early and Ride Losers too Long: Theory and Evidence.' *Journal of Finance* 40:777–90.
Sherman, F. 1994. 'SHERFACS: A Cross-Paradigm, Hierarchical and Contextually Sensitive Conflict Management Data Set.' *International Interactions* 20:79–100.
Shillony, B.-A. 1982. 'The Japanese Experience.' In N. Oren, ed., *Termination of Wars*. Jerusalem: Magnes Press.
Shlaim, A. 1976. 'Failures in National Intelligence Estimates: The Case of the Yom Kippur War.' *World Politics* 28: no. 3:348–80.
———. 1983. *The United States and the Berlin Blockade, 1948–1949: A Study of Crisis Decision-Making*. Berkeley and Los Angeles: University of California Press.
Shubik, M. 1982. *Game Theory in the Social Sciences: Concepts and Solutions*. Cambridge: MIT Press.

Sigal, L.V. 1988. *Fighting to a Finish*. New York: Ithaca.
Simon, H.A. 1984. 'On the Behavioral and Rational Foundations of Economic Dynamics.' *Journal of Economic Behavior and Organization* 5:35–55.
Simone, V., and A.T. Feraru. 1995. *The Asian Pacific: Political and Economic Development in a Global Context*. White Plains, NY: Longman.
Singer, J.D. 1961. 'The Level-of-Analysis Problem in International Relations.' *World Politics*, 14:77–92.
——. 1981. 'Accounting for International War: The State of the Discipline.' *Journal of Peace Research* 18:1–18.
——. 1990. 'Reconstructing the Correlates of War Data Set on Material Capabilities of States, 1816–1985.' In J.D. Singer and P.F. Diehl, eds, *Measuring the Correlates of War*. Ann Arbor: University of Michigan Press.
Singer, J.D., et al. 1979. *Explaining War: Selected Papers from the Correlates of War Project*. Beverly Hills: Sage.
Singer, J.D., S. Bremer and J. Stuckey. 1972. 'Capability Distribution, Uncertainty, and Major Power War, 1820–1965.' In B. Russett, ed., *Peace, War, and Numbers*. Beverly Hills: Sage.
Singer, J.D. and M. Small. 1966. 'National Alliance Commitments and War Involvement, 1815–1945.' *Peace Research Society (International) Papers* 5:109–40.
——. 1972. *The Wages of War 1816–1965: A Statistical Handbook*. New York: John Wiley.
Siverson, R.M. 1980. 'Attributes of National Alliance Membership and War Participation, 1815–1965.' *American Journal of Political Science* 24:1–15.
Siverson, R.M., and P.F. Diehl. 1989. 'Arms Races, the Conflict Spiral, and the Onset of War.' In M.I. Midlarsky, ed., *Handbook of War Studies*. Boston: Unwin Hyman.
Siverson, R.M. and J. King. 1979. 'Alliances and the Expansion of War.' In J.D. Singer and M. Wallace, eds, *To Augur Well*. Beverly Hills: Sage.
Siverson, R. and H. Starr. 1990. 'Opportunity, Willingness, and the Diffusion of War.' *American Political Science Review* 84:47–67.
——. 1991. *The Diffusion of War*. Ann Arbor: University of Michigan Press.
Slovic, P., and S. Lichtenstein. 1983. 'Preference Reversals: A Broader Perspective.' *American Economic Review* 73:596–605.
Small, M., and J.D. Singer. 1976. 'The War-Proneness of Democratic Regimes, 1816–1965.' *Jerusalem Journal of International Affairs* 1:50–59.
——. 1982. *Resort to Arms: International and Civil Wars, 1816–1980*. Beverly Hills: Sage.
Smoke, R. 1977. *War: Controlling Escalation*. Cambridge: Harvard University Press.
Snyder, G.H. 1961. *Deterrence and Defense: Toward a Theory of National Security*. Princeton: Princeton University Press.
——. 1984. 'The Security Dilemma in Alliance Politics.' *World Politics* 36:481–95.
Snyder, G.H., and P. Diesing. 1977. *Conflict Among Nations: Bargaining, Decision-Making and System Structure in International Crises*. Princeton: Princeton University Press.
Snyder, J. 1991. *Myths of Empire*. Ithaca: Cornell University Press.
Snyder, R.C., H.W. Bruck, and B. Sapin. 1962. 'Decision-Making as an Approach

to the Study of International Politics.' In R.C. Snyder, H.W. Bruck, and B. Sapin, eds, *Foreign Policy Decision-Making: An Approach to the Study of International Politics.* New York: Free Press.

Sorokin, P.A. 1937. *Social and Cultural Dynamics, III.* New York: American Book Company.

Spanier, J. 1974. *Games Nations Play: Analyzing International Politics.* New York: Praeger.

Spiro, D.E. 1994. 'The Insignificance of the Liberal Peace.' *International Security* 19:50–86.

Starr, H. 1978. 'A Return Journey: Richardson, 'Frontiers,' and Wars in the 1946–1965 Era.' *Journal of Conflict Resolution* 22:441–67.

———. 1991. 'Joining Political and Geographic Perspectives: Geopolitics and International Relations.' *International Interactions* 17:1–9.

Starr, H. and B.A. Most. 1976. 'The Substance and Study of Borders in International Relations Research.' *International Studies Quarterly* 20:581–620.

Staudenmaier, W. 1987. 'Conflict Termination in the Nuclear Era.' In S. Cimbala and K. Dunn, eds, *Conflict Termination and Military Strategy.* Boulder: Westview Press.

Stein, A.A., and B.M. Russett. 1980. 'Evaluating War: Outcomes and Consequences.' In T.R. Gurr, ed., *Handbook of Political Conflict: Theory and Research.* New York: Free Press.

Stein, J.G. 1975. 'War Termination and Conflict Reduction or, How Wars Should End.' *Jerusalem Journal of International Relations* 1:1–27.

———. 1982. 'The Termination of the October War – A Reappraisal.' In N. Oren, ed., *Termination of Wars.* Jerusalem: Magnes Press.

———. 1985a. 'Calculation, Miscalculation and Conventional Deterrence I: The View from Cairo.' In R. Jervis, R.N. Lebow, and J.G. Stein, eds, *Psychology and Deterrence.* Baltimore: Johns Hopkins Press.

———. 1985b. 'Calculation, Miscalculation and Conventional Deterrence II: The View from Jerusalem.' In R. Jervis, R.N. Lebow, and J.G. Stein, eds, *Psychology and Deterrence.* Baltimore: Johns Hopkins Press.

———. 1992. 'International Cooperation and Loss Avoidance: Framing the Problem.' *International Journal* 47:202–34.

———. 1993. 'The Political Economy of Security Agreements: The Linked Costs of Failure at Camp David.' In P.B. Evans, H. Jacobson, and R. Putnam, eds, *Double-Edged Diplomacy: International Bargaining and Domestic Politics.* Berkeley: University of California Press.

Stein, J.G., and L.W. Pauly. 1993. *Choosing to Cooperate: How States Avoid Loss.* Baltimore: Johns Hopkins University Press.

Stein, J.G., and R. Tanter. 1980. *Rational Decision-Making: Israel's Security Choices, 1967.* Columbus: Ohio State University Press.

Steinberg, B.S. 1991a. 'Psychoanalytic Concepts in International Politics: The Role of Shame and Humiliation.' *International Review of Psycho-Analysis* 18:65–85.

———. 1991b. 'Shame and Humiliation in the Cuban Missile Crisis: A Psychoanalytic Perspective.' *Political Psychology.* 12:653–90.

———. 1996. *Shame and Humiliation: Presidential Decision-Making on Vietnam.* Montreal: McGill-Queen's University Press.

Steinbruner, J.D. 1974. *The Cybernetic Theory of Decision*. Princeton: Princeton University Press.
Steinert, M. 1977. *Hitler's War and the Germans: Public Mood and Attitude during the Second World War*. Athens: Ohio University Press.
Stimson, H.L., 1973. *H.L. Stimson Diaries*. New Haven: Yale University Library: Manuscripts and Archives.
Stimson, H.L., and M. Bundy. 1947. *On Active Service in Peace and War*. New York: Harper.
Stoessinger, J.G. 1985. *Why Nations Go To War*, 4th edn. New York: St. Martin's Press.
Taliaferro, J.W. 1994. 'Analogical Reasoning and Prospect Theory: Hypotheses on Framing.' Paper presented at the annual meeting of the International Studies Association.
Tanter, R. 1966. 'Dimensions of Conflict Behavior Within and Between Nations, 1958–60.' *Journal of Conflict Resolution* 10:41–64.
——. 1974. *Modelling and Managing International Conflicts: The Berlin Crises*. Beverly Hills: Sage.
Taylor, M. 1976. *Anarchy and Cooperation*. London: John Wiley.
Taylor, C.L., and D.A. Jodice. 1983. *World Handbook of Political and Social Indicators*, 3rd edn. New Haven: Yale University Press.
Taylor, S.A., and T. Ralston. 1991. 'The Role of Intelligence in Crisis Management.' In A. George, ed., *Avoiding War: Problems of Crisis Management*. Boulder: Westview Press.
Telhami, S. 1990. *Power and Leadership in International Bargaining: The Path to the Camp David Accords*. New York: Columbia University Press.
Tetlock, P.E. 1987. 'Testing Deterrence Theory: Some Conceptual and Methodological Issues.' *Journal of Social Issues* 43:85–91.
Thaler, R. 1980. 'Toward a Positive Theory of Consumer Choice.' *Journal of Economic Behavior and Organization* 1:39–60.
Thompson, W.R. 1986. 'Polarity, the Long Cycle, and Global Power Warfare.' *Journal of Conflict Resolution* 30:587–615.
——. 1988. *On Global War*. Columbia: University of South Carolina Press.
——. 1995. 'Principal Rivalries.' *Journal of Conflict Resolution*. 39:195–223.
Treverton, G. 1987. 'Ending Major Coalition Wars.' In S. Cimbala and K. Dunn, eds, *Conflict Termination and Military Strategy*. Boulder: Westview Press.
Tsebelis, G., and J. Sprague. 1989. 'Coercion and Revolution: Variations on a Predator–Prey Model.' *Mathematical and Computer Modelling* 12:547–59.
Tversky, A. and D. Kahneman. 1974. 'Judgment Under Uncertainty: Heuristics and Biases.' *Science* 185:1124–31.
——. 1986. 'Rational Choice and the Framing of Decisions.' *Journal of Business* 59:251–78.
——. 1991. 'Loss aversion in riskless choice: A reference dependent model.' *Quarterly Journal of Economics* 41:1039–61.
Tversky, A., P. Slovic, and D. Kahneman. 1990. 'The Causes of Preference Reversal.' *American Economic Review* 80:204–17.
United States Arms Control and Disarmament Agency. Various Years. *World Military Expenditures and Arms Control*. Washington, DC: US Government Printing Office.

Utley, J.G. 1985. *Going to War with Japan, 1937–1941.* Knoxville: University of Tennessee Press.
Van Creveld, M.L. 1989. *Technology and War: From 2000 B.C. to the Present.* New York: Free Press.
———. 1991. *The Transformation of War.* Toronto: Maxwell Macmillan International.
Vasquez, J.A. 1987a. 'The Steps to War: Toward a Scientific Explanation of Correlates of War Findings.' *World Politics* 40:108–45.
———. 1987b. 'Foreign Policy, Learning, and War.' In C. Hermann, C. Kegley, Jr., and J. Rosenau, eds, *New Directions in the Study of Foreign Policy.* Winchester: Allen & Unwin.
———. 1991. 'The Deterrence Myth: Nuclear Weapons and the Prevention of Nuclear War.' In C. Kegley, ed., *The Long Postwar Peace.* New York: HarperCollins.
———. 1993. *The War Puzzle.* Cambridge: Cambridge University Press.
———. 1996. 'The Causes of the Second World War in Europe: A New Scientific Explanation.' *International Political Science Review* 17:161–78.
———. (forthcoming). 'The Realist Paradigm as a Degenerating Research Program.'
Vasquez, J.A., and M.T. Henehan, eds. 1992. *The Scientific Study of Peace and War: A Text Reader.* New York: Lexington Books.
Vertzberger, Y.Y. 1982. 'India's Strategic Posture and the Border War Defeat of 1962: A Case Study in Micalculation.' *Journal of Strategic Studies* 5:370–92.
———. 1984. *Misperceptions in Foreign Policymaking: The Sino-Indian Conflict, 1959–1962.* Boulder: Westview Press.
———. 1990. *The World in Their Minds: Information Processing, Cognition and Perception in Foreign Policy Decisionmaking.* Stanford: Stanford Univesity Press.
Von Neumann, J., and O. Morgenstern. 1947. *Theory of Games and Economic Behavior*, 2nd edn. Princeton: Princeton University Press.
Von Reikhoff, H. 1987. 'Methodological and Historical Problems in Determining Deterrence Success.' *Journal of Social Issues* 43:79–84.
Wagner, R.H. 1989. 'Uncertainty, Rational Learning, and Bargaining in the Cuban Missile Crisis.' In P.C. Ordeshook, ed., *Models of Strategic Choice in Politics.* Ann Arbor: University of Michigan Press.
———. 1993. 'The Causes of Peace.' In R. Licklider, ed., *Stopping the Killing: How Civil Wars End.* New York: New York University Press.
Wallace, M.D. 1973. 'Alliance Polarization, Cross-Cutting, and International War, 1815–1964: A Measurement Procedure and Some Preliminary Evidence.' *Journal of Conflict Resolution* 17:575–604.
———. 1979. 'Arms Races and Escalation: Some New Evidence.' *Journal of Conflict Resolution* 23:3–16.
———. 1981. 'Old Nails in New Coffins: The Para Bellum Hypothesis Revisited.' *Journal of Peace Research* 18:91–5.
———. 1982. 'Armaments and Escalation: Two Competing Hypotheses.' *International Studies Quarterly* 26:37–51.
———. 1990. 'Racing Redux: The Arms Race-Escalation Debate Revisited.' In C. Gochman and A. Sabrosky. eds, *Prisoners of War.* Lexington: Lexington Books.
Wallensteen, P. 1981. 'Incompatibility, Confrontation, and War: Four Models and Three Historical Systems, 1816–1976.' *Journal of Peace Research* 18:57–90.

Wallerstein, I. 1983. 'Crises: The World-Economy, The Movements, and the Ideologies.' In A. Bergesen, ed., *Crises in the World-System*. Beverly Hills: Sage.
Walt, S. 1992. 'Revolution and War.' *World Politics* 44:321-68.
Waltz, K.N. 1959. *Man, the State and War*. New York: Columbia University Press.
———. 1964. 'The Stability of a Bipolar World.' *Daedalus* 93:881-909.
———. 1967. 'International Structure, National Force, and the Balance of World Power.' *Journal of International Affairs* 21:215-31.
Wang, K. 'Presidential Responses to Foreign Policy Crises.' *Journal of Conflict Resolution* 40:68-97.
Ward, M.D. 1984. 'Differential Paths to Parity: A Study of the Contemporary Arms Race.' *American Political Science Review* 78:297-317.
Warner, G. 1974. *Iraq and Syria, 1941*. London: Davis-Poynter.
Watt, D.C. 1989. *How War Came: The Immediate Origins of the Second World War 1938-1939*. New York: Pantheon.
Wayman, F.W. 1984. 'Bipolarity and War: The Role of Capability Concentration and Alliance Patterns among Major Powers, 1816-1965.' *Journal of Peace Research* 21:61-78.
———. 1989. 'Power Shifts and War.' Paper presented at the Annual Meeting of the International Studies Association, London, 1989.
———. 1996. 'Power Shifts and the Onset of War.' In J. Kugler and D. Lemke, eds, *Parity and War*. Ann Arbor: University of Michigan Press.
Wayman, F.W., and D. M. Jones. 1991. 'Evolution of Conflict in Enduring Rivalries.' Paper presented at the Annual Meeting of the International Studies Association, Vancouver, 1991.
Weede, E. 1980. 'Arms Races and Escalations: Some Persisting Doubts.' *Journal of Conflict Resolution.* 24:285-7.
Weigley, R.F. 1973. 'The Role of the War Department and the Army.' In D. Borg and S. Okamoto, eds, *Pearl Harbor as History: Japanese-American Relations, 1931-1941*. New York: Columbia University Press.
Weinberg, G.L. 1994. *A World at Arms: A Global History of World War II*. Cambridge: Cambridge University Press.
White, G.L. 1966. 'Misperception and the Vietnam War.' *Journal of Social Issues* 22:1-164.
Wilkenfeld, J. 1968. 'Domestic and Foreign Conflict Behavior of Nations.' *Journal of Peace Research* 1:56-69.
———. 1975. 'A Time-Series Perspective on Conflict in the Middle East.' In P.J. McGowan, ed., *Sage International Yearbook of Foreign Policy Studies 3*. Beverly Hills: Sage.
———. 1991. 'Trigger-Response Transitions in Foreign Policy Crises, 1929-1985.' *Journal of Conflict Resolution* 35:143-69.
Wilkenfeld, J., M. Brecher, and S. Moser. 1988. *Crises in the Twentieth Century, Volume II: Handbook of Foreign Policy Crises*. Oxford: Pergamon.
Witol, G.L. 1995. *Expected-Utility Theory, Prospect Theory, and War: Explaining Decision Making In The Franco-Prussian War, The Japanese Attack on Pearl Harbor, And The Soviet Invasion of Afghanistan*. Halifax: Centre for Foreign Policy Studies.
Wittman, D. 1979. 'How a War Ends: A Rational Model Approach.' *Journal of Conflict Resolution.* 23:743-63.

Wohlstetter, A. 1959. 'The Delicate Balance of Terror.' *Foreign Affairs* 37:211–34.
Wohlstetter, R. 1962. *Pearl Harbor: Warning and Decision.* Stanford: Stanford University Press.
Wright, Q. 1942. *A Study of War,* 2 vols. Chicago: University of Chicago Press.
Yamamoto, Y. and S.A. Bremer. 1980. 'Wider Wars and Restless Nights: Major Power Intervention in Ongoing War.' In J.D. Singer, ed., *The Correlates of War, Vol. II.* New York: Free Press.
Young, H.P., ed. 1991. *Negotiation Analysis.* Ann Arbor: University of Michigan Press.
———. 1994. *Equity in Theory and Practice.* Princeton: Princeton University Press.
Young, O.R. 1967. *The Intermediaries: Third Parties in International Crises.* Princeton: Princeton University Press.
———. 1968. *The Politics of Force.* Princeton: Princeton University Press.
Zacher, M. 1992. 'The Decaying Pillars of the Westphalian Temple: Implications for International Order and Governance.' In James Rosenau and Ernst-Otto Czempiel (ed.) *Governance Without Government: Order and Change in World Politics.* Cambridge, New York: Cambridge University Press, pp. 58–101.
Zagare, F.C. 1983. 'A Game-Theoretic Evaluation of the 1973 Cease-Fire Alert Decision.' *Journal of Peace Research* 20:73–86.
———. 1987. *The Dynamics of Deterrence.* Chicago: University of Chicago Press.
Zajac, E.E. 1995. *Political Economy of Fairness.* Cambridge: MIT Press.
Zeira, E. 1993. *The October 73 War: Myth Against Reality,* (Hebrew). Tel-Aviv: Yedioth Ahronot.
Zerbinos, M. 1994. 'Internal Conflict and the Democratic Peace.' Paper presented at the Midwest regional meeting of the International Studies Association at Columbus, Ohio, 30 September – 1 October 1994.
Zinnes, D.A. 1976. *Contemporary Research in International Relations.* New York: Free Press.
———. 1980. 'Why War? Evidence on the Outbreak of International Conflict.' In T.R. Gurr, ed., *Handbook of Political Conflict: Theory and Research.* New York: Free Press.
Zinnes, D.A., J.L. Zinnes, and R.D. McClure. 1972. 'Hostility in Diplomatic Communication.' In C. Hermann, ed., *International Crises.* New York: Free Press.

Name Index

Abdolali, N., 52
Abelson, R.P., 298, 299
Abramson, P.R., 278
Achen, C.H., 143
Adomeit, H., 11
Aldrich, J., 204 n.14
Alford, J.R., 277
Allais, M., 104
Allan, P., 11
Allison, G.T., 11, 12
Allison, P.D., 52
Altfeld, M.F., 29 n.5
Alves, M.H.M., 76
Ames, B., 273
Anderson, P.A., 174, 175, 202 n.1, 289
Anderton, C.H., 29 n.5
Andrade, L., 300
Andriole, S.J., 13
Aquino, C., 276, 280, 285
Arkes, H.R., 290
Arrow, K.J., 102
Ashley, R. 28 n.1, 29 n.2
Assad, H. al-, 82, 88-9, 90
Astorino-Courtois, A., 300
Austine, W., 300
Axelrod, R., 35
Azar, E.E., 9, 13, 29 n.4, 59 n.3, 163

Bar-Joseph, U., 270 n.1
Barringer, R.E., 215, 303 n.4
Barzilai, G., 292
Bazerman, M.H., 108, 114 n.10,11, 115 n.14
Begin, M., 310, 311, 312, 313-14, 315
Bell, P.M.H., 220, 221, 222, 223, 224, 225, 226, 227, 229, 232, 233, 235, 239 nn.17,18,19,20, 240 n.28
Ben Yehuda, H., 15, 123
Ben Zvi, A., 25, 247, 248, 249, 250, 255, 270 nn.1,3, 271 nn.14,17,33
Bennett, D.S., 17, 95 nn.23,24, 163, 183-4
Bercovitch, J., 168, 170
Betts, R.K., 140 n.1, 256, 270 n.3
Bickers, K.N., 92 n.2, 292, 303 n.2
Biersteker, T., 28 n.2
Blumer, C., 290
Bobrow, D.B., 14

Boettcher, W., 288, 292, 303 n.6
Borthwick, M., 275
Box, G.E.P., 277
Bracken, P., 11
Brams, S.J., 11, 13, 27, 36, 60 nn.12,13, 145, 146, 160 n.2, 301, 306, 309, 315, 317, 319, 323
Bratton, M., 74
Braun, A., 261, 271 nn.22,25,28
Brecher, M., 11, 12, 13, 15, 18, 22, 29 n.4, 59 nn.3,6, 113, 123, 140 n.1, 141n, 145, 153, 157, 160 n.13, 161 n.19, 163, 168, 169, 170, 171, 172, 185, 187, 210, 214, 215, 230, 239 n.19, 258
Bremer, S.A., 46, 51, 60 n.9, 201, 216, 218, 239 n.15
Brito, D.L., 29 n.5
Brody, R., 207, 215, 240 n.27
Brookshire, D.S., 100
Brown, S., 18
Bruck, H.W., 11
Brussel, G.S., 156
Brzezinski, Z., 312, 313, 314, 323
Bueno de Mesquita, B., 11, 12, 18, 39, 67, 91, 93 nn.6,8, 160 n.3, 218, 239 n.14, 293
The War Trap, 19, 293
Bullock, A., 221
Bunce, V., 273
Bundy, M., 254, 271 nn.19,20
Burke, J.P., 11
Bush, G., 291, 300, 301

Campbell, D.T., 275, 277
Campbell, D., 6, 28 n.2
Caporaso, J.A., 277
Carter, J.E., 311, 313, 314, 323
Chai, S.-K., 77
Chamberlain, N., 221, 230, 233, 240 nn.20,23
Chambers, F.P., 226
Chan, S., 25-6
Chiang Ching-kuo, 276, 282
Choucri, N., 18, 207
Christensen, T.J., 227
Ciano, G., 226, 227, 228, 233
Claude, I., Jr., 18

356

Name Index

Clausewitz, K. von, 17
 On War, 17
Cohen, E.A., 270 n.1, 271 n.33
Cotton, T., 93 n.8
Coursey, D.L., 100
Cox, R., 6
Craig, G.A., 161 n.17
Crawford, V.P., 114 n.10
Cusack, T.R., 213

Daladier, E., 230
Darwin, C., 7
Dawisha, K., 11
Dayan, M., 257, 258, 260–1, 265, 271 nn.21,22, 314–15
DeNardo, J., 74, 75, 77, 78
Der Derian, J., 28 n.2
DeRouen, K., 92 n.2
Deutsch, K.W., 13
Diehl, P., 29 nn.4,5, 35, 36, 46, 52, 64, 95 n.28, 162, 163, 164, 165, 166, 167, 168, 169, 170, 171, 173, 178–9, 182–3, 185, 186, 187, 188, 191, 193, 202 nn.6,7,8,9, 210, 213, 214
Diesing, P., 10, 11, 14, 35, 60 n.11, 271 n.13
Divine, R.A., 233
Dixon, W.J., 273
Doane, M.J., 106, 114 n.5
Dougherty, J.E., 158
Dowty, A., 11

Earle, E.M., 29 n.6
Eberwein, W., 213
Eckstein, H., 13, 270 n.7
Eckstein, S., 76
Einhorn, H.J., 102
Elazar, D., 259, 261, 265
Engels, F., 7
Evans, P.B., 91, 272
Evron, Y., 90

Fabyanic, T., 294
Fagen, R.R., 242
Fahmy, I., 322
Farah, N., 29 n.4
Farnham, B., 114 n.7, 271 nn.15,23, 288
Fearon, J., 174
Feraru, A.T., 275
Feste, K., 163
Finlay, D.J., 163
Fishburn, P.C., 100
Francisco, R., 76
Freedman, L., 88

Friedman, E., 275
Frisch, D., 290
Fry, M.G., 155

Gamson, W.A., 78
Ganguly, S., 271 n.33
Garland, H., 289, 290
Garreton, M.A.M., 76
Geddes, B., 94 n.18
Geller, D.S., 33, 35, 80, 94 n.18, 166, 168
Gelpi, C., 17, 95 nn.23,24
George, A.L., 11, 12, 13, 14, 18, 59 n.6, 111, 144, 160 n.10, 161 n.17, 242, 244, 246, 247, 270 n.7
George, J., 6, 28 n.2
Gerow, L.T., 254
Geva, N., 26–7, 115 n.12, 291, 300, 301
Gibler, D., 238 n.4
Giddens, A., 6
Glassman, J.D., 11
Gochman, C., 13, 14, 179, 202 nn.5,6, 213, 215
Goertz, G., 29 n.4, 35, 36, 46, 52, 64, 95 n.28, 162, 163, 164, 165, 166, 169, 171, 178–9, 182–3, 185, 186, 187, 188, 191, 202 nn.6,8,9, 210
Golan, G., 11
Goldstein, W.M., 102
Gooch, J., 270 n.1, 271 n.33
Greenstein, F.I., 11
Grether, D.M., 102
Grew, J., 247, 251, 258, 271 n.27
Grieco, J., 108
Gurr, T.R., 7, 80, 218

Haas, E.B., 11
Haas, M., 11
Hagan, J.D., 74, 75, 77
Halifax, Lord E., 225, 239 n.20
Hall, D.K., 11, 18
Han, S.-J., 79
Handel, M., 248, 258, 259, 263, 264
Hartman, R.S., 106, 114 n.5
Harvey, F., 6, 22–3, 143, 146, 153, 154, 156, 158, 160 nn.11,12
Hassan (king of Morocco), 89
Hempel, C.G., 207
Henehan, M.T., 238 n.8
Hensel, P.R., 22, 23, 52, 59 n.7, 163, 164, 172, 175, 176, 177–8, 179, 180–1, 185, 186, 187, 188, 189, 194, 200, 201, 202 nn.6,8, 203 n.11, 210

Name Index

Herek, G.M., 11
Hermann, M.G., 272
Hermann, C.F., 12
Hershey, J.C., 114 n.6
Herz, J.H., 18
Heuer, R.J., 271 n.31
Hitler, A., 220–1, 222, 223, 224, 225, 226–7, 228, 229–30, 231, 232, 233–4, 235, 240 nn.20,23,24
Mein Kampf, 220
Hodges, T., 90
Hoffi, Y., 258, 259, 260
Holsti, K.J., 28 n.2, 210
Holsti, O.R., 12, 13, 201, 207, 215, 240 n.27, 242, 290
Hood, R.M., 217
Hoole, F.W., 238 n.5
Hoover, D., 76, 77, 78
Houweling, H.W.,160 n.14, 217
Hovis, J.L., 100
Howard, M., 18
Huang, C., 273, 277
Hughes, H.S., 232
Hull, C., 249, 250, 251, 252–3, 255, 258
Huntington, 274
Hussein, S., 88, 291, 300, 301
Hussein (king of Jordan), 259
Huth, P., 17, 18, 21, 29 n.4, 35, 46, 60 n.9, 91, 93 n.7, 95 nn.22,23,24,25,27, 143, 144, 160 n.10, 166, 168, 173, 178, 179, 210

Ikle, F., 294
Inglehart, R., 278
Intriligator, M.D., 29 n.5
Isard, W., 29 n.5

Jacobson, H.K., 91
James, P., 16, 22–3, 92 n.2, 143, 144, 146, 153, 154, 156, 158, 160 nn.11,12, 168, 169, 170, 171, 172, 185, 213, 215, 292
Janis, I.L., 12
Jervis, R., 12, 18, 60 n.15, 96, 103, 106, 107, 108, 110, 111, 112, 160 n.1, 242, 247, 265, 268, 270 n.5, 271 n.24, 292
Job, B., 92 n.2, 292
Jodice, D.A., 93 n.13
Johnson, L.B., 290
Jones, D.S., 33, 35, 46, 163, 164, 176, 178
Jureidini, P., 59 n.3

Kacowicz, A.M., 312, 313, 317
Kahn, H., 11, 17, 158
On Escalation, 17
On Thermonuclear War, 17
Kahneman, D., 13, 96, 97, 98, 99–100, 101, 102, 103, 104–5, 106, 107, 108, 114 nn.2,4,5, 288, 289, 291, 301
Kaiser, D.E., 220, 222, 223, 225, 239 n.17, 240 nn.22,23
Kam, E., 242, 245, 248, 271 n.32
Kaplan, J., 294
Karsh, E., 88
Kegley, C.W., Jr., 238 n.10, 272
Keller, B.A., 258
Kennedy, P., 214, 219
Keohane, R.O., 106, 108
Khoury, P.S., 94 n.16
Khrushchev, N., 111
Kienle, E., 89
Kilgour, D.M., 11, 13, 93 n.9, 146
Kim Dae Jung, 79, 276
Kim Young Sam, 79, 276, 284
King, J., 217
Kingston, J., 166, 167
Kissinger, H.A., 311, 321
Knetsch, J.L., 99, 100, 103, 106, 107, 114 n.5
Knez, M., 100
Knorr, K., 249, 270 n.6
Knox, F., 252, 255
Kochenberger, G.A., 100
Kolm, S.-C., 309
Kowalewski, D., 76, 77, 78, 79
Kozhemiakin, A.V., 272
Kugler, J., 18

Lake, D., 67
Lalman, D., 11, 18, 67, 91, 93 n.6, 160 n.3
Langer, E.J., 298, 299
Lapid, Y., 28 n.2
Lawson, F., 89, 90
Lazarus, R.S., 12
Lebow, R.N., 10, 11, 12, 13, 16, 18, 59 n.6, 112, 143, 144, 242, 271 n.33
Lee Min Woo, 79
Lemke, D., 166
Leng, R., 11, 13, 14, 16, 40, 59 nn.6,7, 95 n.25, 172, 173, 174, 178, 179, 192, 214, 215, 230
Lenin, V.I., 18
Levite, E., 243, 247, 248, 249, 250, 255, 271 n.10

Name Index

Levy, J.S., 21-2, 83, 92 nn.1,2, 96, 99, 105, 106, 110, 111, 112, 114 n.2, 115 n.15, 160 n.1, 209, 210, 212, 228, 238 n.4, 239 n.13, 244, 270 n.4, 273, 288, 292, 303 n.3
Lewis-Beck, M.S., 277, 279
Lian, B., 92 n.2
Liao, T.F., 204 nn.14,15
Lichtenstein,S., 101, 102
Lieberman, E., 166, 167
Litvinov, M.M., 227
Lobmeyer, H.G., 89
Longrigg, 94 n.16
Luce, D.R., 35
Luebbert, G.M., 29 n.5
Lust-Okar, E., 18, 21, 94 n.16

MacArthur, D., 256
Mann, L., 12
Mansfield, E., 92 n.2
Maoz, M., 89
Maoz, Z., 11, 13, 14, 20-1, 33, 35, 36, 40, 45, 46, 51, 52, 58, 59 nn.2,4,5, 60 nn.9,10,14,15, 166, 172, 175, 176, 177, 178, 181-2, 185, 188, 200, 202 nn.5,6, 213, 214, 218, 290
Marcos, F., 276, 279, 280
Marshall, G.C., 252, 255, 256
Marx, K., 7
Massoud, T., 293
Mattli, W., 36
Maxwell, G., 94 n.16
May, E.R., 269
McClelland, C.A., 11, 13
McClure, R.D., 207
McDermott, R., 110, 114 n.7, 302 n.1
McGowan, P.J., 217
McKeown, T., 174, 175, 202 n.1
McLaurin, R., 59 n.3, 90
McNeil, B.J., 102
Mead, M., 211
Meernik, J., 92 n.2
Meir, G., 261, 265
Merritt, R.L., 303 n.2
Michels, R., 7
Midlarsky, M.I., 209, 217, 218, 220, 230, 239 n.12
Migdal, J.S., 66
Miller, J., 88
Mintz, A., 26-7, 115 n.12, 291, 292, 300, 301
Moll, K.D., 29 n.5
Moon, B.E., 273
Mor, B.D., 13, 20-1, 35, 36, 45, 58, 59

nn.2,4,5, 60 nn.10,14, 172, 176, 177, 178, 181-2, 185, 200
Morgan, P.M., 11, 160 n.1, 256, 271 n.26
Morgan, T.C., 11, 92 n.2, 108, 115 n.14, 239 n.13, 292, 303 n.2
Morgenstern, O., 289
Morgenthau, H., Jr., 246-7, 251, 271 n.12
Morgenthau, H.J., 18, 212
Morrow, J.D., 35, 213
Mosca, G., 7
Moser, S., 145, 153, 160 n.13, 187, 230
Most, B.A., 217
Mueller, J.E., 161 n.19, 225, 299
Mughisuddin, M., 90
Muller, E., 80
Mullik, B.N., 271 n.33
Mussolini, B., 224, 226, 228, 233, 234, 240 n.23
Mylroie, L., 88

Napoleon I, 227
Napoleon III, 238 n.7
Neale, M.A., 108, 114 nn.10,11, 115 n.14
Nelson, F.D., 204 n.14
Newport, S., 289, 290
Nicholson, M., 29 n.3
Nincic, M., 201
Nisbett, R.E., 271 n.32
Nomikos, E.V., 12
Nomura, K., 249, 251, 253, 255
North, R.C., 12, 18, 207, 215, 240 n.27

O'Keefe, M., 74, 77
Oliver, P., 94 n.16
Olson, M., Jr., 272, 278
Oneal, J., 92 n.2, 292
Organski, A.F.K., 18
Ostrom, C.W., Jr., 92 n.2, 238 n.5, 292
Oye, K., 35

Paige, G.D., 11
Paret, P., 17, 29 n.6
Pareto, A., 7
Paul, Prince (regent of Yugoslavia), 234
Pauly, L.W., 108, 115 n.14
Pelowski, A.L., 277
Peterson, S., 91
Pfaltzgraff, R.L., Jr., 158
Phillips, D.L., 6
Phillips, J.L., Jr., 203 n.13
Pillar, P., 295

Name Index

Pipes, D., 82
Platig, R., 4
Plott, C.R., 102
Post, J.M., 12
Powell, C., 301
Powell, R., 11, 35
Pruitt, D.G., 17
Przeworski, A., 275
Putnam, R.D., 91, 272

Quandt, W.B., 311, 312, 313, 314, 322, 323
Quattrone, G.A., 13, 101, 104, 289, 290, 291
Quwatli, S., 78–9

Raiffa, H., 35, 306, 317, 320
Randle, R., 294
Rapoport, A., 16
Ray, J.L., 18, 272
Raymond, G., 238 n.10, 272
Regan, P., 168, 170
Reiter, D., 95 nn.23,24
Reynolds, H.T., 203 n.13
Richardson, J.L., 11, 214, 238 n.6
Richardson, L., 108, 115 n.13
Richardson, L.F., 16, 18, 213, 216, 273
Riker, W.H., 323
Ringer, F.K., 207
Roeder, P., 273
Roh Tae Woo, 276, 282, 284, 285
Roosevelt, F.D., 233, 235, 251, 252, 253, 254
Rosecrance, R., 91, 221, 223, 228, 231, 240 n.24
Rosenau, J., 28 n.2
Ross, D., 110
Ross, H.L., 277
Ross, L., 271 n.32
Rousseau, D., 80, 95 nn.23,24
Roy, A.B., 210
Rummel, R.J., 18, 214
Russett, B., 29 n.4, 51, 60 n.9, 91, 92 n.2, 93 n.8, 143, 144, 160 n.10, 166, 168, 201, 272, 273, 275, 292, 299

Sabrosky, A.N., 218, 220
Sadat, A., 263, 264, 265, 266, 310, 311, 312, 313, 314, 315, 317, 323
Sagen, S.D., 255, 271 nn.10,18
Sample, S.G., 213, 238 n.8
Samuelson, W., 106
Sapin, B., 11

Schelling, T.C., 11, 17, 112, 271 n.30
The Strategy of Conflict, 17
Schroeder, P.W., 227, 228
Schulze, W.D., 100
Schumaker, P., 74, 77, 79
Schwarzkopf, N., 140 n.1, 301
Schweller, R.L., 126
Segal, U., 102
Selten, R., 160 n.3
Senese, P., 210
Shamir, Y., 290
Shefrin, H., 104
Sherman, F., 95 n.29
Shillony, B.-A., 294
Shlaim, A., 11, 244
Shoemaker, P.J.H., 114 n.6
Shubik, M., 60 n.11
Siccama, J.G., 160 n.14, 217
Simon, H.A., 97
Simone, V., 275
Simons, W.E., 11, 18, 247
Sinden, J.A., 100, 106, 114 n.5
Singer, J.D., 9, 13, 14, 46, 185, 187, 228, 238 n.4, 239 n.15
Siverson, R.M., 29 n.5, 93 n.8, 217, 218, 232
Slovic, P., 101
Small, M., 9, 13, 185, 187, 228, 238 n.4
Smith, V.L., 100
Smoke, R., 11, 14, 17, 111, 160 n.10, 242, 244, 270 n.7
Snidal, D., 143
Snyder, J., 91, 92 n.2, 227
Snyder, R.C., 11, 17
Snyder, G.H., 10, 11, 14, 18, 35, 60 n.11, 271 n.13
Sorel, G., 7
Sorokin, P.A., 18
Spanier, J., 13
Spencer, H., 7
Sprague, J., 80
Stalin, J., 221, 228, 233, 234, 239 n.17
Stanely, J.C., 275
Starr, H., 217, 218, 232
Statman, M., 104
Staudenmaier, W., 293
Stein, A., 91
Stein, J.G., 12, 96, 108, 109, 112, 115 n.14, 143, 144, 261, 263, 270 n.1, 271 n.29, 293, 294, 303 n.5, 312
Steinberg, B.S., 11, 12
Steinbruner, J.D., 12
Steiner, Z., 221, 223, 231, 240 n.24
Steinert, M., 240 n.23

Name Index 361

Stimson, H., 246–7, 251, 252, 253, 254, 258, 270 n.8, 271 nn.12,19,20
Stuckey, J., 46, 239 n.15

Taliaferro, J.W., 114 n.7
Tanter, R., 12, 14, 18
Taylor, A.D., 306, 309, 315, 317, 319
Taylor, C.L., 93 n.13
Taylor, M., 35
Telhami, S., 313
Teune, H., 275
Thaler, R., 99, 100, 103, 106, 107, 114 n.5
Thompson, W.R., 59 n.3, 202 n.4
Tiao, G.C., 277
Togman, J., 27
Tsebelis, G., 80
Tversky, A., 13, 96, 97, 98, 99, 100, 101, 102, 104–5, 107, 108, 114 nn.2,4

Utley, J.G., 247, 251, 271 nn.10,18, 288, 289, 290, 291, 300

Van de Walle, N., 74
Vasquez, J.A., 24–5, 51, 163, 201, 209, 210, 211, 213, 215, 218, 220, 221, 222, 225, 227, 237 n.1, 238 nn.2,4,8,9,10,11, 239 n.14, 240 n.26
Vertzberger, Y.Y., 18, 242, 262, 264, 270 n.2, 271 nn.24,33
von Neumann, J., 289

Wagner, A., 90
Wagner, R.H., 36
Walker, R.B.J., 29 n.2
Wallace, M.D., 29 n.5, 213, 214, 223, 273, 284
Wallensteen, P., 214, 238 n.10

Wallerstein, I., 14
Walt, S., 92 n.2
Wang, K., 92 n.2
Ward, M.D., 213
Warner, 94 n.16
Watt, D.C., 220, 221, 223, 224, 225, 226, 227, 228, 231, 233, 239 nn.19,20, 240 n.23
Wayman, F.W., 163, 164, 166, 168, 171, 176, 178, 200, 210, 239 nn.13,14
Weede, E., 29 n.5, 80, 214
Weighley, R.F., 254, 271 n.9
Weinberg, G.L., 221, 232, 239 n.17, 240 n.28
White, G.L., 215
Wilkenfeld, J., 11, 13, 18, 29 n.4, 140 n.4, 145, 153, 160 n.13, 161 n.19, 187, 213, 214, 230, 239 n.19
Wilson, R.K., 108, 115 n.14
Wittman, D., 293, 301
Wohlstetter, A., 158, 159
Wohlstetter, R., 242, 250, 256, 271 n.17
Woller, G., 93 n.8
Woo, C.-K., 106, 114 n.5
Wright, Q., 18

Yamamoto, Y., 216, 218
Young, H.P., 306, 309
Young, O.R., 11, 14

Zacher, M.W., 161 n.18
Zagare, F.C., 93 n.9, 301
Zajac, E.E., 309
Zamir, Z., 261
Zeckhauser, R., 106, 278
Zeira, E., 257, 270 n.1
Zerbinos, M., 272
Zinnes, D.A., 19, 207, 303 n.2
Zinnes, J.L., 207

Subject Index

Adjusted Winner (AW), 27, 306–7, 323
  and Camp David negotiations, 310–18, 322–3
  compared to proportional allocation (PA), 319
  conditions of, 309, 317–18, 320–1, 323
  equitability adjustment in, 309, 310, 317, 321
  manipulability of, 318–19
  and Panama Canal Treaty, 306, 317
  procedure explained, 308–9
  properties of, 309, 321
  and ranking of issues, 319–20
  shortcomings of, 323
  timing of, 321
  winning and losing in, 321–2
  see also Fair division
Alliances, 212–13, 217, 219
  and World War II, 225–9
Arbitration, in prospect theory, 107–8
Arms race
  and escalation to war, 16, 173, 193, 213–14, 273
  and rivalry, 166, 167–8

Balance of power, 19, 125
  and World War II, 227–9
Bargaining, 96
  in prospect theory, 105–13
  superpower, scale of, 154–5
  see also Crisis *entries*
Berlin crises, 203 n.8
Brazil, domestic opposition in, 76
Britain
  and Crimean war, 238 n.7
  and World War II, 220–37
  and Suez crisis, 108

Camp David negotiations, 310–18
  fairness of, 315–18, 322–3
  issues in, 312–15
  see also Adjusted winner
Capabilities, military, relative, 94 n.21, 95 nn.22-3
  assessment of, *see* Surprise attack
  and crisis escalation, 125–6, 132, 137
  shifts in, and rivalry, 171, 200

Command, Control, Communication, and Intelligence (C^3I), 159, 161 n.20
Conflict, international
  data banks on, 11, 28 n.1
  domestic unrest and, 21, 62–4, 81–4, 87–90
  and international crisis, 8–9
  prospect-theory explanations of, 21–2
  territorial changes and, 188, 190–1, 192–3
  see also Crisis; Rivalry; War *entries*
Conflict, protracted (PC), 9–10, 29 n.4, 185
  and war, 10
  and crisis, 10, 124–5, 131, 133, 137, 168–9, 171–2
  and conflict management, 170
  see also Rivalry, enduring
Cooperation, international, and prospect theory, 108–9
Concert of Europe, 216
Correlates of War (COW), 23, 28 n.1, 162, 184–5, 187, 188, 191, 216
Cox regression model, 52
Crisis, foreign policy, 8, 15, 119, 144–5, 153, 155
Crisis, international, 7–9, 11–18, 119, 187–8
  bargaining in, 11, 17, 96, 110, 154–5
  decision-making in, 11, 12–13, 139–40
  initiation of, 11, 84–90
  and international conflict, 8–10
  and levels of analysis, 13–15, 119
  management, 11, 139–40, 158–9, 170
  methodology of research on, 13, 142–5
  multi-stage threat game (MTG) of, 142–3, 145–56
  recurrent, 172–5, 192–3
  topics in study of, 11–12
  pre-Crimean war, 238 n.7
  see also Deterrence; Rivalry, enduring
Crisis, intra-war (IWC), 137
Crisis escalation, 16–18, 22, 84–7
  actor attributes and, 127, 137
  and coping, 137, 139–40
  defined, 119, 130
  domestic unrest and, 81–4, 87–90, 127, 137

362

Subject Index 363

findings on, 130–40
interactor attributes and, 124–6, 131–3, 137
model of, 120–30
perceptual conditions and, 129–30
and probability of war, 130, 215
in recurrent crises, 172–5, 192–3, 214–15
situational attributes and, 127–8, 131–3
system attributes and, 122–4, 131, 133, 137
Critical theory; *see* International Relations theory, postmodern critique of
Cuban missile crisis, 111, 145, 155, 156, 161 n.19, 203 n.8

Decision-making
in crisis, 11, 12–13, 139–40
elimination-by-aspects (EBA) model of, 291
non-compensatory principle of, 26–7, 291
on war termination, 26–7
see also Prospect theory *entries*
Democratic peace
and crisis escalation, 126
and enduring rivalries, 52, 183
and military expenditures, 25–6, 284–7
proposition of, 272–3
see also Democratization *entries*
Democratization, 273
in East Asia, 274, 275–7, 279
Democratization, and military expenditures, 272–5, 283–4
in East Asia, 280–6
model of, 277–9
Deterrence
Chicken model of, 145, 146, 153, 159
and compellence, 144
and crisis, 11, 174–5
multi-stage threat game (MTG) of, 142–3, 145–59
and Mutual Assured Destruction (MAD), 158
and payoff structures, 145–6, 157–8
in prospect theory, 112–13
rational, model of, 157–9
and rivalry, 166–7, 168
studies of, 22–3, 142–5, 157–8
theory, testing of, 142–5, 152–9
Domestic opposition; *see* Opposition, domestic

East Asia, defense spending in, 284–6
and economic growth, 278
and international tensions, 280
and democratization, 274, 275–7, 279, 280–6
see also entries for individual countries
Egypt
and Camp David negotiations, 310–18
Israeli perception of, before 1973 war, 246–9, 256–64, 265–7, 268
and rivalry with Israel, 167
and war initiation in 1973, 264–6
Enduring rivalry; *see* Rivalry, enduring
Expected-utility theory; *see* Prospect theory
Escalation; *see* Crisis escalation *and* War *entries*

Fair Division
criteria of, 307–8
and dispute resolution, 306
see also Adjusted Winner
Falklands/Malvinas war, 111–12
Foreign policy crisis; *see* Crisis, foreign policy
Foreign policy, and domestic policy, 63–4, 87–90, 110
game-theoretic model of, 64–72
impact of domestic coalitions on, 66–7
and 'rally around the flag' effect, 70, 71, 72, 81, 82, 83, 84, 88, 299–300
see also Conflict, international; Crisis escalation; Rivalry, enduring; *and* War *entries*
Foreign policy, overextension of, 65
Framing, 101–5
and deterrence, 112–13
in negotiation and bargaining, 107–9, 111–12
and public opinion, 290
and war termination, 291, 295, 299–302
see also Prospect theory *entries*
France
and Crimean war, 238 n.7
and World War II, 220–37 *passim*

Games
Chicken, 145, 146, 153, 159
Deadlock, 50, 182
and equilibrium concepts, 41, 42, 45, 146

Games – *continued*
  model of enduring rivalry, 38–9, 41–3, 51, 55–9, 60 n.11
  Stag Hunt, 60 n.15
  structure of, and enduring rivalry, 52–5, 181–2
  of superpower rivalry, 145–6
  theory of moves (TOM), 36
  transformation of, 36–7, 44–5, 46, 55–9
  types of game models, 35–6, 41, 45, 60 n.11
German Democratic Republic, domestic opposition in, 76
Germany, in World War II, 220–37
Gulf crisis and war (1990–91), 111, 291, 300–1

International Crisis Behavior (ICB), 23, 28 n.1, 153, 154, 155, 156, 185, 187, 189–90, 191
International Relations theory
  impediments to cumulation in, 4–7, 28 n.1,
  incorporating domestic politics into, 91–2
  postmodern critique of, 5–7, 28 n.2
  progress in, 3–4
  and prospect theory, 113
  and war, 207–9
Interrupted time series, 277
Iraq, invasion of Kuwait (1990), 88
Iranian hostage rescue mission (1979), 110
Israel
  and Camp David negotiations, 310–18
  and Madrid conference, 108–9
  perception of Egypt and Syria, before 1973 war, 246–9, 256–64, 265–7, 268
  and rivalry with Egypt, 167
Italy, in World War II, 220–37 *passim*

Japan
  and attack on Pearl Harbor, 264, 265, 266
  and termination of war against US, 294
  US perception of, before Pearl Harbor, 246–56, 265–6, 267, 268

Lebensraum, 220, 222, 224, 230, 234, 239 n.17
'Long Peace', and role of nuclear weapons, 161 n.19
Loss aversion, *see* Prospect theory

Malaysia, defense expenditures in, 280–2, 285
Mb statistic, 52, 61 n.21
Mein Kampf (Hitler), 220
Militarized interstate disputes (MIDs)
  and crisis, 13–14
  and enduring rivalries, 46, 60 n.17, 180–1, 185–7, 188–201
  initiation of, 84–90
  reciprocated, 60 n.17
  see also War *entries*
Morocco, Green March against Spain (1975), 89–90

1973 Middle East war, *see* Surprise attack
Nonmyopic equilibrium (NME), 41
Nuclear weapons, and the 'Long Peace', 161 n.19

On Escalation (Kahn), 17
On Thermonuclear War (Kahn), 17
On War (Clausewitz), 17
Opposition, domestic
  and crisis escalation, 81–4, 87–90, 127
  determinants of elite response to, 72–81
  and diversionary action, 110

Pearl Harbor; *see* Surprise attack
Philippines, democratization in, 276, 279
  and defense expenditures, 280–2, 285–6
Polish crisis (1939), 231
Power transition
  and rivalry, 166, 167, 168
  theory, 137
  and war, 18
Preferences
  formation and change in enduring rivalries, 34, 36, 37–41, 43–4, 58–9
  reversals, in prospect theory, 102, 300
  specification of, in game models, 145–6
Proliferation, nuclear, 159
Proportional allocation (PA), 319
Prospect theory
  compared to expected-utility theory, 96–105
  and elimination by aspects (EBA), 291
  and framing, 101–5, 107–9, 111–13, 290–1, 295, 299–302

loss aversion, 98–100, 103, 105–9, 111, 112–13, 295
  problems in, 113, 292–3
  and reference dependence, 97–8, 102–3
  and response to probabilities, 103–4, 289–90
  and risk orientation, 97–8, 100–4, 289
  and sunk-cost effect, 290, 300
  as theory of risky choice, 104–5, 288, 289–90
  and the value function, 98–9, 104
Prospect theory, and international politics
  crisis decision-making, 13, 96
  deterrence and compellence, 112–13
  impact of public opinion, 290, 292, 295, 299–302
  international conflict, 21–2
  negotiation and bargaining, 105–9, 295
  perceptions of decline, 109–12
  war termination, 26–7, 288–9, 290, 291, 295, 299–302
Protracted conflict; *see* Conflict, protracted
Public opinion, 240 nn.23,24, 290, 292, 294, 295, 299–302

Regime type, 18, 79–80, 126, 132–3
  see also Democratization, and military expenditures
Relevant dyads, 166
Risk orientation, *see* Prospect theory
Rivalry
  as a case selection mechanism, 165, 166–8, 198, 199
  concept of, 162–4, 186–7
  and conflict management, 170–1
  as a dependent variable, 165, 199
  evolution of, 164–5, 172–84, 186–7, 188–9, 194–201
  as an independent variable, 165, 168–72, 199, 218
  and isolated conflict, 163, 169, 189–91
  Israeli–Egyptian, 167
  operational definition of, 185–7
  proto-rivalry, 164, 169, 170, 179, 189–91
  termination of, 182–4
  see also Rivalry, enduring *entries*; Conflict, protracted

Rivalry, enduring
  and conflict management, 170
  contentious issues and, 181, 189, 194–8, 199, 200
  and crises, 171–5, 189–91, 192–3
  definition of, 34–5, 163–4, 186–7
  domestic politics and, 64, 81–4, 88–90, 201
  evolution of, 20–1, 23, 34, 43–5, 58–9, 172–84, 186–7, 188–9, 192–201
  game-theoretic model of, 37–46
  game-theoretic conceptions of, 35–7
  incidence of, 33, 190, 199
  and militarized interstate disputes, 46, 60 n.17, 171, 180–1, 185–7, 188–201
  preference formation and change in, 34, 36, 37–41, 43–4, 46, 49–51, 58–9
  strategic configuration of, 41–3, 58, 182
  termination of, 182–4
  universe of cases, 46–9, 190
  see also Rivalry; Rivalry, enduring, occurrence of conflict in; Conflict, protracted
Rivalry, enduring, occurrence of conflict in, 45–6, 169, 189–98
  alliance membership and, 52, 55
  challenger's diplomatic-military position and, 84–7
  contiguity and, 51–2, 55, 240 n.21
  joint democracy and, 52, 55
  previous conflicts and, 172–6, 180–1, 188–9, 192–201
  strategic game played and, 52–5, 181–2
  strategic game transitions and, 55–8
  see also Rivalry *entries*; Conflict, protracted

SHERFACS dataset, 95 n.29
Security dilemma, 18–19
South Korea
  democratization in, 276–27, 279
  democratization in, and defense expenditures, 280, 281, 282–5
  domestic opposition in, 79
Soviet Union
  and conflict management, 170
  and Cuban missile crisis, 156
  risk-propensity of, 110
  and rivalry with US, 142–3, 158, 240 n.26

Soviet Union – *continued*
   and Suez crisis, 155–6
   in World War II, 220–37 *passim*
Spain, and Moroccan Green March, 89
Status quo, in prospect theory, 105–13
   and deterrence and compellence, 112–13
   and perceptions of decline, 109–12
   status quo bias, 106
   see also Prospect theory *entries*
'Steps to war' model, 24–5
   see also War *entries*
The Strategy of Conflict (Schelling), 17
Suez crisis, 155–6
Supergame, 35, 60 n.11
Surprise attack, 25
   and capability assessment, 244–6, 253–6, 262–4, 265–70
   cognitive explanations of, 241–3
   and intention assessment, 244–6, 249–53, 256–62, 264–70
   in 1973 Middle East war, 246–9, 256–68
   in Pearl Harbor, 246–56, 264–8
Syria
   domestic opposition in, 78–9
   Israeli perception of, before 1973 war, 246–9, 256–64, 265, 267, 268
   policy toward Israel, 88–9, 90
   state legitimacy in, 82
System structure, and crisis escalation, 122–3

Taiwan, democratization in, 276, 279
   and defense expenditures, 282–3, 285–6
Theory of moves (TOM), 36
Threat perception, 19, 242, 243, 248–9, 269–70

Unitary actor assumption, 64–5, 93 n.5
United States
   and Camp David negotiations, 311
   and conflict management, 170
   and Cuban missile crisis, 156
   perception of Japan, before Pearl Harbor, 246–56, 265–6, 267, 268
   risk-propensity of, 110

   and rivalry with USSR, 142–3, 158, 240 n.26
   and Suez crisis, 155–6
   in World War II, 220–37 *passim*
United Nations, and conflict management, 170

War
   and crisis escalation, 16–18
   defined, 9–10, 187, 209–10
   expansion of, 24, 217–19, 231–36
   in rivalry, 189–91, 192–3, 240 n.21
   scientific explanation of, 207–9
War, causes of, 18–20
   alliances, 212–13, 225–9
   dispute recurrence, 210–11
   and Egypt in 1973, 264, 265, 266
   hard-liners, 214, 215, 224–5
   and Japan in 1941, 264, 265, 266
   military buildups, 213–14, 222–4, 229
   norms, 216, 229–30
   power politics, 211–15
   public opinion, and World War II, 240 nn.23–4
   repeated crises, 214–15, 221–2, 229, 230–1
   and 'Steps to war' model, 24–5
   territorial disputes, 210–11, 216, 220–1, 229
   threat perception, 19, 213, 222
   see also Conflict *and* Rivalry *entries*
War, termination of, 26–7
   and prospect theory, 288–9, 290–1, 295, 299–302
   and public opinion, 294, 299–302
   rational-choice explanations of, 293–5
   simulation of, 295–300, 303–5
The War Puzzle (Vasquez), 209
The War Trap (Bueno de Mesquita), 19, 293
WEIS (*World Event Interaction Survey*), 11, 28 n.1
World system, approach of, 14–15
World War II, 24–5
   characterized, 209
   expansion of, 231–7
   onset of, 220–31, 236
   termination of, 294